THE INFORMED
INVESTOR'S TAX
PLANNING GUIDE

THE INFORMED INVESTOR'S TAX PLANNING GUIDE

Kenneth J. Soderman

IRWIN
Professional Publishing
Burr Ridge, Illinois
New York, New York

Senior sponsoring editor: Amy Hollands Gaber
Project editor: Paula M. Buschman
Production manager: Bob Lange
Designer: Mercedes Santos
Compositor: Wm. C. Brown Communications, Inc.
Typeface: 10/12 Times Roman
Printer: Arcata Graphics/Kingsport

Library of Congress Cataloging-in-Publication Data

Soderman, Kenneth J.
    The informed investor's tax planning guide / Kenneth J. Soderman.
        p. cm.
    Includes index.
    ISBN 0-7863-0186-4
    1. Investments—Taxation—Law and legislation—United States.
2. Tax planning—United States.   I. Title
KF6415.S63   1994
343.7305'246—dc20
[347.3035246]   94–10917

Printed in the United States of America

1 2 3 4 5 6 7 8 9 0 AGK 1 0 9 8 7 6 5 4

To Jill and Jilley

Preface

How to use this book. This book contains an *Encyclopedia of Investment Taxation* and a related *Year-Round Planning Guide*. The Encyclopedia entries are arranged in alphabetical order, and a particular entry may also be located by using the Index. Tax-related entries in the Encyclopedia also covered in the *Year-Round Planning Guide* are cross-referenced to the relevant paragraph in the Guide. A Table of Contents to the *Year-Round Planning Guide* is also provided. See also the Foreword on the Revenue Reconciliation Act of 1993.

Year-Round Planning Guide
Tax-Saver Checklist

Here is a list of a number of tax-saving strategies that may provide individual taxpayers with big tax savings. References are provided to the Year-Round Planning Guide (YPG) chapter in which the strategies, and related issues, are discussed. See also the Foreword on the Revenue Reconciliation Act of 1993.

INCOME SHIFTING

Income shifting can provide tax benefits for many individual taxpayers, in that deduction of expenses may be accelerated into the current year and income may be shifted to the following year to cut current-year taxes. Here are some strategies designed to produce such tax benefits for individual taxpayers (who typically are cash-basis taxpayers).

A. Shifting Income to Family Members in a Lower Tax Bracket

A simple and effective way to accomplish this is to place assets in an account, typically a bank account, under the state's Uniform Gifts to Minors Act (UGMA) or Uniform Transfers to Minors Act (UTMA).

Caution. Note that the transferor relinquishes the legal right to the assets transferred into such an account. Also, children under age 14 may be subject to tax on unearned income at the *parental* tax rate. This commonly is referred to as the "kiddie" tax.

B. Purchases of US Savings Bonds (Series EE)

1. For young children. Even though unearned income of children under age 14 may be taxed at the *parental* tax rate, a child (or any other individual taxpayer) is not currently subject to tax on interest earned on Series EE US savings bonds if an election is made to defer taxation of that interest until disposition of the bonds. See YPG Chapter 10.

2. For prospective retirees. Taxpayers who are planning for retirement should also consider the purchase of Series EE US savings bonds if they expect to be in a lower tax bracket when retired. Tax savings may arise from the election to defer tax by reporting the interest earned on disposition of the bonds. See also YPG Chapter 4.

C. Purchases of Short-Term Treasury Bills and Certificates of Deposit

Make current-year purchases of US Treasury bills or certificates of deposit (CDs) having maturities of 12 months or less that will mature next year. The interest earned will be subject to tax only on maturity.

ACCELERATION OF TAX DEDUCTIONS

An individual taxpayer can cut his or her current-year tax bill by accelerating tax-deductible expenses into the current year in the following ways:

- Accelerate charitable contributions into the current year.
- *Pay December mortgage interest on a principal or second residence in December.* By so doing, a taxpayer can nail down a tax deduction in the current year. Such interest typically is billed by lenders in January of the next year. See YPG Chapter 3.
- *Accelerate the payment of current-year estimated state and local tax payments.* By so doing, a taxpayer can nail down a tax deduction in the current year. *Note:* Such tax payments are added back in determining taxable income for purposes of the alternative minimum tax (AMT). See YPG Chapter 6.
- *Pay tax-deductible expenses at year's end by using a credit card.* By so doing, a taxpayer can nail down a tax deduction in the current year even though the taxpayer pays the credit card bill in the following year.

PURCHASE STATE AND LOCAL BONDS

Individual taxpayers living in states and cities that impose personal income taxes should consider purchasing bonds issued by such jurisdictions. Such bonds generally are exempt from federal, state, and local income taxation. *Caution:* Certain state and local bonds, referred to as "private activity" bonds, may be subject to the alternative minimum tax (AMT) (see YPG Chapter 6). Also, the investment quality of such bonds, as rated by services such as Standard & Poor's and Moody's, should be taken into account by investors.

NET CAPITAL GAINS AND LOSSES

An individual taxpayer who sells a capital asset such as stocks, bonds, or other types of investment property during a year at a gain should consider selling other capital assets that would generate a capital loss. This process, called "netting," can cut the current-year tax bill. An individual taxpayer can net all capital losses against capital gains, but he or she can apply only $3,000 of capital losses against ordinary income in any year. See YPG 2.02. and 2.04.

AVOID WASH SALES

If a taxpayer sells the *same* stock or other securities as those sold at a loss before or after the loss sale (a 61-day rule), the loss will be disallowed for tax purposes. See YPG 2.04.

INTEREST EXPENSE

Obtain a home equity loan, a mortgage on a new home, or mortgage refinancing, the interest on all of which is deductible, subject to limits not applicable to most individual taxpayers, to replace outstanding consumer loans. Interest on consumer loans (e.g., a loan to finance the purchase of an auto used totally for personal purposes, and credit card debt), is *nondeductible* after 1990. Such interest is commonly referred to as "consumer" or "personal" interest.

Another strategy is to liquidate investments to pay off consumer loans. Interest on funds borrowed to make new investments is deductible, subject to limits. *Caution:* In accordance with interest tracing rules prescribed in IRS Regulations for deduction purposes, taxpayers should keep funds borrowed for investment or business purposes separate from funds borrowed for personal purposes. See YPG Chapter 3.

AVOID DISALLOWANCE OF PASSIVE LOSSES

One hundred percent of the taxpayer's aggregate loss from passive activities may be disallowed as a tax deduction. If a taxpayer is involved in a passive activity, such as certain rental operations in which the taxpayer does not actively participate, he or she should consider other investments that generate passive *income,* commonly referred to as passive income generators (PIGs).

Tax-saving strategy. A taxpayer should convert a passive loss into an active loss by *materially participating* in the loss activity (e.g., by participating in it for more than 500 hours during a year).

Another passive loss strategy. A taxpayer who currently has outstanding loans that generate interest subject to the passive loss rules should consider paying off these loans by using the other assets or obtaining a loan against his or her principal or second residence, which would generate current interest deductions. See YPG Chapter 8.

INDIVIDUAL RETIREMENT ACCOUNTS

A. Limits on Deductibility

In general, an individual taxpayer cannot deduct contributions to Individual Retirement Accounts (IRAs) when the taxpayer or his or her spouse is an active participant in an employer-sponsored retirement plan and adjusted gross income exceeds levels specified in the tax law. These levels are $50,000 for married couples filing joint returns and $35,000 for single taxpayers. IRA contributions are only partially deductible when AGI is between $40,000 and $50,000 for joint return filers and between $25,000 and $35,000 for single taxpayers.

B. IRA Planning Tips

If a taxpayer cannot make a fully deductible IRA contribution, income deferral under a § 401(k) plan, if offered by his or her employer, is an attractive tax-saving alternative. This is true because the limit on the deductible contribution is $8,994 for 1993 and $9,240 for 1994 (adjusted yearly for inflation) as opposed to $2,000 in the case of an IRA.

Taxpayers are allowed to withdraw a *nondeductible* IRA contribution without a tax penalty as long as:

- The withdrawn funds are received by the taxpayer before the due date of the tax return for the year in which the nondeductible IRA contribution was made.
- The withdrawn funds include the net income earned on such funds and that income is reported on the taxpayer's return for the year in which the nondeductible IRA contribution was made.

Taxpayers can obtain short-term loans from IRAs *once* each year. Such loans are an *interest-free* alternative to short-term financing from lending institutions, such as banks and finance companies. No tax penalty will result from such a loan if the taxpayer *recontributes* the withdrawn funds to an IRA within 60 days.

RETIREMENT FUND DISTRIBUTIONS

Individual taxpayers have the option of electing five-year averaging for tax purposes with respect to distributions from qualified retirement plans other than individual retirement accounts (IRAs).

Caution. Five-year averaging may not always produce the best tax result. Accordingly, income projections for retirement years should be made to determine the best tax result when a taxpayer is to receive a plan distribution.

Alternative strategy. Roll over the distribution to another qualified plan, *including an IRA,* within 60 days of receipt. See YPG Chapter 4.

LIKE-KIND EXCHANGES

A taxpayer will generally not recognize gain on an exchange of property for "like-kind" property. Gain on such an exchange will, however, be recognized when part of the exchange involves property that is not of like-kind or when debts on the exchanged property are unequal. If such an exchange is delayed, with a second property transferred later than the first, the property must be identified within 45 days and the transfer completed within 180 days of the first property's transfer. Real property qualifies as like-kind property, whether it is improved or unimproved. However, stocks, bonds, notes, partnership interests, interests held in trust, and inventory do not qualify.

$125,000 HOME SALE EXCLUSION

Taxpayers age 55 or over who plan to marry and who own separate homes, one or both of which they plan to sell, can reap big tax savings. Completing the sale(s) before the marriage takes place makes *each* taxpayer eligible to elect to exclude up to $125,000 of any resulting gain. See YPG 2.05.

Contents

Chapter Ten
THE "KIDDIE" TAX AND TRANSFERS TO CHILDREN

I

YEAR-ROUND PLANNING GUIDE

Foreword: The Revenue Reconciliation Act of 1993

On August 10, 1993, the president signed into law the Revenue Reconciliation Act of 1993 (RRA '93), which was narrowly passed by Congress as part of the Omnibus Budget Reconciliation Act of 1993 (H.R. 2264, Title III). Not all RRA '93 provisions are applicable for the 1993 tax year, but some provisions are *retroactive*. A number of these provisions are retroactive to *June 30, 1992,* as indicated below.

Key among these retroactive provisions are increases in the top federal income tax rates applicable to individuals and corporations and the top federal estate and gift tax rates. The tax rate increases and other RRA '93 provisions within the scope of this book and important to individual taxpayers/investors are highlighted and discussed below.

I. SUMMARY OF RELEVANT RRA '93 PROVISIONS

A. Investment Incentive Provisions

- Capital gains exclusion for certain small business stock (RRA '93 § 13113).
- Rollover of gain from sale of publicly traded securities into specialized small business investment companies (RRA '93 § 13114).
- Modification of minimum tax depreciation rules (RRA '93 § 13115).
- Increase in amount of IRC § 179 expensing deduction to $17,500 (RRA '93 § 13116).
- Bonds for high-speed intercity rail facilities (RRA '93 § 13121).
- Extension of qualified small-issue bonds (RRA '93 § 13122).

B. Real Estate Investment Provisions

- Extension of qualified mortgage bonds and mortgage credit certificates (RRA '93 § 13141).
- Extension and modification of the low-income housing tax credit (RRA '93 § 13142).
- Modification of passive loss rules for certain real estate professionals (RRA '93 § 13143).
- Treatment of certain real property business debt of individuals (RRA '93 § 13150).
- Recovery period for depreciation of nonresidential real property increased from 31.5 to 39 years (RRA '93 § 13151).

C. Luxury Excise Tax

- Luxury excise tax on boats, aircraft, jewelry, and furs *retroactively repealed for sales after 1992;* luxury excise tax on automobiles modified and indexed (RRA '93 §§ 13161–13162).

D. Other Provisions

- Alternative minimum tax (AMT) treatment for charitable contributions of appreciated property (RRA '93 § 13171).
- New substantiation and disclosure requirements for charitable contributions (RRA '93 §§ 13172–13173).
- Health insurance deduction for self-employed individuals extended (RRA '93 § 13174).

E. Individual Income and Estate and Gift Tax Provisions

- Top federal income tax rate applicable to individuals increased to 36 percent, with an additional 10 percent surtax applicable to "high-income" taxpayers, resulting in a top tax rate of 39.6 percent, *effective retroactively to January 1, 1993* (RRA '93 §§ 13201–13205).
- "Anti-conversion" provisions added to prevent conversion of ordinary income into capital gain (RRA '93 § 13206).
- Health insurance (HI) wage base cap repealed (RRA '93 § 13207).
- Top federal estate and gift tax rates increased back to 53 percent and 55 percent, *effective retroactively to January 1, 1993* (RRA '93 § 13208).

- Deduction for business meals and entertainment reduced from 80 percent to 50 percent (RRA '93 § 13209).
- Disallowance of deduction for club dues (RRA '93 § 13210).
- Deduction for executive pay over $1 million generally disallowed (RRA '93 § 13211).
- Amount of compensation taken into account for qualified retirement plan benefits and contributions reduced (RRA '93 § 13212).
- Moving expense deduction reduced (RRA '93 § 13213).
- Estimated tax rules for individuals simplified (RRA '93 § 13214).
- Certain taxpayers subjected to tax on 85 percent of Social Security benefits received (RRA '93 § 13215).

F. Business Provisions

- Top federal income tax rate applicable to corporations increased to 35 percent, *retroactively effective to January 1, 1993* (RRA '93 § 13221).

G. Compliance Provisions

- Standard for accuracy-related and preparer penalties raised (RRA '93 § 13251).

H. Treatment of Intangible Assets

- Fifteen-year amortization allowed for goodwill and certain other intangible assets (RRA '93 § 13261).
- Special treatment of certain liquidation payments by partnerships modified (RRA '93 § 13262).

I. Miscellaneous Revenue-Raising Provisions

- Forty-five-day interest-free period for certain refunds expanded (RRA '93 § 13271).
- Deductions denied for travel expenses incurred by a taxpayer's spouse or dependents (RRA '93 § 13272).
- Withholding rate on supplemental wage payments increased (RRA '93 § 13273).

J. Other Revenue-Related Provisions

- Disaster loss relief for individuals whose principal residences were damaged by presidentially declared disasters (RRA '93 § 13431).

II. DISCUSSION AND ANALYSIS OF KEY PROVISIONS

This section provides a discussion and analysis of key RRA '93 provisions highlighted in section I, above, which are within the scope of this book and important to individual investors.

A. Investment Incentive Provisions

1. Capital gains exclusion for certain small business stock (RRA '93 § 13113). In general, RRA '93 allows *noncorporate* taxpayers holding qualified small business stock for over five years to exclude 50 percent of any gain on the sale or exchange of that stock. The amount of gain for which the exclusion is available is limited to the *greater* of:

- 10 times the taxpayer's basis in the stock; or
- $10 million of gain from the stock's sale or exchange.

Fifty percent of the excluded gain is a preference for purposes of the alternative minimum tax (AMT).

The stock must be acquired by a taxpayer at its original issuance, either directly or through an underwriter, for money or other property except for stock, or as compensation for services rendered to the corporation other than as an underwriter of such stock. A *qualified small business* is a subchapter C (regular) corporation having less than $50 million of gross assets from the date of enactment through the date of the stock's issuance. Also, the corporation generally is not allowed to own real property having a value of more than 10 percent of its total assets or portfolio stock or securities having a value of more than 10 percent of its total assets over liabilities.

> **Observation.** Because the gain exclusion is available only with respect to *C* corporation stock, S corporations and their shareholders may find it advantageous to discontinue S elections. Of course, this RRA '93 provision is only one consideration to be taken into account in connection with the discontinuance of an S election. Also, it is important to note that this exclusion applies with respect to qualified small business stock issued *after August 10, 1993*, RRA '93's date of enactment.

The exclusion is available with respect to qualified small business stock disposed of by a partnership, S corporation, regulated investment company (mutual fund), or common trust fund that is taken into account by a partner, shareholder, or participant other than a C corporation. The exclusion will be available if:

- All eligibility requirements for small business stock are met;
- The entity held the stock for more than five years; and
- The partner, shareholder, or participant held an interest in the entity on the date that the entity acquired the stock and all times thereafter before the disposition of the stock.

Effective date. Effective for stock issued after August 10, 1993, RRA's date of enactment.

2. Rollover of gain from sale of publicly traded securities into specialized small business investment companies (RRA '93 § 13114). Under RRA '93, individuals and C corporations may elect not to recognize gain on the sale of publicly traded securities when the sale proceeds are used within 60 days to purchase common stock or a partnership interest in a specialized small business investment company. A *specialized small business investment company* is any partnership or corporation licensed under § 301(d) of the Small Business Investment Act of 1958. The amount of gain that is excludable yearly by individual taxpayers under the election is limited to the lesser of $50,000 or $500,000 reduced by the gain previously excluded under the election. The applicable limits for corporate taxpayers are $250,000 and $1,000,000, respectively. Any gain excluded by a taxpayer under this election reduces the basis of the stock or partnership interest purchased.

Effective date. Effective for publicly traded securities on or after August 10, 1993, RRA '93's date of enactment.

3. Modification of minimum tax depreciation rules (RRA '93 § 13115). RRA '93 makes two major modifications in how *corporations* compute alternative minimum tax (AMT). The first modification is the elimination of the AMT depreciation system used to compute adjusted current earnings (ACE). The second modification provides that AMT and ACE are to be computed using the regular tax rules with respect to charitable contributions of appreciated property.

Effective date. The ACE depreciation computation is repealed for property placed in service after 1993. The computation remains in effect for property previously placed in service. The modification made with respect to charitable contributions of appreciated property is effective for contributions of tangible personal property made after June 30, 1992, and for contributions of other property made after December 31, 1992.

4. Increase in amount of IRC § 179 expensing deduction (RRA '93 § 13116). RRA '93 increases the small expensing deduction under IRC § 179. The increase is from $10,000 to $17,500 of the cost of qualifying property placed in service during the taxable year. The $17,500 deduction ceiling is reduced, but not below zero, by the amount by which the qualifying property placed in service by the taxpayer during a taxable year is greater than $200,000.

Effective date. Effective for property placed in service in taxable years beginning after December 31, 1992.

5. Bonds for high-speed intercity rail facilities (RRA '93 § 13121). RRA '93 exempts from the statutory private activity bond limitations high-speed intercity rail facility bonds issued in connection with government-owned property. The current law volume cap allocation continues to apply for bonds issued for privately owned property.

Effective date. Effective for bonds issued after December 31, 1993.

6. Extension of qualified small-issue bonds (RRA '93 § 13122). The authority to issue qualified small-issue manufacturing and agricultural bonds is retroactively and permanently extended by RRA '93.

Effective date. Effective for bonds issued after June 30, 1992.

B. Real Estate Investment Provisions

1. Extension of qualified mortgage bonds and mortgage credit certificates (RRA '93 § 13141). The authority to issue qualified mortgage bonds and mortgage credit certificates is retroactively and permanently extended by RRA '93. Certain modifications are also made by RRA '93 in connection with the treatment of resale price control and subsidy lien programs, the financing of contract deed agreements, and the financing of two-family residences.

Effective date. The extension of the authority to issue qualified mortgage bonds and mortgage credit certificates is effective after June 30, 1992. The modifications described above are effective on August 10, 1993, RRA '93's date of enactment.

2. Extension and modification of the low-income housing tax credit (RRA '93 § 13142). The low-income housing tax credit is retroactively extended and made permanent by RRA '93. Certain modifications are also made in connection with the credit with respect to full-time students, HOME funds, deep-rent skewing, maximum rent, tenant occupancy, income recertification, tenant protection, and developmental and operational costs.

Effective date. The extension of the low-income housing tax credit is generally effective after June 30, 1992. The modifications with respect to full-time students and developmental and operational costs are effective after June 30, 1992. The modifications with respect to tenant occupancy, income recertification, HOME funds, and tenant protection are effective on August 10, 1993, RRA '93's date of enactment. Elections in connection with deep-rent skewing and maximum rent are required to be made within 180 days after August 10, 1993.

3.   Modification of passive loss rules for certain real estate professionals (RRA '93 § 13143). RRA '93 provides relief from the passive activity loss rules for certain real estate professionals. It does this by treating rental real estate activities in which a taxpayer materially participates as not subject to limitation under the passive activity loss rules if certain requirements are met. Net losses from rental real estate in which a qualifying taxpayer materially participates are allowed to offset income from real property trade or business activities. Also, rental real estate activities are no longer automatically considered to be passive activities.

Real property trade or business activities includes any real property development, redevelopment, construction, reconstruction, acquisition, conversion, rental operation, management, leasing, or brokerage trade or business conducted by individuals and C corporations.

RRA '93 does not alter the definition of *material participation.* Unless a taxpayer elects to treat all rental real estate interests as a single activity, material participation in rental real estate activities is determined separately for each real estate interest held.

A taxpayer qualifies under this passive activity loss relief provision if more than 50 percent of the personal services performed by the taxpayer in a trade or business during the taxable year are in real property trades or businesses in which the taxpayer materially participates, and in which over 750 hours of services are performed.

Observation. For purposes of determining whether the eligibility requirements described above are met, taxpayers will need to carefully track their hours of participation in rental real estate activities.

A closely held C corporation meets the above requirements when more than 50 percent of its gross receipts for the taxable year are derived from real property trades or businesses in which the corporation is considered to materially participate.

An employee's personal services are not considered as being in a real estate trade or business unless such employee holds more than a 5 percent interest in the employer, including ownership by family members under attribution rules.

RRA '93 provides special rules for married taxpayers who file joint returns. Each spouse's personal services are taken into account separately in determining whether the eligibility requirements are met. A spouse's participation is taken into account in determining material participation. Spouses will qualify under this provision when less than 50 percent of their aggregate business services are performed in real property trades or businesses in which either spouse materially participates, as long as more than 50 percent of one spouse's business services qualify.

Effective date.   Effective for taxable years beginning after December 31, 1993.

4.   Treatment of certain real property business debt of individuals (RRA '93 § 13150).   RRA '93 provides new relief for taxpayers with respect to discharges of *noncorporate* indebtedness secured by real property. Such relief previously had been available only to bankrupt and insolvent taxpayers.

An election is provided under RRA '93 under which income recognition can be avoided to the extent that the taxpayer's basis in depreciable real property can be reduced by the amount of the debt discharge. The election is applicable to discharges of qualified real property business indebtedness.

For this purpose, *qualified real property business indebtedness* (QRPBI) generally is any indebtedness secured by real property used in a trade or business. Indebtedness incurred or assumed by a taxpayer after 1992 is eligible for relief under this provision if it was incurred or assumed in connection with the acquisition, construction, reconstruction, or substantial improvement of real property, or in refinancing QRPBI.

The income exclusion under this election is limited to the lesser of:

- The excess of the debt's outstanding principal amount over the secured real property's fair market value (less the amount of any QRPBI secured by the property); *or*
- The basis of depreciable real property held by the taxpayer that can be reduced.

To the extent that the taxpayer's discharge of indebtedness income is greater than the limitation amount, that excess income is recognized, as long as the taxpayer is solvent immediately after the debt is discharged.

The basis reduction under this provision generally applies to all depreciable real property that the taxpayer held immediately before the debt discharge, and generally is made as of the first day of the following taxable year or on disposition of the property, if earlier. The basis reduction is recaptured as ordinary income when the property is disposed of to the extent that it is greater than the amount of reduced depreciation deductions with respect to the property up to the date of disposition.

Observation. This new provision will not apply with respect to debt discharges made in connection with foreclosures or deeds in lieu of foreclosures on real property securing the discharged debt. The reason for this is that the property's basis is reduced immediately before its transfer and the amount of the reduction is recaptured when the transfer occurs.

Effective date. The election is applicable to debt discharges of QRPBI made after December 31, 1992, of individuals, partnerships, S corporations, and fiduciaries, notwithstanding financial condition.

5. Recovery period for depreciation of nonresidential real property (RRA '93 § 13151). RRA '93 extends the recovery period for nonresidential real property from 31.5 years to 39 years.

Note. RRA '93 does *not* affect the 40-year recovery period for nonresidential real property applicable for purposes of the alternative minimum tax (AMT).

Effective date. The extension of the recovery period generally applies to property placed in service on or after May 13, 1993. However, the extension does not apply to property placed in service before January 1, 1994, if the taxpayer or a qualified person entered into a binding written contract to purchase or construct the property before May 13, 1993, or construction of the property was started by or for the taxpayer or a qualified person before May 13, 1993.

C. Revenue-Raising Provisions

1. Individual income and estate and gift tax provisions (RRA '93 §§ 13201–13205). RRA '93 provides for the following federal income tax rate increases for high-income individuals retroactive to January 1, 1993:

1. A new fourth tax bracket of 36 percent applies to:

• Taxable income above $140,000 for married taxpayers filing joint returns.

• Taxable income above $70,000 for married taxpayers filing separate returns.

- Taxable income above $115,000 for single taxpayers.
- Taxable income above $127,500 for heads of households.
- Taxable income of trusts and estates above $5,500.

2. A tax rate of 39.6 percent applies on taxable income over $250,000 for individual tax return filers under any filing status.

3. A 26 percent rate applies to alternative minimum taxable income (AMTI) of up to $175,000, and a 28 percent rate applies to AMTI above that amount. For married individuals filing separate tax returns, the 28 percent rate applies to AMTI more than $87,500 over the exemption amount.

Observation. As a result of RRA '93's changes, many taxpayers will be affected by the squeezing of AMT and regular income tax rates.

4. AMTI exemptions of $45,000 for married taxpayers filing joint tax returns and $33,750 for unmarried taxpayers are provided under RRA '93. An exemption of $22,500 is also provided for married individuals filing separately, estates, and trusts.

5. Permanent extensions are provided by RRA '93 of the limitation on itemized deductions and the phaseout of personal exemptions under current law. The limitation and the phaseout were to have expired in 1996 and 1997, respectively (see discussion below).

6. Also included in the income tax rate increase provisions are rules intended to prohibit certain conversions of ordinary income to capital gain considered abusive for income tax purposes (see detailed discussion below).

Election. Individuals may elect to pay additional 1993 regular federal income tax attributable to RRA '93's hike in tax rates in *installments,* without charge for interest and penalties on the deferred installment payments. This election does not apply for purposes of the alternative minimum tax (AMT).

Note. In *Notice 93–75,* IRB 1993–33, 10/25/93, the IRS provides guidance for individual taxpayers liable for additional 1993 taxes as a result of the tax rate increases enacted under RRA '93. This guidance relates to the making of the installment payment election, and a number of computational examples are provided in connection with installment payments. Form 8841, Deferral of Additional Taxes, is used for tax reporting purposes.

7. Indexing for inflation: The RRA '93 tax rate bracket and surtax thresholds are to be indexed for inflation beginning in 1995.

Note. RRA '93 does *not* affect indexing for the 28 percent and 31 percent tax rates. Those rates remain subject to current indexing rules.

For 1993, the reduction of an individual taxpayer's allowable itemized deductions (see 5 above) begins at $108,450 of adjusted gross income (AGI) and is complete at $230,950 of AGI. For married taxpayers filing separate returns, the AGI threshold is $54,225. Also, for 1993, the amount of the personal exemption and the dependency exemption is set at $2,350. These exemptions are phased out once an individual taxpayer's AGI exceeds an inflation-adjusted level (see 5 above). For 1993, these AGI thresholds are:

- $162,700 for married taxpayers filing joint returns and qualifying surviving spouses.
- $135,600 for heads of household.
- $108,450 for single return filers.
- $81,350 for married taxpayers filing separate returns.

The total exemption amount that otherwise would be allowable is reduced by 2 percent for each $2,500 of AGI, or fraction thereof, in excess of the applicable threshold. For married taxpayers filing separate tax returns, the reduction in the exemption amount is 2 percent for each $1,250 of AGI or fraction thereof.

Observation. The yearly inflation increase in the AGI thresholds can produce significant tax savings for high-income taxpayers. This is because even one additional dollar of AGI can have the *same* effect as an additional $2,500 of AGI.

Effective date. The income tax rate increase provisions described above are effective beginning on January 1, 1993.

2. Income tax planning considerations and strategies for high-income individuals.

a. *Marriage penalty:* The surtax and tax rate increase of 36 percent are harder on married taxpayers than on single taxpayers.

Illustration 1. Ray and Kay, married professionals, have a combined taxable income of $141,000. Of that amount, $100,000 is attributable to Ray and $41,000 to Kay. Because they are joint return filers, their combined taxable income is subject to tax at 36 percent. However, if Ray and Kay were single taxpayers, each would not be taxed at the 36 percent rate.

Illustration 2. Jay and May, married professionals filing a joint return, have a combined taxable income of $300,000. They will be subject to the surtax, with a 39.6 percent rate applicable to $50,000 ($300,000 less the $250,000 threshold). If Jay and May were single taxpayers, they would not be subject to the surtax.

b. *Kiddie tax implications:* With the income tax rate increasing to as high as 39.6 percent, it may make sense for parents to shift income to children age 14 and over, who may be taxed at a rate as low as 15 percent.

c. *Other tax planning considerations and strategies:* For high-income taxpayers, the retroactivity of the tax rate increases will result in additional tax outlays. However, on a prospective basis, there are a number of steps that high-income taxpayers can take to reduce their tax bills:

- Contribute the maximum allowable amounts to tax-deferred retirement plans, such as:

§ 401(k) plans (sponsored by employers).

Keogh plans (typically for the self-employed).

Individual retirement accounts (IRAs).

- Purchase tax-exempt municipal bonds and tax-deferred annuities.

Caution. Not all municipal bonds are exempt from federal income tax. Interest payments on "private activity" municipal bonds are subject to the alternative minimum tax (AMT). As a result, taxpayers should take into account their potential AMT liability when considering a municipal bond investment.

Observation. For taxpayers *not* subject to the AMT, purchases of private activity bonds may be advantageous since the interest yield on these bonds generally is higher than the yield on other municipal bond issues.

Observation. Tax-deferred annuities may also be advantageous for many individual investors. However, there are a number of potential drawbacks with respect to such annuities that should be considered before investing in them. Annuities can involve fees that can negate tax benefits for an individual taxpayer. If a taxpayer wishes to withdraw from an investment in an annuity, he or she may be subject to surrender fees. Also, the issuer of the annuity may decrease the interest rate payable on the annuity. If the purchaser is dissatisfied with that action, he or she may be subject to surrender fees on withdrawal of the funds invested.

3. Treatment of net capital gains (RRA '93 § 13206). The individual income tax rate increases discussed at C.1., above, do *not* apply to net capital gains, which are taxed at a 28 percent maximum rate. RRA '93 provides rules designed to prevent taxpayers from converting ordinary income into capital gain.

Observation.   As a result of the income tax rate increases discussed above, the 28 percent rate applicable to capital gains makes investments in capital gain producing property very attractive for higher income taxpayers.

4. Anti-conversion provisions—ordinary income to capital gain. (RRA '93 § 13206(a)).   Because RRA '93 creates a tax rate differential between ordinary income and capital gains, it also contains rules designed to prevent the conversion of the more highly taxed ordinary income into lower taxed capital gains.

"Conversion transactions."   Under RRA '93, capital gains from the disposition of property that was part of a conversion transaction is generally recharacterized as ordinary income. In general, a *conversion transaction* represents two or more positions taken with regard to the same or similar property, such as in the case of hedges and straddles, where substantially all of the taxpayer's return is attributable to the taxpayer's net investment in the transaction. In this type of transaction, the taxpayer is in the economic position of a lender. The amount generally recharacterized as ordinary income is based on the taxpayer's net investment multiplied by 120 percent of the applicable federal rate (AFR) for the period in which the transaction occurred.

Effective date.   Transactions entered into after April 30, 1993.

5. Repeal of certain exceptions to the market discount rules (RRA '93 § 13206(b)).   On a taxpayer's disposition of a market discount bond, any gain on the disposition is taxable as ordinary income. RRA '93 repeals the prior law exception from this general rule for tax-exempt bonds and market discount bonds issued on or before July 18, 1984.

Effective date.   Bonds acquired after April 30, 1993.

6. Accrual of income by holders of stripped preferred stock (RRA '93 § 13206(c)).   RRA '93 treats a purchaser of stripped preferred stock in generally the same manner that the purchaser of a stripped bond is treated under the original issue discount (OID) rules. The same treatment applies to a person who strips preferred stock and disposes of the dividend rights with respect to that stock. As a result, stripped stock is treated in the same manner as a bond issued with OID equal to:

- The stated redemption price of the stock, less
- The amount paid for the stock.

Any accrued discount is treated as ordinary income and not as interest or dividends. In general, a *stripped* bond or stock is an instrument whose ownership is separate from the right to receive interest thereon. *Stripped preferred stock* is any preferred stock where the ownership of the stock has been separated from the right to receive any dividend that has not yet become payable.

Effective date.   Stripped stock purchased after April 30, 1993.

7.   Treatment of net capital gains as investment income (RRA '93 § 13206(d)).   Noncorporate taxpayers are allowed a deduction for investment interest up to the amount of their net investment income. Before RRA '93, net investment income included a taxpayer's net gain on the disposition of property held for investment. Under RRA '93, in determining deductible investment interest, net capital gains generally are not treated as investment income for purposes of the net investment income limitation. Taxpayers are allowed, however, to include net capital gains in investment income if they elect to reduce net capital gains eligible for the top 28 percent tax rate applicable to capital gains. If net capital gains *are* included in net investment income, that amount of capital gains is *not* eligible for the 28 percent rate. Also, this only applies where the taxpayer is in a higher tax bracket than 28 percent.

Effective date.   Effective for taxable years beginning after December 31, 1992.

8.   Repeal of health insurance (HI) wage base cap (RRA '93 § 13207).   All wages paid to, and all self-employment income earned by, individuals are subjected by RRA '93 to the 2.9 percent Medicare hospital insurance (HI) tax. The Medicare tax with respect to salaried employees is 1.45 percent for employers and employees, respectively. The Medicare portion of the self-employment tax is 2.9 percent for self-employed individuals.

Note.   While the removal of the HI wage base cap can mean a big tax increase for many individual taxpayers, self-employed individuals are permitted to deduct 50 percent of the self-employment tax in arriving at adjusted gross income (AGI) on their federal income tax returns (Form 1040).

Effective date.   The repeal of the HI wage base cap is effective for wages and self-employment income received after December 31, 1993.

9.   Increase in top federal estate and gift tax rates (RRA '93 § 13208).   RRA '93 reinstates the top two federal estate and gift tax rates that expired in 1992.

For taxable transfers over $2,500,000 but not in excess of $3,000,000, the applicable tax rate is 53 percent. For taxable transfers in excess of $3,000,000, the applicable tax rate is 55 percent.

The phaseout of the graduated tax rates and the unified estate and gift tax credit occurs between $10,000,000 and $21,040,000.

The tax rate applicable to generation-skipping transfers is 55 percent.

Effective date.   The increase in the top federal estate and gift tax rates and the phaseout of the graduated tax rates and unified credit is effective for decedents dying, gifts made, and generation-skipping transfers occurring after December 31, 1992.

10. Deduction for business meals and entertainment reduced (RRA '93 § 13209).   RRA '93 reduces the allowable deduction for business meals and entertainment from 80 percent to 50 percent. However, it also provides a break for food and beverage employers by providing such employers with a credit for the amount of employer-paid FICA (Social Security) tax on employee tips that are not treated as wages for federal minimum wage purposes.

Effective date.   The reduced deduction for business meals and entertainment is effective for taxable years beginning after 1993. The FICA credit for food and beverage employers applies to taxes paid after 1993.

11. Deduction of club dues denied (RRA '93 § 13210).   RRA '93 denies a deduction for club dues, including business, social, athletic, luncheon, or sporting clubs. Dues paid with respect to airline and hotel clubs will also be nondeductible. The deduction bar also applies when the club dues are paid in connection with employee recreational expenses.

Effective date.   Taxable years beginning after 1993.

12. Limit on deduction for executive compensation (RRA '93 § 13211).   RRA '93 denies the deduction for certain compensation over $1 million per year paid by a publicly traded corporation to each of its five top officers. Excluded from this deduction limit are compensation payments based on productivity, tax-qualified retirement plan contributions, and fringe benefits.

Effective date.   Effective with respect to compensation that is otherwise deductible by the corporate payer in a taxable year beginning after December 31, 1993. An exception generally applies to compensation paid under a written binding contract in effect on February 17, 1993, and at all times thereafter.

13. Amounts taken into account under qualified retirement plans reduced (RRA '93 § 13212). RRA '93 reduces the limit (under IRC § 401(a)(17) before enactment of RRA '93) on compensation taken into account for purposes of determining benefits under a qualified retirement plan. For 1993, the statutory limit of $200,000 was increased to $235,840, as indexed for inflation. For 1994, the limit is reduced to $150,000, and in subsequent years the limit will be indexed for inflation.

Effective date. The new compensation limit is effective for benefits accruing in plan years beginning after December 31, 1993. Benefits accrued by that date over the limit are grandfathered under RRA '93.

14. Deduction for moving expenses reduced (RRA '93 § 13213). An employed or self-employed individual is allowed to deduct specific expenses incurred in moving his or her residence as a result of obtaining a new job or entering into a new business. Deductible moving expenses include those incurred for:

- Selling, or settling an existing lease on, the individual's previous residence and purchasing, or settling an unexpired lease on, a new residence.
- Moving household goods.
- Expenses for travel, meals and lodging incurred in transporting the individual and his family.
- Expenses for meals and temporary lodging for a stay of up to 30 days near the individual's new job location.

RRA '93 excludes from deductible moving expenses the costs of:

- Househunting trips incurred prior to a move.
- Selling, or settling an existing lease on, the taxpayer's former residence and purchasing, or acquiring a new lease on, a new residence. Such costs would include real estate commissions and legal fees.

What remains deductible with respect to moving expenses after RRA '93 are the expenses of moving household goods and personal effects to a new residence and lodging expenses, but *not meals* incurred in connection with the move.

Observation. Although employed and self-employed individuals are prohibited by RRA '93 from deducting closing costs on residence transfers in connection with employment- or business-related moves, such costs may still result in a tax benefit. This is because closing costs reduce taxable gain realized on the sale of the old residence and increase the tax basis of the new residence.

RRA '93 also provides that a taxpayer can deduct moving expenses only if his or her new job is at least 50 miles farther from the former residence than was the old job. Current law provides a 35-mile deductibility test. In addition, employer reimbursements of moving expenses will be excludable from employees' income.

Effective date. Moving expenses incurred after 1993.

15. Estimated tax rules for individuals simplified (RRA '93 § 13214). The federal estimated tax rules for individuals, including owners of unincorporated business such as sole proprietors, are simplified by RRA '93. The safe harbor available prior to RRA '93, based on the taxpayer's prior-year tax liability, is also repealed.

Individual taxpayers having adjusted gross income (AGI) of $150,000 or less are allowed under RRA '93 to satisfy current-year liability for estimated taxes under a 100 percent "safe harbor." The current year estimated tax liability would be satisfied under this safe harbor if the taxpayer makes estimated tax payments representing 100 percent of the preceding year's tax liability.

A 110 percent "safe harbor" is provided for individual taxpayers having more than $150,000 of AGI. Current-year estimated tax liability would be satisfied if the taxpayer makes estimated tax payments constituting 110 percent of the preceding year's tax liability. These taxpayers may also avoid the underpayment penalty if they make timely estimated tax payments representing 90 percent of the current year's tax liability.

Note. An individual taxpayer's ability to base estimated tax payments on 90 percent of his or her current-year estimated tax liability is *not* affected by RRA '93.

16. Penalties for underpayment of estimated tax. The federal tax withholding tables will *not* be revised for 1993 to reflect RRA '93s federal income tax rate increases and the 10 percent surtax. Estimated tax underpayment penalties that individual taxpayers would otherwise face as a result of these RRA '93 tax rate increases will be waived for 1993. Also, any additional tax owed by an individual taxpayer as a result of the RRA '93 tax rate increases may be paid in three equal installments due on April 15 of 1994, 1995, and 1996. If these installment payments are properly made by the taxpayer, no penalties or interest will be assessed.

17. Taxable amount of Social Security benefits increased to 85 percent for certain taxpayers (RRA '93 § 13215). RRA '93 increases from 50 percent to 85 percent the taxable portion of Social Security and Tier 1 Railroad Retirement benefits for certain taxpayers. Taxpayers subject to this provision would be required to include in gross income the lesser of:

- 85 percent of the taxpayer's Social Security or Railroad Retirement Tier 1 benefits.
- 85 percent of the excess of the taxpayer's income over the applicable threshold amount.

This increase in gross income would apply if the sum of:

- The taxpayer's modified adjusted gross income (MAGI) for the taxable year, *and*
- 50 percent of the Social Security/Railroad Retirement Tier 1 benefits, exceeds the threshold amount.

A taxpayer's MAGI is the taxpayer's adjusted gross income without including:

- Income from US savings bonds used to pay higher education tuition and fees.
- Certain excluded income of US citizens or residents living abroad.
- Tax-exempt interest income received or accrued by the taxpayer.

The threshold amounts are raised by RRA '93 to $34,000 for unmarried taxpayers and $44,000 for married couples filing joint returns from $25,000 and $32,000, respectively. The threshold amount is zero for a married individual who lives with his or her spouse during the taxable year and files a separate tax return.

Effective date.   The above increase in the taxable amount of Social Security and Railroad Retirement Tier 1 benefits is effective for taxable years beginning after December 31, 1993.

D. Provisions Affecting Business Taxpayers

1. Increase in maximum marginal corporate income tax rate (RRA '93 § 13221).   The maximum marginal income tax rate on the income of C corporations is increased by RRA '93 from 34 percent to 35 percent. It also sets the maximum tax rate on net capital gains of C corporations at 35 percent. In addition, taxable income over $15 million is subject to an added tax equal to the lesser of 3 percent of the amount in excess of $15 million or $200,000.

RRA '93 also makes certain modifications to the corporate estimated tax rules (see RRA '93 § 13225).

Effective date. Taxable years beginning after 1992. However, penalties for underpayment of 1993 corporate estimated taxes will be waived with respect to tax underpayments resulting from the RRA '93 changes.

E. Compliance Provisions

1. Standard for accuracy-related and preparer penalties raised (RRA '93 § 13251). A 20 percent penalty is imposed on any part of a tax underpayment attributable to a substantial income tax understatement, negligence, or disregard of tax rules and regulations. In determining whether an income tax understatement is substantial, the amount of the income tax understatement is reduced by any part of such understatement related to an item, if:

- The treatment of such item on the taxpayer's is or was supported by substantial authority; or
- The facts concerning the treatment of the item were adequately disclosed on the return or a statement attached thereto, as long as such treatment was not frivolous (see Reg. § 1.6662–4).

The regulations provide that negligence consists of a taxpayer's failure to:

- Make a reasonable attempt to comply with the federal tax laws;
- Exercise ordinary and reasonable care in preparing a tax return; and
- Maintain adequate books and records or properly substantiate tax return items (see Reg. § 16662–3(b)(1)).

Also, *disregard* of tax rules and regulations consists of any careless, reckless, or intentional disregard of such rules and regulations. The penalty for this does not apply when:

- The taxpayer adequately discloses the return position taken;
- The tax return position taken by the taxpayer is not frivolous;
- The taxpayer has adequate books and records; and
- The taxpayer has properly substantiated items on the return (see IRC § 6662(c), Reg. § 1.662–3(c)).

For purposes of these rules, a frivolous tax return position taken by a taxpayer is a position that is "patently improper." For purposes of the accuracy-related penalty, a new "reasonable basis" rule applies under RRA '93 in place of the "not frivolous" rule under pre-'93 RRA law. As a result, if a taxpayer has a reasonable basis for a tax return position, the penalty for a substantial income tax understatement will not be applied as long as that position is adequately disclosed. Also, the penalty for disregarding tax rules and regulations will not apply when a taxpayer adequately discloses a position on a tax return and there is a reasonable basis for that position.

In the case of the negligence penalty, disclosure will be irrelevant, since a taxpayer generally will not be treated as being negligent with respect to a tax return position as long as there is a reasonable basis for that position, despite disclosure.

Effective date. The new RRA '93 penalty rules apply to tax returns due after December 31, 1993, without regard to any filing extensions.

F. Treatment of Intangible Assets

1. Fifteen-year amortization allowed for goodwill and certain other intangible assets (RRA '93 § 13261). RRA '93 requires a 15-year amortization of the capitalized cost of certain intangible assets ("Section 197 intangibles") acquired and held in connection with the conduct of a trade or business or an activity engaged in for the production of income. Types of intangible property included and excluded under this new rule are specified. Among the important intangible assets included under this rule are goodwill and going-concern value.

"Anti-churning" rules are also provided to prohibit taxpayers from converting any intangible asset that previously was not amortizable into an amortizable intangible asset subject to this new rule.

Effective date. This new rule generally applies to property acquired after August 10, 1993, RRA '93's date of enactment. However, taxpayers may elect, on an all-or-nothing basis, to apply this new rule to all property acquired after July 25, 1991.

2. Special treatment of certain liquidation payments by partnerships modified (RRA '93 § 13262). RRA '93 repeals the special treatment of payments for unrealized receivables, other than unbilled amounts and accounts receivable, for all partners. Such payments will be treated as made in exchange for the partner's interest in partnership property.

Effective date. Generally effective for partners retiring or dying on or after January 5, 1993. An exception is provided with respect to any partner who retires on or after January 5, 1993, if a written contract to purchase the partner's partnership interest was binding on January 4, 1993, and at all times thereafter until its purchase.

G. Miscellaneous Revenue-Raising Provisions

1. Forty-five-day interest-free period for certain refunds expanded (RRA '93 § 13271). RRA '93 extends the 45-day interest-free rule for tax refunds to all types of federal tax returns, including income, employment, excise, estate, and gift tax returns.

Effective date. Effective for tax returns to be filed, without regard to extensions, after December 31, 1993. Effective for amended returns and refund claims filed after December 31, 1994, regardless of the taxable period involved. Effective for IRS-initiated tax adjustments applicable to refunds paid after December 31, 1994.

2. Deductions denied for travel expenses incurred for travel of a taxpayer's spouse or dependents (RRA '93 § 13272). RRA '93 denies a deduction for travel expenses paid or incurred for a spouse, dependent, or other individual who accompanies a taxpayer on business travel, unless:

- The accompanying individual is an employee of the taxpayer;
- The other individual's travel is for a bona fide business purpose; and
- The expenses would otherwise be deductible.

Effective date. Effective for amounts paid or incurred after December 31, 1993.

3. Withholding rate on supplemental wage payments increased (RRA '93 § 13273). The flat percentage withholding rate on supplemental wage payments is increased by RRA '93 from 20 percent to 28 percent. Such payments include bonuses, nonqualified stock option exercises, overtime pay, and commissions.

Effective date. Effective for payments made after 1993.

H. Other Revenue-Related Provisions

1. Disaster loss relief for certain individuals (RRA '93 § 13431). RRA '93 provides disaster loss relief to individuals whose principal residences were damaged by presidentially declared disasters. Under this relief provision, a gain need not be recognized as a result of the receipt of insurance proceeds for unscheduled personal property contained in a taxpayer's principal residence which was involuntarily converted in a presidentially declared disaster.

With respect to any other insurance proceeds for such a residence or its contents, such proceeds may be treated as a common pool of funds. When such a pool of funds is used for the purchase of any property similar or related in service or use to the converted residence, or its contents, the taxpayer can elect to recognize gain only to the extent that the amount of the pool is greater than the cost of the replacement property.

The close of the applicable period for the replacement of involuntarily converted property as a result of a presidentially declared disaster is extended by RRA '93 to four years after the close of the first taxable year in which any part of the gain on conversion is realized.

The above RRA '93 rules apply to residences located in areas suffering a disaster that resulted in a presidential determination that federal assistance was warranted under the Disaster Relief and Emergency Assistance Act.

Note. The Conference Report to RRA '93 indicates that a renter may be eligible for such relief if the rented residence would have been his or her principal residence if owned.

Effective date. Effective for property involuntarily converted as a result of disasters for which a presidential declaration is made on or after September 1, 1991, and to taxable years ending on or after that date.

Chapter One

Introduction

This *Year-Round Planning Guide* (YPG) focuses on tax rules and tax planning strategies of importance to individual investors. The related *Encyclopedia of Investment Taxation,* which follows the YPG, provides summary descriptions of investment terms and tax terms related to investments.

The following nine chapters cover investment tax angles of interest to, and for the benefit of, most individual taxpayers. The intent of this work is not to be a comprehensive research tool for the tax professional. Rather, it is designed to be an easy-to-use reference tool for individual investors and professionals who do not necessarily specialize, or work primarily in the area of, federal income, estate, and gift taxation. The Encyclopedia is designed to provide these users with concise definitions of investment-related tax terms and research references to relevant authorities and to the CCH Standard Federal Tax Reporter. This Guide is designed to highlight tax planning pitfalls and tax-saving opportunities important to most individual investors. Of course, when complex tax issues arise in the course of planning in the areas of federal income, estate, and gift taxation, a competent tax adviser with related expertise should be consulted. *Note:* To ensure complete, up-to-date coverage, please also refer to the Foreword on the Revenue Reconciliation Act of 1993.

Chapter Two

Tax-Wise Use of Investment Favorites

2.01. OVERVIEW

This chapter covers many investments favored by individual investors, such as stocks, bonds, options, and the purchase and sale of a residence. It is designed to help individual investors, with respect to such transactions, to maximize their gains, to best utilize any losses they realize, and to plan future investments with the most favorable tax-wise results.

2.02. CAPITAL GAINS AND LOSSES—WHAT'S LEFT?

A. Inclusion of Capital Gains

The Tax Reform Act of 1986 (TRA '86), starting in 1987, ended the tax-favored treatment of net long-term capital gains. Assets such as investments in stock, bonds, and options are capital assets for purposes of these rules. Before the enactment of TRA '86, 60 percent of such gains were excluded from tax. As a result of TRA '86, individual taxpayers who realize a net long-term capital gain on the sale of such investments are taxed on these gains at the same tax rates as ordinary income. Ordinary income is subject to a top marginal tax rate of 36 percent, while a marginal tax rate of 39.6 percent (i.e., the 36 percent rate plus a 10 percent surtax) applies to taxable income over $250,000. Also, personal exemptions are reduced ratably for every $2,500 of adjusted gross income within a phaseout range of $122,500. The phaseout range is between $162,700 and $285,200 for married taxpayers filing joint returns, $81,350 to $142,600 for married taxpayers filing separate returns, $108,450 to $230,950 for unmarried taxpayers, and $135,600 to $258,100 for heads of households.

Note. RRA '93 raised the top federal income tax rates, but not the 28 percent tax rate applicable to capital gains. However, it also provides anti-conversion provisions designed to prevent the conversion of ordinary income into lighter taxed capital gain. For more details, see the Foreword on RRA '93.

B. What Is a Long-Term Capital Gain or Loss?

A taxpayer has a long-term capital gain or loss on disposition of a capital asset acquired before June 23, 1984, or after 1987 when he or she holds it for more than one year. In the case of a capital asset acquired after June 22, 1984, and before 1988, the taxpayer has a long-term capital gain or loss on the disposition of capital asset when it is held for more than six months. Special rules apply to gains on commodity straddle transactions.

C. Why Is the Capital Gain/Loss and Ordinary Gain/Loss Distinction Still Relevant?

TRA '86 did not legislate out of existence the distinctions among ordinary income, deductions, and losses, and capital gains and losses. Taxpayers must still net their capital gains and losses, and capital losses are still applied against capital gains. A taxpayer with capital losses that are greater than his or her capital gains for a taxable year can offset up to $3,000 of the net capital loss against ordinary income in that year. Any remaining net capital loss is carried forward to future years.

Remember. Long-term and short-term capital gains offset up to $3,000 of ordinary income on a dollar-for-dollar basis. This was not the case before enactment of TRA '86.

Dealer versus investor status. Before the enactment of TRA '86, dealer status was not advantageous tax-wise for individuals such as real estate dealers and antique dealers. This was true because a *dealer's* profits were taxable as ordinary income, whereas an *investor's* profits constituted capital gains, 60 percent of which were excluded from tax if long-term. But after TRA '86, dealers and investors receive the *same* treatment for tax purposes, because the tax rates applicable to capital gains and ordinary income are now the same. Thus, *dealers* now are in a more advantageous position, tax-wise, because any costs they incur in the activity involved are deductible business expenses not subject to deduction limits.

2.03. TAX-WISE USE OF OPTIONS

Individuals can reap investment profits and tax benefits through the intelligent use of options, which are written on issues of common stock popular with investors (e.g., General Motors, IBM).

A. Types of Options

1. Calls. A *call* is an option contract that permits the contract holder to buy a specific number of shares of a specific security (typically stock) at a specific price during a specified period. The purchase price set forth in the contract is referred to as the *strike price,* and the person offering the contract to an investor is referred to as the option *writer.*

Illustration.   An option writer sells a call option to an investor giving the investor the right, but not the obligation, to demand delivery of 100 shares of the stock of Zenith, Inc. at a strike price of $25 per share during a specified six-month period. If, during this period, Zenith's share price increases to $40, the investor would exercise the call option. The cost involved for the investor under these circumstances would be the $25 per share price plus the amount paid for the option. If, however, Zenith's share price drops to $15, the investor does not exercise the option. When this is the case, the option lapses and the writer pockets the option premium (defined at 2.03.B.1)

2. Puts.   Basically, a *put* is an option contract that is the reverse of a call option. It is an option involving the right to sell a specific number of shares of a specific security (usually stock) at a specific price (strike price) over a specified period of time. A buyer of a put option generally speculates that the value of the underlying stock will drop. If the price of the underlying stock does not drop during the period specified under the option, the investor lets the option lapse and the writer pockets the option premium.

Illustration.   Sara Smith buys a Gocorp, Inc. June/50 option. This option, which expires in June, gives her the right, but not the obligation, to sell 100 Gocorp shares at $50 per share, regardless of the market price of Gocorp shares.

Planning point.   A taxpayer may find the use of a put option a successful strategy to protect against a decline in stock prices. For example, suppose the stock of Apex, Inc. currently trades for $30 per share. Michael Moore owns 100 Apex shares, on which he has a substantial gain. However, he is concerned that Apex's shares may drop in price. To protect himself, he buys a put, covering 100 Apex shares, under which he can sell his shares for $25 each. Before the option period expires, the price of Apex shares drops to $20. Accordingly, Moore exercises the put so as to preserve gain on his Apex shares.

3. Straddles. A *straddle* involves a put and a call option on the same underlying stock at the same strike price. Such an option strategy can serve to limit a taxpayer's loss. However, it can also limit a taxpayer's gain. Also, the option strike (exercise) prices may be different in such an arrangement, and this difference is called a *spread*. Special rules apply to "tax straddles" designed to create artificial gains and losses for tax purposes.

4. Covered options. These are options with respect to which the writer owns the underlying security.

5. Naked options. These are options with respect to which the writer does not own the underlying security.

Observation. Naked options involve considerable risk for an option writer. For example, suppose a call option for a stock is written having a strike price of $20 per share. Further suppose that the stock's price climbs to $40 per share within the option period. Under these circumstances, the writer would pocket the option premium, but would also be required to purchase sufficient shares at $40 to satisfy the delivery demand of the option purchaser. Obviously, the cost of such a purchase would substantially exceed the amount of the option premium.

B. Other Aspects of Options

1. Option premium. An *option premium* is the cash consideration an option holder pays to an option writer in exchange for the obligation involved.

2. Closing transaction. This is a transaction involving the termination of an option writer's obligation with respect to the option, other than through the option's exercise or lapse. Ordinarily, this would involve the purchase of an option identical to the original option involved.

C. How Option Writers Are Treated for Tax Purposes

The premium, defined at 2.03.B.1, that a writer of an option receives constitutes taxable income for the writer. The premium becomes taxable income for an option writer at such time as the option lapses, is exercised, or is discharged.

1. Lapsed options. When an option written by a taxpayer expires without being exercised by its purchaser, it lapses. Upon the lapse of an option, the option writer is required to include the option premium in gross income as a short-term capital gain (taxable at the same rate applicable to ordinary income).

2. Exercised options. When a purchaser exercises a call, the sale of the related security is forced. The option premium is then added to the proceeds from the sale of the security.

3. Closing transactions. A writer of a call option has a short-term capital gain or loss when the obligation under the option is extinguished upon the purchase of an identical option in a closing transaction. Under these circumstances, the writer has a short-term capital gain or loss in the amount of the difference between the option premiums.

D. How Option Holders Are Treated for Tax Purposes

1. Sale of an option. When a taxpayer sells an option, his or her gain or loss is the difference between the option premium paid and the sales proceeds received. Its character is long-term or short-term depending on the taxpayer's holding period for the option.

2. Lapse of an option. The lapse of an option is treated for tax purposes as a sale or exchange that produces a short-term capital loss.

3. Treatment of straddles. As noted at 2.03.A.3, a straddle involves a call and a put on the same security, usually at the same strike price. If the strike prices differ, a spread is involved. The investor necessarily realizes a loss on one option and a gain on the other.

Illustration. Shares of Bigco, Inc. are currently trading at $40 per share. Jane Brooks writes both a call and a put with respect to 100 of her Bigco shares. The option purchasers pay her a $1,000 call premium and a $500 put premium. Assume that during the period of the options, Bigco shares rise in price to

$50 per share. Brooks would have a loss with respect to the call, since the stock's price rose, but she would still have a net gain. She would lose $1,000 when the call option purchaser demanded delivery of the underlying stock, but would pocket the $1,000 call premium and the $500 premium for the put, which would lapse. If, however, the price of Bigco shares were to rise above $55 per share, Brooks would incur an overall loss.

2.04. TAX-WISE INVESTMENT STRATEGIES

A. Maximizing the Benefit of "Paper" Losses for Tax Purposes

Taxpayers often hold securities on which they have, at any given time, unrealized paper losses. Such losses, if realized by the taxpayer through sales, can be used to offset gains realized on other investments.

1. Doubling up. However, even if a taxpayer wishes to realize a loss to free up a gain on another investment from tax, he or she may have confidence that the loss position will ultimately turn around. A taxpayer who sells a security at a loss cannot repurchase the security ("substantially identical" property) within 30 days of the sale and utilize the loss for tax purposes. The above loss prohibition rule also applies when a taxpayer purchases the security within 30 days prior to the sale. Under these circumstances, the taxpayer would have to add the loss to his cost basis for the newly purchased security. This result occurs because of *wash sale* rules under the tax law (see 2.04.C).

Note. The wash sale rules apply only to *losses* on investments. Thus, a taxpayer who sells investment property at a *gain* must recognize the gain even if substantially identical property is acquired 30 days before or after the sale.

It is still possible for the taxpayer to realize this loss, however. It may be done through a simple strategy referred to as *doubling up.* A taxpayer can double up by buying an identical amount of the security on which he or she wishes to realize a loss, waiting *31 days,* and then selling the original holding to realize the loss. By so doing, a taxpayer has a deductible loss and the opportunity to benefit from any future appreciation of the security as a result of the purchase.

2. Losses on mutual fund shares. Many mutual fund sponsors allow investors to move invested funds among the various funds that they sponsor without charge or at a low cost. This can prove to be beneficial, tax-wise, for an investor in that he or she can recognize a loss on a mutual fund investment without having to withdraw funds from the sponsor's group of funds. And the taxpayer can shift funds back into the original fund and still have a loss for tax purposes, as long as he or she waits 31 days before doing so.

Caution. With respect to mutual fund investments that a taxpayer buys and sells in various lots, he or she should take care in identifying lots purchased and sold so that a desired tax result will be achieved. Usually, the best way for a taxpayer to do this is to specifically identify lots bought and sold; the IRS will ordinarily respect such identification. Otherwise, the IRS may apply its own method for identifying shares sold, typically on a first-in, first-out basis. This can work to a taxpayer's disadvantage, tax-wise, in that earlier-acquired shares often have a lower tax basis (cost) and may thus produce a larger taxable gain.

B. Short Sale Rules

1. What is a short sale? A short sale involves an investor's sale of stock that is not intended for delivery when the sale is made. If the taxpayer actually owns the stock sold, the sale is called a short sale *against the box*— see 2.04.B.4.

2. Why enter into a short sale? A taxpayer might enter into a short sale when he or she thinks a security will decline in value. The taxpayer would sell the security, which he or she does *not* own. The taxpayer's securities broker would then borrow a sufficient amount of the security for the purpose of delivering it to the buyer.

The taxpayer must later "cover" the short sale by purchasing the same amount of the security sold and returning it to the lending party. If the taxpayer is able to purchase the security for a lower price than the short sale price, he or she has a gain in the amount of the price differential, less, of course, brokerage commissions and any applicable taxes. If the taxpayer's purchase price is higher than the short sale price, a loss results.

3. How is gain or loss on a short sale treated for tax purposes? A taxpayer does not recognize gain or loss on a short sale until the security is delivered to close the sale transaction. Whether the gain or loss is a long-term or short-term capital gain or loss is determined by the taxpayer's holding period for the security delivered to cover the short sale.

Substantially identical stock. If a taxpayer holds, for less than the long-term capital gain holding period (currently, more than one year), stock that is "substantially identical" to stock involved in a short sale, either when the sale is made or when it is closed, special rules apply. Under these rules, a taxpayer's gain on the closing of the short sale is short-term. Also, the taxpayer's holding period for the "substantially identical stock" begins on the earlier of the date the short sale is closed or the date of sale, gift, or other disposition. If the taxpayer holds the "substantially identical stock" for more than the long-term capital gain holding period, his or her loss on the closing of the short sale is treated as a long-term capital loss. For purposes of these rules, and the wash sale rules, discussed at 2.04.C, "substantially identical" securities are those that are not different in any material feature or in a number of material features considered together.

4. Short sales "against the box." Such a short sale involves a security that the taxpayer already owns. A taxpayer might enter into a short sale against the box to realize a gain on a security in one taxable year and to avoid recognizing it for tax purposes until the following taxable year.

Illustration. Charles Wilson owns 500 shares of Apex, Inc., a stock that is a favorite growth stock for many securities analysts and on which there has been considerable appreciation. Wilson arranges to have his securities broker sell his Apex shares short in December 1990. This transaction fixes Wilson's gain. In January 1991 Wilson closes out the short sale by delivering his 500 Apex shares. So Wilson's gain becomes a recognized gain for tax purposes in 1991, rather than in 1990.

Watch this. Wash sale rules provided under the tax law, discussed at 2.04.C, also apply to short sales. As a result, if a taxpayer who sells substantially identical stock, or makes another short sale of a substantially identical stock or security, within 30 days before or after closing a short sale is not allowed short sale losses for tax purposes.

C. Wash Sale Rules

Under these rules, a taxpayer loses his or her deduction with respect to a security sold at a loss if he or she purchases the same or substantially identical securities within 30 days before or after the sale that produced the loss. Thus, a 61-day rule applies.

A wash sale would occur on the date that a securities broker executes a sell order for a taxpayer, referred to as the *contract date*. A wash sale does *not* occur on the date that delivery of the stock sold is made. The date on which the delivery of the stock is made is referred to as the settlement date.

Caution. These rules can be particularly troublesome for a taxpayer who disposes of several lots of a security simultaneously. If some lots are sold at a loss and others at a gain, and the security is reacquired within the 61-day period, the taxpayer will be faced with nondeductible losses and taxable gains.

D. Purchases of Municipal Bonds

Municipal bonds (i.e., bonds issued by state and local governmental units) have traditionally been investment favorites because the interest paid on them is exempt from federal income tax. This interest may also be exempt from state and local taxes as well, as would be the case when the purchaser resides within the issuer's territory. For example, interest on a regular New York City municipal bond would be totally tax-exempt to a New York City resident.

1. Risk factor. The yield on municipal bonds is affected by general market factors affecting interest rates. For example, if market interest rates are generally declining, the market value of a bond should increase because its interest rate will usually be attractive in comparison. However, if market interest rates are generally rising, the market value of a bond should decline because its interest rate will usually not be attractive in comparison. Bond values may also be affected by other factors, notably the evaluation of the issuer's creditworthiness by ratings agencies such as Moody's Investors' Service and Standard & Poor's.

2. Treatment of interest expense and other carrying charges. A taxpayer is generally *not* allowed to deduct expenses and interest incurred to purchase or carry municipal obligations that are free of federal income tax. This is the case whether there is a *direct or indirect* relationship between the taxpayer's borrowing and the carrying of the tax-exempt obligations. For example, if a taxpayer enters into a margin loan with his or her securities broker to purchase securities generating *taxable* income, the IRS may find such a relationship ineligible for interest deduction purposes when the taxpayer retains tax-exempt obligations.

3. Exception for private activity bonds. As provided under the Tax Reform Act of 1986 (TRA '86), the interest income on certain municipal bonds is not exempt from the alternative minimum tax (AMT). These bonds, referred to as *private activity bonds* (PA bonds), are discussed in detail in Chapter 6, Minimizing the Bite of the Alternative Minimum Tax. They are issued by governmental units for such purposes as mass commuting facilities and water and sewage projects.

The rules applicable to PA bonds generally apply to bonds issued on or after September 1, 1986, although certain exceptions apply. If a taxpayer purchases a bond issued before September 1, 1986, in the secondary market (i.e., not as an original issue purchaser), interest payments on such a bond continue to be free of federal income tax as long as it was tax-exempt when issued.

RRA '93.   RRA '93 exempts from the private activity bond volume limitations bonds issued with respect to government-owned property. See the Foreword on RRA '93.

Planning point.   If a taxpayer's regular federal income tax liability is more than his or her AMT liability, PA bonds may be a good investment. They can be a superior investment to regular municipal bonds for such taxpayers because they usually have higher interest yields. The amount of PA bonds that such an individual should purchase without incurring an AMT liability would generally be based on the amount of taxable income, other AMT preferences, and AMT exemptions available. Typically, wealthy individuals having few or no AMT preferences will benefit from the purchase of PA bonds.

Another AMT point.   When a taxpayer incurs expenses and interest for the purpose of purchasing and carrying PA bonds, which give rise to an AMT preference, such expenses and interest *reduce* his or her AMT preference. For *regular tax* purposes, however, such expenses and interest charges generally are *not* deductible, as discussed above.

Note.   Another requirement imposed by recent tax law changes is that taxpayers must now report the municipal bond interest they receive during a taxable year on their federal income tax returns, even though it is *not* subject to federal income tax.

E. Purchases of US Government Obligations

These instruments are also traditional favorites of individual investors. Although interest paid thereon is subject to federal income tax, such interest is exempt from state and local income tax. And because these instruments are backed by the federal government, they provide a high degree of investment safety.

Note. As discussed in Chapter 3, a taxpayer's deduction of investment interest is limited to his or her investment income plus an additional statutory allowance phased out after 1990. The interest income on US government obligations increases a taxpayer's investment income and therefore can boost a taxpayer's investment interest deduction.

1. US Treasury bills. These instruments, commonly referred to as *T-bills,* are purchased by an investor at an amount below face value, and at maturity their face value is paid. The discount (i.e., the difference between the investor's purchase price and the amount paid at maturity) is the equivalent of interest income. These instruments can be purchased in a minimum denomination of $10,000, with additional increments of $5,000 available. They have 13-week, 26-week, and 52-week maturities.

Tax break. A taxpayer can purchase a T-bill in the current taxable year and can elect to defer the tax on the income earned until the following taxable year.

2. US Treasury bonds and notes. These instruments, commonly referred to as *T-bonds* and *T-notes,* are, unlike Treasury bills, issued by the US Treasury at face value. The Treasury pays the holder interest every six months after the date of the issuance of the instrument. The interest payments are taxable to the holder on receipt.

T-notes have maturities of 2, 4, 5, 7, and 10 years. If a T-note has a maturity of less than four years, the minimum denomination available for purchase is $5,000, with $1,000 increments available. For T-notes with longer maturities, and for T-bonds, the minimum denomination available for purchase is $1,000, with $1,000 increments available. T-bonds have maturities of 10, 20, and 30 years.

3. US savings bonds. U.S. savings bonds are offered in two series: EE and HH. Interest earned on these bonds, as is the case with other US obligations, is exempt from state and local tax. Series EE US savings bonds are offered to investors at a discount of 50 percent from face value in denominations from $50 to $10,000. They can be redeemed, after a six-month holding period has elapsed, at a premium over their purchase price or, at maturity, at face value. These bonds are described in detail in the Encyclopedia, and the tax planning opportunities they offer in connection with transfers of wealth to children are discussed in Chapter 10.

Note. The interest rate paid on Series EE US savings bonds is adjusted semiannually in November and May of each year. This adjustment provision is designed to provide investment stability in that it is made in response to money market interest rates.

Further note. If a taxpayer has elected to report US savings bond interest currently, an IRS Revenue Procedure permits taxpayers to periodically elect out of such reporting. This Revenue Procedure, current reporting, and deferral of interest income on US savings bonds are discussed in detail in Chapter 10, in connection with transfers to children. This Revenue Procedure (Rev. Proc. 89–46) is reproduced in Appendix A of this book.

Series HH US savings bonds are offered by the Treasury at par value, and interest payments on them are made semiannually. They can be purchased *only* in exchange for the old Series E or the current Series EE US savings bonds. They are offered in $500, $1,000, $5,000, and $10,000 denominations and have 10-year maturities. Interest income earned on these bonds is currently taxable to the holder. A detailed description of these bonds is provided in the Encyclopedia of Investment Taxation.

F. Tax Shelters—What's Left?

Recent tax legislation has severely limited the ability of taxpayers to reap tax benefits through the use of tax shelters. In simple terms, tax shelters were investment vehicles designed to provide investors with tax benefits that, on a dollar-for-dollar basis, often exceeded the investment outlay.

The Tax Reform Act of 1986 (TRA '86) was a key element in restricting tax shelters. Other recent tax legislation has provided further restrictions. Of these restrictions, the most significant are the at-risk rules and the passive loss rules. Under the passive loss rules, discussed in detail in Chapter 8, losses from a taxpayer's passive activities generally can offset only income from such activities. Passive activities include rental activities and other activities in which the taxpayer's active participation does not exceed certain statutory thresholds. Some exceptions apply, notably with respect to certain rental real estate activities. Under the at-risk rules, a taxpayer's loss deductions with respect to an investment are, in general, limited to the amounts that he or she invests or borrows with respect to which there is personal liability, referred to as *recourse debt,* subject to certain exceptions. The at-risk rules are discussed in detail in Chapter 9.

Particulary with respect to real estate tax shelters, investors once found depreciation write-offs appealing. Under recent tax legislation, depreciation write-offs have been restricted, particularly with respect to the lengthening of the period over which the property can be depreciated. Depreciation methods, the accelerated cost recovery system (ACRS), and the modified accelerated cost recovery system (MACRS), under which the cost of an investment may be recovered, are described in detail in the Encyclopedia of Investment Taxation.

G. Other Considerations

Other investments and investment tax strategies are discussed in other parts of this book, both in the Encyclopedia of Investment Taxation and in the chapters of the Year-Round Planning Guide as indicated in the following list.

- Maximizing the deductibility of interest paid, including investment interest and "qualified residence interest"—Chapter 3.
- Retirement planning and withdrawals of funds from qualified retirement plans, including individual retirement accounts—Chapter 4.
- The tax-wise use of life insurance—Chapter 5.
- Minimizing the alternative minimum tax—Chapter 6.
- Hobby loss deduction limits—Chapter 7.
- Avoiding the pitfalls of the passive loss rules—Chapter 8.
- Avoiding the pitfalls of the at-risk rules—Chapter 9.
- The "kiddie tax" and wealth transfers to children—Chapter 10.

The balance of this chapter will be devoted to tax aspects of ownership of a personal residence.

2.05. MINIMIZING THE TAX BITE ON THE SALE OF A PERSONAL RESIDENCE

Many taxpayers have much, if not most, of their wealth tied up in their personal residences. Much of this wealth is attributable to the residence's appreciation in value during the period of ownership. When this wealth is tapped at the time of the residence's sale, the tax bite can be significant. The discussion in this series of paragraphs is designed to help taxpayers minimize that tax bite.

A. Overview of the Applicable Rules

The gain on the sale of a taxpayer's personal residence is *not* currently taxable; rather, the tax on that gain is *deferred* if conditions specified in the tax law are met. These conditions are as follows:

* The total gain will escape current tax when an amount equal to the proceeds of the residence's sale, net of expenses incurred with respect to the sale, is reinvested in a replacement residence within a replacement period specified in the tax law. (In general, for many taxpayers this is a period of two years before, or two years after, the sale—see 2.06.)
* The gain will partially escape current tax when only a portion of the sale proceeds are invested in a replacement residence. The portion of the sale proceeds not so invested are subject to tax in the year of sale as a capital gain.

Illustration. Charlene Parker purchased a home in 1988 that served as her principal residence. Her tax basis in the home is $100,000. In September of 1993 Parker sells the home for $120,000 and purchases a replacement residence. *Result:* Parker's realized gain is $20,000 ($120,000–$100,000). None of this realized gain will be taxed as long as Parker pays $120,000 or more for the replacement residence. If Parker pays less than $120,000 for the replacement residence, she will be liable to tax. For example, if she pays $100,000 for the replacement residence, she will be taxed on the entire gain. If she pays $110,000 for the replacement residence, she will pay tax on $10,000.

Note. The Tax Court has allowed deferral under § 1034 in a case involving a depressed real estate market (*Clapham*, 63 TC 505). Here, the taxpayer moved out of his old home two years before buying a replacement. The taxpayer continued to attempt to sell it and intermittently rented it. He finally sold the old house nine months after he bought the new one.

B. What Is Considered a "Personal Residence"?

The following are considered "personal residences" for purposes of the nonrecognition-of-gain rules described above:

Houses.	Houseboats.
Condominiums.	Housetrailers.
Cooperative apartments.	Yachts.

C. Special Rule for Surviving Spouses

The tax law allows nonrecognition-of-gain treatment to a surviving spouse whose spouse died after their former residence was sold but before a replacement residence is purchased. This rule applies to sales or exchanges made after 1984 in taxable years ending after 1984.

To qualify under this rule, the spouses must have been married on the date of death of the deceased spouse, *and* the surviving spouse must use the replacement residence as his or her principal residence.

Note. This is the case whether or not the former principal residence was held jointly by the spouses or by only one of the spouses.

D. Divorced Spouses

Under the facts of an IRS private letter ruling (8911015), issued at the request of taxpayers, a married couple who filed joint tax returns sold their personal residence and elected to defer the gain on the sale. However, they divorced within the replacement period without purchasing a replacement residence. Under the divorce agreement between these taxpayers, any gain recognized with respect to the sale was to be split evenly between them. The husband later purchased a residence within the two-year replacement period, but the wife did not. The cost of the husband's residence equaled 80 percent of the realized gain on the marital residence. According to the IRS, on these facts, 50 percent of the adjusted sales price of the marital residence and the realized gain thereon is taken into account by the husband in determining the deferral of gain. The husband is also required to include the amount of the gain realized by his ex-wife on an amended tax return, since she did not purchase a replacement residence within the two-year period.

Note. In the private letter ruling discussed above, the IRS also indicated that the former spouses were *jointly and severally liable* for tax, interest, and penalties owing with respect to the gain on the sale of the marital residence.

Caution. Private letter rulings cannot be relied upon as precedent; they are relevant only to the taxpayer(s) involved. However, they are indicative as to what positions the IRS may take on the tax issue(s) involved.

E. Exclusion Available for Home Sellers over Age 55

The sale of a residence by a taxpayer who is over age 55 at a gain is subject to special rules under the tax law. Such a taxpayer is permitted to elect to exclude up to $125,000 of gain on the sale. (In the case of married persons who file separate tax returns, only up to $62,500 can be excluded from tax.) This exclusion is available even though the taxpayer does not purchase a replacement residence. To qualify for this exclusion, the taxpayer's residence is required to be owned or used by him or her as a personal residence for a minimum of three of the five years before its sale. These rules apply only to gain on the sale of a residence; a loss on such a sale cannot be deducted.

After using this exclusion, a taxpayer may still take advantage of the rollover rules with respect to gain that is more than the exclusion amount.

Illustration. Robert Walker turned age 56 in June 1993. In August 1993 he sold his personal residence, receiving net proceeds of $150,000. He had purchased the residence in 1985 at a cost of $100,000. If he elects the over-55 exclusion, Walker can exclude his $50,000 gain from tax.

Note. The rules applicable to "fixing-up" expenses do not come into play when this exclusion is elected (see 2.11).

1. Once-in-a-lifetime chance. An individual taxpayer is allowed to make this exclusion election only *once* in his or her lifetime. In the case of a married couple, only one exclusion election is allowable for the lifetime of *either* spouse. As a result, if one spouse has made the election prior to his or her current marriage, he or she cannot make the election with respect to a residence owned jointly with a spouse. But if spouses each *individually* made the election prior to their marriage, the elections are not voided. Also, electing spouses who divorce are not entitled to a subsequent election. In such a case, the election cannot be made by a new spouse of either, unless the new marriage is ended before that new spouse sells his or her residence in a sale that qualifies under the exclusion rules.

Observation. When two taxpayers who are over age 55 are thinking of marriage, and each has a residence that they wish to sell, they should consider delaying their marriage until after their homes are sold in order to maximize the benefit of the exclusion. The amount of difference in tax between the sale of residences by unmarried persons and married couples, when the exclusion is elected, may be as high as $49,500. This figure is the result of applying the top marginal tax rate of 39.6 percent against the $125,000 exclusion amount unavailable.

2. Three-of-five-year requirement. For meeting the three-of-five-year requirement, discussed above, a taxpayer is considered to dwell in his or her principal residence during the five-year period even when he or she is required to enter a qualified facility for care (e.g., a licensed nursing home). To qualify under this rule, applicable to residence sales after September 30, 1988, the taxpayer is required to have owned and actually lived in the residence as a principal residence for a minimum of one year during the five-year period.

Remember this. The one-time exclusion for home sellers age 55 or over can be used together with the deferral rule under Code § 1034, resulting in potentially big tax saving on the sale of a residence.

2.06.   REPLACEMENT PERIOD REQUIREMENT FOR NONRECOGNITION OF GAIN

A. General Rule

A taxpayer who lives in a residence that he or she purchased within two years before or within two years after selling his or her former residence may be able to defer tax on gain from that sale. To obtain nonrecognition treatment, the statutory replacement period rules must be complied with strictly.

B. Special Rule Applicable to Residences under Construction

A special rule applies to residences under construction. Under this rule, such a residence is considered as having been purchased under the general nonrecognition rules applicable to the purchase of a replacement residence only if construction is complete within two years after the sale of the former residence.

Important. Once the statutory replacement period has passed, *no* additional time will be allowed a taxpayer to obtain a replacement residence and take advantage of the nonrecognition rules. This is the case even when the failure to make the replacement is due to circumstances beyond a taxpayer's control, such as a delay in completion of construction.

C. Exceptions

1. Foreign homes. The statutory replacement period is *suspended* for taxpayers having foreign tax homes or who are on extended active duty with the US armed forces. However, under this exception, the period of suspension cannot exceed four years after the date the residence is sold.

2. Special exception for sales after July 18, 1984. For sales of residences after July 18, 1984, the replacement period can be extended for certain taxpayers. The period can be extended to the later of:

- Eight years after the date the residence is sold in the case of a US armed forces member stationed in a foreign country, or who is required to live in government quarters at a remote location.

- One year after the last day that the armed forces member is stationed in a foreign country or is required to live in government quarters.

2.07. NONRECOGNITION TREATMENT NOT ELECTIVE

With respect to the gain on a taxpayer's sale of his or her residence, tax-deferred rollover treatment under the nonrecognition rules is *mandatory*. The taxpayer *cannot elect* this treatment. However, a taxpayer can *avoid* this treatment by failing to meet the statutory conditions, such as the replacement period.

Observations. For the majority of taxpayers it makes sense to comply with the statutory conditions and obtain the tax deferral break rather than recognize gain on the sale of a residence. However, there are some cases in which the taxpayer would want to recognize the gain. For example, suppose a taxpayer has a net operating loss carryover. He or she could recognize the gain, offset the loss against the gain, and, as a result, free up the gain from eventual tax and utilize the loss carryover, whose value might otherwise have been wasted.

2.08. EFFECT OF NONRECOGNITION TREATMENT

A. Tax Deferral

The effect of the nonrecognition treatment is tax deferral for the taxpayer whose sale of his or her residence meets the statutory conditions. This deferral can be permanent if the taxpayer owns the replacement home at the time of his or her death. Also, the tax can be deferred numerous times if the taxpayer purchases several residences over time, as long as he or she meets the statutory conditions with respect to each replacement.

B. Sale of Residence within Two Years of Prior Sale

A taxpayer cannot receive tax-free rollover treatment with respect to the sale of a principal residence when he or she sold another principal residence within two years prior to the second sale. But a taxpayer can still enjoy tax-free rollover treatment from selling a principal residence within the two-year period as a result of a move to a new principal place of work if the taxpayer meets certain requirements under the moving expense deduction rules, notably the 35-mile distance requirement.

2.09. CONDEMNATION OF TAXPAYER'S RESIDENCE

A. Nonrecognition Alternatives

If a taxpayer's residence is condemned by a governmental unit or the taxpayer sells the residence under threat of such condemnation, he or she has two nonrecognition alternatives available for tax purposes:

* The taxpayer may elect tax-free rollover treatment under the nonrecognition rules applicable to replacement residences under Code § 1034, described above.

* Otherwise, the taxpayer's gain resulting from the condemnation or sale of the residence under threat of condemnation will not be recognized for tax purposes to the extent the proceeds are reinvested in another residence (i.e., "similar or related property" under the tax law), and nonrecognition treatment is elected by the taxpayer under the tax rules applicable to involuntary conversions.

B. How the Replacement and Involuntary Conversion Rules Differ

Although nonrecognition treatment may be enjoyed by a taxpayer with respect to the sale of a principal residence under threat of condemnation or through condemnation, nonrecognition treatment differs under the tax rules applicable to involuntary conversions and those applicable to the replacement of a principal residence. The differences are as follows:

* A taxpayer is given a longer replacement deadline under the involuntary conversion rules. In general, replacement property must be acquired in accordance with these rules within two years after the first taxable year in

which any part of the related gain was realized by the taxpayer unless the taxpayer can show reasonable cause for failure to timely file and the actual filing is made within a reasonable time after the initial time limit.

Important break.   If there is an involuntary conversion of property used in a business, a taxpayer is allowed three years in which to replace the converted property.

But watch this.   If a taxpayer acquires property before other property that he or she holds is condemned, or is sold under threat of condemnation, that other property will not qualify as replacement property under the involuntary conversion rules.

- Under the involuntary conversion rules there is no allowance for fixing-up expenses.
- The involuntary conversion rules are not necessarily mandatory in operation. They are mandatory in operation when property is directly converted by a taxpayer into replacement property. They are not mandatory, but can be elected by a taxpayer, when the taxpayer converts property into cash and later into replacement property. On the other hand, the nonrecognition rules applicable to the voluntary replacement of a taxpayer's principal residence are mandatory in operation as long as the requirements under those rules are met.

2.10.   TAXPAYER'S BASIS FOR THE REPLACE-MENT RESIDENCE

A taxpayer's basis for the replacement residence is its purchase price minus any gain not recognized on the sale of the former residence. In the case of a newly constructed residence, the costs of land and construction are used instead of the purchase price.

Illustration 1.   David Johnson had a $60,000 basis in his former residence, which he sold for $85,000. His replacement residence cost $85,000. Johnson's basis for the new residence is $60,000, which is the $85,000 cost less the $25,000 not taxed under the nonrecognition rules.

Illustration 2.   Suppose that Johnson in Illustration 1 paid $88,000 for the replacement residence. In this case, Johnson's basis in the new home would be $63,000, which is $88,000 cost less the $25,000 not taxed under the nonrecognition rules.

Illustration 3. Suppose that Johnson in Illustration 1 paid $82,000 for the replacement residence. In this case, Johnson's basis for it would be $60,000, which is $82,000 cost less $22,000 of gain not recognized.

A taxpayer's basis for the replacement residence also includes any mortgage debt he or she assumes.

Illustration 4. Ann Page sells her home for $65,000, realizing a $15,000 profit. To purchase a replacement residence, she pays $30,000 in cash and obtains a $50,000 mortgage. Consequently, her basis for the replacement residence is $65,000, which is $80,000 total cost less the $15,000 unrecognized gain.

When the purchaser of the taxpayer's former residence assumes, satisfies, or gives the taxpayer a mortgage, the amount of the mortgage is treated as being part of the sale proceeds.

If the gain on the sale of his or her residence is a taxable gain, a taxpayer is allowed to deduct the residence's tax basis and any selling expenses from the sales price. For this purpose, the tax basis of the residence is for most taxpayers its cost. Cost may be reduced by depreciation *only* if the residence was used for business purposes or was rented. Also, for this purpose, selling expenses would typically include commission of a real estate broker, legal fees, advertising expenses, transfer taxes not otherwise deductible, and recording fees.

In determining the adjusted basis of a replacement residence, a taxpayer increases its purchase price (cost) by expenses incurred in connection with the purchase, such as closing costs, legal fees, appraisal fees, and title insurance. Also added in arriving at the residence's adjusted basis are amounts expended by the taxpayer for replacements, improvements, and alterations that materially add to the value of the residence, extend its useful life, or enable it to be adapted for another use.

Note. If the work done on the residence is *extensive,* the purchasing taxpayer is allowed to capitalize its cost. This is so even though part of the work, by itself, would otherwise constitute a nondeductible, noncapitalizable repair.

2.11.   SPECIAL TREATMENT OF FIXING-UP EXPENSES

Fixing-up expenses can be applied to reduce the gain recognized on the sale of a residence when a taxpayer replaces the residence or is over age 55. In general, the taxpayer's gain on the sale is the amount realized less the residence's tax basis. For this purpose, the amount realized is the sale price reduced by expenses incurred in connection with the sale. *Qualified* fixing-up expenses can also be deducted from the amount realized in determining the gain to be recognized by the taxpayer.

Qualified fixing-up expenses are expenses incurred for repairs done to make a residence more salable. They are qualified *only* if all the following conditions hold:

- They are incurred for work performed within 90 days before the contract to sell the residence was entered into. For this purpose, it is immaterial when title passes, but the contract involved must be one under which the sale actually takes place. If the work is performed prior to the 90-day period, the related expenses are *not* qualified fixing-up expenses. This is the case even if payment for that work is made during the 90-day period.
- Payment is made no later than 30 days after the date of the residence's sale. This date is *not* the contract date.
- They are not otherwise deductible, do not represent a capital expenditure added to the residence's basis, and are not taken into account in determining the amount realized by the taxpayer on the sale of the residence.

Note.   It is immaterial whether the fix-up work is done, or payment for it is made, in the same taxable year in which the sale occurs.

Chapter Three

Maximizing Deductions for Interest Paid

3.01. OVERVIEW

This chapter discusses how to maximize the deductibility of interest paid by taxpayers. The following paragraphs cover the basics of the interest deduction rules, focusing primarily on the deductibility of investment interest and qualified residence interest. Also discussed are below-market interest and no-interest loans, which are subject to special rules provided under the tax law.

3.02. DEDUCTIBILITY OF INTEREST—BASIC RULES

A. Nondeductible Interest Paid

Nondeductible interest is interest paid or accrued with respect to the purchase of:

- Bonds generating tax-exempt interest income.
- A life insurance, endowment, or annuity contract with a plan of systematically borrowing cash value increases.
- A "single premium" life insurance contract (under which nearly all premiums are paid within four years of purchase of the policy or by a large prepayment).
- Shares in a mutual fund (regulated investment company) distributing only tax-exempt (or interest related to distributions of partially tax-exempt) dividends.

B. "Delayed" Interest

A taxpayer is required to spread prepayments of interest over the years to which the interest payments relate. A taxpayer is also allowed to deduct interest payable with respect to a margin account when it is actually paid, and this may occur when the securities broker with whom the account is maintained collects dividends or interest on assets in the account. In addition, a taxpayer may deduct interest with respect to a refinanced loan when the interest is paid in a separate transaction at the time the new loan is negotiated.

3.03. INTEREST-TRACING RULES

Under Temporary Regulations issued by the IRS, interest allocation rules are provided to prevent the sheltering of income from personal services and portfolio (in general, investment) income. These tracing rules generally apply to interest expenses paid or accrued in a taxable year beginning *after December 31, 1986,* irrespective of when the taxpayer incurred the underlying debt. With respect to expenditures made *on or before August 3, 1987,* any expenditure made from an account within 90 days after debt proceeds are deposited or received in cash can be treated as made from the debt proceeds. Such expenditures are *not* subject to the 15-day rule that generally applies under the Temporary Regulations to expenditures made after August 3, 1987. Also, under a transition rule, debt outstanding on December 31, 1986, that is properly attributable to a business or rental activity is allocated to the assets held for use or sale to customers of that business or activity.

Further, under the Temporary Regulations, a taxpayer's debt is allocated among his or her expenditures without any statutory limits on the deductibility of interest being taken into account. In applying the statutory limits applicable with respect to passive activities and nonbusiness interest, nondeductible interest expense is *not* taken into account. However, a taxpayer is allowed to deduct qualified residence interest, discussed later in this chapter, irrespective of how he or she allocates interest expense under the Temporary Regulations.

These important and complex interest-tracing rules provided under the Temporary Regulations are discussed in detail below.

A. How the Interest-Tracing Rules Work—Overview

The Temporary Regulations (Temp. Reg. § 1.163–8T) providing interest-tracing rules were prompted by rules requiring allocation of interest for purposes of the following interest deduction limits enacted in the Tax Reform Act of 1986 (TRA '86):

- The phased-in curtailment, ending after 1990, of deductions for personal interest (e.g., credit card and personal loan interest).
- Limits on credits and the deductibility of losses from passive activities.
- Restrictions on the deductibility of investment interest.

B. How Debt Is Allocated—Generally

Under the Temporary Regulations, debt is allocated by tracing disbursements of the debt proceeds to specific expenditures made by a taxpayer for the following purposes:

* Use in a trade or business.
* Use for investment purposes.
* Use in passive activity.
* Use for personal purposes.

Accordingly, when such debt is allocated, the related interest expense is then subject to the limit applicable to the particular category of expenditure involved. Thus, for example, if debt is incurred for personal purposes of the taxpayer, the interest paid with respect to that debt is subject to the deduction limits applicable to personal interest, and that debt is totally nondeductible beginning in 1991.

> ***Note.*** The type of property that is used by the taxpayer to secure debt is immaterial for purposes of the interest allocation rules.

C. Specific Debt Allocation Rules

Three basic debt allocation rules are specified under the Temporary Regulations. These regard:

* Debt proceeds deposited to the taxpayer/borrower's account.
* Debt proceeds not paid over by the lender to the taxpayer/borrower.
* Debt proceeds distributed by the lender to the taxpayer/borrower in cash.

1. Debt proceeds deposited in taxpayer's account. Initially, under the Temporary Regulations, when debt proceeds are deposited in a taxpayer/borrower's account, that deposit is considered as held by the taxpayer/borrower for *investment* purposes. If the taxpayer applies those proceeds for another of the purposes listed at 3.03.B, however, reallocation to that particular type of expenditure is required. As a result, a pro rata allocation of the interest on such debt must be made with respect to each type of expenditure involved.

When a taxpayer spends funds from an account that contains debt proceeds, the expenditure is treated under the Temporary Regulations as having been made from such proceeds *before* any unborrowed amounts in the account at the time of expenditure and any amounts subsequently deposited to that account.

The nature of the expenditure will govern the deductibility of the interest on the debt. For example, if the expenditure is made for personal purposes, the interest is personal (consumer) interest, which is totally nondeductible after 1990.

When a taxpayer's account contains only debt proceeds and interest earned on those proceeds, an amount spent from such an account may be treated as being made first from the account interest. To the extent that such expenditure is treated as having been from the account interest, it is not taken into account for purposes of the ordering rules.

When a taxpayer makes a payment from a checking account, the payment is treated as made at the time the check is written. However, for this rule to apply, the check must be mailed or delivered by the taxpayer within a reasonable time period. But if the check does not clear within a reasonable time after the date that it was written, the related expenditure may be considered as having been made by the taxpayer at a later date.

Key Exception.   Expenditures made by a taxpayer from an account within 15 days after the deposit of debt proceeds in that account can be treated as made out of such debt proceeds. Consequently, if a taxpayer makes a personal expenditure from such an account before making an expenditure related to a trade or business expenditure, the related debt *can* be allocated to the trade or business expenditure as long as it is made within 15 days after the related funds were originally deposited in the taxpayer's account.

When proceeds of multiple loans are deposited by a taxpayer in the same account, the loan proceeds are treated under the Temporary Regulations as deposited in the account in the order that the loans are made. When a taxpayer obtains multiple loans at the same time, those loans can be treated as obtained in any order.

Note.   In the case of adjustable rate loans, with respect to which interest does not accrue at the same rate on the full amount of the loan, each part of the loan for which interest accrues at a different rate is treated as a separate loan requiring separate allocation. And, *significantly,* this rule is also applicable to a taxpayer's lines of credit and other similar continuous borrowings.

2. Debt proceeds not paid to taxpayer.   If loan proceeds are received by someone other than the taxpayer, the Temporary Regulations treat them as if the taxpayer used them for the purpose for which they were used by the other party. This also is the case with respect to debts assumed when property is purchased or sold and no loan proceeds are disbursed to the taxpayer.

3. Debt proceeds received in cash. Any cash expenditure made by a taxpayer within 15 days of receipt of cash debt proceeds can be treated as if made from such proceeds as of the date the taxpayer receives them. When a taxpayer spends cash from cash debt proceeds later than the 15th day after their receipt, such expenditures are treated as having been made for *personal* purposes.

Watch this! A cash withdrawal from an account by a taxpayer that is treated as an expenditure from debt proceeds under the Temporary Regulation is treated as debt proceeds received by the taxpayer in cash. If the taxpayer does not use these proceeds with 15 days after their receipt for a purpose other than a personal one, they are treated as *used for personal purposes.* As a result, the interest on the debt will be treated as *personal interest.*

4. Incurring debt to carry debt. When a debt is used by a taxpayer to pay the cost of carrying debt, including interest payments, debt allocation involves substitution. If debt proceeds are used to pay interest on a taxpayer's other debt, the debt from which the proceeds are paid is allocated to the same expenditure that generated the interest expense. If debt proceeds are used to pay carrying costs on the related debt, except with respect to interest expense, such proceeds are allocated in accordance with the remaining amount of that debt.

D. Rules on Reallocation of Debt

1. Which debts must be reallocated? Under the Temporary Regulations, there must be a reallocation of debt allocated by a taxpayer to an expenditure when:
- The proceeds of the related debt are applied to a different kind of expenditure.
- Debt proceeds are capitalized with respect to an asset held by a taxpayer, and the proceeds from the sale of that asset are otherwise applied.
- The character of an activity in which the taxpayer is involved changes. In this case the taxpayer's expenditures in connection with the earlier activity must be reallocated to the new activity. This could occur, for example, when the change involves a shift from a passive activity to one in which the taxpayer materially participates.

In these three situations, the amount of debt required to be reallocated under the Temporary Regulations is not more than the proceeds obtained on the disposition of the related assets or their fair market value at the time of the change. To the extent such proceeds are more than the amount of the related debt, reallocation is required under the general rules of the Temporary Regulations applicable when debt proceeds are deposited in a taxpayer's account.

2. When is reallocation required? In determining when a debt is required to be reallocated, a taxpayer is allowed to treat all expenditures made from his or her account during any calendar month as made on the later of

- The first day of that month.
- The date the debt proceeds involved are deposited in his or her account.

Note. For purposes of this reallocation rule, a taxpayer can take advantage of the alternative *only* if *all* expenditures from the particular account during the same month are treated in the same manner.

Recommendation. A taxpayer's segregation of loan proceeds greatly simplifies the task involved with respect to the tracing rules of the Temporary Regulations. The taxpayer's burden will further be eased by maintaining separate accounts for each type of expenditure made with respect to borrowings.

E. Debt Repayments

1. Ordering rules. When a debt incurred by a taxpayer is allocated to more than one expenditure (see 3.03.C.1), repayment of such debt is treated as having been made in the following order:

- Personal expenditures.
- Investment and passive activity expenditures.
- Expenditures made with respect to a rental real estate passive activity in which the taxpayer materially participates.
- Expenditures in connection with a former passive activity.
- Trade or business expenditures.

These ordering rules are designed to minimize statutory interest deduction limits. Accordingly, debt repayments are first applied in the order of debt subject to the most severe deduction limits—debt incurred for personal, investment, and passive activity purposes. Repayments are then applied to other activities.

2. Multiple type of expenditures. When a taxpayer's debt is allocated to multiple type of expenditures, repayment of that debt is treated as having been made in the order in which the original debt was allocated or reallocated.

3. Refinancing. In the case of a refinancing of debt, the amount of the new debt incurred is allocated to same expenditure with respect to which the original debt was incurred. To the extent that the proceeds of the refinancing are more than the amount of the original debt, allocation is made in accordance with the general rules of the Temporary Regulations.

F. How Interest Expense Is Allocated

The Temporary Regulations require taxpayers to allocate interest accruing on debt to the expenditure(s) to which the debt was required to be allocated under the rules described above. This is the case without regard to when the taxpayer actually pays such interest.

A simplified procedure is provided under the Temporary Regulations with respect to compound interest (i.e., interest charged on interest owed on the underlying debt). When a taxpayer is required to reallocate debt during a taxable year, compound interest on that debt is permitted to be allocated between the original and later expenditures involved on a pro rata basis. This pro rata allocation is based on the number of days during the year (12 30-day months) that the debt was allocated to each expenditure.

> *Watch this.* When interest expense is allocated to an expenditure under the Temporary Regulations, it is *not* later reallocated. This is the case even if the related debt *is* reallocated. This rule produces a record-keeping problem for taxpayers with respect to interest expense.

3.04. TREATMENT OF DISCOUNT ON MARKET DISCOUNT BONDS

Interest that a taxpayer pays or accrues to purchase or carry a market discount bond (defined at 3.04.C) can, in general, be deducted to the extent that the bond generates interest income. For this purpose, interest income includes original issue discount (OID). To the extent that the related interest expense is more than the interest income earned by the taxpayer on such a bond, the deductibility of that excess interest expense will, in general, be deferred until the taxpayer disposes of the bond.

> *RRA '93.* RRA '93 provides anti-conversion rules designed to prevent the conversion of ordinary income to lower taxed capital gains. One of these rules extends the market discount rules to acquisitions after April 30, 1993, of tax-exempt bonds and bonds which were issued on or before July 18, 1984, (previously grandfathered under the rules). See the Foreword on RRA '93.

A. Determining the Amount of Interest Expense Deferred

To determine the amount of interest expense deferred with respect to the market discount bond, the taxpayer must first determine the related *net direct interest expense*. To arrive at this amount, the total of interest and OID on the bond includable in the taxpayer's gross income for the taxable year is subtracted from the taxpayer's interest expense during the taxable year incurred to purchase or carry the bond. The taxpayer then subtracts the amortization of the market discount for the taxable year, or part thereof, during which the taxpayer holds the bond. The remainder, which is the net direct interest expense is currently deductible, and deductibility of the part offset by the amortization of the market discount is deferred.

B. Treatment of Deferred Interest upon Disposition of a Market Discount Bond

A taxpayer who disposes of a market discount bond is allowed to deduct any prior interest expense deferred on the bond in the year of sale.

C. Which Bonds Are Considered Market Discount Bonds?

All bonds are subject to the market discount rules, with the following statutory exceptions:

- Original issue discount (OID) bonds.
- US savings bonds.
- Tax-exempt bonds.
- Short-term obligations having a fixed maturity date of up to 12 months (6 months for those acquired before 1988) from the issue date.
- Certain installment obligations.

D. What Is Market Discount?

Market discount is defined under the tax law as the excess of the stated redemption price at maturity of a bond subject to the market discount rules, over the taxpayer's basis for the bond at the time it was acquired. Market discount is considered to be zero under these rules when it is less than one-fourth of 1 percent (.0025) of the stated redemption price of a bond subject to these rules times the number of full years remaining until the bond matures.

Observation. Market discount usually arises when there is a general rise in market interest rates because market values of bonds will typically decline as a result.

E. Recognizing Market Discount as Interest

1. Accrual of market discount. A taxpayer has two ways available to accrue market discount over the term to maturity of a bond subject to the market discount rules:

- The taxpayer may accrue it in an equal amount for each day. Such an amount is determined through dividing the market discount by the days remaining until the bond matures.
- The taxpayer may accrue it in a daily amount yielding a constant amortization rate based on his or her tax basis for the bond.

2. Treatment of recognized gain. Any gain recognized by a taxpayer on disposition of a market discount bond issued after July 18, 1984, is treated as interest income to the extent of market discount accrued during the period that the taxpayer held the bond. Gain in excess of that amount will generally be treated as capital gain.

3. Current inclusion of market discount in interest income. As an alternative to the accrual methods described at 3.04.E.1, a taxpayer can currently include in interest income for the taxable year that year's amortization of market discount on a bond subject to the market discount rules. If this method is elected by a taxpayer, his or her basis for such a bond is increased by the market discount on it included in income. In the year the taxpayer sells the bond, only the amortization of market discount for that year is included in interest income.

Watch this. A taxpayer who makes this alternative election may be able to deduct more interest earlier, but his or her ability to do this depends on how the limit on the deductibility of investment interest will apply. Also, this election is binding on a taxpayer with respect to all market discount bonds purchased during the election year and thereafter.

Recommendations. Election of this alternative may be beneficial for taxpayers having capital loss carryovers because gains on the disposition of such bonds, qualify as capital gains, can be offset against such carryovers.

F. Treatment of Original Issue Discount

1. Definition. When a bond is issued at a price below its stated redemption value at maturity, the price difference is called *original issue discount* (OID). In general, amortization of OID is currently includable in an investor's taxable income.

2. Impact of OID on market discount. The impact of OID on market discounts is as follows: for a bond acquired through original issue after July 18, 1984, the market discount rules will *not* apply unless the taxpayer's tax basis for the bond is less than its issue price, or the bond was issued in a corporate reorganization in exchange for a market discount bond. When a bond does have OID and market discount, a taxpayer determines the market discount by calculating the total OID, which is income for all holders before he or she purchased the bond, and subtracting from total OID his or her tax basis for the bond at the time of purchase from its issue price.

G. Treatment of Interest on Short-Term Obligations

Discount on a short-term obligation is accrued by, and currently taxable to, taxpayers under the following circumstances:

- The obligation is held by accrual basis taxpayers, banks, mutual funds, common trust funds, and certain pass-through entities.
- The obligation is part of a hedging transaction.
- The obligation is a stripped bond (i.e., one on which the income portion is separated from principal) or interest coupons held by a taxpayer who stripped them from the bond.
- The obligation is held by a taxpayer primarily for sale to customers in the ordinary course of a trade or business.

For short-term obligations not listed here, such treatment is not mandatory but may be elected by a taxpayer.

1. What is a short-term obligation? For purposes of these rules, a short-term obligation is an obligation having a fixed maturity date up to a maximum of *one year* from the date on which it is issued.

2. Determining the amount of interest expense deferred. In determining the amount of interest deferred on a short-term obligation, a taxpayer first must determine the net direct interest expense (see 3.04.A). From this amount, the taxpayer then subtracts (1) the amortization of acquisition discount for the year, or part thereof, that the obligation was held by the taxpayer and (2) interest, other than interest related to the determination of acquisition discount, accrued, but not included in income, under the taxpayer's method of accounting (cash method for most individual taxpayers). The result is the deductible amount of net direct interest expense. Deduction of the amount offset by the two amounts subtracted from net direct interest expense is deferred.

3. Recognizing discount as interest. Taxpayers who are on the cash basis, such as most individual taxpayers, do not include in income, but must accrue, acquisition discount or OID over the remaining term of a short-term obligation. The accrual may be made by the taxpayer using either of two methods:

* The taxpayer may use an equal daily amount, determined by dividing the discount amount by the number of days remaining until the obligation matures.
* Alternatively, the taxpayer may use a daily amount yielding a constant amortization rate based on his or her tax basis for the obligation.

4. Treatment of recognized gain. On the disposition of a short-term obligation, any gain recognized by the taxpayer is treated as interest income to the extent that discount was accrued during the period he or she held the obligation. Gain in excess of that amount will generally be treated as capital gain.

5. Current inclusion of acquisition discount or OID in income. A taxpayer can elect to include amortization of acquisition discount or OID for the year currently in interest income. Interest paid by the taxpayer is currently deductible to the extent not otherwise limited by the investment interest rules. Also, when the taxpayer disposes of the obligation, he or she includes in interest income only the amount of discount amortized in the year in which the disposition occurs.

Watch this. The election to include acquisition discount or OID in interest income currently is binding on the taxpayer with respect to all short-term obligations acquired in the year of the election and thereafter.

3.05. AMORTIZATION OF BOND PREMIUM

Bond premium is the excess amount that an investor pays for a bond over the bond's face value. A taxpayer may elect to amortize this premium. The amortization will not be deductible, however, when the bond is tax-exempt.

If the taxpayer so elects, the amortization is treated as follows:

• *For bonds acquired before October 23, 1986,* it is treated as a miscellaneous itemized deduction that is not subject to the deduction limit of 2 percent of the taxpayer's adjusted gross income that generally applies to such deductions under current tax law.

• *For bonds acquired after October 22, 1986, but before January 1, 1988,* it is treated as an interest expense that is subject to deduction limits applicable to investment interest or, alternatively, as an offset to interest income earned on the bond.

• *For bonds acquired after December 31, 1987,* it is treated as an offset to interest income earned on the bond.

If the taxpayer elects to amortize, he or she must reduce the tax basis of the bond by the amount of the amortization. Accordingly, the taxpayer's gain will be greater, or loss smaller, on the disposition of a bond subject to the election.

Watch this. A taxpayer is bound by this election with respect to all bonds of a similar type acquired in the election year and thereafter.

3.06. MAXIMIZING THE DEDUCTIBILITY OF INVESTMENT INTEREST

A. What Is Investment Interest?

Interest paid by a taxpayer for the purpose of making and/or holding investment property is subject to deduction limits. Property held by a taxpayer for investment purposes basically generates portfolio income, which includes dividends, interest, royalties, or annuity income, *and* the net gain from the sale or exchange of property acquired by a taxpayer for generation of portfolio income or for potential appreciation in value. A taxpayer's investment interest also includes his or her respective share of investment interest paid by S corporations, partnerships, trusts, and estates in which he or she has an interest.

B. How the Investment Interest Limits Work

Investment interest does not include any interest taken into account in determining a taxpayer's passive activity income or loss. Nor does it include interest properly allocable to a rental real estate activity in which the taxpayer actively participates. It also does not include qualified residence interest.

Deductible investment interest is limited to the taxpayer's net investment income for the year. Excess investment interest can be carried over indefinitely for deduction purposes. A carryover can be deducted in a later taxable year only to the extent that the taxpayer's net investment income exceeds investment interest incurred in the later taxable year. The deductibility of interest paid or incurred by a taxpayer in conducting a trade or business is not subject to this limit, although it may be subject to the passive loss rules.

Note. Investment interest is not subject to the limit on itemized deductions applicable to certain high-income taxpayers.

Illustration. Sue Smith, a single individual, has 1993 investment income of $14,000, comprised of dividends and a net gain on the sale of investment property. Sue incurred directly connected expenses, other than interest, of $1,000 with respect to this income. She also incurred $16,000 of investment interest expense.

Here is how Sue determines her 1993 net investment income and her deductible investment interest expense:

Total investment income	$14,000
Less: investment expenses other than interest	(1,000)
Net investment income	13,000
Less: investment interest expense	(16,000)
Excess 1993 investment interest expense	$3,000
($16,000 − $13,000)	

For 1993, Sue can deduct only $13,000 of investment interest expense, the amount of her net investment income. The excess investment interest of $3,000 is carried over for deduction in 1994 or a later taxable year.

RRA '93. Effective for taxable years beginning after December 31, 1992, RRA '93 excludes net capital gain from the definition of investment income for purposes of the computation of a taxpayer's net investment income. Taxpayers are, however, permitted to elect to include net capital gain in investment income and forgo the benefit of the 28 percent top tax rate on capital gains with respect to the amount included.

Observation. In computing the applicable deduction limit for investment interest, a taxpayer does *not* take into account any investment expenses connected with investments that generate tax-exempt income (e.g., many municipal bonds). Such expenses are nondeductible under the tax law. Other nondeductible investment expenses for purposes of these rules include costs that increase the tax basis of property or are used in determining gain or loss on its sale (e.g., state and local transfer taxes, certain brokerage commissions, and legal fees).

3.07. QUALIFIED RESIDENCE INTEREST

For a great many taxpayers who own their homes, and have loans outstanding against those homes, the tax rules applicable to "qualified residence interest" are of critical importance. Although the impact of these rules is most severe with respect to taxpayers having home mortgage loans in amounts in excess of $1 million, they also have a significant impact on taxpayers having smaller mortgage loans. For taxpayers having smaller mortgages, these rules can kick in, for example, when they refinance existing mortgages, obtain home improvement loans, and incur debt under certain other circumstances, as discussed below. The qualified residence interest rules generally apply to loans obtained *after October 13, 1987.*

Major tax trap! Interest on a home mortgage loan that does not qualify as qualified residence interest may be treated as personal (consumer) interest. Personal interest is *totally nondeductible.*

A. Deductibility of Interest on Mortgage Loans Obtained on or before October 13, 1987

In general, a taxpayer is allowed to deduct all interest paid on a mortgage obtained on a qualified residence *on or before October 13, 1987.* A taxpayer is also allowed to deduct all interest paid on a mortgage obtained after that date when the purpose of that mortgage is to *refinance* a mortgage obtained before that date, to the extent of the balance of the refinanced loan as of the date of the refinancing.

Such qualifying loans must be secured by the taxpayer's "qualified residence" during the full loan term. In a case of refinanced mortgage, these rules will apply only until the original mortgage loan is satisfied. In general, with respect to these loans, the period involved will not be more than 30 years after the date that the taxpayer obtained the original mortgage. For refinancings extending beyond that period, the rules applicable to mortgage loans obtained after October 13, 1987, apply.

B. Deductibility of Interest on Mortgage Loans Obtained after October 13, 1987

When a taxpayer obtains a mortgage on a qualified residence (defined at 3.07.C) *after October 13, 1987,* the mortgage is characterized under the tax law as either "acquisition indebtedness" or "home equity indebtedness." Loan interest will not be deductible under the qualified residence interest rules to the extent that "acquisition indebtedness" is over $1 million or "home equity indebtedness" is over $100,000. In the case of married taxpayers filing separate tax returns, these dollar limits are $500,000 and $50,000, respectively.

1. What is acquisition indebtedness?   Under the tax law, *acquisition indebtedness* is defined as debt incurred by a taxpayer for the purpose of acquiring, constructing, or the substantial improvement of a qualified residence and secured by such residence. A refinancing may also constitute acquisition indebtedness to the extent that its amount is not more than the balance of the original loan on the date of the refinancing.

2. What is home equity indebtedness?   *Home equity indebtedness* is any debt, other than acquisition indebtedness, secured by a taxpayer's qualified residence, to the extent that the residence's fair market value is more than the related amount of acquisition indebtedness.

C. What Is a Qualified Residence?

Under these interest deduction rules, the threshold consideration is whether mortgage financing is secured by a qualified residence. If the residence financed so qualifies, the interest paid is deductible, subject to limits discussed below.

Otherwise, the interest paid may be deductible in part, either as interest incurred in the conduct of a trade or business or as personal interest, which is subject to severe deduction limits.

1. Taxpayer's principal residence.   In general, residential loan interest incurred by a taxpayer may be deductible only with respect to the taxpayer's principal residence and a second residence as designated by the taxpayer on a yearly basis, as discussed at 3.07.C.2. A taxpayer's *principal residence* is his or her residence that qualifies for tax-free rollover treatment under Code § 1034, discussed at 2.05.E. Any other residence of the taxpayer could be considered a second residence.

Note.   When a married couple does not file a joint tax return, each spouse can designate only *one* residence as a qualified residence for purposes of these rules, unless *each* spouse consents to the treatment of both by one of them.

2. Taxpayer's second residence.   In addition to a taxpayer's principal residence, interest incurred with respect to a loan on a second residence may qualify as qualified residence interest. To qualify, such a second residence must be used by the taxpayer during a taxable year *for the greater of 14 days or 10 percent of the days that it is rented at fair rental value.*

Watch this.   A taxpayer's residence is considered *rented* for purposes of these rules if (1) the taxpayer offers it for rental or resale or (2) repairs or renovates it for rental purposes.

For purposes of the rules applicable to second residences, the definition of *residence* includes a free-standing residence, a condominium, trailer, recreational vehicle, houseboat, or other similar facility providing sleeping accommodations and cooking and toilet facilities.

A taxpayer is allowed to designate another residence as his or her second residence for purposes of the qualified residence interest rules for a taxable year. Such a designation *can* be made under any of the following circumstances.

- The taxpayer acquires a new residence and elects to have it treated as a second residence for purposes of these rules.
- The taxpayer sells a residence designated as a second residence or starts to treat it as his or her principal residence.
- The taxpayer has a principal residence that ceases to qualify as such, but does not qualify as a second residence.

Note. A taxpayer who has entered into a time-sharing arrangement with respect to a property may still qualify under the qualified residence interest rules with respect to such property.

3. Treatment of loans obtained with respect to residence under construction. If a taxpayer incurs interest with respect to a loan obtained for the purpose of constructing a residence, a special deduction rule applies. Under this rule, a residence under construction is treated as a taxpayer's qualified residence for interest deduction purposes for up to 24 months, as long as it qualifies as such when it is ready for occupancy.

D. Election out of the Qualified Residence Interest Rules

A taxpayer is allowed to elect out of the qualified residence interest rules. By so doing, he or she can treat indebtedness as *not* secured by a qualified residence. This election may make sense for a taxpayer when debt is incurred to acquire investment property or with respect to a residence used in a trade or business.

Watch this. Once this election is made, it *cannot* be revoked without the permission of the IRS.

E. Treatment of "Points"

1. Purchase or improvement of qualified residence. Points charged on a home mortgage loan by a lender may generally be deducted in the year paid when they relate to the purchase or improvement of the taxpayer's principal residence and points are typically charged in the area and are not excessive in amount. However, if points are withheld from the loan proceeds, they are not deductible in full in the year the mortgage is obtained but are amortized over the loan term.

2. Refinancings. Points paid in connection with refinancing of a home mortgage must generally be deducted by a taxpayer over the term of the new loan. To the extent that the points paid relate to improvements made by the taxpayer to his or her principal residence, they may be deducted currently.

Under a recent appeals court decision, which reversed the US Tax Court, taxpayers were allowed to currently deduct points paid for the purpose of securing a new, long-term home mortgage loan after short-term financing expired (*Huntsman*, 8th Cir., 1990).

Caution. The ruling in *Huntsman* can be relied on in the area of the Eighth Circuit as precedent. The IRS, however, has expressed disagreement with the ruling and will likely litigate elsewhere with respect to this issue.

Important. Remember that the IRS treats points as deductible when paid in connection with the purchase or improvement of a taxpayer's *principal residence.* It does not treat as deductible when paid points incurred with respect to a second residence, a home equity loan, a line of credit, or a refinancing of a taxpayer's personal residence.

Safe harbor. To ensure current deductibility of points paid in connection with the purchase or improvement of a personal residence, cash basis taxpayers should comply with the safe harbor procedures provided by the IRS (see *Rev. Proc. 92–12*). To come within this safe harbor, points must be paid directly by the taxpayer with respect to the purchase of a principal residence and are designated as such on the settlement statement, computed as a percentage of the amount borrowed, and conform with business practices where the residence is situated.

How points are paid may affect deduction. When a borrower pays points at the time the mortgage loan is closed with separate, unborrowed funds, the points will be currently deductible as long as statutory requirements are met. If the borrower finances the points, the IRS has set forth different deduction rules for loans used to buy a principal residence and those used for the improvement of a principal residence.

For points charged in connection with a loan used to buy a principal residence, borrowers are treated as having paid points directly when they provide cash at or before the loan closing at least equal to the amount of points charged. The cash cannot have been borrowed as part of the loan transaction (*Rev. Proc. 92–12*).

For loans used to improve principal residences, a current deduction is not available unless the points are paid with funds other than those obtained from the lender (*Rev. Rul. 87–22, 1987–1 CB 146; Rev. Proc. 92–12*).

3.08. TAX TREATMENT OF BELOW-MARKET AND INTEREST-FREE LOANS

Code § 7872 applies to loans providing for an interest rate that is below market. Under it, the difference between the loan rate and the market rate (i.e., the interest forgone) is treated (1) as if transferred to the lender from the borrower, *and then* (2) as if transferred again from the borrower to the lender as interest.

A. Which Loans Are Subject to the Below-Market Interest Rules?

The below-market interest rules of § 7872 apply to two principal types of loans:

• Demand loans.
• Gift loans.

1. Demand loans. These loans differ from term loans, which are made for specified periods. Under § 7872, they are defined as "any loan which is payable in full at any time on the demand of the lender, any loan if the benefits of the interest arrangements of such loan are not transferable and are conditioned on the future performance of substantial services by an individual, and any loan with an indefinite maturity."

2. Gift loans. These are loans bearing below-market interest with respect to which the interest forgone is treated as a gift. For this purpose, forgone interest is the excess of:

• The interest that would have been payable on the loan for the period involved if (*a*) loan interest accrued at the applicable federal rate, and (*b*) the loan interest were payable annually on the last day of the calendar year.
• Any loan interest payable that is properly allocable to that period.

3. Other specific types of loans covered by the below-market rules. The following specific types of loans also are covered by the below-market interest rules:

• *Compensation-related loans.* These are below-market loans between an employer and employee that are related to the employee's direct or indirect performance of services for the employer. They may also be made between an independent contractor and the party for whom he or she provides services.
• *Tax-avoidance loans.* These are below-market loans having interest terms for which the principal purpose is federal tax avoidance. For purposes of this rule, tax avoidance is considered to be the principal purpose of the loan interest arrangement when it is a key factor in terms of structuring the transaction between the parties as a below-market loan.

- *Below-market loans between a corporation and a shareholder,* whether direct or indirect.
- *Other loans.* In general, these involve any other loan arrangement that potentially has a significant effect on the federal tax liability of the borrower or lender.

B. Exceptions to the Below-Market Rules

1. De minimis exception. A $10,000 de minimis exception from the below-market interest rules applies to

- Gift loans between individuals, except when such a loan is used in purchasing, or carrying, income-producing property.
- Compensation-related loans.
- Loans between a corporation and a shareholder.

Note. For purposes of compensation-related loans and loans between a corporation and shareholder, applicability of the exception is determined on a daily basis. Also, the de minimis exception does *not* apply to tax-avoidance loans.

2. Limit on interest accrual for certain gift loans. With respect to a gift loan made directly between individuals, interest treated as transferred again by the borrower to the lender at the end of a taxable year is limited to the borrower's net investment income for the year. For purposes of this limit, when the borrower has less than $1,000 of net investment income for a year, it is treated as zero. Consequently, in such a case, there will be no retransferral of interest.

Also, if there is more than one gift loan between individuals, the taxpayer/borrower's net investment income is allocated pro rata among such loans. This allocation is based on the amount of interest otherwise treated as referred. This limit applies only when the total amount of such loans is $100,000 and tax avoidance is not their principal purpose.

3. Gift tax exclusion. As provided under Code § 2503, the first $10,000 of a donor's gifts to a donee is not taken into account in determining the total gifts made during a year for gift tax purposes. For gift tax purposes, a married couple can elect to split gifts, treating them as having been made one-half by each, thereby in effect doubling this exclusion. However, for purposes of the below-market interest rules, a married couple is considered to be *one* person.

C. Application of Rules: Gift Loans

1. Gift demand loans. With respect to this type of loan, the lender, who typically is an individual, is treated as having taxable income from the loan for a taxable year. This income is the amount represented by the difference in interest that would have been charged at the applicable federal rate and the amount of interest actually received with respect to the loan.

The borrower, who also typically is an individual, is generally entitled to deduct the interest treated as earned by the lender, as long as he or she itemizes deductions for tax purposes.

For gift tax purposes, the lender is considered to have made a gift of the forgone interest to the borrower.

2. Gift term loans. For income tax purposes, the treatment of these loans is the same as that applicable to gift demand loans, for both the borrower and the lender. However, the treatment of these loans for gift tax purposes differs. With respect to these loans, for gift tax purposes, the forgone interest is the equivalent of the amount by which the loan amount exceeds the present value of all loan payments discounted at the applicable federal rate.

D. Application of Rules: Other Loans

1. Regular demand loans. These loans include compensation-related and corporation-shareholder loans, as described at 3.08.A.3. With respect to these loans, the lender is treated as having income for a calendar year in the amount of the difference between (*a*) the amount of interest that would have been charged at the applicable federal rate and (*b*) the amount of interest actually received. The lender is entitled to deduct as compensation the amount of interest considered to be received.

The borrower recognizes taxable income at the end of the year in the amount of the difference between (*a*) the interest actually charged and (*b*) the interest determined by use of the applicable federal rate. The borrower is also entitled to deduct as interest, subject to applicable deduction limits, the amount treated as received by the lender. In the case of a loan between a corporation and a shareholder, a taxable dividend results to the shareholder in the amount of interest imputed with respect to which the corporation is not entitled to a deduction.

2. Regular term loans. In the case of a compensation-related loan, the lender is entitled to deduct, when the loan is made, the difference between the amount of the loan and the present value of required loan payments, discounted at the applicable federal rate. The lender recognizes this difference as taxable interest income over the term of the loan. If the borrower is a shareholder of the corporate lender, the shareholder receives a dividend with respect to which the corporate lender is not entitled to a deduction.

The borrower recognizes compensation income when the loan is made in the amount of the difference computed above. The borrower is also entitled to deduct related interest expense over the loan term in the amount imputed to the lender.

3.09. TAX CONSIDERATIONS IN MAKING LOANS TO RELATIVES

A. In General

Many taxpayers are not careful in ensuring that loans to relatives will be respected for tax purposes. To be assured a bad debt deduction if such a loan turns sour, the loan should be evidenced by a formal note and secured, interest should be charged to, and received from, the borrower. Negative income and gift tax consequences (see discussion at 3.08) may be avoided if an adequate rate of interest is charged with respect to such a loan.

B. Treatment of Interest

When the lender is required to include interest on a loan in gross income, the ability of the borrower to deduct the interest for tax purposes generally depends upon how the borrower uses the loan proceeds (see 3.03).

1. If the loan proceeds are used in the borrower's trade or business, the interest is deductible as trade or business interest. However, if the loan proceeds are used in a passive activity, current deduction of the loan interest paid is limited (see Chapter 8).

2. If the loan proceeds are used for investment purposes, the loan interest may be deductible as investment interest, subject to certain limits. A taxpayer is allowed to deduct investment interest only to the extent of net investment income, with any excess carried over for possible deduction in later years (see 3.06).

3. If the loan is secured by a taxpayer's residence, the loan interest may be deducted as follows:

- Where the loan proceeds are used to purchase, build, or substantially improve up to two qualified residences or to refinance debt incurred for such purposes, the loan interest is deductible on up to $1,000,000 of such debt; and

- Where the loan qualifies as home equity debt, the loan interest is deductible on up to $100,000 of such debt, regardless of the purpose for which the loan proceeds are used (see 3.07).

4. If the loan proceeds are used for personal purposes, e.g., purchase of a car for personal use, interest paid on the loan is totally nondeductible personal interest.

C. Loan Cancellation or Forgiveness

1. Gifts. If a lender cancels or forgives all or part of a loan as a gift, the borrower is not required to report any amount to gross income as a result of the cancellation or forgiveness. However, the lender may be subject to gift tax as the result of the cancellation or forgiveness.

It is possible for the lender to avoid gift tax in such a situation in two ways:

- Use of the annual $10,000 per donee gift tax exclusion; or
- Use of the unified credit against the gift tax.

2. Discharge of indebtedness. If cancellation or forgiveness of a loan is not made by a lender as a gift, the borrower may be required to include in income discharge of indebtedness income. However, if a debt is discharged in bankruptcy or the borrower is insolvent, discharge of indebtedness income may be excluded from the borrower's income.

D. Satisfaction of Loan with Property

When a borrower transfers property to a lender in satisfaction or a debt, the transfer is considered to be a repayment of the debt up to the fair market value of the property transferred. The lender would realize gain on the transfer if the value of the property transferred is greater than the outstanding amount of the debt. Also, the lender's basis for the property transferred is its fair market value. As far as the borrower is concerned, gain or loss is determined by the difference between the borrower's basis for the property transferred and the outstanding amount of the debt.

E. Worthlessness of Loan

1. In general. To sustain a bad debt deduction, a lender must prove that:

- The debt was bona fide, and
- The debt became totally worthless in the year for which the bad debt deduction was claimed with respect to it.

For nonbusiness bad debts, a bad debt deduction is claimed for the taxable year in which the debt becomes totally worthless. The deduction of the nonbusiness bad debt produces a short-term capital loss.

Total worthlessness of a debt is determined based on all the surrounding facts and circumstances. Such facts and circumstances include the value of the debt collateral and the debtor's financial condition. Also, the fact that repayment of a debt is not yet due does not preclude a bad debt deduction.

2. What is a bona fide debt for deduction purposes? A bona fide debt is one based on a valid and enforceable obligation between borrower and lender to pay a fixed or determinable sum of money. There must also be a reasonable expectation, intention, and belief that the debt will be repaid based on all the facts and circumstances when it is incurred.

Factors cited by the courts in determining whether a debt is bona fide include the following:

- Interest charged.
- The existence of a note or other evidence of indebtedness such as a written loan agreement.
- Records of the parties treating the transaction involved as a loan.
- Security or collateral.
- Fixed repayment schedule.
- Demand for repayment.
- Actual repayments.
- Solvency of the borrower at the time the transaction is entered into (see e.g., *A.R. Goldstein*. TC Memo 1980–273).

Chapter Four

Tax Planning for Retirement

4.01. INDIVIDUAL RETIREMENT ACCOUNTS (IRAs)

A. Establishing an IRA

An eligible individual taxpayer can establish an IRA, and make contributions to it for a taxable year, no later than the due date of his or her federal income tax return, without regard to filing extensions, for that taxable year. An IRA account can be established in several ways. These include establishing any of the following:

- A trust account or a custodial account.
- A trust account under a prototype plan approved by the IRS set up by a bank, stockbroker, insurance company, or similar entity.
- An account with the taxpayer's employer or union.

An individual taxpayer may establish more than one IRA account. However, there are statutory limits to the amount that can be contributed without penalty, as discussed below.

B. Deductible IRA Contributions

1. How much is deductible. An individual taxpayer's ability to make tax-deductible IRA contributions is based on two conditions:

- The amount of the taxpayer's adjusted gross income (AGI).
- Whether or not the taxpayer is an active participant in a retirement plan sponsored by his or her employer.

If the individual does not participate in an employer-sponsored retirement plan, an income tax deduction is allowable for IRA contributions of up to the lesser of $2,000 or 100 percent of the taxpayer's compensation. Such a contribution can be made by a married taxpayer filing a joint tax return with his or her spouse, as long as the spouse is not an active participant in an employer-sponsored retirement plan.

If a married taxpayer files a separate tax return and is not an active participant (see 4.01.B.2) in an employer-sponsored retirement plan, although his or her spouse is, he or she is entitled to the full tax-deductible IRA contribution allowable under the tax law as long as the spouses did not live together at any time during the taxable year.

If an individual taxpayer does actively participate in an employer-sponsored retirement plan, or files a joint or separate tax return with a spouse who is an active participant in an employer-sponsored retirement plan, the amount deductible as an IRA contribution may be reduced below the maximum statutory limit. The reduction is based on the amount of the taxpayer's AGI and depends on whether that amount falls within a phaseout range.

When the individual taxpayer is an active participant in an employer-sponsored retirement plan, his or her tax-deductible IRA contribution is reduced or totally eliminated. For single individuals, unmarried filers, and heads of households, the deductible IRA contribution begins to be phased out when AGI exceeds $25,000, and is totally eliminated when AGI reaches $35,000 (a $10,000 phaseout range).

Illustration.   Jill Greene is a single individual who has $20,000 of compensation and $30,000 of AGI for the current year. She is also an active participant in a retirement plan sponsored by her employer. Her AGI exceeds the phaseout range by $5,000, so the maximum amount that she can deduct for the current year as an IRA contribution is $1,000 [($5,000 ÷ $10,000) × $2,000]. See also the discussion of nondeductible IRA contributions at 4.01.C. For married individuals filing joint tax returns and surviving spouses, the deductible IRA contribution begins to be phased out when AGI exceeds $40,000 and is totally phased out when AGI reaches $50,000 (also a $10,000 phaseout range).

Illustration.   The Burkes file a joint tax return for the current year. Jim and Mary Burke each receive compensation of $18,000, and their adjusted gross income for the year is $42,000. Mary is an active participant in an employer-sponsored retirement plan, but Jim is not. Under these circumstances, Jim and Mary each may deduct up to $1,600 of their IRA contributions because the AGI on their joint return exceeds the phaseout range floor by $2,000. So they divide $8,000 by $10,000 and multiply by $2,000 to arrive at their deductible IRA contribution amounts for the current year.

Note. For purposes of determining the amount of reduction of the allowable IRA contribution deduction, any reduction amount that is not a multiple of $10 is required to be reduced to the next lowest $10.

2. Who is an "active participant"? For purposes of these rules, an active participant is an individual who is an active participant in any of the following:

- A qualified pension (including Keogh), profit-sharing, or stock-bonus plan.
- A qualified annuity plan.
- A plan established by the US government or by a state or political subdivisions, agencies, or instrumentalities thereof (subject to an exception for an eligible state deferred compensation plan).
- A simplified employee pension (SEP).

The definition of *active participant* includes participants who are not vested with respect to employer contributions. Also, an individual eligible to participate in a defined benefit plan, but who refuses to participate in such a plan, is treated under the tax law as an active participant in the plan.

3. IRA contributions of recipients of Social Security payments. According to the IRS, a taxpayer who receives Social Security benefits computes his or her IRA deduction limit using the following rules:

- Do *not* take into account any IRA contributions for the taxable year.
- Do take into account any taxable Social Security benefits received during the taxable year.

See IRS Announcement 88–38, 1988–10 I.R.B. 60.

C. Nondeductible IRA Contributions

If a taxpayer cannot make tax-deductible contributions to an IRA as a result of the deduction limits covered above, he or she generally can make *nondeductible* contributions to an IRA. These nondeductible contributions, however, are also subject to limits.

1. Limit. A taxpayer is allowed to make nondeductible contributions to an IRA up to the lesser of the excess of (1) $2,000, or $2,250 for married individuals maintaining an IRA and a spousal IRA, respectively, or (2) 100 percent of compensation, over the allowable IRA contribution deduction.

2. Election. A taxpayer may elect *not* to deduct for tax purposes the amount of IRA contributions for a taxable year that would otherwise be tax deductible. If the taxpayer so elects, his or her deduction limit for nondeductible contributions can be increased by the contribution amount that otherwise would have been deductible.

3. "Designated" nondeductible IRA contribution. This is any contribution made by a taxpayer to an IRA for a taxable year that he or she designates as not deducted. A taxpayer making an IRA contribution that is designated as nondeductible for a taxable year or who receives an IRA distribution during a taxable year must provide certain information on his or her tax return. This information includes:

- The amount of designated nondeductible IRA contributions made by the taxpayer for the taxable year.
- The total of all prior years' designated IRA contributions not previously withdrawn by the taxpayer.
- The total balance of all of the taxpayer's IRAs maintained at the end of the calendar year ending with or within the taxable year.
- The amount of IRA distributions received by the taxpayer during the taxable year.

Caution. If this required information is not provided on the taxpayer's return, all the taxpayer's IRA contributions are deemed *deductible*. Accordingly, such contributions will be treated as *taxable* when they are withdrawn, unless the taxpayer can demonstrate, to the satisfaction of the IRS, that they were *nondeductible* when made.

4. Reporting. A taxpayer is required to use IRS Form 8606 to report the information listed at 4.01.C.3, and the form allows computation of the taxable amount of an IRA distribution made during the taxable year. This form is filed with the individual federal income tax return, Form 1040, by a taxpayer who makes a nondeductible IRA contribution.

In connection with nondeductible IRA contributions, individual taxpayers should retain the following:

- A copy of the Form 1040 filed for each year in which such a contribution is made.
- The Form 5498 received by the taxpayer from his or her IRA trustee for each year he or she makes a contribution to, or receives a distribution from, an IRA.
- Form 1099R for each year during which the taxpayer receives a distribution from an IRA.

5. Tax-saver (spousal IRAs). Before the limits on deductible IRA contributions were enacted in the Tax Reform Act of 1986, married taxpayers, employing spousal IRAs as an investment strategy, could place most of the funds invested in the IRA of the spouse having the larger amount of compensation income. For example, an executive could contribute the maximum tax-deductible contribution of $2,000 to his own IRA and $250 to a spousal IRA opened for his nonworking spouse. After the enactment of the TRA '86 contribution limits, married spouses with spousal IRAs may wish to rethink their investment strategies. It may be advisable, for many of these couples, to make the larger contribution to the IRA of the spouse having the lower amount, or no amount, of compensation income. By so doing, the couple can increase the amount of *nondeductible* IRA contributions. As a result, should the spouses want or need to withdraw IRA funds prematurely, those nondeductible contributions could be withdrawn free of tax (see discussion of IRA withdrawal rules at 4.01.D). Of course, any *deductible* IRA contributions are includable in the taxpayer's taxable income on withdrawal.

6. Excess IRA contributions. A taxpayer's IRA contributions exceeding the allowable deduction amount, without taking into account the limit applicable to active participants in employer-sponsored plans, not withdrawn before the due date, including extensions, of the taxpayer's return are subject to a penalty of 6 percent. This excess amount, however, can be deducted in a subsequent taxable year up to the allowable deduction ceiling amount, subject to a reduction for any IRA contributions made by the taxpayer during that taxable year.

D. IRA Withdrawals

A taxpayer is permitted to withdraw any IRA contributions made during a taxable year if all the following conditions are met:

- Such contributions are received by the taxpayer before the due date, including extensions, of his or her income tax return for that taxable year.
- No deduction is claimed with respect to such contributions.
- No earnings are received by the taxpayer with respect to such contributions. (Any such earnings are includable in the taxpayer's gross income for the taxable year in which such contributions are made.)

Amounts withdrawn by a taxpayer from an IRA before he or she reaches age 59½ may be subject to a 10 percent penalty prescribed under the tax law in addition to the regular income tax owing with respect to such amount, except in the case of withdrawals of excess IRA contributions. The 10 percent penalty does not apply with respect to IRA distributions made as a result of the IRA owner's death or disability.

1. Time requirements for IRA distributions. IRA distributions must commence no later than April 1 of the year following the calendar year in which the IRA owner reaches age 70½. This rule also applies with respect to pre-1987 accumulated tax-deductible contributions to an IRA. If the IRA owner reaches age 70½ and distributions are less than those required under the tax law, a 50 percent penalty applies to the extent that the amount of the distribution is less than the prescribed amount.

If an IRA owner who is age 70½ or older has multiple IRAs, the minimum required distribution is computed separately for each IRA. The minimum distribution can be made in one of the following ways:

• It can be made separately from each IRA account of the taxpayer.

• The minimum distributions with respect to all of the taxpayer's IRAs are determined, and then the *total* minimum distribution can be taken out of one or more of the IRAs.

The latter of these alternatives is available to IRA owners and IRA *beneficiaries*. Accordingly, an individual who is both an IRA *owner* and an IRA *beneficiary* can meet the minimum distribution rule by having the minimum required distribution made from the *owned* IRA rather than the IRA in which there is an interest held as a beneficiary.

Note. For recalculation of the minimum IRA distribution for the next year, the amount actually distributed from each IRA in which the taxpayer has an interest reduces each such IRA's year-end account balance for the preceding year.

2. Use of joint beneficiaries to extend minimum IRA distribution amounts. Minimum required distribution from IRAs, discussed at 4.03.B, can be extended if an IRA owner designates a joint beneficiary and distributions are made over the individuals' joint lives. Here's how this works. The taxpayer determines the minimum distribution required from each of his or her IRAs separately and then combines those amounts. If the joint beneficiaries on the taxpayer's multiple IRAs are not the same, actual distributions should be taken from those IRAs whose joint beneficiaries have the shortest life expectancies.

3. Computing the taxable amount of an IRA distribution. In determining the amount of an IRA distribution that must be included in gross income, a taxpayer must do the following:

• Treat every IRA owned as a single contract.

• Treat all IRA withdrawals made during a taxable year as a single distribution.

- Compute the contract value, which is determined by including all IRA distributions made during the calendar year, income thereon, and the investment in the contract as of the close of the calendar year in which the taxable year begins.
- Not have the total amount of IRA withdrawals excludable from taxable income exceed his or her investment in the contract.

The amount of IRA distribution includable in a taxpayer's gross income is determined by taking the following steps:

- Step 1: determine the amount of IRA withdrawals for the taxable year.
- Step 2: determine the total of *nondeductible* IRA contributions made in any taxable year, less any prior-year tax-exempt IRA withdrawals.
- Step 3: add the balances of all IRAs held at the close of the taxable year, adding withdrawals made during the year (from step 1).
- Step 4: determine the percentage excludable from gross income (step 2 amount ÷ step 3 amount).
- Step 5: determine the total amount of IRA withdrawals excludable from gross income (step 1 amount X step 4 amount).
- Step 6: determine the amount includable in gross income (step 1 amount − step 5 amount).

Illustration.   Beginning in 1986, Charles Merriman opened IRA accounts to which he made contributions. In 1986, 1987, and 1988, Charles made tax-deductible IRA contributions of $2,000. In 1989 he made a deductible IRA contribution of $500 and a nondeductible IRA contribution of $300. In 1990, he made a deductible IRA contribution of $500 and a nondeductible IRA contribution of $700. Finally, in 1991 and 1992 he made nondeductible IRA contributions of $1,000 and $2,000, respectively. Thus, Charles has made a total of $7,000 in deductible IRA contributions and a total of $4,000 in nondeductible IRA contributions. Charles withdraws $3,000 from an IRA account in 1992; he did not make any tax-free IRA withdrawals in prior years. The year-end balances in his IRA accounts, including interest on the amounts contributed, amounted to $17,000. He includes $2,400 in gross income as a result of the $3,000 IRA withdrawal. This amount is determined as follows:

- Step 1: determine the amount withdrawn from IRAs during the year—$3,000.
- Step 2: determine the amount of *all* nondeductible IRA contributions made, reduced by prior-year tax-free withdrawals—$4,000.

- Step 3: add the amount determined in step 1 to the total year-end IRA account balances—$17,000 + $3,000 = $20,000.
- Step 4: divide the amount determined in step 2 by the amount determined in step 3 to arrive at the percentage used to determine the amount of the withdrawal(s) excludable from tax—$4,000 ÷ $20,000 = 20%.
- Step 5: determine the amount of the IRA withdrawal *excludable* from the taxpayer's gross income by multiplying the amount determined in step 1 by the amount determined in step 4—$3,000 X 20% = $600.
- Step 6: determine the amount of the IRA withdrawal *includable* in the taxpayer's gross income by reducing the withdrawn amount(s) determined in step 1 by the excludable amount determined in Step 5—$3,000 − $600 = $2,400.

E. IRA Considerations for Self-Employed Individuals

A self-employed individual who maintains a Keogh (H.R. 10) plan is considered to be covered under a qualified plan. As a result, such an individual's IRA contributions may be nondeductible for tax purposes, in whole or in part. Also, for purposes of determining the allowable amount that can be contributed to an IRA, a self-employed individual's compensation includes the net earnings from his or her self-employment. A discussion of qualified plans for self-employed persons is provided at 4.02.

F. IRA Rollovers

1. Lump-sum and partial distributions. Individual taxpayers' lump-sum distributions from qualified plans are accorded tax-free treatment if such distributions are reinvested in an IRA within 60 days of the time that the lump-sum distribution from the qualified plan is made. This is referred to as a tax-free *rollover*.

A portion of such a lump-sum distribution may also be rolled over into an IRA and accorded tax-free treatment. If this is done, the part not rolled over into an IRA is taxable for the recipient in the current year. However, when such amounts are withdrawn from the IRA, including a lump-sum withdrawal, they are not eligible for five-year averaging or capital gains treatment that may have applied if the rollover had not been made. See the discussion at 4.03.

A tax-free rollover is also available for a partial distribution from a retirement plan if the following conditions hold:

- The distribution represents at least 50 percent of the employee's balance in the plan.
- It is not part of a series of periodic payments.
- It is not made on account of the employee's death or separation from service with the employer.
- Tax-free rollover treatment is elected by the employee.

Note. When a taxpayer rolls over any part of a partial distribution from a qualified plan, capital gains or forward averaging treatment is not available with respect to any future distribution(s) from such a plan (see the discussion of distributions from qualified plans at 4.03). Also, any unrealized appreciation on securities of the participant's employer distributed from such a plan will be subject to tax when distributed.

Important. Distributions that the tax law requires to be made from an IRA (e.g., distributions made after the taxpayer reaches age 70½) *cannot* be rolled over into another IRA.

Note. Under a special provision, funds deposited in certain troubled financial institutions may be rolled over into an IRA (or another qualified plan) even though the rollover is not made within 60 days of the date on which the distribution is made. For purposes of this provision, the 60-day period does not include any time during which the account is frozen. Also, a minimum of 10 days after the release of funds in such an account is allowed to a taxpayer to complete a rollover to an IRA. This exception applies only with respect to funds frozen on at least one day during the 60-day period following the distribution.

2. Availability and amount of IRA rollover. A rollover to an IRA is available to participants in qualified plans, their spouses, and persons entitled to plan benefits under Qualified Domestic Relations Orders (QDROs).

The maximum amount that can be rolled over into an IRA from a qualified plan is the fair market value of the distribution that is eligible for a rollover reduced by the participant's cost basis in his or her plan account.

Note. The surviving spouse of the participant in a qualified plan may also be eligible to benefit from the $5,000 death benefit exclusion under Code § 101(b).

3. Additional IRA rollover provisions. The spouse of a deceased participant in a qualified plan who receives a distribution from the participant's plan account may roll the distribution over to an IRA. However, such a distribution *cannot* be rolled over to other qualified plans. Also, the spouse of a deceased plan participant who receives a distribution of the total amount in the participant's plan account as a result of the plan's termination may roll over the distribution to an IRA. But other persons who inherit an IRA account as a result of the owner's death *cannot* roll the account's funds into an IRA and must pay income tax on those funds as ordinary income.

Lump-sum distributions received from a § 403(b) annuity (generally available for employees of public schools and charitable organizations) can be rolled over in whole or in part to an IRA or to another § 403(b) annuity within 60 days of the distribution in the same manner as a rollover of amounts from a qualified plan.

4. Benefits of IRA rollovers. These are a number of benefits to a taxpayer from rolling over amounts distributed from a qualified plan to an IRA:

- Flexibility with respect to funds invested in an employer plan when the participant separates from service with the employer.
- The ability to have the invested funds continue to grow free of tax in the IRA until the taxpayer reaches age 70½.
- The ability with an IRA to make certain investments (e.g., the purchase of certain annuities such as a variable annuity) not available to other qualified plans.
- Unlike other qualified plans, no requirement that a married IRA plan participant have the *written* consent of his or her spouse to designate a person other than that spouse as a beneficiary with respect to plan benefits.

5. Disadvantages of IRA rollovers. The chief disadvantage in rolling over account balances from a qualified plan into an IRA is that any distributions from an IRA are subject to current tax as *ordinary income*. Tax advantages applicable to qualified plan distributions (see 4.03) such as capital gains treatment under special rules in the tax law and forward averaging are not available with respect to IRA distributions.

Note. The tax advantages noted above can be restored, however, when the IRA account is treated as a "conduit" and the funds are again rolled over into a qualified plan that is not an IRA. To qualify under this rule, the rollover IRA and other IRAs of the taxpayer must be maintained separately.

G. Premature IRA Distributions

An IRA owner who receives a distribution from his or her IRA before reaching age 59½ can be subject to a 10 percent penalty tax in addition to the regular income tax payable with respect to the amount distributed. But this penalty can be avoided if withdrawals from the IRA are made in substantially equal periodic payments spread over the IRA owner's life or the joint lives of the IRA owner and his or her designated beneficiary as prescribed in tables issued by the IRS.

Observation. Apparently, the life expectancy involved is not computed each year, but the initial life expectancy is reduced by each succeeding year. Note, however, that once payouts from the IRA commence, it may be difficult for a taxpayer to make any payout change without incurring a penalty.

H. "Collectibles"

IRA account funds invested in "collectibles" are treated, in general, as IRA distributions, and the cost of such items are includable in the IRA owner's gross income and subject to applicable penalties. However, investments in gold and silver coins issued by the US government and acquired after 1986 are eligible for exclusion. Also, coins issued by a US state that are acquired by an IRA account after November 10, 1988, are permissible IRA investments.

I. Simplified Employee Pension Plans (SEPs)

These plans are IRAs established by employees to which their employers make contributions. The employer, when making contributions, must not discriminate in favor of certain employees, such as highly paid employees. For SEP contribution purposes, the employer can take into account the employer's share of Social Security (FICA) taxes, as long as such taxes are taken into account for each employee who has a SEP; an employer can thus make large SEP contributions to accounts of highly paid employees and minimal contributions to other employees' accounts.

1. Deduction limits. SEP deduction limits are the lesser of 15 percent of employee compensation up to a specified limit or $30,000 per year adjusted for inflation. The annual compensation limit applicable to SEPs for 1993 is $235,840. This limit is adjusted for inflation.

RRA '93:   The Revenue Reconciliation Act of 1993 reduced the limit to $150,000 with respect to benefits accruing in plan years beginning after 1993. The limit will be indexed for inflation. See the Foreword on RRA '93.

Note.   An employer also can deduct his or her own IRA contribution, (i.e., up to $2,000 or $2,250) with respect to a spousal IRA.

2.   Contribution rules.   An employer who sponsors a defined benefit pension plan for self-employed persons is *not* allowed to make SEP contributions. And if *any* eligible employee will not participate, an employer cannot establish a SEP for any employee.

An employer who makes contributions to a SEP in a year must make contributions for each employee who reached age 21 and was employed by the employer in at least three of the five immediately preceding calendar years. But a sponsoring employer is not required to make SEP contributions for a calendar year for an employee whose compensation is below a specified limit, which is adjusted for inflation yearly.

3.   Deferral limits.   There is a limit on amounts that a participant in a SEP may elect to defer. This limit is indexed for inflation each year.

4.   Small SEPs.   A small SEP is available when an employer has 25 or fewer employees at any time. Under such a SEP, an employee can elect to receive cash in lieu of a SEP contribution, as long as 50 percent or more of eligible employees so elect. The percentage that can be deferred by highly paid employees is limited to 1.25 times the average deferral percentage of other eligible employees.

5.   Salary-reduction SEPs.   A SEP may include an elective salary-reduction (i.e., deferral) arrangement, under which an employee may elect to have a specific percentage of his or her pre-tax compensation set aside in a deferral account for his or her benefit or paid in cash. An amount deferred is not included in the employee's gross income, but a cash payment would be. The limit on an employee's elective deferrals is the same as under a § 401(k) plan. The limit on compensation to be taken into account, initially $200,000, is indexed yearly for inflation after 1989. For 1993, the compensation limit is $235,840. Also, the maximum deferrable amount is $8,994 for 1993 and $9,240 for 1994. *RRA '93*: The Revenue Reconciliation Act of 1993 reduced the compensation limit to $150,000 with respect to benefits accruing in plan years beginning after 1993. The limit will be indexed for inflation. See the Foreword on RRA '93.

These other rules are also applicable with respect to salary-reduction SEPs:

- Fifty percent or more of eligible employees must make the salary-reduction election.

- A special nondiscrimination rule applies with respect to deferrals of highly paid employees, under which the deferral percentage for such employees cannot be more than 1.25 times the average of deferral percentages for other eligible employees who are not considered highly paid.

- Any excess deferrals must be distributed to participants in cash.

- Salary deferral account SEP contributions are treated as compensation for Social Security (FICA) tax purposes.

6. Special rules for integrated plans. An employer is not allowed to make contributions to an employee SEP account that is integrated with Social Security for any year in which the employer maintains another integrated plan in which such an employee is a participant.

If an employer does not sponsor an integrated plan at any time during a year, Social Security contributions may be treated as SEP contributions, but only if Social Security contributions are so treated with respect to each employee who is a SEP participant.

7. Other rules applicable to SEPs.

- In general, SEPs are subjected to the tax rules that apply to IRAs, except for contribution limits.

- A sponsoring employer must make contributions to its SEP for *every* employee who is eligible for SEP participation in a year. Such eligible employees include individuals who are no longer employed by the employer when the SEP contribution is made; deceased employees; and former employees who cannot be located.

- A SEP may include or exclude self-employed individuals.

- If an employee for whom an employer is required to make contributions to a SEP did not establish an IRA, or closed an IRA, before the employer made its current year SEP contribution, the employer must establish an IRA for that employee.

- An employer can use a calendar year or its own fiscal year for a SEP.

- A SEP is not required to be established by an employer until a SEP contribution is made. A SEP contribution for a particular year is required to be made by the employer within 3½ months after the end of that year.

- When contributions made by the employer for highly paid employees are over the maximum allowable amount, excess contribution rules for cash-or-deferred arrangements (CODAs) apply, and a 10 percent tax applies to any excess contribution amount.

4.02. RETIREMENT PLANNING FOR SELF-EMPLOYED INDIVIDUALS

A. Keogh Plans

An individual who is self-employed, such as a doctor, lawyer, or sole proprietor of a business, is permitted to establish a retirement plan. Typically, such self-employed individuals establish Keogh plans, which are also referred to as H.R. 10 plans. Such plans offer benefits similar to qualified plans sponsored by corporate employers. Keogh plans are subject to the same rules as corporate plans with respect to qualification (including rules applicable to top-heavy plans, as discussed at 4.02.L), account vesting, and contribution and benefit limits.

> *Note.* A self-employed individual may be able to establish a simplified employee pension (SEP). SEPs are discussed at 4.01.I.

B. Tax Advantages of Keogh Plans

1. Deductible amounts. Self-employed individuals are allowed to deduct amounts contributed to Keogh plans, subject to contribution limits described at 4.02.C. This enables such individuals to deduct *investment* funds. Also, the earnings on funds invested in the plan are *not* taxable until the funds are distributed.

2. Flexibility. A self-employed individual has considerable flexibility with respect to the structure of a Keogh plan. The plan can be established to achieve specific investment goals of the individual, or it can be a master plan sponsored by a financial institution, securities broker, insurance company, or a professional association, for example. Also, the trustee of the plan need not be a financial institution; the self-employed individual or any other individual can serve as the plan's trustee.

C. Contribution Limits

The percentage contribution limit is applied to the earned income of the participant *after* the contribution to the plan has been taken into account.

1. Profit-sharing plans. Contributions by self-employed individuals to profit-sharing Keogh plans are limited to 15 percent of earned income, up to $30,000, after the contribution to the plan. As a percentage amount, this is 13.043 percent of precontribution earned income.

2. Money purchase plans. Contributions by self-employed individuals to money purchase Keogh plans are limited to 25 percent of earned income, up to $30,000, after the contribution to the plan. This amounts to 20 percent of the self-employed individual's earned income before the plan contribution.

3. Limits for common-law employees. The applicable limit for profit-sharing plans is 15 percent of earned income before the contribution. The applicable limit for money purchase plans is 25 percent of earned income before the contribution.

Note. Under money purchase Keogh plans, a fixed percentage of earned income, up to the $30,000 limit, must be made to each participant's account each year.

The applicable limit for combination profit-sharing and money purchase plans is 25 percent of earned income before the contribution.

Observation. Under the above rules, plan contributions for common-law employees of a self-employed individual can be larger than for the employer in terms of the percentage of earned income involved.

RRA '93. Under RRA '93, the maximum compensation that can be taken into account for purposes of determining benefits from and contributions to a qualified plan ($235,840 for 1993) is reduced to $150,000. This limit is indexed for inflation in later years. This provision applies to plan years beginning after December 31, 1993. For more details, see the Foreword on RRA '93.

D. Coverage Requirements

To be a qualified plan under the tax law, a Keogh plan must meet one of the following:

- A percentage test.
- A classification test.

Note. These requirements are met as long as they are met by the plan on at least one day of each quarter of the year.

1. Percentage test. For plan years beginning before 1989, to meet this statutory test, a Keogh plan must benefit 70 percent or more of the sponsoring employer's employees, and at least 80 percent of all employees eligible for plan benefits, as long as 70 percent of all of the sponsoring employer's employees are eligible for plan benefits. For purposes of this test, employees not meeting minimum age and minimum service requirements specified in the plan as conditions for participation may be excluded.

For plan years beginning after 1988, a Keogh plan must meet one of the following minimum coverage tests to be a qualified plan:

- *Percentage test.* The plan must benefit at least 70 percent of all non–highly paid employees.

- *Ratio test.* The plan must benefit a percentage of non–highly paid employees who represent at least 70 percent of the percentage of highly paid employees covered.

- *Average benefits test.* This test is met when the average benefit percentage for non–highly paid employees is at least 70 percent of that percentage for highly paid employees, *and* the classification test, discussed at 4.02.D.2, is met.

These rules are satisfied as long as the plan benefits the lesser of 50 employees or 40 percent or more of all employees of the sponsoring employer. For this purpose, employees under a collective bargaining agreement and employees not satisfying minimum age and service requirements for plan participation purposes may be excluded.

2. Classification test. This test is met by a Keogh plan if the plan benefits employees within an employer classification that the IRS finds does not discriminate in favor of highly paid employees. In general, discrimination under a plan is determined under all of the facts and circumstance. Certain employees can be excluded by an employer for purposes of this test, including those covered by a collective bargaining agreement and nonresident aliens who receive no US-source income.

Note. Certain plan requirements (e.g., that employees must submit to a physical examination or agree to wage withholding) will not disqualify the plan.

E. Employees Who "Benefit" under the Plan

Under IRS regulations, an employee is considered to benefit under a plan if he or she accrues a plan benefit during a year. Such an employee must also receive a current allocation or accrue an additional benefit under the plan. This does not include an employee who is only eligible to accrue a plan benefit or to receive an allocation under the plan.

When a plan involves elective contributions, after-tax employee contributions, or matching contributions, an employee benefits from the plan only if one of the following holds:

- The employee is currently eligible to make elective contributions [under § 401(k) plans].
- The employee is eligible to make after-tax contributions or to receive matching contributions under the plan.

F. Plan Minimum Age and Service Requirements

To be qualified, a plan cannot require, for purposes of participation, that an employee's period of service with the sponsoring employer be longer than the later of the date (1) the employee attains age 21; or (2) he or she completes (a) one year of service with the employer, or (b) two years of service if the plan permits full vesting of accrued benefits for employees having two years of service or less. For purposes of these rules, a plan participant can be excluded if he or she does not accrue a plan benefit or allocation only because he or she does not meet (1) a minimum service requirement; or (2) a plan requirement that he or she be employed by the sponsoring employer on the last day of the year to receive an allocation, *and* he or she terminates employment during the year and has 500 hours or less of service with the employer.

G. Plan Distributions

A participant cannot receive benefits from a Keogh plan without incurring a penalty before he or she attains age 59½. However, a penalty will not apply if the distribution from the plan is made on account of the participant's death or disability. Distributions from the plan are required to begin no later than April 1 of the year after the calendar year in which the participant attains age 70½, even if the employee continues employment with the employer sponsoring the plan. Such distributions may be made periodically, in which case they are taxable as annuity payments, or in a lump sum. (See 4.03.C.4 for a discussion of tax planning for lump-sum distributions.)

A nondeductible 50 percent excise tax applies when required minimum distributions are not made from a plan after 1988. This tax applies to the amount by which the actual plan distribution is below the minimum amount required to be distributed.

H. Excise Tax on Nondeductible Plan Contributions

A self-employed person who makes contributions to a plan in excess of the allowable limit as an employer is subject to a 10 percent excise tax. This tax will not apply, however, when plan contributions made on behalf of such a person exceed his or her earned income as a result of the tax law's minimum funding rules.

I. Tax Reporting Rules

1. Contributions. The employer deducts contributions for himself or herself on line 27 of Form 1040. The employer's contributions for his or her employees are deducted on Schedule C of his or her Form 1040.

2. Plans. Most self-employed persons employ fewer than 100 employees. This discussion addresses the reporting rules of such employers.

Form 5500EZ can be used by a single-participant plan. Such a plan covers the taxpayer and his or her spouse, as long as the business is wholly owned by the taxpayer or his or her spouse, or partners in business partnerships and their spouses. For plan years beginning in 1989, Form 5500EZ is not required to be filed by employers having one of the following:

- A single-participant plan with $100,000 or less in assets at the end of the plan year.
- Two or more single-participant plans having a total of $100,000 or less in assets at the end of the plan year.

However, if the employer has more than one single-participant plans having total assets exceeding $100,000, he or she must file a Form 5500EZ for each such plan for 1989.

J. Integration with Social Security

A plan that is integrated with Social Security is required to provide a minimum plan benefit for employees whose compensation is less than the Social Security wage base.

K. Estate Tax on Plan Benefits

Benefits from a Keogh plan are subject to the estate tax if payable to the employee's estate, related to an owner-employee's nondeductible plan contributions, or distributed in a lump sum. If distributed in a lump sum, the tax rules applicable to lump-sum distributions apply (see 4.03).

L. Treatment of Top-Heavy Plans

A top-heavy Keogh plan is a plan in which the present value of accrued plan benefits for "key employees" (as statutorily defined) is more than 60 percent of account balances of all employees covered under the plan. Special rules apply to compensation includable under the plan with respect to covered employees as well as vesting provisions. Vesting can be either three-year vesting (i.e., entitlement to 100 percent of benefits after three years' participation) or six-year vesting (i.e., the vested amount increases beginning in year 2 by 20 percent increments up to 100 percent in year 6).

4.03. DISTRIBUTIONS FROM QUALIFIED RETIREMENT PLANS

A number of provisions of the tax law in general are designed to prevent the manipulation of qualified plans for purposes other than providing retirement income for plan participants. Accordingly, the tax law applies penalties to certain plan distributions and certain tax-sheltered income accumulations that do not meet this objective. The penalties, as discussed below, apply to the following:

- Premature plan distributions.
- Distributions less than the minimum required under the tax law.
- Excess plan distributions.
- Excess income accumulations in qualified plans.

A. Premature Plan Distributions

    1. Penalty tax. When any participant receives a distribution from a qualified retirement plan before reaching age 59½, he or she may be subject to a 10 percent excise tax plus any income tax payable with respect to the amount distributed. However, certain important exceptions apply, as discussed at 4.03.A.2.

The 10 percent penalty tax is based on the amount of the distribution includable in the participant's gross income for tax purposes. Accordingly, the penalty tax does *not* apply to any recovery of the participant's basis in his or her plan account, or any amounts rolled over by the participant into another qualified retirement plan or an individual retirement account (IRA). The 10 percent penalty tax does apply, however, to a "hardship" distribution from a § 401(k) plan to a participant who has not reached age 59½ at the time and who is not disabled. See discussion at 4.01.F.

2. Exceptions to 10 percent penalty tax. The following six exceptions apply to relieve a qualified plan participant from liability for the 10 percent penalty tax on a premature distribution from such a plan:

- Distributions made from the plan on account of the participant's disability or death.
- Distributions made from the plan of substantially equal periodic payments over the participant's life or life expectancy or over the joint lives or life expectancies of the participant and his or her designated beneficiary (discussed further at 4.03.A.3).
- Distributions made from the plan after a participant separates from service with the employer after having reached age 55.
- Distributions made from the plan under a qualified domestic relations order (QDRO) to an alternate payee who is the participant's former spouse or child.
- Distributions made from the plan to pay tax-deductible medical expenses of the participant.
- Certain distributions made to the participant from employee stock ownership plans (ESOPs).

3. "Substantially equal periodic payments" exception. This exception typically is used by plan participants who retire before reaching age 55. Use of an annuity or installment payments will satisfy this exception, as described below.

Annuities. To qualify for purposes of this exception, an annuity must meet the following requirements:

- Payments must be made on at least an annual basis.
- Payments are to be made over the participant's life or life expectancy or joint lives or life expectancies of the participant and his or her designated beneficiary.
- Payments cannot be increased substantially.

Installment payments. Installment payments of plan benefits afford investment flexibility to retiring participants. To qualify for purposes of this exception, the installment payments must be made at least on an annual basis and must be made in amounts that remain at a constant level before the later of five years from the time payments commence *or* the recipient reaches age 59½. Exceptions: Changes in installment payments made as a result of the following factors will not cause the payments to fail to qualify as substantially equal periodic payments:

- Benefit increases given retired employees.
- Cost-of-living adjustments (COLA).
- Death of the participant's beneficiary.
- End of any Social Security supplemental payments.

Caution. Once payments have begun, if payments later fail to be substantially equal periodic payments, a recapture tax of 10 percent will apply.

B. Insufficient Distributions

As described below, certain minimum distribution requirements apply with respect to distributions from qualified plans. If these minimum distribution requirements are not met, a 50 percent penalty applies to the amount by which the plan distribution actually made is below the minimum distribution required under the tax law. In general terms, these requirements are as follows:

- Distributions must begin as of a specific date.
- Distributions must be made within specific periods.
- Distributions of the minimum required amount must be made after distributions are required to begin.

1. Date distributions must begin. Distributions from a qualified plan to a participant must begin no later than April 1 of the year in which that participant attains age 70½. If a participant attained age 70½ before 1988, he or she is allowed to defer distributions until April 1 of the year after retirement. The IRS has also indicated that April 1, 1990, is the date that distributions from qualified plans must begin for participants attaining age 70½ in 1988.

There is a special rule for any participant who owns at least 5 percent of the sponsor of qualified plan. The date that distributions from the plan must begin with respect to such a participant is April 1 following the year in which he or she attains age 70½. This rule applies irrespective of the date on which such an owner-participant retires.

2. Required distribution periods. Under the tax law, the period within which distributions from a qualified plan must be made is based on whether the distributions from the plan are *lifetime distributions* or *distributions made to beneficiaries after the death of the participant.*

When **lifetime distributions** are to be made from a qualified plan, minimum yearly distributions must be made over the distributee participant's life expectancy *or* the life expectancies of the participant and his or her designated beneficiary. The tax law provides for a minimum distribution incidental benefit (MDIB), beginning in 1989, when the participant's designated beneficiary with respect to qualified plan benefits is *not* the participant's spouse. For purposes of this rule, Prop. Reg. § 1.401(a)(9)–2 provides a table of joint life expectancies. Under this table, a plan participant's beneficiaries are considered to be 10 years younger than the participant. As a result of this table in the Proposed Regulations, required minimum distributions are substantially increased.

In the case of **distributions made after the participant's death,** the timing of distributions required to be made is based on whether or not plan distributions commenced during the participant's lifetime. If plan distributions commenced *before the participant's death,* his or her beneficiary cannot delay, but can *speed up,* distribution of the benefits remaining in the participant's account. If the participant *dies before distributions from the plan commence,* plan benefits generally must be distributed within five years of his or her death. However, there are exceptions to this rule:

- If the participant's beneficiary is *not* his or her spouse, plan distributions can be made over the beneficiary's life expectancy as long as they commence within one year of the participant's death.

- Plan distributions made to a participant's spouse may be made over the spouse's life expectancy, as long as the distributions commence by the date that the participant would have attained age 70½.

- The surviving spouse of a plan participant may roll over the amount in the participant's account to an IRA.

Note. When the deceased participant's spouse is younger than the deceased participant, a rollover of the balance in the participant's account into an IRA defers required distributions to April 1 of the year in which the deceased participant's spouse attains age 70½.

3. Required minimum plan distributions. The tax law prescribes required annual minimum distributions from qualified plans after distributions are required to begin. The minimum distribution requirement can be met in either of two ways: an *annuity* or *installment payments.*

Annuities. For purposes of this minimum distribution requirement, an annuity must satisfy the following four tests:

- Payments under the annuity must be made at least annually.
- Its term cannot exceed the plan participant's life or life expectancy or the joint lives or life expectancies of the participant and his or her designated beneficiary.
- Payments under the annuity must commence no later than the date they are required to commence under the tax law.
- Payments cannot be substantially increased.

Installment payments. If distributions from a qualified plan are not made under an annuity, as described above, they must be made in installments on at least an annual basis to meet the minimum distribution requirement. To qualify, the installment payments must commence no later than the date that payments from the plan are required to commence under the tax law. The minimum amount required to be distributed from the plan is determined by dividing the participant's *plan account balance* by the participant's life expectancy or the joint *life expectancies* of the participant and his or her designated beneficiary. The key terms are defined as follows:

- *Account balance.* For this purpose, the participant's account balance is his or her account balance on the first day of the year in which the distribution from the plan is made. But for the first required distribution (by April 1), the participant's account balance on the first day of the preceding year is used.
- *Life expectancies.* For this purpose, a participant's life expectancy or the joint life expectancies of the participant and his or her spouse can be redetermined each year. Thus, the participant and his or her spouse can receive lifetime payments without entering into an annuity arrangement. Also, this provides investment flexibility and enables the participant and spouse or estate to receive the full amount of benefits available to him or her under the plan.

Caution. Joint life expectancies *cannot* be redetermined when the participant's designated beneficiary is *not* his or her spouse. Under regulations, the participant can redetermine his or her life expectancy annually, but the life expectancy of the beneficiary who is not the participant's spouse cannot be so redetermined.

C. Excess Distributions

1. Penalty tax. A 15 percent penalty tax applies with respect to excess distributions from qualified plans. Such a distribution is the amount by which annual distributions to, or on behalf of, a participant exceed $150,000 or a base amount, whichever is greater. The base amount, originally $112,500, is indexed for inflation. The indexed amount for 1993 is $144,551. But see the discussions of the special exemption for surviving spouses and of the "grandfather" rule at 4.03.D.3.

Important. The 15 percent penalty does *not* apply with respect to amounts that are rolled over tax-free to another qualified plan or with respect to amounts representing a recovery of the participant's basis in his or her plan account.

Caution. A deferral by a participant of the initial distribution from a qualified plan to save taxes may result in the imposition of the 15 percent excess distribution penalty.

2. Payments made under a qualified domestic relations order (QDRO). Payments made under a QDRO to the spouse or former spouse of a plan participant are included in the gross income of the spouse or former spouse, *not* the gross income of the participant.

Planning tip. In the case of a divorce, a plan participant should consider having any alimony payments made from his or her qualified plan benefits. In such a case, *each* spouse is subject to the $150,000 floor annually, and thus the 15 percent penalty may be avoided.

3. Interaction with 10 percent penalty on premature plan distributions. The 10 percent penalty on premature distributions from qualified plans, discussed at 4.03.A.1, reduces the 15 percent penalty on excess distributions from qualified plans. Thus, in effect, the 10 percent penalty can be eliminated.

4. Lump-sum distributions. These distributions can qualify for favorable tax treatment through the use of 10-year averaging, under transition rules in the tax law, or through five-year averaging currently available under the tax law. If five-year averaging is elected by a plan participant, the floor amount for purposes of this penalty is generally increased fivefold (however, see 4.03.D.3).

Planning tip. In general, plan participants will not find averaging to be advantageous tax-wise when a lump-sum distribution from a plan is more than $500,000. But election of such treatment may help the participant to avoid or minimize the 15 percent excess distribution penalty.

D. Excess Accumulations

1. Penalty tax. A 15 percent penalty applies to excess accumulations in qualified plan accounts of deceased participants. An excess accumulation is defined as the excess of the value of the deceased participant's plan benefits over the value of a hypothetical annuity. This annuity is treated as paid over the life expectancy of the deceased participant immediately before his or her death. Annual payments are considered to be the same as the floor amount, discussed at 4.03.C, that applies at the time of the participant's death.

Note. For this purpose, annuity factors are provided in the regulations applicable to the federal estate tax—see Reg. § 20.2031–7(f).

2. Special exemption for surviving spouses. A spouse who survives a plan participant may elect out of the 15 percent penalty applicable to excess plan accumulations. This can be done only if the surviving spouse is the beneficiary of at least 99 percent of the decedent's benefits from all qualified plans, individual retirement accounts (IRAs), and § 403(b) annuities in which the decedent was a participant. If the surviving spouse so elects, the decedent's benefits are added to those of the surviving spouse for purposes of determining whether there is an excess distribution or accumulation subject to a penalty.

If the surviving spouse does not so elect, or cannot so elect because he or she is not the sole beneficiary of the decedent's benefits, those benefits are subject to the 15 percent excess accumulation penalty except for distributions after death. Distributions after death are not subject to the 15 percent excess distribution penalty, discussed at 4.03.C.1.

Caution. This special penalty exemption is available *only* as long as the benefits of the surviving spouse are not commingled with the decedent spouse's benefits.

3. "Grandfather" rule. The 15 percent excess distribution and accumulation penalties can be avoided or minimized under a grandfather rule applicable to a qualified plan participant's benefits accrued in his or her plan account as of *August 1, 1986*. Amounts grandfathered under this rule can be recovered by the participant under one of two methods:

• An attained age method.
• A discretionary method.

In general, the grandfather rule could have been elected on a tax return filed for a taxable year ending *before 1989* by a participant with an accrued plan benefit as of August 1, 1986, over $562,500. If the election was made, the portion of each distribution made to the participant attributable to the August 1, 1986, accrued benefit will not be penalized. If the election was not made, the $150,000 limit applies.

Note.   Once the grandfathered amount is exceeded, a plan participant can still benefit from the annual floor amount with respect to the excess distribution and excess accumulation penalties. As noted above, this floor currently is $150,000, and this amount should increase in the future as a result of indexing for inflation.

Chapter Five

Tax-Wise Use of Life Insurance

5.01. TAX AND FINANCIAL ADVANTAGES AVAILABLE THROUGH LIFE INSURANCE

The purchase of life insurance policies can enable taxpayers to save taxes and realize certain financial benefits, as highlighted here and discussed in detail later in this chapter. The use of life insurance trusts can also provide significant tax and financial benefits.

A. Ability to Provide Financially for the Decedent's Heirs and/or Beneficiaries

For the vast majority of taxpayers, the chief reason for the purchase of life insurance policies is to provide financial resources and, it is hoped, financial security for designated beneficiaries. Typically, the purchaser's goal is to provide financially for his or her heirs—ordinarily family members—in the event of his or her death, particularly an untimely death.

Also, life insurance can allow the purchaser to provide bequests that are comparable in value. For example, if a parent bequests an interest in a business to one heir, he or she can provide bequests of comparable value to other heirs through life insurance proceeds.

B. Liquidity for the Decedent's Estate

Life insurance proceeds can cover the tax liabilities and administrative expenses of the estate of a taxpayer/decedent, thereby lifting a potentially heavy financial burden from heirs and/or beneficiaries. This is a primary benefit of a taxpayer's purchase of a life insurance policy and is typically the lowest-cost way of covering expenses of his or her estate.

C. Increased Current Income for Retirees

Typical retirement plans allow the participant the option of receiving a higher amount of income from the plan during retirement or providing a larger amount of distributions to designated beneficiaries after his or her death. Through the purchase of life insurance, a plan participant who elects to receive higher current retirement income can provide financial resources to heirs and/or beneficiaries after his or her death.

D. Source of Funding a Child's Education

Life insurance can provide funding for a child's education in the event of the death of the insured parent or through a loan against the cash value of a cash-value life insurance policy (see 5.04.B).

> *Note.* Interest paid on insurance policy loans is subject to tax deduction limits as personal interest. This interest is *totally nondeductible* after 1990.

E. Source of Funding of Charitable Contributions

A taxpayer may make a contribution to a charity after his or her death by designating the charity as beneficiary of a newly purchased life insurance policy or one currently in force. Also, a taxpayer may make a current contribution to a charity, for which a tax deduction could be obtained, and provide for financial resources in his or her estate through the purchase of life insurance.

F. Benefits for Married Couples

A married couple may use life insurance to benefit from the unlimited marital deduction allowed for federal estate tax purposes. To realize this benefit, many married couples seek to postpone the payment of this tax until the death of the surviving spouse. A way to accomplish this is through an insurance product developed relatively recently, a life insurance policy commonly referred to as a *second-to-die* policy. Under this type of policy, married partners are jointly insured, and policy benefits are payable after the death of the surviving (second-to-die) spouse.

Note. Second-to-die policies are advantageous only when the unlimited marital deduction applies. There also are certain disadvantages to such policies, notably a potential lack of estate liquidity when the first spouse dies. Some insurers have created variations on these policies to address these disadvantages, such as providing the surviving spouse with cash to cover expenses arising from the other spouse's death, or adding the benefit payable with respect to the first-to-die spouse to the surviving spouse's policy.

G. Loans

Many life insurance policies having cash value, particularly those issued in past years, offer favorable, or at least market-competitive, interest rates on loans available under such policies against cash value. Such loans can be particularly valuable to policyholders not otherwise readily able to obtain a loan.

H. Benefits for Owners of Closely Held Businesses

Life insurance can provide a number of benefits to owners of closely held businesses. A popular way for such an owner to arrange for the orderly transfer of the business is by use of a buy-sell agreement funded by life insurance.

Buy-sell agreements typically provide that the heirs of an owner of a closely held business are to sell the interests in the business that they inherit to the remaining owners at a specified price. These agreements serve to set the value of the owner's interest for federal estate tax purposes and the amount that the heirs will receive for their inherited interests. By using life insurance to fund such an agreement, the business will have the resources to purchase the heirs' interests.

Note. Many rules and strategies under the federal income and estate tax laws apply with respect to ownership interests in closely held businesses. A detailed discussion of tax and estate planning for owners of such businesses is beyond the scope of this Guide.

I. Benefits for Terminally Ill Individuals

The IRS has issued proposed regulations under § 7702 allowing tax-free receipt of life insurance benefits paid during an insured's lifetime due to a terminal illness expected to result in the insured's death within 12 months. Such "living benefits" are of two types, accelerated death benefits and accident and health benefits based on the occurrence of certain morbidity risks.

5.02. WHAT IS LIFE INSURANCE, FOR TAX PURPOSES?

A. Requirements

To enjoy tax-favored status under the tax law, an insurance arrangement involving an individual's life must meet statutory requirements. The Internal Revenue Code (§ 7702) provides that life insurance contracts issued after 1984 must qualify as such under state law. Such contracts must also meet either a cash value accumulation test or a guideline premium test and a cash value corridor test. Life insurance contracts issued before 1985 generally were required to involve the shifting and distribution of risk to enjoy tax-favored status. The tax-favored status of life insurance is discussed in detail in the remainder of this chapter.

• Cash value accumulation test. This test is met if the life insurance policy's cash surrender value cannot exceed the net single premium required to fund policy benefits. Accordingly, a number of investment-oriented life insurance policies fail this test.

• *Guideline premium test.* This test is met if the sum of policy premiums paid exceeds the guideline single premium when the policy is issued, or the total of guideline level premiums at the testing date. The tax law specifies the guideline amounts, which are, in general, designed to prevent premium payments from exceeding the amount required to fund the benefits that the policy provides.

• *Cash value corridor test.* This test is met if the benefits provided under the policy are never less than an "applicable percentage" of the policy's cash surrender value as set forth in the tax law. This percentage varies inversely with the insured's attained age.

B. Failure to Meet Code Requirements

1. Treatment of cash value buildup. If the requirements set forth in the Code (under § 7702) are not met by a life insurance policy, the yearly buildup of the policy's cash value must be included in income by the policyholder for federal income tax purposes. The buildup amount is determined by deducting the premiums paid on the policy by the policyholder during the year from the sum of the policy's cash value and the cost of insurance coverage under it during that year.

Watch this. Whenever a life insurance policy fails to meet the requirements specified in the Code, *all* income generated under the policy becomes taxable to the policyholder.

2. Treatment of death benefits. When a life insurance policy fails to meet the Code requirements, the death benefit under the policy is considered to be life insurance only to the extent that it is more than the cash value of the policy. The cash value of the policy cannot be excluded from income tax in the hands of policy beneficiaries.

Watch this. The cash value will also be subject to federal estate tax when the policy does not meet the Code requirements.

C. Special Rules for "Modified Endowment Contracts"

Recent tax law changes created unfavorable tax consequences for "modified endowment contracts." Such contracts are life insurance contracts that meet Code (§ 7702) requirements but fail another statutory test referred to as the *seven-pay test.* This test is failed if accumulated payments under the contract are more than the total of net level payments required for funding benefits after payment of such net level payments at *any time* during the first *seven* years of the contract.

Under such contracts, amounts paid are treated by the recipient first as income and second as a return of capital invested. This treatment applies regardless of whether the amount was received as a loan.

Watch this. An additional 10 percent income tax applies to amounts received under modified endowment contracts.

5.03. FAVORABLE TAX ATTRIBUTES OF LIFE INSURANCE

A. Income Tax

Life insurance is generally not subject to income taxation, either during the insured's life or at his or her death. Thus, it can enable an insured to accumulate wealth during life and to pass on that wealth to beneficiaries at no income tax cost. This will be covered in more detail in later sections of this chapter.

B. Estate Tax

The proceeds of life insurance policies may be exempt from the federal estate tax. They are exempt from this tax as long as they are not payable to, or for the benefit of, the insured's estate, *and* the insured, at death, did not hold any "incidents of ownership" (see 5.06.B) in the life insurance policy.

C. Gift Tax

The insured may transfer an insurance policy on his or her life without imposition of the federal gift tax. In general, the value of a life insurance policy during the insured's life is much lower than the policy's face amount (i.e., the amount payable to the insured's beneficiaries at his or her death). Thus, if gifts of life insurance are made during the insured's life, there is a benefit for the insured with respect to the unified federal estate and gift tax credit and annual exclusions from the federal gift tax. As a result, an insured person may be able to substantially cut the federal estate tax that would otherwise be due after his or her death.

D. Generation-Skipping Tax

It may also be possible to avoid imposition of the federal generation-skipping transfer tax (commonly referred to as the GST; see 5.09.E) on proceeds of a life insurance policy as the result of an annual exclusion and an exemption from this tax.

5.04. TYPES OF LIFE INSURANCE

Because there are numerous types of life insurance policies offered that afford investment and tax planning flexibility, life insurance should be a key estate planning tool for many taxpayers.

A. Term Life Insurance

A term life insurance policy's face amount is payable to the insured's designated beneficiary or beneficiaries if the insured's death occurs within a specified term of years. At the end of that specified term, the policy is no longer in force. Such a policy has no cash value and generates no investment earnings, but policy premiums are generally much lower than those on other types of life insurance.

Many insurers offer several popular modifications of the basic term insurance. These include

- Convertible term insurance, which provides the option of converting the policy to another form of insurance (usually cash-value life insurance, such as whole life).
- Decreasing term insurance.
- Renewable term insurance, which permits the renewal of life insurance coverage for another term after the expiration of the insured's current term of coverage.

Group term insurance. A group term life insurance policy, typically held by employers and professional or fraternal organizations, for example, for the benefit of their employees or members, generally provides the lowest-cost life insurance coverage. The cost reduction is obtained because the insurer's risk is spread over a group of individuals.

B. Cash-Value Life Insurance

1. Whole life insurance. This type of life insurance coverage typically provides for premium payments and the death benefit to remain at a steady level during the life of the insured. In general, it involves decreasing term insurance *and* an increasing savings fund that generates interest income. The interest earned, the rate of which is specified in the policy and often guaranteed by the insurer, builds up the policy's cash value. This cash value may be redeemed by the holder of the policy, or a loan may be taken out against it or applied to policy premium payments.

Many insurers offer modifications of the basic whole life insurance coverage. These include

- Limited-payment life insurance policies.
- Single-premium whole life insurance policies.
- Variable life insurance policies.

2. Universal life insurance. This type of cash-value life insurance is quite similar to the basic "whole" life insurance, except that it usually affords the opportunity for a larger buildup of cash value. It typically enables the policyholder to alternate between whole life and term life insurance coverage and to increase or decrease coverage under the policy. Term life insurance coverage may be limited while the policy's cash value is increased with tax-favored treatment on the cash buildup.

Note. Whole life insurance policies and universal life insurance policies are either participating or nonparticipating. If the policy is *participating,* the policyholder is entitled to participate in the earnings of a *mutual* insurance company, to the extent that those earnings exceed payouts to policyholders. If the policy, whether issued by a mutual insurance company or one owned by stockholders, is nonparticipating, the income buildup thereon does not exceed the specified interest rate.

3. Endowment life insurance policies. This is a type of cash-value insurance under which policy premiums typically exceed those payable on other types of life insurance policies. The policyholder is no longer required to pay premiums on the policy after a specified term. At the end of that term, the cash value of the policy will be equal to its face amount.

4. Annuity contracts. Many insurers offer annuity contracts under which the holder, the *annuitant,* receives immediate or future payments over either a specified period of his or her life, rather than at *death,* as under the standard life insurance policy.

5. Life insurance for business owners and executives. Tax and financial planning strategies for owners/executives of small businesses, particularly closely held businesses, typically involve life insurance. As noted earlier, closely held businesses often use life insurance to fund buy-sell agreements designed to provide for orderly transfers of interests held therein. Businesses also frequently purchase "key man" life insurance policies on the lives of key personnel to fund any payments from the business to the insured's beneficiaries at death and to cover any decrease in the earnings of the business as a result of his or her death.

Another type of insurance commonly used by businesses is "split-dollar" life insurance, which is not a pure form of life insurance. Rather, it is an arrangement providing a special treatment of ownership and payments with respect to cash-value life insurance. This involves, in the typical case, a split of benefits payable under the policy between an employee who needs life insurance and a business having the financial resources to make premium payments on the policy. Thus, the insured has the needed life insurance coverage and the employer is entitled to the later return of the premium payments (i.e., its investment in the policy).

C. "Living Benefits" Policies

Some life insurance companies offer policies that allow for the payout of policy face value before the insured's death, under certain circumstances. These policies provide the typical death benefits as well as living benefits. The living benefits would cover the costs of medical care and long-term care, usually in cases where the insured develops a terminal or catastrophic illness.

To resolve uncertainty over the tax treatment of such benefits, the IRS has provided guidance in the form of proposed regulations (see Prop. Reg. § 1.7702–2). In general, these proposed regulations cover two categories of benefits: qualified accelerated death benefits (QADBs), and additional benefits

(ABs). QADBs are excluded from a recipient's income, as they are treated as paid by reason of death. The proposed regulations also set forth conditions under which ABs can be excluded from a recipient's income.

Note. As this Guide covers tax and financial planning strategies from the viewpoint of an individual investor, a complete discussion of the use of life insurance by businesses is beyond its scope. The preceding summary is intended only as an overview providing highlights of the tax-wise use of life insurance by businesses, particularly by closely held businesses, and the benefits of that use to owners, executives, and other key employees.

5.05. INCOME TAXATION OF LIFE INSURANCE PROCEEDS

A. Treatment of Benefits

When a person covered under a life insurance policy dies, the policy beneficiary or beneficiaries can receive the policy proceeds in either of two ways, which have differing income tax consequences:

• Lump-sum distribution.

• Deferred payment.

1. Lump-sum distributions. As a general rule, the Internal Revenue Code provides that proceeds of a life insurance policy received by a beneficiary as a result of the insured's death are *not* subject to federal income tax. This rule applies to the full death benefit distributed under the policy whether the beneficiary is the insured estate, an individual, a corporation, a partnership, or a trustee of a trust.

Observation. It is important to emphasize that the federal income exemption applies to the *full* amount of the policy proceeds distributed as a result of the insured's death, including the amounts relating to the insured's insurance coverage, the savings element of the policy (referred to as the *policy reserve*), and the income earned on the latter.

2. Deferred-payment settlements. After the death of an insured individual, a beneficiary of the life insurance policy may elect to have the proceeds remain with the insurer. If the beneficiary so elects, investment earnings on the amount retained by the insurer are includable in the beneficiary's gross income for federal income tax purposes. Payments to the beneficiary under such an arrangement are made in installments. The portion of each such installment representing the death benefit owed to the beneficiary as a result of the insured's death are not subject to income taxation, whereas the balance, representing income earned after the insured's death, is.

Types of deferred-payment settlements available to life insurance policy beneficiaries include:

• *Installments payable over the beneficiary's life.* Under this type of settlement, payment of the amount held by the insurer is made in pro rata payments based on the beneficiary's life expectancy. Such payments are not subject to federal income taxation in the beneficiary's hands, *as long as* the insurer does *not* guarantee minimum payout in the case of the beneficiary's death or a refund.

• *Installments made over a specified period.* If a beneficiary elects to receive periodic payments under a life insurance policy rather than a lump-sum distribution, the amount retained by the insurer is subject to proration over the total period over which the periodic payments are to be made. The amount so prorated by the insurer is excludable from the beneficiary's gross income for federal income tax purposes.

• *Interest payable on death benefit.* If an insurer retains the death benefit payable under a life insurance policy and, per agreement, is to pay interest on that amount, the interest received by the policy beneficiary is includable in his or her gross income for federal income tax purposes.

3. Exception for policies transferred for value. The exemption from federal income taxation does *not* apply under certain circumstances where a life insurance policy is transferred by the policyholder in return for some valuable consideration, such as cash. When this exception applies, the amount of proceeds excludable from income tax by a beneficiary cannot be more than the amount paid for the transfer of the policy and any premiums or other amounts paid by the transferee after the transfer.

Watch this. A policy may be deemed to have been transferred for value even though its transferor does not receive cash or other property as a result of the transfer. For example, this may be the case where a transferor has taken out a loan against the policy and then makes a gift of the policy.

The exception to the general rule exempting life insurance policy proceeds from federal income taxation does *not* apply when a policy is transferred for value to the insured, to an insured's partner, to a partnership in which the insured is a partner, or to a corporation in which the insured is a shareholder and/or officer.

Another exception to the exception applies when the basis of the policy in the transferee's hands is determined by reference to its basis in the transferor's hands, in whole or in part.

B. Other Tax Deductions Available with Respect to Life Insurance Policies

1. Life insurance obtained for personal reasons. When a taxpayer acquires a life insurance policy for personal reasons, such as to provide financial resources for his or her family in the event of his or her death, premiums paid on the policy are *not* deductible for federal income tax purposes.

2. Interest expense incurred.

Personal interest. If an individual taxpayer takes out a loan against a life insurance policy on his or her life acquired for personal reasons, the interest paid on that loan is treated, for federal income tax purposes, as personal interest. This interest is *totally* nondeductible.

Business-related or investment-related interest paid. When interest paid on a life insurance policy loan is related to an investment or to a trade or business, or is paid by a corporation, the following deduction limits apply:
• No deduction is allowed with respect to a loan related to the purchase or the holding of a single-premium life insurance, endowment, or annuity policy. For purposes of this rule, a life insurance policy qualifies as a single-premium policy if substantially all of the policy premiums are paid within four years of the date that the policy was purchased.
• No deduction is allowed with respect to a loan related to the purchase or the holding of a life insurance or endowment policy or annuity contract when the systematic direct or indirect borrowing of some or all of the increases in cash value is intended. However, this deduction limit does not apply if no portion of four of the first seven annual policy premiums are financed by debt, if interest paid on any debt related to the policy is $100 or less, if the debt was incurred due to an unexpected loss of income or increased financial obligations, or if the debt is related to a trade or business.
• No deduction is allowed for debt exceeding $50,000 incurred on policies purchased or held that insure the lives of persons having a financial interest in a trade or business conducted by a taxpayer, or employees thereof.

3. Treatment of dividends. A holder of a life insurance policy can use any dividends payable on the policy to pay premiums that are due or to buy additional life insurance coverage, can allow them to accumulate with the insurer, or can receive them in cash. As a general rule, these policy dividends are not subject to federal income taxation unless paid on modified endowment contracts and annuity contracts. With respect to the latter contracts, all dividends paid in cash are subject to federal income taxation in the amount that the policy's cash value exceeds the total premiums paid. Also, with respect to such contracts, dividends withdrawn by the holder are subject to federal income taxation in the amount that they exceed aggregate premiums paid on the policy.

4. Premiums paid on group term life insurance. As a general rule, when an employer pays premiums on an insurance policy insuring the life of an employee, the premiums represent taxable income to the employee, as long as the policy benefits are payable to the employee or his or her beneficiary. However, there are exceptions to this rule, notably the income exclusion provided under Code § 79.

Under this exclusion, employer-paid premiums on a group term life insurance policy may be excluded from income for tax purposes within specified limits. Excludable premium payments are

- Those paid on the first $50,000 of insurance.
- Those paid by the employee.
- Those paid with respect to a retired, disabled employee.
- Those paid on a policy having the employer as beneficiary or charitable organization as *sole* beneficiary.

5.06. ESTATE TAXATION OF LIFE INSURANCE PROCEEDS

Proceeds of a life insurance policy are included in the gross estate of a deceased insured if the policy proceeds are receivable by the insured's estate or for its benefit, or by any other beneficiary as long as the insured held incidents of ownership in the policy at the time of his or her death. For this purpose, such incidents of ownership to be defined are those held solely by the insured or those held with another person or persons.

Note. The treatment of proceeds of a policy held by a decedent on the life of *another* person is somewhat different. In such cases, the amount includable in the decedent's gross estate is the *value* of the policy. This amount, in most cases, is less than the death benefit payable under the policy.

A. Proceeds Receivable by or for the Benefit of the Insured's Estate

These are life insurance proceeds that are receivable by the executor or administrator of the insured's estate or directly by the estate. Insured parties often provide for this application of policy proceeds to provide liquidity for their estates. Proceeds so applied are includable in the gross estate of the deceased insured.

Watch this. To the extent that the insured's estate receives benefits under the policy, the related policy proceeds are required to be included in the deceased insured's gross estate. This can present a problem when an insured requires the proceeds of a life insurance policy on his or her life to be applied against the debts, taxes, and other expenses of his or her estate. To the extent that the proceeds are so applied, they are includable in the insured's gross estate.

Planning point. If the insured does not require that the proceeds of the insurance policy on his or her life be applied to the payment of debts, taxes, and other expenses, but a general authorization is given to make purchase of assets or to enter into loans, the potential problem just described should be avoided.

Also, if a beneficiary of the policy is required to pay administration expenses and debts of the deceased insured's estate from policy proceeds, the amount of the proceeds so applied are required to be included in the deceased insured's gross estate.

B. What Are "Incidents of Ownership" in an Insurance Policy?

As noted earlier, the proceeds of a life insurance policy are included in an insured's gross estate if he or she, alone or with one or more other persons, had incidents of ownership in the policy. Under the Internal Revenue Code and related regulations, *incidents of ownership* refers to the right of the insured or his or her estate to the policy's economic benefits.

1. Reversionary interest. Such an interest is treated as an incident of ownership if its value is more than 5 percent of the policy's value immediately before the decedent's death.

Note. This involves the potential receipt of a life insurance policy or its benefits by the insured or his or her estate, as well as the insured's potential disposition of same.

2. Ability to borrow against the policy. This is considered by the IRS to constitute an incident of ownership in a life insurance policy. Accordingly, the proceeds of such a policy are includable in the gross estate of the deceased insured. (See IRS Revenue Ruling 79–129.)

3. Use of the policy as loan security. When an insured assigns a policy on his or her life as security for a loan, he or she is considered to have incidents of ownership in the policy. However, when the insured has transferred *all* incidents of ownership in the policy, its proceeds are not includable in the insured's gross estate if the transferee subsequently assigns the policy for the purpose of obtaining a loan on behalf of either the transferee or the insured, unless, prior to the transfer, there was an agreement that such a loan would be obtained.

4. Incidents of ownership when the policy is held in trust. The insured is considered to hold incidents of ownership in a life insurance policy if the policy is held by a trust with respect to which the insured is a beneficiary. Also, when an insured transfers a policy on his or her life to a trust, the insured is considered to have incidents of ownership in the policy if he or she can alter, amend, terminate, or revoke that trust, *or* can designate the persons to receive the trust's benefits. For purposes of the latter rule, the insured will be treated as having incidents of ownership in the policy even if he or she is *not* a beneficiary of the trust.

5. Incidents of ownership reacquired. An insured may reacquire incidents of ownership in a life insurance policy, after transfer of such incidents, through an occurrence beyond his or her control. This could occur, for example, when an insured transfers all incidents of ownership to a beneficiary, and the beneficiary, at death, passes the policy to a trust of which the insured is a trustee. Under such circumstances, if the insured were to die while serving as trustee, the policy proceeds generally would not be included in the insured's gross estate.

Note. If, at his or her death, the insured is unable to exercise the incidents of ownership in a policy insuring his or her life—if, for example, the insured is incompetent at the time he or she becomes an heir to an estate whose assets include the policy—the policy proceeds are generally includable in the insured's gross estate.

C. Transfer of a Life Insurance Policy within Three Years of the Insured's Death

If an insured makes a gift of a policy on his or her life within three years of death, the proceeds of that policy will be included in his or her gross estate for federal estate tax purposes, *even though* the insured, at death, did not have any incidents of ownership in the policy, and the policy benefits were not receivable by, or for the benefit of, his or her estate.

Note. The amount included in the deceased insured's estate does *not* include the amount of any premium paid by the *donee* after the gift of the policy. The IRS probably will not permit this, however, if the premium payments are made with funds gifted by the insured.

D. Taxable Amount of Policy Proceeds

When the proceeds of a life insurance policy are paid in a lump sum on the death of the insured, the amount payable under the policy is includable in the gross estate of the deceased insured. When the policy proceeds are payable through an annuity, special rules apply. Under these rules, the amount of an optional lump-sum payment is includable in the gross estate of the deceased insured. However, if the life insurance policy does not provide a lump-sum payment option, the policy's face value is included in the gross estate of the deceased insured. Also, for purposes of these rules, if the policy has no face value, the includable amount is that used by the insurer in determining the annuity's value.

5.07.   MARITAL DEDUCTION FOR FEDERAL ESTATE TAX PURPOSES

The marital deduction allowable under the federal estate tax law applies to a lump-sum payment under a life insurance policy made to the spouse of a deceased insured. The marital deduction is also allowable if the policy proceeds are payable to a "QTIP trust" or under a qualifying power of appointment.

Where proceeds of a life insurance policy are not paid in a lump sum to the surviving spouse of the insured, qualification of such proceeds for the federal estate tax marital deduction are dependent on the policy's terms. The proceeds of a life insurance policy can qualify for the marital deduction for purposes of the federal estate tax in the following ways:

The insured should make his or her spouse the *sole* beneficiary.

The proceeds of the life insurance policy should be payable so as to qualify under an exception to the terminable interest rule under the Internal Revenue Code:

• The proceeds are payable to a QTIP trust.
• The proceeds are payable to a power-of-appointment trust.
• The proceeds are payable to the insured's surviving spouse only if that spouse survives the insured by six months and does not die as a result of a common disaster that caused the death of the insured.
• The policy provides a settlement option meeting an exception to the terminable interest rule as long as (1) The policy proceeds are payable to the insured's surviving spouse in installments or are held by the insurer subject to its agreement to pay interest to the insured's surviving spouse; (2) The installment or interest payments are made at least annually and begin within 13 months of the insured's death; (3) During the life of the insured's surviving spouse, installments or interest are payable *only* to that surviving spouse; (4) Amounts payable under the life insurance policy are subject to an unrestricted power of appointment in the hands of the insured's surviving spouse exercisable by himself or herself or his or her estate; and (5) No one can appoint the proceeds of the insurance policy to a person other than the insured's surviving spouse.

5.08. FEDERAL GIFT TAXATION OF LIFE INSURANCE

An insured may transfer ownership of a policy on his or her life to beneficiaries other than his or her spouse, usually to his or her children or to a trust established for their benefit. Such a transfer is subject to the federal gift tax, and if the transferee continues to pay policy premiums, such payments also constitute gifts subject to this tax.

Observation. A gift of an insurance policy from one spouse to another may be made and will accomplish the goal of avoiding imposition of the deferral *estate* tax on the policy proceeds in the estate of the deceased insured. As a general rule, however, it is most advantageous for the insured to retain control of the policy insuring his or her life and designate his or her spouse as beneficiary of that policy. By so doing, the maximum benefit of the marital deduction allowed for federal *estate* tax purposes (see 5.07) can be realized.

Further observation. If an insured is considering making a gift of a policy on his or her life, he or she should also seriously consider taking out a loan against the policy. By so doing, the insured can withdraw the equity in the policy, and gift tax would be avoided on the *net* policy proceeds. *Caveat:* If the insured takes out a policy loan, the deductibility of the loan interest is limited as personal interest. Such interest is totally nondeductible. However, the ability to withdraw the equity in the policy should be a more important consideration than the deductibility of interest on a policy loan in most cases.

A. Valuation for Gift Tax Purposes

1. Newly issued or paid-up life insurance policies. In the case of such policies, valuation for federal gift tax purposes is established based on the sale of the policy involved or of a comparable policy issued by the same insurer.

2. Other existing policies. In the case of such policies, regulations issued by the Internal Revenue Service provide the valuation method. (See Reg. § 25.2512–6.)

B. Gifts of Life Insurance Policies: Planning Considerations

An insured can reap tax benefits from a gift of a policy on his or her life.

1. Gift tax versus estate tax. The value of a life insurance policy during an insured's life, especially the value of a *term* insurance policy having no cash value, typically is much less than the death benefit (face amount) payable to beneficiaries. Accordingly, an insured can obtain a substantial tax benefit by making a gift of such a policy, paying the gift tax on the *lifetime* value rather than having the policy's face amount included in his or her taxable estate for purposes of the federal estate tax.

2. Gift tax exclusion. In general, a gift tax exclusion applies to gifts of up to $10,000 *for each individual to whom a gift is made.* This is an exclusion allowed *each year,* and a married couple can treat such a gift as made equally by each spouse, if they so elect. Accordingly, up to $20,000 in value of such a gift can be excluded with respect to *each* recipient.

Premium payments made with respect to the policy after the gift is made are also subject to the annual gift tax exclusion.

3. Stepped-up basis. Unlike property that is gifted to another by a tax-payer, which has the same basis for federal tax purposes as it did in the taxpayer's hands, a gift of a life insurance policy, in effect, has a stepped-up basis. This is because the amount of the death benefit paid under the policy is the same as the basis.

4. Marital deduction. If an insured transfers a life insurance policy to his or her spouse, the policy proceeds are eligible for the unlimited marital deduction for federal gift tax purposes.

Observation. Such a transfer is generally not advantageous because the same estate tax benefit can be achieved by the insured's naming his or her spouse as beneficiary of the policy. If such a transfer is made, the insured would lose control of the policy *without* any additional tax benefit.

5.09. LIFE INSURANCE TRUSTS

A. What Is a Trust?

In general, a trust involves the division of ownership of property between one or more trustees and beneficiaries. Under legal rules applicable to trusts, the trustee(s), typically a financial institution such as a bank, holds formal title to the property placed in the trust by the maker of the trust (referred to as the *settlor*) for the purpose of investing the assets placed therein for the benefit of the trust beneficiaries. The trustee, in accordance with law, is a fiduciary required to fairly and carefully manage the trust assets for the trust beneficiaries. The trust beneficiaries, under legal rules, are considered to hold equitable interests in the trust's assets. Such equitable interests constitute the legal right to income earned by the trust assets.

B. Why Create a Trust?

There are a number of reasons for a taxpayer to consider the establishment of a trust, including a life insurance trust:

• A trust takes advantage of experienced financial management on the part of the trustee, typically a financial institution, such as a bank. Legal requirements apply to trustees that are designed to protect the financial interests of trust beneficiaries.

• By transferring assets to a trust, the maker of the trust can avoid subjecting those assets to the probate process at his or her death. This usually saves legal fees and time involved with probate proceedings and can avoid disputes among beneficiaries. (*Note:* Property transferred to a trust is still exempt from probate even when the transferor is a life beneficiary of the property and/or has the power to revoke the trust during his or her life.)

• The maker of the trust can provide for multiple and future beneficiaries. By creating a trust, an individual can provide income to his or her descendants, for example.

C. What Are the Tax Advantages of Establishing a Trust?

Tax laws enacted in recent years have limited federal income tax advantages from the use of trusts. In addition, the advantages of a trust for federal estate and gift tax purposes have been limited by the generation-skipping transfer tax (GST) (see 5.09.E). Certain significant tax breaks remain, however.

1. QTIP trust. Benefits can be achieved by taxpayers through the use of qualified terminable interest property (QTIP) trusts, for purposes of the marital deduction available for federal estate and gift tax purposes. In brief, this is because, although an *unlimited* marital deduction is not generally available for terminable interest, a transfer of such an interest *will* qualify for the unlimited marital deduction when it is made to a QTIP trust and all of its income is payable to the transferor's spouse over the transferor's life. The property remaining in the trust at the transferor's death may then be distributed as he or she wished.

2. Subchapter S trust. A qualified Subchapter S trust can be advantageous to a shareholder in an S corporation in that such a trust (in addition to *individuals* specified in the Internal Revenue Code) can be a shareholder in the corporation. This may afford tax planning flexibility to an S corporation shareholder. (*Note:* A complete discussion of tax planning for S corporations and their shareholders is beyond the scope of this Guide.)

D. What Is a Life Insurance Trust?

A life insurance trust is a trust that is the beneficiary of an insurance policy on the life of an individual. There are various types of life insurance trusts.

1. Funded trusts. A funded life insurance trust receives other assets in addition to one or more insurance policies on the life of an individual. After the death of the insured, the trustee distributes the proceeds of the life insurance policy and any other assets transferred to the trust as directed by the instrument (document) that established the trust.

2. Unfunded trusts. An unfunded life insurance trust generally holds no assets other than one or more life insurance policies on the life of an individual. After the death of the insured, the trustee distributes the proceeds of the life insurance policy as directed by the instrument (document) that established the trust.

Watch this. The laws of some states may not permit certain unfunded life insurance trusts, such as trusts not owning the life insurance policy but merely designated as beneficiary of the policy. Accordingly, the law of the state in which a life insurance trust is to be established should be researched. Usually, such laws may be satisfied by transferring a minimal amount of other assets to the life insurance trust.

3. Revocable life insurance trusts. A trust may be revocable; that is, the maker (grantor) may end it and retrieve the trust property. Such trusts are also frequently referred to as *living trusts.* At the maker's death, such a trust becomes irrevocable.

Funded revocable life insurance trusts are created for the primary purpose of avoiding probate with respect of the trust assets. They provide no benefits taxwise. A taxable transfer to the trust assets occurs only when the trust becomes irrevocable after the maker's death or another event. If the trust becomes irrevocable as a result of the maker's death, the trust assets (including policy death benefits) are included in the maker's gross estate for federal estate tax purposes. If the trust becomes irrevocable during the maker's life, the maker is treated as having made taxable gifts to the trust's beneficiaries for federal gift tax purposes.

Tax break. The marital deduction allowable for federal estate tax purposes may reduce or entirely eliminate federal estate tax on the trust assets.

Note. When premiums on a life insurance policy in such a trust are paid by someone other than the maker of the trust, the premium payments are treated as taxable gifts to the maker for federal gift tax purposes.

4. Irrevocable life insurance trusts. Unlike revocable life insurance trusts, irrevocable life insurance trusts afford *significant* potential tax savings for individuals. Creation of such a trust has a downside, however, since the maker forever relinquishes all interests in the trust assets.

Since the deposit of assets into such a trust involves a completed transfer, it constitutes a taxable gift to the trust's beneficiaries for federal gift tax purposes. The valuation of such a gift is determined under principles discussed in 5.08.A.

Watch this. The annual gift tax exclusion for gifts of up to $10,000 per donee per year is *not* available with respect to gifts of *future interests.* In general, such interests include remainder interests, reversions, and others that are to take effect in the future. Beneficiaries' interests in irrevocable life insurance trusts are usually considered to constitute future interests, since these trusts are designed to provide benefits for the beneficiaries after the insured's death.

Salvaging the exclusion: the "Crummey" power. The annual gift tax exclusion may be salvaged by avoiding the future interest problem through use of the *Crummey* power. This power takes its name from a court case in which its use was approved [*Crummey* v. *Com.*, 397 F.2d 82 (9th Cir. 1986)].

By use of the Crummey power, additional assets placed in an irrevocable life insurance trust (i.e., a life insurance policy or amounts to be used to pay policy premiums) will be considered a *present,* rather than a future, interest. This is accomplished by giving trust beneficiaries the power to *demand* that the additions be paid to them.

To ensure that the present interest requirement is met, the life insurance trust should do all the following:

- Give to beneficiaries a noncumulative power to annually withdraw any additions to trust principal.

- Promptly give beneficiaries written notice of annual additions to trust principal so that the power to withdraw may be exercised.

- Specify a time limit within which the power may be exercised.

- Provide for the automatic lapse of the withdrawal power when it is not exercised within the specified period.

- Place a limit on the amount a beneficiary may withdraw annually.

- Give the trustee the power to make elected withdrawals through distributions of insurance policies, cash, or other property.

The withdrawal limit is established based on the amount of the annual exclusion allowed per donee for federal gift tax purposes. Also, 30 days is a typical time period established for exercise of the withdrawal power.

Gift tax implications of Crummey power. The Crummey power can result in a taxable gift to the beneficiary of an irrevocable life insurance trust. This is because the power can be exercised for the beneficiary's *own* benefit. As such, the power is considered to be a general power of appointment, for federal gift tax purposes, up to the withdrawable amount. The release or exercise of the power by a beneficiary can constitute a taxable gift to that beneficiary.

If there is a lapse of such a power, as a general power of appointment, it is considered a release constituting a taxable transfer for federal gift tax purposes. It is so treated to the extent that the trust assets to which the power applies exceed the greater of $5,000 or 5 percent of the asset value from which withdrawals under lapsed powers could have been paid (the "five and five rule").

The marital deduction allowed spouses under the federal gift tax law generally is not applicable to a life insurance policy transferred to a trust. This is because a spouse's interest is considered a terminable interest, since it is contingent on surviving the maker of the trust, and also because such trusts typically have multiple beneficiaries.

In addition, the "gift-splitting" election, under which a gift made by an individual can be treated as made jointly with his or her spouse, generally will not be available. This is the case when the value of the spouse's interest in the trust cannot be determined and the trust has multiple beneficiaries.

Estate tax implications of Crummey power.   Estate tax rules similar to those just discussed with respect to the federal gift tax apply to beneficiaries of irrevocable life insurance trusts providing for a Crummey power. Thus, property subject to the power, as a general power of appointment, generally will be included in the gross estate of a deceased beneficiary. Similar rules (i.e., the five and five rule) also apply with respect to lapsed Crummey powers. However, the lapse rules, for these purposes, apply only to lapses that occur during the beneficiary's lifetime. Thus, if a beneficiary of an irrevocable life insurance trust dies when he or she could have exercised a Crummey power, he or she will be treated as holding the power at death. Accordingly, amounts subject to the Crummey power will be included in his or her gross estate: the five and five rule will *not* apply.

For proceeds of a life insurance policy held in trust *not* to be included in the insured individual's gross estate, the policy proceeds cannot be received by the executor of the insured's estate or for its benefit, and the deceased insured cannot hold any incidents of ownership in the policy at death.

Other federal estate tax considerations include:

• *Retained interests.* If the maker of such a trust retains interests in or powers over the life insurance trust so that its assets are included in his or her gross estate, the proceeds of the life insurance policies held by the trust will also be included in his or her gross estate.

• *Transfers to a life insurance trust within three years of the transferor's death.* When an insured transfers a policy on his or her life to an individual or trust within three years of death, the policy proceeds are included in his or her gross estate for federal estate tax purposes.

Income tax implications of Crummey power.   A beneficiary of an irrevocable life insurance trust is subject to federal income tax on the amount withdrawable under the Crummey power. This is because the beneficiary is considered, for these purposes, to be an owner of the trust up to such amount.

If the life insurance trust is *funded,* the maker must include in his or her taxable income any trust income used to pay premiums on policies insuring his or her life or that of his or her spouse.

As a practical matter, such beneficiaries will not have an income tax problem with respect to a Crummey power. This is because these life insurance trusts typically are funded or minimally funded and, consequently, generate little or no taxable income.

There are no income tax consequences for beneficiaries from the payment of premiums on a life insurance policy held by such a trust or a transfer of a life insurance policy to such a trust, as these are tax-exempt gifts.

E. Generation-Skipping Tax (GST) Implications of Life Insurance Trusts

Generation-skipping transfers are subject to tax at the *highest* federal state tax rate—currently 55 percent. This tax is referred to as the *generation-skipping tax* (GST). Under these tax rules, an exemption of $1,000,000 per donor (transferor) is provided. This tax generally applies to generation-skipping transfers, including those relating to life insurance trusts.

1. What transfers are subject to the GST?   The following transfers are subject to the GST:

• *Direct skip.* This refers to a transfer made directly to a "skip person" when no intervening interest is given to a "non-skip person." For this purpose, a *skip person* is one who is at least two generations younger than the donor.

• *Taxable termination.* A taxable termination takes place when there is a termination of an interest in property that causes a transfer to a skip person. Such a termination may result from the release of a power, the passage of time, or death.

• *Taxable distribution.* A taxable distribution is any distribution from a trust to a skip person that is not a direct skip or taxable termination.

2. Transfers to an irrevocable life insurance trust.   In general, the creation of an irrevocable life insurance trust, the transfer of a life insurance policy to the trust, the payment of premiums on the policy, or the death of the insured do not constitute transfers subject to the GST, as long as the trust beneficiaries are not all skip persons. When the trust beneficiaries include non-skip persons (e.g., the maker's spouse and/or children), a transfer will not be subject to the GST until the interests of non-skip persons in the trust are terminated or distributions from the trust are made to skip persons.

Chapter Six

Minimizing the Bite of the Alternative Minimum Tax

The alternative minimum tax (AMT) was enacted as part of the Tax Reform Act of 1986 (TRA '86). This tax is broader in its scope and coverage than the minimum tax it replaced and affects the investment decisions of many taxpayers, preventing them from escaping tax entirely. The AMT's key feature is that it involves a *prepayment* of tax; that is, it results in earlier payment of tax in connection with a transaction to which its rules apply than would be the case under the parallel regular tax rules.

The AMT applies to individuals, regular (C) corporations, estates, and trusts. This chapter focuses on how the AMT applies to individuals and affects their investment decisions.

6.01. FEATURES OF THE AMT

A. Alternative Minimum Taxable Income

The AMT is computed on the basis of alternative minimum taxable income (AMTI). AMTI is determined by adding or subtracting AMT adjustments and adding AMT preferences to regular taxable income before deduction of a regular tax net operating loss, if any. Adjustments and preferences are key features of the AMT and are described in the following sections. The computation of the AMT is also described.

Important. A taxpayer's income from a lump-sum plan distribution (taxable under Code § 402(e)) is *not* taken into account for AMT purposes. For coverage of lump-sum distributions from qualified plans, see Chapter 4.

B. AMT Adjustments

Adjustments for certain items entail the substitution of AMT treatment for regular tax treatment. These adjustments may increase or decrease AMTI, whereas AMT preferences only increase AMTI. In addition to increasing or decreasing taxable income for purposes of computing AMTI, adjustments can affect an asset's basis, and they may result in a timing difference for purposes of the AMT credit and in a difference in the gain or loss on the sale of an asset for purposes of the AMT and the regular tax.

The following are adjustments to be made by individuals for purposes of the AMT:

- Itemized deductions, the standard deduction, and personal exemptions.
- Excess depreciation on real property placed in service after 1986.
- Excess depreciation on personal property placed in service after 1986.
- Installment sales.
- Passive activity losses.
- Long-term contracts.
- Farming losses.
- Circulation, research, and experimentation expenses.
- Mining exploration and development costs.

These adjustments will be discussed in more detail in 6.03.

C. AMT Preferences

AMT preferences refer to items accorded preferential treatment for regular tax purposes, and are additions to taxable income for AMT purposes. The preferences are as follows:

- Charitable contributions of appreciated property.
- Certain tax-exempt interest income.
- Accelerated depreciation and amortization of property before 1987.
- Incentive stock options.
- Intangible drilling costs.
- Percentage depletion.

These preferences will be discussed in more detail in 6.03.

RRA '93. RRA '93 generally repeals the AMT preference for charitable contributions of appreciated property made after December 31, 1992. The AMT preference for contributions of tangible personal property is retroactively repealed for contributions made after June 30, 1992. For more detail on RRA '93 AMT changes, see the Foreword on RRA '93.

D. AMT Exemptions

The tax law provides taxpayers with exemptions from the AMT. In the case of married couples who file joint tax returns and surviving spouses, the exemption is $45,000, beginning in 1993. In the case of single taxpayers or heads of households, the exemption is $33,750, beginning in 1993. In the case of married taxpayers filing separate tax returns, the exemption is $22,500, beginning in 1993.

However, at specified income levels, the AMT exemption is phased out. For married couples filing joint returns and for surviving spouses, the exemption begins phasing out when the AMTI is more than $150,000, and it is totally phased out when AMTI reaches $310,000. In the case of single taxpayers and heads of households, the exemption begins to phase out when AMTI is more than $112,500, and it is totally phased out when AMTI reaches $232,500. In the case of married taxpayers filing separate tax returns, the exemption begins to phase out when AMTI is more than $75,000, and it is totally phased out when AMTI reaches $155,000.

E. AMT Credit

Because of the prepayment aspect, an AMT credit is allowed. For a taxable year, this credit is the amount by which the AMT exceeds the taxpayer's regular tax liability as a result of timing differences (deferral preferences). In accordance with its prepayment aspect, these differences generally result from the acceleration of income and the deferral of deductions under AMT.

The AMT credit cannot reduce an individual's regular tax liability below his or her AMT liability as tentatively computed. Such AMT liability represents the tax that must be paid by the taxpayer, even though the AMT credit would reduce his or her regular tax to an amount less than his or her regular tax liability.

Note. When a taxpayer has general business credits or foreign tax credits for the taxable year, or is carrying over such credits, these credits offset the taxpayer's regular tax liability for AMT credit purposes.

As stated previously, timing differences—*deferral preferences*—produce the AMT credit. These include all AMT adjustments and preferences described here, *except:*

- Itemized deductions not allowed against the AMT.
- Charitable contributions of appreciated property.
- Interest on private activity bonds subject to the AMT.
- Percentage depletion.

F. Net Operating Losses

A taxpayer may have a net operating loss (NOL)—that is, an excess of deductions over income, for a taxable year. A deduction for such a NOL is available for regular tax *and* AMT purposes. For regular tax purposes, a NOL can be carried back to the 3 taxable years preceding the loss year and can be carried forward for 15 years after the loss year. Similar rules apply, with certain modifications, for AMT purposes.

For taxable years beginning after 1986, a taxpayer's NOL for regular tax purposes is (1) modified in accordance with adjustments required for AMT purposes, and (2) reduced by preference items, except the preference for charitable contributions of appreciated property. The AMT NOL, as so modified, cannot be more than 90 percent of AMTI. For purposes of this rule, AMTI is computed without taking the AMT NOL into account.

> *Note.*   If a taxpayer elects to carry forward a NOL for regular tax purposes, such an election also applies for AMT purposes.

G. AMT Foreign Tax Credit

The only credit that can offset an individual's AMT liability is an AMT foreign tax credit. This credit differs from the foreign tax credit available for regular tax purposes in that it is computed based on AMTI rather than regular taxable income, and the tax against which the credit is offset is the taxpayer's tentative AMT before reduction by this credit. This credit cannot offset more than 90 percent of a taxpayer's tentative AMT before application of this credit or the AMT NOL deduction.

H. Elections

Individual taxpayers are permitted a number of elections involving the acceleration of income or the deferral of deductions. Such elections equalize the AMT and regular tax treatment of the items involved, and, if they are made, such items will not give rise to AMT preferences.

1. **Depreciation.** Taxpayers are permitted to elect to depreciate assets under an alternative depreciation system (ADS). Depreciation under this system is an alternative to the generally applicable rules under MACRS (modified accelerated cost recovery system). Under ADS, the depreciation method is 150 percent declining balance. With respect to depreciable useful lives, 40 years is the applicable period for real property and, for personal property, the applicable period is the asset depreciation range (ADR) midpoint life or, otherwise, 12 years. This election can be made on a year-to-year basis and is made separately for each parcel of real property.

Important. When this election is made for a taxable year for a class of personal property or real property, it *cannot* be revoked.

2. **Intangible drilling costs (IDCs).** For AMT purposes, a taxpayer may elect to deduct intangible drilling costs (IDCs) otherwise deductible under the regular tax rules. For taxable years beginning after 1989, amortization of IDCs is allowed over a five-year period; otherwise a 10-year amortization period applies.

3. **Expensing election under Code § 179.** Under the regular tax rules, a taxpayer can elect to expense up to $10,000 of qualifying property used in a trade or business. This election does *not* give rise to any adjustments or preferences for purposes of the AMT.

4. **NOL carrybacks.** When a taxpayer elects to carry back a net operating loss for regular tax purposes, the taxpayer is bound by that election for purposes of the AMT.

6.02. COMPUTATION OF THE AMT

The AMT is computed for individuals, subject to the exemptions described, as follows:

Step 1. Start with the taxpayer's taxable income, which for this purpose for the vast majority of individual taxpayers, is gross income less all available deductions, other than for a net operating loss (NOL).

Step 2. Add or subtract AMT adjustments.

Step 3. Add AMT preferences.

Step 4. Subtract any NOL available for AMT purposes. The result is AMTI.

Step 5. Subtract the applicable AMT exemption. The result is net AMTI.

Step 6.   Apply the 21 percent AMT rate to net AMTI.

Step 7.   Subtract any available AMT foreign tax credit. The final result is AMT liability for the taxable year.

The AMT credit available for carryover is then determined.

Observation. RRA '93 increases the AMT rate beginning in 1993 to 26 percent on AMTI up to $175,000 ($87,500 for married taxpayers filing separately) and 28 percent for AMTI over $175,000. In contrast, the top regular tax rate is 36 percent on taxable incomes over $140,000 for married taxpayers filing joint tax returns and $115,000 for single taxpayers. A marginal tax rate of 39.6 percent (i.e., the 36 percent rate plus a 10 percent surtax) applies to taxable incomes over $250,000. (Note: These amounts will be adjusted for inflation beginning in 1995.)

This can create a planning opportunity for taxpayers subject to the AMT. For such taxpayers, it may be advantageous to have additional income and fewer deductions, such as miscellaneous expenses and taxes, in a year in which they will be subject to the AMT. However, if the taxpayer is also subject to the AMT in the following year, this strategy probably will not be advantageous, and income deferral probably will be warranted.

6.03.   DETAILS OF AMT ADJUSTMENTS AND PREFERENCES

A. Adjustments

1.   **Itemized deductions, standard deduction, and personal exemptions.** In computing AMTI, an individual must add back itemized deductions, the standard deduction (if he or she took this deduction in computing taxable income), and personal and dependency exemptions claimed. Taxpayers are allowed the following deductions in computing AMTI:

- Medical expenses, to the extent that they exceed 10 percent of the taxpayer's adjusted gross income (AGI).
- Qualified residence interest, subject to stationary deduction limits.
- Investment interest, to the extent that it does not exceed investment income.
- Charitable contributions, subject to statutory deduction limits.

- Casualty losses, to the extent that they exceed 10 percent of the taxpayer's AGI.
- Certain miscellaneous deductions, such as gambling losses, estate taxes paid on income with respect to a decedent, moving expenses, amortizable bond premiums, short sale deductions, deductions related to annuities where their payments end before the taxpayer's investment is recovered, and deductions related to cooperative housing corporations. Other miscellaneous deductions are generally nondeductible for AMT purposes.

2. Personal interest. No deduction is allowed for personal (consumer) interest for AMT purposes. Such interest is totally nondeductible.

3. Certain state, local, and foreign taxes. Some state, local, and foreign taxes not incurred in connection with a trade or business activity are added back by individual taxpayers when computing AMTI. These include income and real property taxes.

4. Passive activity losses. Passive activity losses and credits can *only* offset passive activity income.

Also, passive losses must be adjusted in accordance with the AMT rules. Thus, AMT adjustments and preferences, such as for depreciation, must be taken into account in determining the amount of loss deductible for AMT purposes.

5. Other adjustments.

- Excess depreciation on real estate placed in service after 1986.
- Excess depreciation on personal property placed in service after 1986.
- Installment sales.
- Long-term contracts.
- Circulation, research, and experimentation costs.
- Mining exploration and development costs.
- Farm losses.

B. Preferences

1. Charitable contribution of appreciated property. Charitable contributions of certain appreciated capital and business use assets held for more than one year do not cause a taxpayer to recognize gain for regular tax purposes. But, the amount by which the value of such an asset is greater than its basis is taken into account as a preference for purposes of the AMT. An exception to this rule was provided for contributions of tangible personal property that were made after 1990 and before July 1, 1992.

RRA '93 retroactively reinstated this exception for charitable contributions of tangible personal property made *after June 30, 1992,* and eliminated the tax preference for charitable contributions of any capital gain or business use property, whether real or personal, made *after December 31, 1992.*

2. Incentive stock options. An individual taxpayer's exercise of an incentive stock option (ISO) gives rise to a preference for AMT purposes. The preference is the bargain element of the ISO, that is, the amount by which the ISO's fair market value exceeds the exercise price when it is exercised. The taxpayer is also required, under AMT rules, to adjust the basis of stock acquired through the exercise of an ISO after 1986. The required adjustment is a basis increase in the amount of the preference income that is generated by the exercise of the ISO.

3. Certain tax-exempt interest income. The AMT applies to otherwise tax-exempt interest income earned by a taxpayer on private activity bonds. These bonds are those defined under Code § 142 and issued after August 7, 1986 (with certain transitional exceptions). Such bonds include those issued to finance projects such as sewage disposal facilities, solid waste disposal facilities, mass commuting facilities, water facilities (other than for irrigation), and qualified multifamily residential rental projects.

Observation. Private activity bonds usually pay a higher rate of interest than other tax-exempt bonds and can be a very attractive investment for an individual who has a higher regular tax liability than AMT liability.

4. Intangible drilling costs. An AMT preference can arise from an individual taxpayer's oil, gas, or geothermal activities. The amount of this preference is the amount by which the taxpayer's excess intangible drilling costs (IDCs) exceed 65 percent of the net income of the taxpayer's oil, gas, or geothermal properties. For this purpose, a taxpayer's excess IDCs represent those deductible for regular tax purposes, less a normative deduction. The normative deduction is the amount that the taxpayer would have deducted under 120-month straight-line amortization or under an elective cost depletion method. Also, a taxpayer's net income from such natural resource properties is the gross income from all such properties held by the taxpayer, less deductions other than excess IDCs. Any deductions related to nonproducing properties—dry wells— are not taken into account.

Election. To avoid the AMT preference, a taxpayer may elect after 1989 to amortize IDCs over five years, beginning with the month in which the costs are paid or incurred. Before 1989, a 10-year amortization election was available.

5. Percentage depletion. For taxpayers owning natural resource property, such as oil, gas, or geothermal wells, or mineral properties, the tax law permits deductions for the depletion of such property. The taxpayer is allowed deductions based on either cost depletion or percentage depletion.

Under cost depletion, a taxpayer determines his or her deductible amount by dividing the adjusted basis of the producing property by total reserves and multiplying the product by production for the year. Under percentage depletion, the taxpayer's deduction is based on a percentage, set forth in the tax law, of gross income from the producing property.

Percentage depletion is beneficial, tax-wise, for most taxpayers in that it can allow a taxpayer to deduct an amount exceeding the cost of a producing property. Because of this benefit, the tax law provides for an AMT preference with respect to percentage depletion. The amount of this preference is the excess of the taxpayer's percentage depletion for regular tax purposes over the basis of *each* subject natural resource property held by the taxpayer at the end of a year. The preference is determined separately for each such property, and will not arise until the total of depletion allowable and claimed by the taxpayer on a property exceeds the property's adjusted basis.

6. Accelerated depreciation and amortization of property placed in service before 1987. Because of the benefit obtained from previously allowed acceleration of depreciation and amortization, current tax law treats these as AMT preferences.

Chapter Seven

Avoiding Deduction Limits on "Hobby" Losses

7.01. WHAT ARE "HOBBY" LOSSES?

An activity engaged in by a taxpayer for a purpose other than making a profit, usually called a *hobby,* is, for tax purposes, an activity that fails to meet two tests set forth in the tax law (Code § 183):

- The profit presumption test.
- The profit motive test.

These tests will be described later. If they are not met, a taxpayer's deductions with respect to the activity will be limited.

A. What Can a Taxpayer Deduct with Respect to a Hobby?

If a taxpayer is engaged in an activity for a purpose other than making a profit, he or she may still deduct the following items related to that activity:

- Items allowed a taxpayer with respect to *any* activity, including itemized deductions, notably interest, subject to applicable deduction limits (see Chapter 3), and taxes.
- Items deductible as trade or business expenses (under Code § 162) or expenses for the production of income (under Code § 212), to the extent that the activity generates sufficient gross income against which to offset such items.

The activity can produce a loss for tax purposes if allowable itemized deductions exceed the gross income generated.

What is gross income for purposes of the hobby loss limits? *Gross income* includes gross receipts and gain resulting from the sale, exchange, or other disposition of property employed in an activity. Also included in gross income is capital gain resulting from the sale of property connected with the activity and rental income generated by such property.

B. What Is an Activity for Purposes of the Hobby Loss Limits?

A taxpayer may engage in multiple activities, which may or may not be treated as separate. The following criteria are set forth in the income tax regulations as to what constitutes an *activity* for purposes of these rules:

* The extent to which undertakings of a taxpayer are economically and organizationally interrelated.
* The extent to which undertakings of a taxpayer are similar.
* The business purpose involved in carrying on the various undertakings separately or together in a trade, business, or investment context.

In general, a taxpayer's characterization of multiple undertakings either as a single activity or as separate activities will be respected by the IRS if reasonable under the particular circumstances.

Income and deductions for separate activities of a taxpayer are segregated in determining if an activity is engaged in for profit, and in applying the limits when it is determined not to have been engaged in for profit.

If a taxpayer's activities are determined to be separate, an income or deduction item may relate to more than one activity. In such a case, the items is allocated among the activities involved on a reasonable basis applied consistently by the taxpayer each year.

What activities are subject to the hobby loss deduction limits? The following types of activities often run afoul of the hobby loss distinction:

* Farming.
* Breeding and showing animals, such as horses and dogs.
* Racing of animals, such as horses and dogs.
* Collecting activities, such as coin, stamp, or antique collecting.
* Writing and publishing.
* Creating and displaying works of art.
* Rental of vacation homes.

This is not an all-inclusive list, but it suggests activities that typically face IRS scrutiny and loss of deductions under the hobby loss limits. The IRS is likely to zero in on such activities if they are conducted by a taxpayer only on a part-time basis, if they involve recreational aspects, and if they require infusions of funds form other income sources.

Watch this. If a taxpayer's activity does not attain the level of a trade or business, any deductions taken with respect to an office in his or her home in connection with the activity can be lost.

Note. A recent Supreme Court decision has made it more difficult for many taxpayers to qualify for home office deductions. According to the High Court, taxpayers who work out of a home office but usually perform services at other business locations must prove that they perform their most important and significant work at home to qualify for home office deductions. This ruling applies to those taxpayers claiming a home office as a principal place of business (*Soliman,* S Ct 1993).

7.02. PROFIT PRESUMPTION TEST

To prove that he or she is engaged in an activity for profit, a taxpayer can resort to the profit presumption test. With this test, the burden of proof that the taxpayer is not engaged in the activity for profit is placed on the IRS.

Under this test, the taxpayer is presumed to have a profit motive for an activity if the gross income from that activity exceeds its deductions for at least *three* years in a period of *five* consecutive years. If the activity involves breeding, training, showing, or racing of horses, its gross income must exceed its deductions for at least *two* years in a period of *seven* consecutive years.

A taxpayer may elect to delay determination of the profit presumption under this test until the *fifth* year that the activity is engaged in, or the *seventh* year for an activity involving horses as just described. By so electing, a taxpayer extends the statutory period in which the IRS can assess a tax deficiency with respect to the activity for two years after the due date of the taxpayer's return for the fifth (or seventh) year. The election is made by filing Form 5213 with the IRS.

7.03. PROFIT MOTIVE TEST

If a taxpayer cannot meet the presumption test with respect to an activity, he or she can attempt to prove that the activity is engaged in for profit under the particular facts and circumstances. The regulations set forth factors relevant in this regard. Any one or more of these factors, however, do not necessarily determine profit motive. The factors in the regulations are as follows:

- How the activity is conducted by the taxpayer. It is generally favorable for the taxpayer if an activity is conducted in a businesslike manner, similar to profitable activities of a like nature, if complete books and records are maintained, and if operations are geared toward generation of a profit.
- The expertise of the taxpayer and his or her advisers with respect to the activity.
- The time and effort spent by the taxpayer in connection with the activity. It is generally favorable for the taxpayer to show that he or she has spent considerable time in connection with the activity or has engaged competent persons in this regard. Also helpful is the absence of personal or recreational aspects to the activity.
- The taxpayer's expectation that assets employed in the activity will increase in value.
- The taxpayer's success in conducting other activities, whether or not they are similar to the one in question.
- The taxpayer's history of income and losses with respect to the activity.
- Any profits earned in the activity. Considerations in this regard are the amount invested in the activity and the value of assets therein.
- The taxpayer's finances. It is generally not favorable for a taxpayer to have substantial income from sources other than the activity in question.
- The extent to which the activity involves recreation and the extent to which the taxpayer derives personal pleasure from it.

7.04. WHAT IS DEDUCTIBLE IF AN ACTIVITY IS DEEMED A HOBBY?

If a taxpayer's activity does not satisfy either the profit presumption test or the profit motive test, it is deemed a hobby subject to deduction limits. As stated earlier, two types of deductions remain available to the taxpayer.

Type one. Deductions allowable to the taxpayer irrespective of the activity. These are generally itemized deductions such as property taxes.

Type two. Deductions allowable with respect to a profitable activity. This type of deduction is broken down into deductions that do and those that do not have an impact on the basis of assets employed in the activity.

A. Type One Deductions

Type one deductions allowable to the taxpayer include the following:

- Property taxes.
- Interest (subject to applicable deduction limits).
- Theft losses.
- Casualty losses.
- Bad debts.
- Losses on worthless securities.
- Costs of tax advice and tax return preparation.
- Charitable contributions (subject to applicable deduction limits).
- Medical expenses (subject to applicable deduction limits).
- Other miscellaneous deductions.

B. Type Two Deductions

1. Deductions not affecting the basis of assets. These deductions are allowable to a taxpayer to the extent of the activity's profit:

- The nondeductible part of type one deductions, except to the extent that adjustment to basis of assets is required.
- Wages and salaries.
- Rent.
- Repairs and maintenance.
- Insurance.
- Materials.
- Utilities.
- Fees of outside consultants.
- Animal feed.

Watch this. To the extent that such deductions are not allowable to the taxpayer for a year, they are lost forever.

2. Deductions affecting the basis of assets. If an activity has a profit after deduction of items in the preceding list, the following items affecting the basis of assets therein are allowable to the extent of such profit:

- Depreciation and amortization.
- Partial losses relating to assets, including the nondeductible portion of type one deductions.
- Partially worthless debts.

If only part of these deductions are allowable, and they have multiple sources, the taxpayer is required to make an allocation. The deduction limit for the taxable year is allocated in the ratio of the allowable deduction for each item if the activity were a business, to the total of deductions affecting basis allowable if the activity involved were a business.

Note. Basis adjustment is required only with respect to items actually allowed as deductions.

Chapter Eight

Passive Loss Rules

8.01. PASSIVE ACTIVITY

A. Definition

Simply defined, a *passive activity* is an activity involving the conduct of either (1) a trade or business with respect to which a taxpayer *does not materially partici- pate* or (2) a rental activity. The so-called passive loss rules are codified in Code § 469, and further guidance is provided under regulations issued by the IRS.

A passive activity includes the following activities in which there is *no mate- rial participation* by the taxpayer:

- Research and experimentation.
- Any trade or business activity.
- Any activity resulting in expenses incurred for the production of income (under Code § 212).
- *Any rental activity,* even if the taxpayer materially participates in such activity.

Not included is a working interest in an oil or gas property held directly by a taxpayer or through an entity with respect to which the taxpayer's liability is not limited.

B. What Is an Activity?

In general, the passive loss rules apply to an *activity*. Under these rules, passive activity income and losses are determined for each activity; material participa- tion by a taxpayer for purposes of the loss deduction limits is determined on the basis of each activity; loss carryovers are allocated among a taxpayer's activi- ties; and, when there is a disposition of an activity, loss carryovers can be de- ducted from active and portfolio income. Also, in general, each separate undertaking of a taxpayer is considered an activity under these rules.

However, according to the *General Explanation of the Tax Reform Act of 1986* (TRA '86)—the "Blue Book"—the "determination of what constitutes a separate activity is intended to be made in a realistic economic sense. The question to be answered is what undertakings consist of an integrated and interrelated economic unit, conducted in coordination with or reliance upon each other, and constituting an appropriate unit for the measurement of gain or loss" (p. 245). Similar undertakings under common control are therefore combined for a taxable year when any of the following conditions are met.

- Taxpayer owns either a direct, or a substantial indirect, interest in each undertaking.
- Taxpayer would be considered to materially or significantly participate when such undertakings are combined.
- Taxpayer owns interests in such undertakings through the same pass-through entity (e.g., corporation, partnership).

Effect of proposed PAL regulations issued May 10, 1992. On May 10, 1992, the IRS issued new proposed regulations (Prop. Reg. 1.469–4) under the passive activity (PAL) rules. These proposed regulations are more flexible in approach, in contrast to earlier temporary regulations, which provided for a mechanical grouping of a taxpayer's undertakings, initially by geographic location.

The proposed regulation provide a facts-and-circumstances approach under which one or more business activities or rental activities are treated as a single activity if the activities represent an appropriate economic unit for measuring gain or loss for purposes of the passive loss rules.

The proposed regulations permit a taxpayer to use any reasonable method of applying the relevant factors and circumstances in grouping activities. In general, the following factors are the most important:

- Similarities and differences in types of business.
- The extent of common control.
- The extent of common ownership.
- Geographic location.
- Interdependence between the activities.

C. What Is an Undertaking?

As noted above, an *undertaking* is a key factor under the passive loss rules. An undertaking is the smallest part of an activity. It may be an activity or only a part of an activity.

1. Location. In general, business operations are considered to be part of a single undertaking if conducted at the same location, or within close proximity thereto, and owned by the same person.

Illustration 1. David Martin owns a camera repair shop and a store where cameras, film, and photographic equipment are sold. Both businesses are conducted at the same location. They are treated as a single undertaking.

Illustration 2. Christina Smith owns a bakery and a delicatessen that are operated at separate locations a few miles away from each other. These businesses will generally not be treated as a single undertaking.

Note. Even though multiple businesses of a taxpayer are not conducted at the same location, those businesses may be considered a single activity under Regulations in certain circumstances.

• *Fixed location.* If a taxpayer's business operations are not conducted at a *fixed* location, or if they are conducted at one or more businesses of customers, those operations are combined with the most closely associated undertaking.

• *Support operations.* In general, business operations that support other business operations are considered part of the operations so supported.

2. Combined rental and nonrental operations. Such operations are considered to constitute a *single* rental or nonrental undertaking, if (1) the rental or nonrental operation produces in excess of 80 percent of the total gross income of the operations, *or* (2) one of the following exceptions applies, so that a rental operation is considered a *nonrental* operation:

• Customer use of the property involved averages seven or fewer days during a year.

• Average customer use of the property involved is more than 7, but not more than 30, days and significant personal services are provided.

• Extraordinary services are provided to customers and the use of the property involved is incidental to customers' receipt of services. (Cleaning, maintenance, security, improvements, long-term repairs, and other necessary and routine services with respect to the property are *not* taken into consideration.)

• Any rentals made are only incidental with respect to nonrental activities.

- During business hours, rental property is available for customers' nonexclusive use.
- The taxpayer owns a partnership, joint venture, or S corporation conducting a nonrental activity with respect to which assets are provided.

3. Oil and gas undertakings. Any oil or gas well owned by a taxpayer is considered to be separate from other activities of the taxpayer, as long as (1) the well is a working interest held by the taxpayer either directly or through an entity with respect to which, in general, the taxpayer's liability is not limited; and (2) the taxpayer does not materially participate in the activity involving the oil or gas well.

D. What Is a Similar Undertaking?

Under IRS regulations, trade or business undertakings are considered to be *similar* if operations in each such undertaking are predominantly in the same line of business, or such undertakings are vertically integrated.

For purposes of these rules, *predominant* means operations generating more than 50 percent of gross income from each undertaking. Also, *vertical integration* means that the supplier ordinarily provides over 50 percent of the services or property used in the undertakings. For example, if a taxpayer owns a dairy farm and has a retail store for the sale of milk and ice cream produced at the farm located several miles away, those operations would be considered to be vertically integrated and thus a single activity.

Illustration. Charles Douglas owns two liquor stores, operated at separate locations and deriving 100 percent of their income from liquor sales. The stores are treated as part of a single activity.

E. Undertakings Controlled by the Same Interest

Under IRS regulations, undertakings are considered to be controlled by the same interests as long as the undertakings can be shown to be controlled by the same interests under the particular facts and circumstance, *or* over 50 percent of each undertaking is owned, directly or through pass-through entities (e.g., partnerships and S corporations), together by five or fewer persons. In determining ownership of an undertaking under the 50 percent test, the greater of a partner's capital or income interest is used for purposes of determining that partner's ownership interest in the particular undertaking.

F. Combination of Dissimilar Activities

Where trades or businesses are under common control, their aggregation is permitted under IRS regulations even if they are not similar, *as long as they constitute integrated business activities*. Under the regulations, multiple undertakings may be treated as a single integrated business when:

- The same person owns the multiple operations.
- The multiple operations are conducted at the same location.
- Similar operations are conducted by other taxpayers at the same location.
- All operations conducted are treated as a single business in accounting records.
- Undertakings of other taxpayers are treated under their accounting records as a single business.
- Products and services are commonly provided together, even though they could be provided through separate undertakings.
- Multiple (two or more) operations serve the same customers.
- Two or more of the operations have the same trade name.
- Common personnel, equipment, and/or facilities are used by the operations.
- The operations are coordinated or some of their activities are interdependent.
- Economic viability of an operation is dependent on one or more of the other operations.
- An operation is incidental to the conduct of one or more of the other operations.

G. Professional Service Undertakings

Professional service undertakings are subject to the passive loss rules. Such an undertaking is one generating over 50 percent of its gross income from rendering services in the fields of accounting, actuarial science, architecture, consulting, engineering, health care, law, or the performing arts.

Undertakings of this nature are considered the same activity under the regulations as long as they are controlled by the same interests, or offer *significant similar* or *significant related* services. Services performed in each profession specified above generally are treated as similar. Such services are treated as significant under the regulations as long as over 20 percent of an undertaking's gross income is attributable to them. Also, services are significantly related when one undertaking produces over 20 percent of the gross income of another undertaking.

H. Rental Real Estate Activities

With exceptions discussed below, a taxpayer's rental real estate activities are generally considered to be passive activities. Under the regulations, a taxpayer is permitted to treat rental real estate undertakings as a single activity or as separate activities. To quality as separate activities, undertakings are able to be transferred under state and/or local law. With respect to property held by a pass-through entity (e.g., a partnership or an S corporation), the separate undertakings are treated separately on the entity's tax return.

Watch this. When a pass-through entity's rental real estate properties are treated by the entity as a single undertaking, a taxpayer who is an investor in that entity must follow that treatment on his or her own tax return. Also, when such a property or properties are treated as part of a single activity, the tax return treatment *cannot* be changed. Thus, if one real property treated as part of a single activity is disposed of, related suspended losses *cannot* be deducted because suspended losses can be deducted only when there is a disposition of an entire activity or entire interest in the entity involved.

Exceptions. Rental real estate undertakings that are required under the regulations to be treated as separate activities are (1) a vacation home or other dwelling unit that is the taxpayer's residence and (2) a rental real estate undertaking with respect to which less than 30 percent of the property's unadjusted basis can be depreciated under Code § 167.

RRA '93. RRA '93 provides relief from the passive loss rules for certain real estate professionals who materially participate in rental real estate activities. For details, see the Foreword on RRA '93.

I. Separating Undertakings

1. Election to treat separately upon disposition. As a general rule, suspended losses from an activity may be deducted by a taxpayer only when there is a disposition of the taxpayer's entire interest in the activity. Yet under IRS regulations, a taxpayer may treat multiple undertakings as a single activity when determining the extent of his or her participation under the passive loss rules, but elect to treat them as *separate* when there is a disposition of an undertaking. This election is made by filing a written statement, as prescribed by the regulations (Temp. Reg. § 1.469–4T(o)), with the taxpayer's return for the year that the undertaking is acquired and with respect to which the election is made.

Important. A taxpayer's time devoted each year to *all* undertakings that would be combined, despite an election to treat undertakings as separate activities, is aggregated for purposes of determining the taxpayer's level of participation, as discussed at 8.01.J.

2. Limits on election. If a taxpayer treated multiple undertakings as part of a single activity on a tax return for his or her first taxable year *after August 9, 1989,* those undertakings cannot later be separated. Accordingly, this election cannot be made by (1) taxpayers who had undertakings as of August 9, 1989, with respect to which the election was not made, or (2) taxpayers who enter into undertakings after that date and who treat such undertakings as a single undertaking on the tax return for the first taxable year involved.

J. Material Participation Tests

1. Definition. The determination of whether a taxpayer's activity is active or passive is determined under material participation tests. For these purposes, Code § 469 provides that *material participation* is participation that is regular, continuous, and substantial.

2. Specific tests. Seven material participation tests have been set forth by the Internal Revenue Service in temporary regulations:
• The taxpayer's participation in an activity exceeds 500 hours in a taxable year.
• The taxpayer's participation is substantially all of the participation in the activity during the taxable year, even though that participation is *less* than 500 hours. For purposes of this test, other owners, employees, and other participants in the activity are taken into account.
• The taxpayer's participation in the activity in a taxable year exceeds 100 hours, and this level of participation is not less than any other participant's participation in the activity.
• The activity involved is one or more of multiple "significant participation" activities in which the taxpayer spends more than 500 hours during a taxable year. Such an activity is defined as a trade or business in which a taxpayer's participation exceeds 100 hours during a taxable year.
• For *any* 5 of the immediately preceding 10 taxable years, the taxpayer materially participated in the activity. *Special rule for farmers:* For purposes of this test, a farmer's material participation for five of eight years that immediately precede death, disability, or retirement is sufficient. Also, the farmer's surviving spouse is treated as materially participating after the farmer's death.

• The activity involved is a personal service activity, and the taxpayer materially participated in such activity in *any* of three earlier taxable years. For purposes of this test, a *personal service activity* is, in general, any trade or business with respect to which capital is *not* a material income-producing factor. Such an activity includes accounting, law, consulting, health care, actuarial science, engineering, and performing arts. *Observation:* If a taxpayer's activities change over a period of years, this test and the previous one, may still be satisfied. This should be the case, pursuant to temporary regulations, as long as the taxpayer's current activity has an undertaking in a trade or business substantially similar to an undertaking included in an activity in which the taxpayer materially participated in the applicable five-year or three-year period.

• Based on the particular facts and circumstances involved, the taxpayer's participation is regular, continuous, and substantial. The conditions of this test are that (1) the taxpayer must be involved in the activity's operations and make a significant contribution to such operations; (2) the activity must be the principal trade or business of the taxpayer; (3) the taxpayer must spend time at the location of the activity; and (4) the taxpayer must have knowledge or experience with respect to the activity's operations. For purposes of this test, a taxpayer's participation in managing an activity might not be taken into account when he or she has an employee who manages the activity. It is likely that it will not be taken into account if the employee spends more time in the activity than the taxpayer.

Important. Participation of a taxpayer's *spouse* is also taken into account for purposes of determining whether or not the *taxpayer's* participation in an activity is material. This rule can help a taxpayer to meet one of the above tests when his or her own participation in an activity is below the required level.

K. Treatment of Oil and Gas Working Interests

An oil or gas working interest is *not* treated as a passive activity if such an interest is held directly by the taxpayer or held through entities not limiting liability. The taxpayer is *not* required to materially participate with respect to such an interest. However, a working interest held by a taxpayer as a limited partner or by an S corporation is generally *not* subject to this exception. For purposes of this exception, a *working interest* is a working or operating mineral interest in a parcel or tract of land on which operation and development costs generally fall.

Caution. Passive losses may result if a taxpayer who has a working interest changes his or her form of ownership of the interest to a form in which liability is limited.

L. Limited Partnership Interests

A limited partner in a partnership is generally considered *not* to materially participate with respect to partnership activity. However, under IRS temporary regulations, a limited partner *is* considered to materially participate in an activity *when:*

- His or her participation in the activity exceeds 500 hours in a taxable year.
- He or she materially participated in the activity for any 5 of the preceding 10 years.
- He or she materially participated in a personal service activity in any three prior taxable years.
- He or she owns a general partnership interest for the entire year in the *same* partnership in which he or she is a limited partner.

Observation. If a taxpayer generates income from an interest in a limited partnership, material participation may not be beneficial. This is true because the passive income generated may be used to offset other passive losses.

Watch this. For purposes of proving material participation in an activity, the regulations do *not* require a taxpayer to maintain contemporaneous records with respect to the activity. However, a taxpayer should maintain such records if the taxpayer's material participation in an activity is determined based on the 5-out-of-10-year test or the 3-year test (see 8.01.J.2).

8.02. TREATMENT OF PASSIVE INCOME AND LOSS

A. Passive Activity Gross Income (PAGI)

Passive activity gross income results from the conduct of passive activities, but does not include the following:

- Compensation received by the taxpayer for *personal services,* including earned income, property transferred to the taxpayer for the performance of personal services, income from an employees' trust or annuity, payments received by the taxpayer from employer retirement and/or deferred compensation plans, taxable Social Security benefits received by the taxpayer, and any other personal service income received by the taxpayer.
- *Portfolio* income that is not received by a taxpayer in the ordinary course of his or her trade or business, including interest; dividends received by the

taxpayer with respect to stock held in a regular (C) corporation; dividends received by the taxpayer with respect to stock held in an S corporation, to the extent of such corporation's earnings and profits; annuities; royalties received with respect to intangible assets; and gains on the disposition of properties that generated portfolio and/or investment income *not* in the ordinary course of a taxpayer's trade or business.

- The *nonpassive* part of net positive tax adjustments made under Code § 481, as a result of a taxpayer's change in accounting method.
- Income received from oil and gas working interests that produced *nonpassive* losses in earlier years.
- *Miscellaneous income* received by the taxpayer, including (1) state, local, and/or foreign income tax refunds; (2) income received as a result of the business use of a taxpayer's residence; (3) income received with respect to a covenant not to compete; (4) income received with respect to copyrights, patents, and artistic, literary, or musical works; (5) dividend income received by cooperative patrons; (6) certain income received with respect to low-income housing projects; (7) other income, based on the taxpayer's particular circumstances.

Observation. A taxpayer who has unused passive losses offsets such losses with passive income. Thus, such a taxpayer should make efforts to have profitable activities generate *passive* income.

The IRS has ruled that discharge of indebtedness is treated as income from a passive activity to the extent the discarded debt's proceeds were being used in a passive activity when the discharge occurred (Rev. Rul. 92–92).

PAGI does not include any gross income attributable to the reimbursement of a casualty or theft loss, if the reimbursement is included in gross income as the reimbursement of a loss deducted in a prior taxable year and if the loss deduction was not a passive activity deduction (Reg. 1.469–2(c)(7)).

B. Deductions Attributable to Passive Activities

Such deductions result from passive activities and include deductions that are carried over from previous taxable years.

Temporary regulations do not allow the following items as passive activity deductions:

- Expenses connected with compensation arising from personal services.
- Expenses connected with portfolio income.
- Losses arising from the disposition of property, not in the ordinary course of the taxpayer's trade or business, that produce investment or portfolio income.
- Expenses connected with business or rental use of a taxpayer's residence.

- Carryover passive activity losses that are fully recognized as a result of a taxpayer's disposition of the related activity, or the taxpayer's entire interest in such activity.
- State, local, and foreign income taxes and war profits and excess profits taxes.
- Miscellaneous itemized deductions (which are subject to a deduction limit of 2 percent of an individual taxpayer's adjusted gross income).
- Charitable contributions.
- Net operating loss (NOL) carryovers.
- Capital loss carryovers.
- Deductions subject to at-risk and basis limitation rules (Code §§ 465, 704(d), 1366) for taxable years beginning before 1987.
- With respect to net negative adjustments made under Code § 481 (required by changes in accounting method), the amount related to nonpassive activities.

According to final regulations, passive activity deductions generally do not include loss deductions from fire, storm, shipwreck, or other casualty or theft, if losses that are similar in cause or severity do not recur regularly in conducting the activity (Reg. Sec. 1.469–2(d)(2)).

C. Suspended Losses for Passive Activities

When a taxpayer's losses from passive activities (held either directly or through a pass-through entity such as a partnership or S corporation) cannot be deducted from income from such activities in the current year, or passive credits cannot be offset against a taxpayer's regular tax arising from passive activities, the losses or credits are carried over until the passive activities generate sufficient income against which to apply them. However, if a taxpayer *actively* participates in a *rental real estate activity,* up to $25,000 of annual losses can be deducted from the taxpayer's *active and portfolio income,* or passive credits in the equivalent amount may be offset by the taxpayer against his or her regular tax.

1. **Limitation on use of deductions and credits.** If a passive activity was entered into by a taxpayer *prior to October 23, 1986,* losses or credits arising from such an activity may be used to offset taxable income from *nonpassive* activities. TRA '86 provides deduction limits, providing for a deduction phaseout, as follows: 1987, 65 percent; 1988, 40 percent; 1989, 20 percent; 1990, 10 percent; 1991 and later years, 0 percent.

Observation. If a taxpayer has suspended passive losses, he or she should consider entering into an activity that produces passive income. By so doing, the taxpayer can utilize the suspended losses and save taxes. And if a taxpayer is involved in an activity that is profitable, reduction or termination of involvement in such activity (so that the activity becomes a passive one) may enable the taxpayer to deduct suspended passive losses.

2. Allocation of suspended passive losses among activities. A taxpayer's net passive loss resulting from multiple activity is allocated among such activities for purposes of determining any passive loss carryforwards. The IRS, under regulations, generally requires allocation of such losses on the basis of the amount of the net loss for the taxable year from each activity producing a loss.

3. Recharacterization rules. When an activity of a taxpayer is passive under the regulations, income generated from such activity can be recharacterized as nonpassive or *portfolio* income in accordance with the following rules:

• The taxpayer does not materially participate in one or more activities with respect to which he or she spends more than 100 hours during the taxable year. If such an activity, or activities, generate net income in a taxable year, an amount of gross income equal to such net income is treated as *nonpassive.*

• When a taxpayer has a rental activity in which customers use nondepreciable (i.e., less than 30 percent of unadjusted basis) property, gross income generated from that activity equal to its net income is treated as *portfolio* income.

• With respect to a money-lending business in which a taxpayer owns an interest, but in which he or she does not materially participate, part of the gross income from the business is required to be treated as *portfolio* income.

• When a taxpayer develops rental property that is disposed of within 12 months of its first rental use, gross income from such rental equal to net rental income (including any gain on the property's disposition) is treated as *nonpassive.*

• When property is rented to a trade or business in which the taxpayer materially participates, gross income from the rental up to net rental income is treated as *nonpassive.*

• Royalty income from qualified property is generally *portfolio* income if received with respect to an interest in an entity that created and developed the property prior to the taxpayer's investment.

D. Rental Real Estate Exception

An exception applies under the passive loss rules for a taxpayer and his or her spouse who *actively participate* in rental real estate activities. Some or all of such losses may be deducted from active income and/or portfolio income, subject to the following limits:

- A maximum of $25,000 for an individual taxpayer and his or her spouse.
- A maximum of $12,500 for married individuals filing separate tax returns.
- No deduction allowed when married individuals who file separate tax returns live together at *any* time during the taxable year.
- See also the limit for high-income taxpayers discussed at 8.02.D.2.

If a taxpayer has less than $25,000 of such losses, or $12,500 in the case of separate filers, passive activity credits may be utilized.

1. What is active participation? There is no formal definition of *active participation* with respect to the passive loss rules in the Internal Revenue Code or regulations, although it involves a level of participation less than material participation. Active participation may be considered to involve the making of significant management decisions, which would include setting rental terms and approving new tenants and expenses made with respect to the rental property, for example. (See IRS *Publication 925.*)

2. Limit applicable to high-income taxpayers. For certain taxpayers with a high amount of adjusted gross income (AGI), the $25,000 deduction (and equivalent credit) limit is reduced. It is reduced by 50 percent of the amount by which the taxpayer's AGI is more than $100,000. The applicable limit is $200,000 for taxpayers claiming tax credits with respect to low-income housing projects and qualified rehabilitation projects. For purposes of this rule, AGI is determined without taking into account deductions for contributions to individual retirement accounts (IRAs) and simplified employee plans (SEPs). If married taxpayers file separate returns, the AGI limit is $50,000, or $100,000 with respect to the available credits, as described above. Also, under the RRA of 1989, the AGI limits applicable to high-income taxpayers do *not* apply with respect to interests acquired *after December 31, 1989,* in a pass-through entity or with respect to property placed in service after that date on which low-income housing credit is claimed.

E. Changes in the Level of a Taxpayer's Participation in an Activity

Under the material participation tests in the regulations, an activity may still be considered *not* to be a passive activity, which is subject to the passive loss rules, *even* if the taxpayer ceases to materially participate in that activity (see 8.01.J.2).

   1. Change to passive activity. If, however, the activity is determined to have become a *passive* activity, losses incurred in the activity are subject to the passive loss rules. However, losses incurred in the activity in earlier years are carried over in a net operating loss if they were not previously used by the taxpayer. Any such unused losses carried over can be deducted against other income of the taxpayer.

   2. Change to nonpassive activity. If, under these tests, the activity is determined to have become *nonpassive,* any losses that were suspended when the activity was passive are deductible against any income currently generated by the activity. Also, any credits of the activity that were suspended offset any regular tax arising from the activity. To the extent that the activity generates losses in excess of income and credits in excess of regular tax, such items may be applied against profitable passive activities.

   Note. These excess losses and credits, discussed above, retain their *original* character, even though the activity's character (i.e., passive or nonpassive) changes.

F. Dispositions of Property Used in an Activity

When there is a disposition of an interest in property used in a passive activity, the resulting gain or loss for the taxpayer involved is *passive*. The taxpayer takes that passive gain or loss into account in determining his or her total current-year gain or loss from passive activities.

   Note. A taxpayer's interest in a partnership or stock held in an S corporation is not treated as property for purposes of these rules. However, the regulations provide that the rules *do* apply when the property involved is held by a pass-through entity (e.g., partnership or S corporation) in which the taxpayer has an interest.

Observation. The gain or loss resulting from the disposition of property by which an activity is passive *only* if the activity is *passive* when the disposition occurs. Thus, if a taxpayer is involved in other passive activities, it may be advantageous to delay a disposition of an activity's property that would produce a gain or to ensure that the regulations' material production tests are failed in the year that such a disposition occurs.

G. Taxable Dispositions of Passive Activities

As a result of the passive loss rules, losses and credits arising from activities deemed passive could conceivably be carried forward for an indefinite period. A taxpayer may currently benefit from such losses, and possibly such credits, if he or she disposes of his or her *entire* interest in the passive activity generating such losses of credits.

Upon disposition of the activity at a loss, the taxpayer determines his or her share of income or loss from the activity for the taxable year and deducts or adds carryover losses. If there is a net loss, such loss is added to the loss resulting from the disposition of the interest. The resulting loss is applied against net income or gains from *all* of the passive activities in which the taxpayer has an interest. Any resulting loss is deductible against the taxpayer's other taxable income.

H. Passive Activity Credits

Passive activities can give rise to tax credits. Such credits can only offset regular tax arising from a taxpayer's *passive* activities, and any credits that cannot be used in the current year must be carried over.

1. Limitations. When a passive activity produces tax credits, a number of credits may be limited to the taxable year (i.e., they cannot be carried over). Such credits include the possession tax credit, drug testing credit, nonconventional fuel credit, general business credit, alcohol fuel credit, credit for increasing research activities, and the low-income housing credit.

Note. As a practical matter, the general business credit and the low-income housing credit would generally be predominant for many individual investors.

Watch this. Any passive loss carryovers are first applied against current-year passive activity gross income, and only then can passive activity credits be applied.

Observation. When a taxpayer is engaged in multiple activities, it is advisable for a taxpayer *not* to materially participate in one or more profitable activities unless he or she does not materially participate in one or more activities (therefore deemed passive) that generate tax credits.

2. Suspended credits. In general, any credits carried over from passive activities are suspended until a taxpayer has sufficient *passive* income against which to offset them. However, a taxpayer may utilize a passive activity credit earlier when property used in a passive activity is sold. In such a case, if the property's basis was reduced by the unused credit, the taxpayer can elect to restore it to basis at the time of sale. The result is a larger loss or lower gain on the sale.

I. Transfers of Passive Activity Interests as a Result of a Taxpayer's Death or Gift

1. Death of an owner of an interest in a passive activity. When a taxpayer who owns an interest in a passive activity dies, a loss from the activity may be deductible against nonpassive income. To the extent that the decedent owner's heir steps up the basis of the interest in the activity as a result of the decedent owner's death, however, the loss is not deductible with respect to the decedent owner.

2. Gift of an interest in a passive activity. When a taxpayer makes a gift of an interest, or a partial gift of an interest, in a passive activity, the taxpayer is not entitled to deduct a loss related to the activity. The person to whom the interest, or partial interest, in the activity is gifted is entitled to increase the basis of the interest carried over from the donor by the amount of loss related to the interest gifted.

J. Sales of a Passive Activity Interest to a Related Party

A taxpayer cannot benefit from losses generated by a passive activity when he or she sells the activity, or an interest therein, to a related party. A taxpayer cannot deduct such losses until the related party transferee transfers the activity or interest therein to an *unrelated* person.

For this purpose, a "related party" is defined under Code §§ 267(b) and 707 (b)(1), the latter relating to partnerships. The relationships typically relevant to individual taxpayers in this regard are described in the following list; however, other relevant relationships are described in the Code sections. Relationships *typically* relevant to individual taxpayers are:

- Spouses, brothers and sisters (whether of whole or half blood), children and other lineal descendants, and parents and other ancestors.
- A person and a corporation in which the person, directly or indirectly, owns more than 50 percent of the corporation's outstanding stock.
- The grantor and fiduciary of a trust.
- The fiduciary and beneficiary of a trust, the fiduciary of a trust and beneficiary of another trust having the *same* grantor, and the fiduciary of a trust and a corporation in which over 50 percent of the corporation's outstanding stock is owned, directly or indirectly, by or for the trust or its grantor.
- A partnership and a person owning, directly or indirectly, an interest of over 50 percent in partnership capital or profits.

Chapter Nine

Avoiding the Pitfalls of the At-Risk Rules

9.01. WHAT ARE THE AT-RISK RULES?

A. Overview

The Internal Revenue Code places limits on the amount of losses deductible by taxpayers with respect to an activity. Such losses are limited to the amount that a taxpayer has "at risk" in the activity. In simple terms, this is the actual amount that the taxpayer could lose as a result of being involved in the activity.

The at-risk rules apply to individual taxpayers and closely held corporations. Their purpose is to prevent these taxpayers from offsetting income from trades, businesses, or professional practices against losses from activities in which their investments are primarily financed by nonrecourse loans. Nonrecourse loans are, in general, those for which the debtor is not personally liable.

Note. If such a loss is determined to be deductible under the at-risk rules, its deductibility is then further determined under the passive loss rules, discussed in Chapter 8.

Under the at-risk rules, the deductible loss is limited to the amount of cash contributed to the activity by the taxpayer, the adjusted basis of other property contributed to the activity by the taxpayer, amounts borrowed by the taxpayer for use in the activity when the taxpayer has personal liability with respect to the borrowing, and any property not used in the activity pledged by the taxpayer as security for the borrowing. In addition, a taxpayer is not considered to be at risk with respect to amounts protected against loss by stop-loss arrangements, guarantees, nonrecourse financing, and similar protective arrangements.

B. Activities to Which the At-Risk Rules Apply

Holding, producing, or distributing motion picture films or video tapes.

Farming, which includes cultivation of land; raising or harvesting agricultural or horticultural commodities, other than trees not bearing fruits or nuts; and raising, shearing, feeding, caring for, training, and/or management of animals.

Leasing of property covered by Code § 1245. In general, this involves depreciable or amortizable property (some of which is not relevant to individual investors), including:

• Personal property.

• Tangible property (other than buildings or their components) used in manufacturing, production, or extraction; in providing transportation, communications, electrical energy, gas, water, or sewage disposal services; or for research or bulk storage with respect to any of these activities.

• Real property amortized under Code § 169, pollution control facilities; Code § 179, expense election with respect to business assets; Code § 185, railroad grading and tunnel bores; Code § 188, child care facilities; Code § 190, removal of barriers to handicapped and elderly persons; Code § 193, tertiary injectants; and Code § 194, reforestation expenses.

• Single-purpose agricultural structures for livestock (including poultry) or horticultural structures (including commercial production of plants and mushrooms) and equipment required for production and related products.

Oil and gas exploration or exploitation.

Geothermal deposit exploration or exploitation.

Other trades, businesses, or income-producing activities including real estate (subject to rules discussed in 9.02) placed in service by the taxpayer after 1986.

Note. For the first five activities listed, the at-risk rules apply separately. For purposes of these rules, trades or businesses are combined when their management involves the *active participation* of the taxpayer.

9.02. HOW THE AT-RISK RULES APPLY TO REAL ESTATE

Real estate placed in service before 1987 is, in general, not subject to the at-risk rules. However, these rules *do* apply to real estate used in a business if the business activity is considered to "hold" that property and provide personal property and/or services.

A. What Is the Holding of Real Estate?

The use of real estate in the activities listed in 9.01.B is *not* treated as *holding* real estate. Real estate assets employed in such an activity are subject to at-risk rules applicable to the activity.

1. Real property used by a taxpayer in a trade or business. The use of real property in a trade or business or in an income-producing activity is considered to constitute the holding of real estate for purposes of the at-risk rules provided in the Internal Revenue Code. Such real estate placed in service *before 1987* is considered to be *separate* from other facets of the taxpayer's trade, business, or other income-producing activity.

2. Living space. With respect to real estate used for living accommodations, if incidental services are provided, as in the case of a hotel, the activity is considered the holding of real estate in total.

B. Tax Treatment

For tax purposes, real estate and other activities are treated separately as follows:

Step 1. Determine the deductions related to each activity of the taxpayer involved.

Step 2. Allocate income to each taxpayer activity based on the ratio of each deduction to total deductions of the activities.

Step 3. Using a reasonable method, allocate any joint expenses to the activities.

9.03.   AMOUNT AT RISK

A taxpayer is considered to be at risk with respect to an activity to the extent of cash and the adjusted basis of property the taxpayer contributed to the activity.

Note. A property's adjusted basis for purposes of determining loss is figured as if it were sold immediately after it was contributed.

Planning point. If a taxpayer is involved in an activity subject to the at-risk rules, consideration should be given to making a contribution to the activity of property with a high adjusted basis—preferably, of property having an adjusted basis higher than fair market value. By so doing, the taxpayer can increase the amount of deductible losses with respect to the activity.

A. Property Encumbered by Debt

When a taxpayer contributes property to an activity subject to the at-risk rules, and that property is encumbered by debt (e.g., a bank loan), the taxpayer's amount at risk includes the amount of such property's adjusted basis *only* to the extent that the taxpayer is *personally liable* for repayment of such debt.

B. Other Debt-Related Rules

A taxpayer is also considered to be at risk with respect to amounts borrowed in connection with the related activity, as long as one of the following conditions is met:

• The taxpayer is *personally liable* on such debt.

• The taxpayer pledged property not used in the activity to secure the debt.

Note. With respect to the second condition, the amount considered to be at risk is limited to the property's net fair market value. For this purpose, *net fair market value* is the fair market value of the property on the date of such pledge, reduced by any earlier or superior creditor claims on the property.

Watch this. If a taxpayer incurs debt with respect to property *not* used in an activity subject to the at-risk rules, the amount of such debt is *not* considered at risk when the ownership of such property is financed, directly or indirectly, by debt incurred with respect to property used in the activity.

Investor and "related person" loans. Debt is *not* considered to be at risk when the creditor has *any* interest in an activity subject to the at-risk rules *other than as a creditor.* Related persons are subject to this rule and are defined as the following:

• A spouse, parents, other ancestors, children, other lineal descendants, brothers, and sisters (of both whole and half blood).

• An individual and a corporation of which over 10 percent of the outstanding stock value is owned, directly or indirectly, by such individual.

• Two corporations that are members of the same controlled corporate group (under a 10 percent ownership test).

• A maker (grantor) and fiduciary (trustee) of a trust (or fiduciaries of multiple trust), as long as the trusts have the same maker.

• A beneficiary and fiduciary of a trust, or the beneficiary of one trust and the fiduciary of another as long as *both* trusts have the same maker (grantor).

- A trust fiduciary (trustee) and a corporation of which more than 10 percent of the outstanding stock value is owned, directly or indirectly, by or for the trust or by or for the maker (grantor).
- Certain organizations having tax-exempt status organized for charitable or educational purposes and the persons directly or indirectly controlling them.
- A partnership and a corporation, as long as the same persons hold over 10 percent of the value of the corporation's outstanding stock and an interest of over 10 percent in the partnership's capital or profits.
- An S corporation and a C corporation, or two S corporations, as long as the same persons own over 10 percent of the value of *each* corporation's outstanding stock.
- A partnership and a person owning, directly or indirectly, an interest of over 10 percent in the partnership's capital or profits.
- Two partnerships, as long as the same persons own, directly or indirectly, an interest of over 10 percent in capital or profits of the partnerships.
- Taxpayers engaged in businesses under common control.

For purposes of this rule, constructive ownership rules apply. These rules (also commonly referred to as *attribution* rules) are as follows:

Rule 1. Shareholders of a corporation, partners in a partnership, and beneficiaries of a trust or estate are treated as owning their respective shares of stock owned, either directly or indirectly, by or for the entity (i.e., corporation, partnership, trust, or estate).

Rule 2. An individual is treated as owning any stock owned, either directly or indirectly, by or for his or her spouse, parents, other ancestors, children, other lineal descendants, and brothers and sisters either of whole or half blood.

Rule 3. An individual owning stock in a corporation (other than ownership as specified under rule 2) is treated as owning any stock in that corporation, either directly or indirectly, by or for a partner of that individual.

Rule 4. Any stock treated as owned under rule 1 is also treated as owned *directly* for purposes of rules 1, 2, and 3. However, stock treated as owned under rule 2 or rule 3 will not again be attributed to another person under either rule 2 or rule 3.

C. Amounts Not at Risk

The Internal Revenue Code also specifies amounts not considered to be at risk. In general, these involve arrangements in which the taxpayer's loss is limited or in which the taxpayer is protected against loss.

1. Nonrecourse debt. This is debt with respect to which the taxpayer is not personally liable, that is, debt for which the lender cannot look to the taxpayer's personal assets for repayment.

Note. Qualified nonrecourse financing secured by real property is a key exception (see 9.04).

2. Loss limitations. These limitations consist of the following:

- Stop-loss arrangements.
- Guarantees.
- Other arrangements designed to limit an investor's loss with respect to an investment.

For this purpose, a stop-loss arrangement involves the limiting of an investor's at-risk amount to his or her actual potential loss.

Exception. An investor's at-risk amounts are *not* limited under a buy-sell agreement regarding his or her interest in an activity that does *not* protect him or her against loss.

Important. Although it provides protection against loss with respect to an activity, a taxpayer's carrying of liability or casualty insurance will *not* cause his or her at-risk amounts to be limited.

9.04. SPECIAL RULES APPLICABLE TO REAL PROPERTY: QUALIFIED NONRECOURSE FINANCING

Qualified nonrecourse financing obtained by a taxpayer with respect to real property does *not* run afoul of the at-risk limitations, whereas *nonrecourse debt* generally does.

To constitute qualified nonrecourse financing, financing must meet the following criteria:

- It is incurred by the taxpayer to hold real property.
- It is secured by real property used in the activity involved.
- It is obtained by the taxpayer from a "qualified person" or from federal, state, or local governments or instrumentalities thereof, or it is guaranteed by such a government or instrumentality thereof.

- It is *not* convertible debt.

For purposes of the last requirement, a *qualified person* is a creditor meeting the following criteria:

- It is actively and regularly engaged in money lending, such as a bank or savings and loan association.
- It is not a related person with respect to the taxpayer (see 9.03.B).
- It is not the party from whom the taxpayer acquired the property involved, and it is not related to the seller of that property.
- It does not receive any fees as a result of the taxpayer's investment in the property involved, and it is not related to any party receiving such fees.

Key exception. If the financing of the purchase of the property involved is basically similar to that obtainable by unrelated parties, and otherwise is commercially reasonable, the taxpayer/borrower and the lender can be related parties.

9.05. EFFECT OF LOAN REPAYMENTS

The effect of loan repayments on a taxpayer's at-risk amount depends on whether the related loan is recourse or nonrecourse.

A. Recourse Loans

Repayment of loans related to an activity on which the taxpayer is personally liable and that, as a result, increased his or her at-risk amount, does not affect the at-risk amount when the repayment is made with funds from *outside* the activity.

If the repayment is made with assets *inside* the activity, the taxpayer's at-risk amount will be reduced. If such inside assets used for repayment are *noncash*, the taxpayer's at-risk amount is reduced by the amount of the adjusted basis of those assets.

If a taxpayer obtains nonrecourse financing for purposes of repaying recourse debt related to an activity, his or her at-risk amount is reduced by the amount of the repayment.

B. Nonrecourse Debt

1. Use of property outside activity. When a taxpayer obtains recourse financing, and such debt is secured by his or her property outside an activity subject to the at-risk rules, his or her at-risk amount increases in the amount of that debt. When such debt is repaid, the taxpayer's at-risk amount will not be affected unless the repayment is made with assets inside the activity.

2. Use of property inside activity. For nonrecourse financing that did not increase a taxpayer's at-risk amount (i.e., financing secured by property inside an activity subject to the at-risk rules), repayment of such debt with funds outside the activity usually increases the taxpayer's at-risk amount. Repayment of such debt with property used inside the activity will not affect the taxpayer's at-risk amount. The taxpayer's at-risk amount also will not be affected when such debt is repaid with funds that would not increase the amount if contributed to the activity subject to the at-risk rules.

3. Proceeds of nonrecourse debt used outside subject activity. Repayment of nonrecourse debt with funds outside an activity subject to the at-risk rules will increase a taxpayer's at-risk amount if the loan proceeds were employed outside the activity.

9.06. HOW THE AT-RISK LIMITS WORK

A. Deductible Losses

The at-risk rules do *not* apply to activities that generate a profit. They apply to activities generating losses, as follows:

Losses are determined using all permitted deductions, including loss carry-overs resulting from at-risk limits.

Losses are deducted on the tax return of the taxpayer who holds an interest in the related activity, in the following amounts:

- When losses generated by an activity subject to the at-risk rules are below the taxpayer's at-risk amount, *all* such losses are deductible, and the taxpayer's at-risk amount is reduced by the losses deducted.

- When losses from such an activity are more than the taxpayer's at-risk amount, the taxpayer deducts such losses up to his or her total at-risk amount.

- Losses that the taxpayer cannot deduct are carried over *indefinitely* until fully used.

Loss carryovers. Since losses carried over under the at-risk rules are deductible by a taxpayer who holds an interest in an activity subject to these rules, such losses are applied to income later generated by that activity. Excess losses can be deducted with respect to the taxpayer's at-risk amount in later taxable years.

Recommendation. A taxpayer having loss carryovers under the at-risk rules should consider increasing investments in subject activities that generate income. By so doing, the losses may be deducted.

B. Other Considerations for Taxpayers with Respect to the At-Risk Rules

* The period of time between an increase and a decrease in the taxpayer's at-risk amount.
* The nature of the activity and practices therein different from normal business practices.
* The use of amounts increasing the taxpayer's at-risk amount toward the end of the taxable year.
* Contracts between parties involved in the subject activity.
* Unanticipated events causing a decrease in the taxpayer's at-risk amount.

C. Interplay with Other Tax Rules

The at-risk rules generally affect other tax rules as follows:
* They take precedence over the tax rule applicable to partnerships. Also, whereas the tax rules applicable to partnerships may cause the basis of a partner's interest in a partnership to be increased by his or her share of nonrecourse debt incurred, the at-risk amount generally will not be increased by that amount.
* The at-risk rules are generally not taken into consideration in determining adjusted basis for computing gain or loss on the sale of property.
* A taxpayer's at-risk amount is increased by the amount of tax-exempt income, and decreased by related expenses, of the subject activity.
* The passive loss rules may take precedence over the at-risk rules, so that a loss deductible under the at-risk rules may be nondeductible under the passive loss rules.

D. Loss Recapture

In general, losses from an activity do not reduce the amount a taxpayer has at risk with respect to that activity. However, the following may reduce the taxpayer's at-risk amount:

- Distributions made to the taxpayer in excess of that amount.
- A shift of liabilities from recourse to nonrecourse status.
- A guarantee or another limit on the taxpayer's risk of loss with respect to the activity.

Amount recaptured. The amount taken into income and treated as a deduction by a taxpayer with respect to an activity cannot be more than the total at-risk losses deducted by the taxpayer after December 31, 1978, less negative at-risk amounts previously included in income by the taxpayer.

9.07. DISPOSITIONS OF ACTIVITIES SUBJECT TO THE AT-RISK RULES

A. Sale of an Interest in an Activity

If a taxpayer recognizes a gain on the sale of an interest in an activity subject to the at-risk rules, or the entire subject activity, that amount represents income from that activity for purposes of the at-risk rules. Such an amount increases the taxpayer's at-risk amount, and consequently, loss carryovers created as a result of the at-risk rules can be offset against it. Also, in determining the amount realized on the disposition of an activity, nonrecourse notes secured by property used in that activity are taken into account.

B. Disposition through Foreclosure Proceedings

In general, when a foreclosure occurs and secured debt exceeds the basis of the taxpayer's interest, gain is recognized, and loss carryovers may be utilized.

C. Disposition through Gifts

When a taxpayer receives an interest in an activity subject to the at-risk rules, he or she assumes the donor's basis for purposes of determining gain or loss on its subsequent disposition. When the donor is relieved of liabilities with respect to the activity, a gift of his or her interest therein may result in recognized gain. Any related suspended losses may be applied against such a gain. Also, any loss carryovers unused by the donor on disposition of the interest in the subject activity are included in the donee's basis for that interest. Finally, in general, the donee's at-risk amount is increased by any gift tax paid with respect to the gift, but the total amount of the increase cannot be more than the excess of the donee's basis for the interest over the amount considered to be "paid" by the donee, including related liabilities.

The "Kiddie" Tax and Transfers to Children

10.01. THE "KIDDIE" TAX

As a result of the Tax Reform Act of 1986 (TRA '86), tax-saving techniques of income shifting to children were severely limited. Before TRA '86, it was generally easy for parents to make asset transfers to children under age 14 resulting in a conversion of income otherwise taxable at higher rates to unearned income, taxable at a lower rate. This chapter will discuss how TRA '86 restricted this tax shelter and how transfers to children can be made at the lowest tax cost under current law.

A. General Rule

Under the kiddie tax, enacted as part of TRA '86, a child having no earned income pays federal income tax on his or her *unearned* income, such as interest and dividends, to the extent that it exceeds $600. The child's tax liability is determined as if a portion of the unearned income had been received by his or her parent(s).

Such unearned income received by the child is free of tax, up to $600. The amount of unearned income from $600 to $1,200 is taxed to the child at the rate applicable to the *child*. Unearned income of the child *over $1,000* is taxed at the rates applicable to the parent(s). In the latter case, the parent(s) has a choice with respect to reporting such income.

When the child reaches age 14, these rules do *not* apply. Then the child, as an unmarried individual, is required to file a federal income tax return reporting his or her gross income exceeding a specified amount.

B. Computation

In computing the kiddie tax, the standard deduction for a child under age 14 is limited to the greater of $600 or his or her *earned income*. There is a "general offset" equal to the greater of the allowable standard deduction or, if deductions are itemized, deductions directly connected with the production of unearned gross income. This amount is deducted in making the kiddie tax computation and, in effect, allows $600 of unearned income to be excluded from tax and taxes the $600 of unearned income at the rate applicable to the child. The result is the child's net unearned income.

The child's net unearned income is then added to the parent's (parents') taxable income. The parental tax is then recomputed, and a hypothetical parental tax liability is determined. The excess of this hypothetical tax over the actual parental tax liability is the tax on the child's net unearned income. That amount and the tax on the child's other income constitute his or her total tax liability for the year.

When there is more than one child under age 14, the net unearned income of all such children is combined and added to the parental taxable income. The resulting increase in the parental tax liability is then apportioned among the children, based on the ratio of the net unearned income of each child over the total net unearned income of all the children.

Examples of kiddie tax computation. The Conference Report to TRA '86 provides seven examples regarding computation of the kiddie tax. *Note:* As originally enacted, the threshold amounts of unearned income were $500 and $1,000. These amounts are indexed for inflation, as indicated above. These examples are reproduced here.

Example 1. If the child has $400 of unearned income and no earned income, the child's standard deduction is $400, which is allocated against the child's unearned income, so that the child has no federal income tax liability.

Example 2. If the child has $900 of unearned income and no earned income, the child's standard deduction is $500, which is allocated against the first $500 of unearned income. The child's net unearned income is $400. Because the child's net unearned income is less than $500, the net earned income is taxed at the child's rates.

Example 3. If the child has $1,300 of unearned income and no earned income, the child's standard deduction is $500, which is allocated against unearned income. The child has net unearned income equal to $800, of which the first $500 is taxed at the child's rates and the remaining $300 is taxed at the top rate of the parents.

Example 4. If the child has $700 of earned income and $300 of unearned income, the child's standard deduction is $700, of which $300 is allocated against unearned income and $400 is allocated against earned income. The child has no net unearned income, and the remaining $300 of earned income is taxed at the child's rates.

Example 5. If the child has $800 of earned income and $900 of unearned income, the child's standard deduction is $800, of which $500 is allocated against unearned income and $300 is allocated against earned income. The child has net unearned income of $400. Because net unearned income is less than $500, the child's net unearned income is taxed at the child's rates. The remaining $500 of earned income also is taxed at the child's rates.

Example 6. Assume the child has $300 of earned income and $1,200 of unearned income, and itemized deductions of $400 (net of the 2 percent floor) that are directly connected with the production of the unearned income. The child has $400 of other deductions. Because the deductions directly connected with the production of the unearned income ($400) are less than the maximum amount of deductions ($500) that are allocated against unearned income, $500 of the $800 total deductions are allocated against unearned income. Therefore, the child has net unearned income of $700 ($1,200 of unearned income less $500), of which $500 is taxed at the child's rates and $200 is taxed at the parents' rate.

Example 7. Assume the child has $700 of earned income and $3,000 of unearned income, and itemized deductions of $800 (net of the 2 percent floor) that are directly connected with the production of the unearned income. The child has $200 of other deductions. The entire amount of deductions relating to the production of unearned income is allocated against his or her unearned income, because this amount ($800) exceeds $500. Therefore, the child has net unearned income equal to $2,200 ($3,000 of unearned income less $800), of which $500 is taxed at child's rates and $1,700 at the parents' top rate. The child has $200 of deductions, which is allocated against earned income. The remaining $500 of earned income is taxed at the child's rates.

C. Reporting Rules: TAMRA Election

As originally enacted under TRA '86, the kiddie tax involved reporting on Form 8615, Computation of Tax for Children Under Age 14 Who Have Investment Income of More than $1,000, attached to separate tax returns for each child under age 14 with unearned taxable income. However, the Technical and Miscellaneous Revenue Act (TAMRA) of 1988 provided optional reporting rules.

In particular, TAMRA allows an election to report the unearned income of children under age 14 on the parents' Form 1040. If this election is made and the following requirements are met, Form 8615 need not be prepared, and separate Forms 1040 for each child under age 14 need not be filed.

Parent(s) may elect to report a child's unearned income on the parental tax return as long as the following conditions are met:

- The child's gross income for the taxable year comprises *only* interest and dividends, including Alaska Permanent Fund dividends.
- Such income of the child is between $500 and $5,000.
- *No estimated tax payments were made under the child's name and Social Security number during the taxable year,* including the application of the preceding year's tax overpayment to the current-year estimated tax.
- The child is not subject to backup withholding.

The election is made by filing Form 8814, Parent's Election to Report Child's Interest and Dividends, with the parental return. By so doing, a child's taxable unearned income in excess of $1,000 is added to the parental gross income. As a result, the parent(s) will pay a tax of 15 percent of the child's income in excess of $500 but not over $1,000. (Note: The use of Form 8814 to report a child's unearned income does *not* affect the tax rate applicable to that income in any way.)

Observation.   This election will generally be most advantageous for parents with children having only small amounts of unearned income.

Watch this.   Although the TAMRA change and Form 8814 were designed to simplify the tax filing burden related to unearned income of children, there are certain disadvantages arising from reporting on this form. The following disadvantages should be carefully considered by parents before this form is used.

Higher adjusted gross income (AGI) for parent(s). Use of Form 8814 will result in the addition of a child's unearned income to the parental AGI. The increase in AGI can cause reduction or elimination of certain itemized deductions, where items are deductible only to the extent that they exceed specified percentages of AGI:

- *Casualty loss deductions.* Casualty losses are deductible only to the extent that they exceed 10 percent of a taxpayer's AGI.
- *Medical expense deductions.* Medical expenses are deductible only to the extent that they exceed 7.5 percent of a taxpayer's AGI.

- *Miscellaneous itemized deductions.* These items include unreimbursed employee business expenses (i.e., union and professional dues); deductible home office expenses; expenses relating to investment income or property (i.e., fees for investment advice); expenses for tax advice and return preparation; appraisals relating to casualty losses or charitable contributions of property; and expenses incurred in connection with a hobby, to the extent of income from that hobby. Such items qualify for deduction as itemized deductions as long as they exceed 2 percent of the taxpayer's AGI.

Child's loss of deductions. When parent(s) elect to report a child's unearned income using Form 8814, they will not be able to take advantage of the increased standard deduction available for a blind child. Also, the parent(s) cannot take advantage of any itemized deductions otherwise allowable to a child, such as for investment expenses.

State tax considerations. In states that base the state income tax on AGI for federal income tax purposes, which may involve certain state adjustments but not comparable kiddie tax rules, the use of Form 8814 could increase the parental state tax liability.

D. Ways to Minimize the Bite of the Kiddie Tax

There are a number of investment vehicles available that can alleviate the impact of the kiddie tax.

1. US savings bonds. The purchase for a child of Series EE US savings bonds that will mature after he or she reaches age 14 can be advantageous for purposes of the kiddie tax. If such bonds are redeemed after the child reaches age 14, accrued bond interest may then be taxable at the *child's* (lower) tax rate. This will be the case unless an election was made to include the accrued bond interest in income in each taxable year.

Election. If the election with respect to accrued interest was made, taxpayers were bound in the past by such election with respect to *all* such bonds owned. Recently, however, the IRS issued procedural rules under which taxpayers can more easily effect a change.

Under Rev. Proc. 89–46 (1989–33 I.R.B. 28), the IRS allows taxpayers to change their method of reporting the interest income (i.e., the annual increase in value) of Series E or EE US savings bonds. The rules prescribed under this revenue procedure provide flexibility for taxpayers, enabling them to quickly and simply change from annual reporting of such income to deferring tax thereon. Taxpayers who comply with these rules will be deemed by the IRS to have obtained its consent for a change in the method of accounting for such income.

Under Code § 454 and regulations thereunder, the interest of Series E or EE US savings bonds need not be reported annually for tax purposes by a cash-basis taxpayer. The taxpayer is allowed to report the total bond interest (i.e., the increase in value) at the earlier of the date of disposition, redemption, or maturity. Alternatively, the taxpayer may elect to have the interest taxed each year. The election is made on the taxpayer's return and can be made for any taxable year. As a general rule, with the exception of the rules prescribed by the IRS in Rev. Proc. 89–46, such an election is binding with respect to all Series E and EE US savings bonds held by the taxpayer.

As a general rule, if a taxpayer has made this election, he or she must request IRS permission to change the method of reporting (i.e., a change in accounting method). Such a request is made by filing Form 3115, Application for Change in Accounting Method, with the IRS within 180 days after the beginning of the taxable year during which the taxpayer's proposed change in method of reporting is to be made. With respect to the reporting of Series E and EE U S savings bond interest, however, the IRS has *waived* this requirement in Rev. Proc. 89–46 for taxable years beginning *on or after January 1, 1989.*

Under Rev. Proc. 89–46, the IRS permits taxpayers to change from a method of reporting as interest income the annual increase in Series E or EE US Savings Bond redemption value. The change permitted is to a method under which the total increases, less any previously reported increases, are reported for tax purposes in the taxable year in which they are realized, by the earlier of such bonds' disposition, redemption, or final maturity. The taxpayer is allowed to change the reporting method again *after five years.*

To qualify for the automatic change allowed under Rev. Proc. 89–46, the taxpayer is required to file a current Form 3115 with his or her Form 1040 for the taxable year in which the reporting change is desired. The Form 3115 must also comply with requirements specified in Rev. Proc. 89–46. (See Appendix A.)

2. Municipal bonds.   Municipal bond investments for children also offer advantages with respect to the kiddie tax. The interest on these bonds is generally free from federal income tax and, depending on the issue, may also be free of state and local income tax. As long as such bonds are held until the child reaches age 14, any gain on their sale is taxable at the *child's* tax rate.

Note.   Certain municipal bonds, called *private activity* bonds, are subject to the alternative minimum tax. (See Chapter 6.)

3. Equities. Purchase of stocks and other securities that produce little or no current income, such as "growth" stocks, can also eliminate or minimize the bite of the kiddie tax. Any increase in their value can be taxed at the *child's* rate, as long as they are held until the child reaches age 14.

4. Other non–income-producing assets. Parents can invest for children in other assets, such as a parcel of land, that do not produce currently taxable income. Again, if such assets are held until the child reaches age 14, any appreciation in value will be taxed at the *child's* rate.

5. Single-premium whole life insurance policies. Investments in such policies for children can be advantageous for purposes of the kiddie tax. For coverage of these policies see Chapter 5.

10.02. TAX-SAVING OPPORTUNITIES THROUGH TRANSFERS TO CHILDREN

A. Overview

Parents transfer funds to their minor children for two main reasons: first, to provide them with resources, perhaps a fund for college education; and second, to reduce the tax bite on the income those funds would generate in their own hands. The Tax Reform Act of 1986 (TRA '86) made it harder for parents to achieve the second goal. However, tax-saving opportunities still remain with respect to transfers of assets to children, although other considerations such as control over transferred assets under state law, must be taken into account and may take precedence over tax savings.

B. Objectives and Considerations

A transfer of assets by parents to minor children may be motivated by one or more of the following objectives and considerations.

* To shift taxable income on the transferred assets from the parents to the minor child. (*Note:* The tax-saving opportunities from such a transfer have been restricted by the kiddie tax enacted as part of TRA '86, discussed in 10.01.)
* To shift future appreciation on the transferred assets to the minor child.

- To give control over the transferred assets to the legal representative of the minor child under state law and, ultimately, to the child when he or she reaches majority.
- To provide for the support and/or education of the minor child.
- To take the transferred assets out of the parental estate(s) to reduce estate tax or the generation-skipping tax (GST).

Key consideration. In making a transfer to a minor child, a key consideration for the transferring parent should be avoidance of gift tax or the use of the unified credit allowed against the gift tax and estate tax. To accomplish this, such a transfer should be geared to qualify for the statutory gift tax exclusion. Techniques to achieve this will be discussed.

C. Transfers that May Be Tax-Unwise

The following transfers to children may not be advantageous from the viewpoint of the parent(s) making the transfer.

1. Gifts to children. A gift from a parent to a child is easily accomplished and qualifies for the annual gift tax exclusion of $10,000 per donee, since it represents a gift of a present interest. However, a *major disadvantage* of such a transfer is that, under law, the parent relinquishes control over the transferred assets to a child who is not competent to deal with them. Thus, the child cannot sell, lease, mortgage, exchange, or otherwise dispose of those assets until attaining the age of majority. Further, once the child attains the age of majority, he or she is totally free to deal with those assets, perhaps in a manner unsatisfactory to the donor parent.

Note. Under the laws of most states, a parent is *not* the legal guardian of property owned by a child. In general, a court-appointed legal guardian, subject to state law restrictions, would manage such property under court supervision.

2. Joint ownership of property with children. Joint ownership can easily be arranged by a parent who wishes to give an interest in property to a child. However, such an arrangement's income, gift, and estate tax consequences depend on state law requirements. For example, if a parent establishes a joint bank account with a child, the child's taxability on a portion of that account depends on how state law treats joint ownership arrangements. Further, if the parent is allowed to withdraw the entire amount in the account without the consent of a minor child, this will not constitute a completed gift for gift tax purposes. Also, the value of the account may be includable in the parent's estate for estate tax purposes, if he or she predeceases the minor child who is the joint owner, even if a completed gift has been made with respect to the account.

3. Revocable trust. By creating a revocable trust, a parent can transfer property to a minor child and retain complete control over that property. A major disadvantage to the creation of such a trust is that the maker (grantor) is considered to hold the trust assets for purposes of federal income, estate, and gift taxation. However, such a trust may be useful in providing for support or education of a minor child if a parent is absent or ill.

4. Totten trust. A parent may wish to establish for the benefit of a child a Totten trust, so named after a court case. This is a revocable trust, taking the form of an account in a bank or savings and loan association, that provides for the passing of its balance upon death of the maker (grantor) to a specified beneficiary. The disadvantage of such an account is that it does not represent a completed transfer for income, estate, or gift tax purposes, since it is revocable.

5. US savings bonds. A parent may wish to provide funds to a child through an investment in US savings bonds. These bonds may be registered in a variety of ways, and the manner in which they are registered determines whether or not a gift is made.

If a US savings bond is registered jointly in the names of a parent and a minor child, a completed gift does not occur until the child redeems the bond without any obligation to that parent with respect to it. When a parent purchases such a bond and registers it jointly with a minor child, the *parent* is taxable on the income earned thereon, even if the child redeems the bond. (Federal income tax implications with respect to investments in US savings bonds are discussed in 10.01.D.1.)

D. Transfers that May Be Tax-Wise

The following transfers of assets to children may make sense for parents, from legal and tax standpoints.

1. Transfers under the Uniform Gifts to Minors Acts. The states have adopted, in varying forms, the Uniform Gifts to Minors Act (UGMA). Some states later adopted a variation, the Uniform Transfers to Minors Act (UTMA). Transfers made, and the attendant tax consequences, are basically the same under either law.

Under the UGMA, assets may be transferred to a custodian for the benefit of a minor child. These assets are managed by the custodian and can be distributed by the custodian in accordance with the relatively broad powers typically prescribed by state law.

Observation. Transfers under the UGMA or the UTMA should not involve a substantial amount of assets. Generally, transfers of substantial assets to minor children should be made in trust.

Note. The following are the *only* assets that can be transferred for the benefit of a minor child under the UGMA:

- Cash.
- Securities.
- Insurance policies.
- Annuity contracts.

Such a transfer of assets qualifies for the annual exclusion allowed for federal gift tax purposes. The transferred assets are included in the estate of the minor child for estate tax purposes if he or she should die before the end of the custodianship. Also, the income generated by the transferred assets is taxable to the minor child.

Watch this. Income from assets transferred to a minor child will be taxable *to the transferor parent* to the extent that that income is used to satisfy a parent's legal obligation of support with respect to the transferee child.

UGMA advantages. A transfer of assets from a parent to a child under the UGMA is quite simple. The transfer simply requires a declaration that it is made to the custodian "as custodian for" the minor child transferee under the UGMA of the particular state. In general, UGMA transfers are beneficial to parents wishing to transfer relatively small amounts to children and avoid expenses related to the establishment and maintenance of trusts.

Another advantage of an UGMA transfer is that the parent may keep control over the property by transferring it, under UGMA, to himself or herself or to his or her spouse as custodian. However, when a parent makes himself or herself (or spouse) custodian under UGMA, if he or she (or his or her spouse) dies before the minor child beneficiary, the transferred property *is* included in the parent's (or spouse's) estate for federal estate tax purposes.

Major disadvantage of transfers under the UGMA. For many parents, a major disadvantage and principal concern regarding a transfer to a minor child under the UGMA is that the assets so transferred *must* be distributed to the child when he or she reaches the age of majority. The attendant problem is that the child, particularly when the applicable age of majority is only 18, usually will not have the capacity to manage the assets and the income they generate, and may dissipate them.

2. Transfers under the Uniform Transfers to Minors Act. There are many similarities between the Uniform Gifts to Minors Act (UGMA) and the Uniform Transfers to Minors Act (UTMA), which has been adopted by a number of states. However, the UTMA differs from the UGMA in the following ways:

• There is no limitation on the type of assets that may be transferred for the benefit of a minor child.

• Under the UTMA, assets can be transferred to the custodian by third parties, such as trusts and estates; an obligor of the child beneficiary, such as an insurer; or the legal representative of such child.

• The age at which the subject assets must be distributed to the child beneficiary can be 21. The transferor may, however, provide for distribution between ages 18 and 21, if he or she so wishes.

The disadvantages involved with the UTMA are the same as those noted for the UGMA.

E. Transfers in Trust to a Minor Child

In general, if parents wish to transfer substantial amounts of assets to children, a trust should be established. A trust can provide flexibility in terms of distributions and administration. Also, depending on how the trust is drafted, tax benefits may be obtained.

Cautionary note. Recent tax laws have restricted the benefits of the use of trusts established for the benefits of children. TRA '86 reduced the income tax bite with respect to trusts but restricted certain advantages, as follows:

• All trusts are required to adopt the calendar year as a taxable year, eliminating the possibility of tax deferral through the use of a different taxable year. (This rule, however, does not apply to some tax-exempt trusts.)

• Trusts are required to make quarterly estimated tax payments.

- A generation-skipping tax (GST) can restrict the benefits of transfers in trust.
- Benefits of transfers to minor children through the use of short-term "Clifford" trusts were terminated for most taxpayers.

1. Transfers to § 2503(c) trusts. A gift to a trust for the benefit of minor children qualifies for the present interest annual exclusion, under Code § 2503(c), as long as:

- The assets transferred and the income thereon may be expended by or for the (child) beneficiary until he or she reaches age 21.
- Assets and the income accumulated thereon, to the extent not previously expended, are distributed to the child beneficiary when he or she reaches age 21.
- If the child beneficiary dies, the assets and the related income are required to be distributed to the beneficiary's estate or in accordance with an appointment made under a general power of appointment.
- Such a trust may continue after the child beneficiary reaches age 21, and the annual gift tax exclusion may still be available. The exclusion will be available as long as the beneficiary has a right to compel distributions from the trust.

Note. All property that can be managed by a trustee may be transferred to a trust under § 2503(c).

2. Transfers to § 2503(b) trusts. The advantage of a transfer to a Code § 2503(b) trust is that a gift in trust can be separated into a present income interest and a remainder interest. The annual exclusion, applicable for purposes of the federal gift tax, is available with respect to the present value of the income interest. The remainder interest is a future interest in trust.

The income interest's value is determined under IRS actuarial tables. The value of an income interest is determined on the basis of an interest rate that is 120 percent of the applicable federal midterm rate for the month containing the valuation date.

The disadvantage of a transfer to a § 2503(b) trust is that the payment of income to the child beneficiary is required. This disadvantage can be overcome by having the trust provide that the trustee may accumulate or distribute trust income until the child beneficiary reaches age 21, at which time all income would be distributed to the beneficiary. As a result, the income interest, prior to the time the child beneficiary reaches age 21, qualifies for the annual exclusion.

Caution. The annual exclusion will not be available with respect to the value of the remainder interest involved. Also, trust arrangements usually are administratively more expensive and complex.

3. Transfers to Crummey trust. Transfers of assets to a Crummey trust provide great flexibility to the transferor. The mechanics of this type of trust, named after a court case, are discussed in greater detail in Chapter 5.

Under a Crummey trust, the minor child beneficiary is provided a limited withdrawal power. This limited withdrawal power represents a present interest in the trust, so that gifts to the trust qualify for the annual exclusion. To so qualify, the following requirements must be met:

- The trust beneficiary must be adequately informed of his or her right to demand a withdrawal from the trust.
- The trust beneficiary must be provided an adequate period to make his or her withdrawal demand.
- The trust must have sufficient assets to cover the beneficiary's withdrawal demand.

Caution. If the trust beneficiary's withdrawal right involves more than $5,000, a lapse of his or her withdrawal right (i.e., the failure to withdraw) may result in negative consequences with respect to the federal estate, gift, and income taxes.

F. Other Planning Considerations

If a family conducts a business, the potential for income shifting exists through the use of a family partnership, an S corporation, or the employment of a child in the family business.

1. Family partnerships. In general, the tax rules applicable to family partnerships are the same as those applicable to other types of partnerships. The following rules also apply:

- The partnership interest must involve capital as a material factor in generating income.
- The transfer of the partnership interest involved must be a valid and complete transfer.
- The child/donee must receive a distributive share of partnership income, subject to reduction for reasonable compensation paid to the donor.
- The formalities applicable under state and local laws must be observed.

Observation. A family limited partnership may be beneficial, tax-wise, with respect to the use of losses from passive activities. An interest in a family limited partnership can produce passive *income* for the child partner. When a parent transfers to a child an interest in passive activities that produce losses, such losses can offset passive income generated by the family partnership.

2. S corporations. Election of S corporation status may hold advantages. To qualify as an S corporation:

- The corporation must be a US corporation having no more than 35 shareholders.
- Only individuals, estates, and qualified trusts may hold shares in the corporation.
- The corporation can have only one class of stock.
- All shareholders of the corporation must agree to the making of the election.

Use of qualified Subchapter S trusts (QSSTs). A QSST may be established to hold stock in an S corporation for the benefit of a shareholder's child. Such a trust must involve a bona fide interest with respect to the child and also meet the following requirements:

- The trust must constitute a grantor trust with respect to the trust beneficiary.
- Only *one* income beneficiary is allowed for *each* such trust.
- The QSST must distribute the trust corpus only to the income beneficiary during the life of that beneficiary, even if the QSST terminates.
- The trustee *and* trust beneficiary must consent to the election of S corporation status.

3. Gift leaseback arrangements. In general, this involves the transfer of assets used in the trade or business of a parent to a trust established for the benefit of his or her child. The trust then leases the property back to the grantor (parent), and the grantor is entitled to a deduction for the rent as a business-related tax deduction.

Caution. These arrangements have been under IRS and federal court scrutiny. In general, the IRS will not contest such arrangements if the lessee is not the grantor of the trust.

ENCYCLOPEDIA OF
INVESTMENT TAXATION

This Encyclopedia includes alphabetical listings of investment terms and tax terms related to investments. It and the related Year-Round Planning Guide focus primarily on individual investors and investments made by such investors: purchases of stocks and bonds, bank certificates of deposit, partnership interests, and real estate investments, for example. Many entries are cross-referenced to the Year-Round Planning Guide (YPG), which elaborates on related tax planning issues. Tax-related entries provide references to the relevant supporting authority: Internal Revenue Code (Code), Treasury Regulations (Reg.), and court cases. The tax-related entries are also cross-referenced to the relevant paragraph in the current Commerce Clearing House, Inc. (CCH) *Standard Federal Tax Reports*.

Note.   Please refer to the Foreword on the Revenue Reconciliation Act of 1993 (H.R. 2264), enacted August 10, 1993. Provisions of this act modify certain rules discussed here.

A

accelerated cost recovery system (ACRS)   This is a mandatory method for depreciation of tangible personal property placed in service after 1980 and before 1987. It permits a rapid recovery of the cost of such property through the use of fixed recovery schedules over periods specified in the tax law. These schedules are reproduced in Appendix B. ACRS is a simple method by which to depreciate assets, and under ACRS salvage value is irrelevant and the concept of useful life is considerably less important than under previous law.

In general, ACRS *recovery property* includes most types of new and used tangible depreciable property placed in service after 1980 and before 1987. However, if property is placed in service after July 31, 1986, and before 1987, a taxpayer may elect to use the modified accelerated cost recovery system (MACRS) rather than ACRS.

Computation of Amount Deductible under ACRS

Under ACRS, a taxpayer may recover the unadjusted basis of eligible recovery property over an applicable recovery period of 3, 5, 10, 18, or 19 years. The recovery periods are set forth in tables, and recovery percentages are given for each year in the recovery period. These tables are reproduced in Appendix B. The taxpayer computes the ACRS deduction by multiplying the unadjusted basis of the particular recovery property by the applicable prescribed percentage.

Recovery property.   This terms refers to tangible, depreciable property placed in service after 1980 and before 1987. In general, it includes the following property, acquired new or used, during that period:

- *3-year property* includes automobiles, light-duty trucks, and some special tools.
- *5-year property* includes equipment such as office furniture and fixtures.
- *10-year property* includes certain real property, such as mobile homes, and certain public utility property.
- *15-year real property* includes all real property, except for real property designated as 5-year or 10-year property. This class has two subclassifications: low-income housing and all other 15-year property (but see following *Note*).

Note: If real property was placed in service after May 8, 1985, and before January 1, 1987, a 19-year recovery period applies, except for low-income housing subject to the 15-year recovery period. If such property was placed in service after March 15, 1984, and before May 9, 1985, an 18-year period applies, except for low-income housing as described above.

Recovery periods.   A deduction for cost recovery is available for the first taxable year in which eligible property is placed in service, no matter when such property was actually placed in service. For assets disposed of during a taxable year, no cost recovery deduction is allowable. Statutory recovery percentages for the various recovery periods are as follows:

- *3-year recovery property:* 25 percent for the first year, 38 percent for the second year, and 37 percent for the third year.
- *5-year recovery property:* 15 percent for the first year, 22 percent for the second year, and 21 percent for the third year through the fifth year.
- *10-year recovery property:* 8 percent for the first year, 14 percent for the second year, 12 percent for the third year, 10 percent for the fourth through the sixth year, and 9 percent for the 7th through the 10th year.
- With respect to *15-year real property,* recovery percentages apply based on when the subject property was placed in service.

Components of real property.   The cost of components of real property (e.g., plumbing and wiring) is generally recovered in the same way as the cost of the building that includes such components. The same recovery period and method used with respect to the building must also be used with respect to the components.

A "substantial improvement" made to real property is treated separately, not as a component. Thus, a 15-year recovery period may be used with respect to such an improvement.

Automobiles and other listed property. Cost recovery deductions are limited with respect to listed property, including automobiles and personal computers, as specified in the Treasury Regulations (Reg. §§ 1.280–1T to –7T), when such property is not used predominantly (i.e., over 50 percent) for business purposes. Also, even if an automobile is used more than 50 percent for business purposes, additional cost recovery deduction limits apply. The automobile deduction caps are subject to adjustment for inflation for automobiles placed in service after 1988.

For listed property subject to ACRS, deductions are generally determined under the straight-line method provided under ACRS. Longer recovery periods, which generally reflect the earnings and profits lives of such property, also apply. Thus, for listed property otherwise qualifying as three-year and five-year ACRS property, the recovery periods are 5 years and 12 years, respectively. If the property fails to satisfy the business use requirement in a taxable year after it is placed in service, cost recovery deductions are subject to recapture by the IRS.

Conventions

For property subject to ACRS, one-half year's depreciation is allowed when it is placed in service, without regard to how long it is held by the taxpayer, unless the mid-quarter convention applies. No deduction is normally allowed under ACRS for the year of disposition of subject personal property, but under the mid-month convention, prorate deductions are allowed in the years of acquisition and disposition of subject property.

Half-year convention. Under this convention, property is considered for cost recovery purposes to have been placed in service or disposed of in the middle of the taxable year. This convention applies to property other than residential rental property and nonresidential real property.

Mid-month convention. Under this convention, property is considered to be placed in service or disposed of during the middle of a month, and the cost recovery deduction is determined based on the number of months during the taxable year that the property was in service. This convention applies to residential rental property and nonresidential real property.

Mid-quarter convention. Under this convention, all subject property placed in service during any quarter of a taxable year is considered to be placed in service at the midpoint of that quarter. This convention applies to property other than residential real property and nonresidential real property, as long as more than 40 percent of the aggregate bases of the subject property is placed in service during the *last three months* of a taxable year. For purposes of this convention, property placed in service and disposed of within the same taxable year is disregarded.

(Code § 168; CCH ¶ 11,001 et seq.; YPG 2.04.F; Appendix B)

See also **anti-churning rules; basis; depreciation; modified accelerated cost recovery system (MACRS); recapture.**

accounting methods Most taxpayers use one of two principal accounting methods: the cash receipts and disbursements method (cash basis) or the accrual method (accrual basis). Included among other permissible accounting methods are the installment method and the long-term contract method. Individual taxpayers are typically cash-basis taxpayers. Most business entities are required under the tax law to use the accrual method; since 1986 tax shelters, C (regular) corporations, and partnerships have had to use the accrual method. A change in a taxpayer's accounting method generally requires consent of the IRS.

(Code § 446; CCH ¶ 20,606)

See also **accrual basis; cash basis; partnership.**

accounting periods A taxpayer calculates taxable income on the basis of the taxpayer's annual accounting period. For most individuals, this period is the calendar year. Many business entities use a fiscal year, which is an accounting period of 12 months ending on the last day of a month other than December, or an annual accounting period varying from 52 to 53 weeks (52–53-week year).

The tax law prescribes special rules for partnerships, S corporations, and personal service corporations (PSCs). Partnerships and S corporations can elect a taxable year other than the year prescribed by the tax law if they make payments to the IRS to cover the value of the tax deferral to the partners or shareholders of these entities resulting from the use of a year other than the required taxable year. PSCs may elect a taxable year that is different from the required taxable year, but certain deductions may have to be deferred for amounts paid to employee-owners if the PSC fails to distribute certain amounts to them by December 31 of a taxable year (Code § 444; CCH ¶ 2754).

Taxpayers may apply to change accounting periods from a calendar year to a fiscal year, or vice versa, or to a different fiscal year. Application for a change is generally made by filing Form 1128 with the IRS. If a change is made, a short-period return is required for the period running from the end of the old year to the beginning of the new year. Special rules apply to short periods resulting from a change to a 52–53-week year.

(Code § 441; CCH ¶ 20,302)

See also **partnership; S corporations.**

accrual basis The accrual basis is a permissible accounting method. Accrual-basis taxpayers, including many business entities, include in gross income all income accrued (i.e., income *earned* rather than received) during the taxable year. Income accrues at the time (1) all events occur that fix the right to receive it and (2) its amount can reasonably be estimated (Code § 446; CCH ¶ 2761).

Accrual-basis taxpayers can generally deduct expenses when (1) all events occur that determine the fact of the liability for the expense, (2) the amount can be determined with reasonable accuracy, and (3) economic performance occurs (i.e., property or a service is provided or property is used).

(Code § 461(h); CCH ¶ 21,801)

See also **accounting methods.**

acquisition discount This is a discount on short-term obligations acquired after July 18, 1984; it must be included in income by accrual-basis taxpayers and certain other taxpayers, such as regulated investment companies (mutual funds) and certain pass-through entities. For such acquisitions made after September 27, 1985, this accrual requirement applies to interest on such obligations, other than interest taken into account in determining acquisition discount.

(Code § 1281; CCH ¶ 32,920J; YPG 3.07.B)

See also **discount; market discount; original issue discount.**

acquisition indebtedness See **qualified residence interest.**

adjusted basis See **basis.**

adjusted gross income (AGI) To arrive at adjusted gross income, an individual taxpayer subtracts from gross income (i.e., all income not expressly excluded from tax) all deductions for adjusted gross income. Included among these deductions, specified in the Internal Revenue Code, are

- Expenses not reimbursed by employers.
- Losses from sales or exchanges of property.
- Deductions attributable to rents and royalties.
- Deductions for self-employed retirement plans.

(Code § 62; CCH ¶ 6001)

ADRs See **American depositary receipts.**

alternative depreciation system (ADS) Depreciation deductible in computing alternative minimum taxable income (AMTI) is calculated by using the alternative depreciation system (ADS). For property placed in service after 1986, the ADS is used for purposes of the alternative minimum tax (AMT) instead of the depreciation method used by the taxpayer for regular tax purposes.

ADS limit depreciation for real estate to the amount of straight-line depreciation over a 40-year period. For most other property, a 150 percent declining balance method is used, with a switch to straight-line when it results in a larger deduction. The difference between the ADS depreciation amount and the regular tax depreciation is an AMT preference. If ADS is elected for *regular tax* purposes, an AMT adjustment will not arise.

(Code § 56; CCH ¶ 5200; YPG 6.01.H)

See also **alternative minimum tax (AMT); AMT preferences; depreciation.**

alternative minimum tax (AMT) All taxpayers, including individuals, are potentially subject to the alternative minimum tax (AMT) if they have a substantial amount in AMT preferences or positive AMT adjustments. An AMT liability will arise only if the amount of AMT determined exceeds the taxpayer's regular tax liability.

Computation of the AMT involves starting with the taxpayer's taxable income for regular tax purposes, adding or subtracting certain AMT adjustments, adding any AMT preferences, subtracting any AMT net operating loss (if applicable), and subtracting an AMT exemption to arrive at alternative minimum taxable income (AMTI). AMTI is then multiplied by 24 percent to determine the AMT. This amount (tentative AMT) can be reduced by an AMT foreign tax credit, if applicable.

RRA '93.   For 1993, the AMT is increased by RRA '93 from 24 percent to 26 percent on AMTI up to $175,000, $87,500 for married taxpayers filing separate tax returns, and to 28 percent for AMTI over $175,000. For more detail on RRA '93 AMT changes, see the Foreword on RRA '93.

(Code § 55; CCH ¶ 580; YPG 6.01 et seq.)

See also **AMT adjustments; AMT credit; AMT exemption; AMT foreign tax credit; AMT net operating loss (NOL); AMT preferences.**

American depositary receipts (ADRs) American depositary receipts (ADRs) are negotiable receipts that are typically backed by 1 to 10 of the underlying shares of stock in a foreign corporation held by an issuing foreign bank. ADRs are traded and transferable in the same manner as US securities, and they may also be transferred into the underlying stock of the foreign corporation.

(YPG 2.02)

AMT See **alternative minimum tax (AMT).**

AMT adjustments The first step in computing the alternative minimum tax (AMT) is to start with taxable income for regular tax purposes and then add or subtract AMT adjustments. Some typical AMT adjustments affecting individual taxpayers are:

- Itemized deductions.
- Excess depreciation on real and personal property placed in service after 1986.
- Certain installment sales.
- Passive activity losses.

These adjustments serve to "average"; that is, they prevent taxpayers from being subject to the same income for both AMT and regular tax purposes.
(Code § 56; CCH ¶ 5200; YPG 6.01.B; 6.03.A)
See also **alternative minimum tax (AMT).**

AMT credit If a taxpayer has an alternative minimum tax (AMT) liability payable, a credit is allowed against the taxpayer's *regular tax* liability in later years. The AMT credit for a taxable year is the amount by which the AMT exceeds the taxpayer's regular tax for that year. It can be carried forward indefinitely, but it cannot be carried back.
(Code § 53; CCH ¶ 5002; YPG 6.01.E)
See also **alternative minimum tax (AMT).**

AMT exemption Taxpayers are not subject to the alternative minimum tax (AMT) if their incomes do not exceed certain specified levels. For individuals, this exemption, based on their tax return filing status, phases out when a specified income level is reached. The amounts of AMT exemptions for individuals are as follows:

- Married persons filing jointly and surviving spouses: $40,000.
- Single persons: $30,000.
- Heads of households: $30,000.
- Married persons filing separately: $20,000.

The applicable exemption amount is reduced by 25 cents for each dollar that the taxpayer's alternative minimum taxable income (AMTI) exceeds the following amounts:

- $150,000 for married persons filing jointly and surviving spouses.
- $112,500 for single persons and heads of household.
- $75,000 for married persons filing separately.

No exemption is available if AMTI exceeds $310,000 for married persons filing jointly and surviving spouses, $232,500 for single taxpayers and heads of households, or $155,000 for married persons filing separately.

RRA '93. For 1993, RRA '93 increases the AMT exemption from $40,000 to $45,000 for married taxpayers filing joint tax returns, from $30,000 to $33,750 for single taxpayers and heads of households, and from $20,000 to $22,500 for married taxpayers filing separate tax returns. For more detail on RRA '93 AMT changes, see the Foreword on RRA '93.

(Code § 55; CCH ¶ 5100; YPG 6.01.D)

See also **alternative minimum tax (AMT).**

AMT foreign tax credit This is the only credit available to individual taxpayers to offset liability for the alternative minimum tax (AMT). This credit is computed in a different manner than the foreign tax credit allowed for regular tax purposes because it is based on alternative minimum taxable income (AMTI) and is taken against the taxpayer's tentative AMT (i.e., AMT before reduction by this credit). The credit cannot offset more than 90 percent of the taxpayer's tentative AMT, not counting reduction by the credit, or by the AMT net operating loss.

(Code § 59(a)(1)(C); CCH ¶ 5400; YPG 6.01.G)

See also **alternative minimum tax; AMT net operating loss (NOL).**

AMT net operating loss (NOL) Individual taxpayers whose deductions exceed their income may have a net operating loss (NOL) for regular tax and alternative minimum tax purposes. For regular tax purposes (under Code § 172), the NOL can be carried back 3 years from the loss year and then forward for 15 years. A taxpayer may, however, forgo a carryback and elect to use the carryforward period of up to 15 years (for both AMT and regular tax purposes). The same basic NOL rules that apply for regular tax purposes also apply for purposes of the alternative minimum tax (AMT), with certain modifications.

For years beginning after 1986, the regular tax NOL is modified for AMT purposes as follows:

- AMT adjustments are added or subtracted.
- AMT preferences are subtracted, except for the AMT preference for charitable contributions of appreciated capital gain property.

These modifications for AMT adjustments and preferences are not made to alternative minimum tax NOLs carried forward from pre-1987 taxable years to post-1986 taxable years.

The AMT NOL, as modified, cannot exceed 90 percent of alternative minimum taxable income (AMTI), computed without taking the alternative minimum tax NOL into account. This rule applies to carrybacks and carryforwards with respect to taxable years beginning after 1986.

(Code § 56(d); CCH ¶ 5200; YPG 6.01.F; 6.01.H.4)

See also **alternative minimum tax (AMT); AMT adjustments; AMT preferences.**

AMT preferences Benefits received by taxpayers from certain deductions, lower tax rates, and exclusions are considered preferences for purposes of the alternative minimum tax (AMT). In general, the AMT preference is the amount of the benefit received less the benefit otherwise allowed. AMT preferences that are added to a taxpayer's taxable income to arrive at alternative minimum taxable income (AMTI) include

- The bargain element on the exercise of an incentive stock option (ISO).
- The excess of intangible drilling costs deducted over 65 percent of net income from oil, gas, and geothermal properties.
- Percentage depletion deducted exceeding the taxpayer's investment in oil, gas, and geothermal properties.
- Charitable contributions of appreciated capital gain property.
- Interest on certain private activity bonds.
- Excess depreciation on property placed in service before 1987.

These preferences are added to the taxpayer's regular taxable income and modified by AMT adjustments to arrive at the taxpayer's AMTI.

RRA '93. RRA '93 generally repeals the AMT preference for charitable contributions of appreciated property made after December 31, 1992. The AMT preference for contributions of tangible personal property is retroactively repealed for contributions made after June 30, 1992. For more detail on RRA '93 AMT changes, see the Foreword on RRA '93.

(Code § 57(a); CCH ¶ 5300; YPG 6.01.C; 6.03.B)

See also **alternative minimum tax (AMT); AMT adjustments; private activity bonds.**

annuities Annuities are insurance contracts that provide for regular payments to be made to the annuitant (the insured) beginning at a fixed date and continuing for a term of years or over the annuitant's life. Payments under the contract include interest and principal sufficient to reach the amount guaranteed. The amount of principal returned is excluded, and the interest included, in the annuitant's gross income for tax purposes.

Individuals may enter into joint and survivor annuity contracts. Under these contracts, the first annuitant receives a fixed monthly income during his or her life and the second annuitant receives the same amount after the first annuitant's death. Individuals may also enter into a joint life annuity, under which fixed monthly payments are made until the first annuitant's death.

Actuarial tables are provided by the IRS. These tables are used to determine the expected return under annuity contracts that are based on individual life expectancies.

(Code § 72; CCH ¶ 6100; YPG 5.04.B.4)

anti-churning rules These are rules under the accelerated cost recovery system (ACRS) and the modified accelerated cost recovery system (MACRS) designed to prevent churning transactions. In a churning transaction, the original user of depreciable property would attempt to place the property in service at a date later than the original placed-in-service date in order to bring the property under ACRS or MACRS. Property churned under ACRS is required to be depreciated under pre-ACRS rules, and property churned under MACRS must be depreciated under ACRS.

RRA '93. New anti-churning rules were enacted as part of RRA '93 to prevent conversion of ordinary income into lighter taxed capital gain. See the discussion in the Foreword on RRA '93.

(Code § 168(e),(f); CCH ¶ 11,001)

See also **accelerated cost recovery system (ACRS); modified accelerated cost recovery system (MACRS).**

at-risk rules A taxpayer's loss deductions from an activity cannot exceed the amount that the taxpayer has at risk in that activity at the end of the taxable year. The taxpayer is considered at risk to the extent of money or the adjusted basis of property contributed to the activity and loans with respect to which the taxpayer is personally liable, or for which the taxpayer is personally liable, or for which property (other than that used in the activity) was pledged.

For this purpose, an *activity* is generally any activity engaged in by a taxpayer in conducting a trade or business or for the production of income. The taxpayer's deductible loss for the taxable year with respect to the activity reduces the taxpayer's investment at risk (but not to less than zero) for later taxable years.

The at-risk rules are applicable to the following taxpayers:

• Individuals.

• Partners in partnerships.

• S corporation shareholders.

• Estates.

• Trusts.

- Personal holding companies.
- Some closely held C (regular) corporations. (Closely held C corporations are generally covered only if owned by five or fewer individuals and if they do not actively engage in the leasing of certain equipment. Some active closely held C corporations, however, are not subject to the at-risk rules if engaged in a "qualifying business" as statutorily defined. Other C corporations are *not* covered by the at-risk rules.)

For purposes of these rules, a loss constitutes the excess of permitted deductions over income received or accrued from covered activities. Such deductions can include a taxpayer's losses that were disallowed under these rules in earlier taxable years.

Covered Activities

The at-risk rules currently apply to the following activities:

- Activities of a trade or business engaged in for the production of income.
- Farming.
- Exploration and exploitation of oil and gas properties and geothermal deposits.
- Equipment leasing.
- Holding, producing, or distributing motion pictures or video tapes.

Aggregation Rules

In general, the at-risk rules cover the latter four covered activities listed above on a separate, rather than an aggregate, basis. Also, those activities may generally be aggregated when constituting all or part of a trade or business if there is active participation by the taxpayer in managing each such activity. Temporary IRS regulations also permit aggregation of certain S corporation and partnership activities.

For the first covered activity listed above, the at-risk rules generally apply separately to each such activity. However, separate activities may be aggregated if they constitute a single trade or business of a taxpayer and if the taxpayer actively participates in management of the trade or business. For a trade or business conducted by a partnership or S corporation, activities may be aggregated when at least 65 percent of losses for a taxable year are required to be allocated to partners or shareholders actively participating in management. (*Active participation* is determined based on the particular facts and circumstances involved.)

Real Estate

The at-risk aggregation rules apply to losses incurred with respect to real property acquired after December 31, 1986. Also, for losses incurred with respect to real property placed in service after 1986, a statutory exception to the at-risk rules applies for qualified nonrecourse financing. This financing is generally secured by the real property and is provided by lending organizations with respect to which no personal liability exists. Also, real estate activities of multiple partnerships may be aggregated for purposes of the at-risk rules and considered as a single activity with respect to a partner, as long as that partner actively participates in the management of all those partnerships.

At-Risk Amounts

Under the at-risk rules, the amount considered at risk in an activity is the total of the following:

- The money and the adjusted basis of any property contributed to the activity.
- Amounts borrowed for use in the activity, as long as the taxpayer is personally liable for the amounts borrowed, or pledged property not involved in the activity to the extent of the fair market value of the taxpayer's interest in such property.

A taxpayer is not considered at risk when protected against loss under arrangements such as guarantees and nonrecourse loans. A corporation is generally treated as being at risk in connection with amounts borrowed from its shareholders for purposes of financing an activity.

The taxpayer's at-risk amount with respect to borrowings is not increased if either of the following is true:

- The lender owns an interest in the activity, other than as a creditor.
- The lender is related to a person owning an interest in the activity, other than the taxpayer.

A taxpayer's at-risk amount can be increased and decreased, based on losses incurred with respect to the activity involved and any additional amount that the taxpayer places at risk. If a taxpayer's loss with respect to the activity involved exceeds the taxpayer's at-risk amount, the deductible loss is limited to the year-end at-risk amount. The nondeductible loss amount is then carried over to a future year in which its deduction is allowed under the at-risk rules.

When a taxpayer's at-risk amount reaches zero, additional losses with respect to the activity involved are nondeductible until the taxpayer provides additional at-risk amounts. A taxpayer can do this by contributing additional funds or property to the activity involved, by obtaining a loan with respect to which there is personal liability, or by pledging property to be used in such activity. Also, any withdrawals by the taxpayer decrease the at-risk amount, and income distributed from the activity will not increase the taxpayer's at-risk amount.

Recapture Rules

Losses allowed to a taxpayer under the at-risk rules can be recaptured when the taxpayer's at-risk amount falls below zero as a result of protective arrangements or an increase of nonrecourse debt. When the taxpayer's at-risk amount falls below zero, income is recognized to the extent that the taxpayer's basis is reduced with respect to the activity involved. The recapture, however, is limited to the excess of losses allowed in earlier taxable years with respect to the activity over amounts previously recaptured.

Proposed IRS Regulations

The IRS has issued lengthy and complex Proposed Regulations with respect to the at-risk rules dealing with general principles, at-risk activities, increases and decreases in at-risk amounts, ordering and timing, and transfers and dispositions of interests.

(Code § 465; CCH ¶ 21,850; YPG 9.01 et seq.)
See also **basis; tax shelters.**

B

bad debt A debt becomes bad when the debt, a loan, or an amount due for services rendered or the sale or rental of property becomes uncollectible. To be deductible, the debt must have had a value when originally incurred, and a true debtor-creditor relationship must have existed.

If the bad debt arises from a business activity, it is fully deductible. Such a debt, for individuals, is a deduction "for" adjusted gross income and is thus deductible even if deductions are not itemized. If the debt arises from a nonbusiness activity (e.g., a loan made to friend or relative), it is treated as a short-term capital loss subject to deduction limits.

(Code § 166; CCH ¶ 10,501; YPG 2.02)
See also **adjusted gross income; capital gains and losses.**

bankruptcy   Bankruptcy laws provide relief for debtors who are unable to repay their debts. In bankruptcy, a debt can be liquidated completely, repayment can be postponed, or the debt can be reduced to a level at which repayment becomes possible. Bankruptcy proceedings are designed to prevent harassment of the debtor and to enable creditors to obtain at least partial repayment.

Two types of bankruptcy proceedings are available for most individuals under Chapters 7 and 13 of the federal bankruptcy code. Chapter 7 provides for liquidation, and proceedings may be commenced under it involuntarily by creditors or by the debtor. The federal bankruptcy court appoints a trustee to oversee the liquidation of the debtor's assets. Certain debts, however, cannot be discharged:

- Certain taxes and customs duties (e.g., unpaid withholding and Social Security taxes and related penalties).
- Debts resulting from fraud, embezzlement, or larceny.
- Alimony, child support, and separate maintenance.
- Willful and malicious tort liability.
- Student loans of less than five years.

At the end of the proceedings, the debtor is discharged by the court, and any previous judgments against the debtor are voided. If a bankruptcy filing is made, the debtor cannot make another bankruptcy filing for six years. Also, a bankruptcy filing usually severely restricts the debtor's ability to obtain credit.

Certain assets of the debtor are exempt from liquidation, including a limited amount of equity in the debtor's home, a car (up to a limited value), certain personal property, and benefits such as Social Security and unemployment compensation.

Chapter 13 provides for debt adjustment in a proceeding under which the debtor is allowed to retain his or her property and assigns a part of his or her income to satisfy debts in full or in part. The debtor files a monthly budget plan with the court, which can approve or modify it, and a trustee is then appointed to control the debtor's income.

Once repayment under the plan is made, the debtor is discharged. However, debts that cannot be discharged under Chapter 7, listed earlier, also cannot be discharged under Chapter 13. A debtor can convert a Chapter 13 proceeding to a Chapter 7 proceeding at any time.

Tax Implications

In a Chapter 7 bankruptcy proceeding, a separate taxable entity is created. This entity, referred to as the *bankruptcy estate,* consists of the debtor's property held by the trustee in bankruptcy. This is also the case with respect to a Chapter 11 bankruptcy proceeding, which involves a *business* reorganization. However, no separate taxable entity is created under a Chapter 13 bankruptcy proceeding. The trustee is responsible for the filing of a tax return, on a calendar or fiscal year basis, when a bankruptcy estate is created. The individual debtor who makes a bankruptcy filing, however, must file his or her own personal federal income tax return (Form 1040).

The IRS is statutorily empowered to immediately assess tax not otherwise assessed when a taxpayer enters into a bankruptcy proceeding.

(Code §§ 1398, 6871; CCH ¶ 33,800 and ¶ 41,410)

basis In determining depreciation on property, gain or loss upon its sale, and bad debt and casualty loss deductions, a taxpayer must refer to the property's basis and adjusted basis. In many cases, a taxpayer's basis for property is its cost. However, a taxpayer can have a basis other than cost if the property is acquired other than by purchase, such as by exchange, by inheritance, or as a gift.

Taxable Exchanges

If the property is acquired in a taxable exchange, the property's basis is generally the property's fair market value (FMV) at the time of the exchange. If the property is acquired in a nontaxable exchange, its basis is generally the adjusted basis (see the following discussion) of the property, "boot" received, additional costs incurred in the exchange, and any gain recognized by the taxpayer. The basis is reduced by any cash and/or boot received and any loss recognized by the taxpayer on the exchange.

Inherited Property

If the property is inherited, its basis is generally its FMV at the time of the decedent's death. However, the property's basis may be its value on an alternate valuation date if the executor so elects. This date is generally six months after the date of the decedent's death. However, if the estate owes no federal estate tax, the alternate valuation date cannot be used.

Gifts

If the property was received as a gift, its basis differs for purposes of determining gain or loss. If the property is sold at a gain, the donee's basis is the basis of the donor or the last preceding owner by whom it was not received by gift. If the property is sold at a loss, the donee's basis is the lower of the basis of the donor or the last preceding owner by whom it was not received by gift, or the FMV of the property at the time of the gift.

Adjusted Basis

The taxpayer's basis for property held may be adjusted if, for example, improvements are made or depreciation is taken on the property. In determining gain or loss on the disposition of the property, adjustments are made for such items to arrive at the taxpayer's adjusted basis for the property. The taxpayer's basis cannot be reduced below zero.

(Code §§ 1011, 1012, 1014, 1015, 1016; CCH ¶ 29,641 et seq.; YPG 2.02; 2.10)

See also **boot; estate tax; exchange; fair market value; gift tax.**

basis for depreciation   For property placed in service before 1981, qualifying for the accelerated cost recovery system (ACRS) (1981–86), or qualifying for the modified accelerated cost recovery system (MACRS) (post-1986), the basis for depreciation is generally the basis used in determining gain or loss on a disposition of the property without adjustment for prior depreciation (Code § 168(d); CCH ¶ 11,001).

For property placed in service before 1981 or not qualifying for ACRS, the basis for depreciation is its adjusted basis (i.e., net of depreciation) (Code § 167(g)).

The basis for depreciation for property received from a decedent is its fair market value (FMV) at the time of the decedent's death. However, if the executor of the estate elected the alternate valuation date under Code § 1014 with respect to the property, the basis for depreciation is its value on that date, less any depreciation after that date (CCH ¶ 29,720).

If personal use property is converted into income-producing property, the basis for depreciation is its adjusted basis or FMV when converted, whichever is less.

(Reg. § 1.167(g)–1; CCH ¶ 11,001)

See also **accelerated cost recovery system (ACRS); depreciation; modified accelerated cost recovery system (MACRS).**

blue-chip stocks   These stocks are considered the highest-quality common stocks, typically involving minimal risk and high dividend payments for the investor. Examples include the 30 stocks in the Dow Jones Industrial Average and traded on the New York Stock Exchange, such as stock of the General Motors Corporation and of International Business Machines (IBM).

(YPG 2.02)

See also **capital asset; capital gains and losses.**

bond   A bond is a debt instrument that generally qualifies as a capital asset for its holder. Tax rules generally applicable to other securities, notably stock, also apply to bonds, such as rules governing holding period and basis.

Bonds may be issued at a premium or at a discount to their par values. Typically, bonds constitute fixed-income investments, generally entitling the holder to a fixed rate of return. Some issues are hybrid instruments that have certain equity characteristics.

Bond prices and values vary in accordance with factors affecting the bond market. For example, when interest rates rise, the value of a bond with a fixed-rate coupon is likely to decline in market value. When interest rates decline, the value of such a bond is likely to rise.

Bond prices, values, and returns also vary depending on their quality as determined by a bond rating service, such as Standard & Poor's or Moody's Investors Service, Inc. A corporate bond with Moody's highest rating, Aaa, for example, will provide a lower rate of return than a bond with its lowest rating, C. The additional return on a lower-rated issue is designed to compensate the investor for the relative risk involved. Also, if a bond's rating is downgraded, its market price will generally decline.

There are many types of bonds. Three principal types are:

- *Corporate bonds,* which are generally taxable by federal, state, and local governments. Such bonds include mortgage bonds, debenture (unsecured) bonds, and convertible bonds (YPG 2.02).
- *Federal government bonds,* which are generally subject to federal income taxation but not state and municipal taxation, and which have maturities of over 10 years (YPG 2.04.E).
- *State and municipal government bonds,* which are generally exempt from federal, state, and municipal taxation. (YPG 2.04.D).

Within these three principal categories are various types of bonds, such as stripped bonds, private activity bonds, and zero-coupon bonds.

Each type of bond covered in this Encyclopedia has its own listing, and reference should be made to the listings of various types of bonds (e.g., zero-coupon bond).

See also **bond discount; bond premium.**

bond discount The amount of discount on a bond is, in general, the difference between the bond's face (par) value and the price paid for it by the investor. A discount bond generally is redeemed at par value upon maturity. An example of a discount bond is a US savings bond.

Special rules are provided in the Internal Revenue Code for certain types of bond discount:

- Acquisition discount.
- Market discount (YPG 3.04).
- Original issue discount (OID) (YPG 3.04).

See also Encyclopedia listings for the preceding items.

bond funds   These are mutual funds that invest in bonds of various types, such as corporate bonds, junk bonds, and tax-exempt municipal bonds. Units in these funds can be purchased through securities brokers or mutual fund groups, with a commission charge. The value of the units may be affected by market forces, such as swings in interest rates.

It is important to note that although a fund's bond portfolio may contain tax-exempt bonds, the related fund income distributed to the shareholder may be considered to lose its tax-exempt status for state and local tax purposes in some jurisdictions.

(YPG 2.02; 2.04)

See also **capital gains and losses; junk bonds; mutual funds.**

bond premium   This is the excess amount an investor pays for a bond over the bond's face value. For tax-exempt bonds, the premium is amortized, and no deduction is available for an amortizable bond premium. For taxable bonds, amortization of premium may be elected. If the amortization election is not made, the premium must be treated as part of the taxpayer's basis for gain or loss on sale or redemption of the bond. If the election is made, the basis must be reduced by the amortizable bond premium.

(Code §§ 171, 1016; CCH ¶ 11,850, ¶ 29,760)

boot   This is cash or other property received in a tax-free exchange of property that does not qualify for tax-free treatment. Any gain on such an exchange is recognized up to the amount of cash and/or fair market value of the other non-qualifying property exchanged, and any loss cannot be recognized.

(Code §§ 351, 1031; CCH ¶ 16,401 et seq., ¶ 31,501 et seq.)

See also **exchange.**

C

calls   See **options.**

capital asset   Section 1221 of the Internal Revenue Code specifies that a capital asset is any property except:

1. Stock in trade or other property properly included in inventory.
2. Property held primarily for sale to customers in the ordinary course of the taxpayer's trade or business.
3. Depreciable property used in a trade or business.
4. Real property used in a trade or business.
5. Copyrights; literary, musical, or artistic compositions; letters; memoranda; or similar property held by any of the following:
   - A taxpayer who created the property through his or her personal efforts.

- A taxpayer for whom the letter, memorandum, etc., was prepared or produced.
- A taxpayer who receives such property from its creator.

6. Accounts or notes receivable acquired by the taxpayer in the ordinary course of a trade or business either of the following ways:

- For services rendered.
- From the sale of inventory, stock-in-trade, or property held for sale to customers in the ordinary course of the trade or business.

7. US government publications received without charge or at a price lower than that charged to the general public.

Note, however, that special rules apply to qualified business property that is a "Section 1231 asset," and a portion of gain on the disposition of depreciable assets may be subject to ordinary income rather than capital gain treatment under the depreciation recapture rules. Also, special rules apply under Internal Revenue Code § 1237 to subdividers of real property (CCH ¶ 32,290 et seq.; 32,390; YPG 2.02).

The following items may receive capital gain or loss treatment in the hands of an individual investor:

- *Options,* such as puts and calls, generally give rise to the same type of gain or loss on their sale or exchange as would arise from the sale or exchange of the underlying property. When an option lapses and a loss is incurred, the option is generally treated as having been sold or exchanged on the day that it lapsed. But this rule does not apply with respect to a loss from the lapse of a put option bought on the same day as the stock bought to fulfill the option contract (YPG 2.03).

- *Partnership interests* are partly capital assets and partly ordinary income assets. The ordinary income portion is the portion related to partnership ordinary income-producing assets, such as partnership accounts receivable and substantially appreciated inventory.

- *Property held for the production of income* but not used in a trade or business qualifies as a capital asset.

- *Real property* held for personal use qualifies as a capital asset.

- *Regulated futures contracts and forward contracts* are subject to a special rule under which a termination of rights or obligations in such contracts (cancellation, expiration, lapse, etc.) is treated as a sale or exchange.

- *Securities, stock, bonds, notes, debentures, and so on* generally qualify as capital assets for individual investors, unless they fall into one of the exceptions listed. Under special rules, small business stock and small business investment company stock are not treated as capital assets when sold at a loss.

See also **bond; capital gains and losses; options; partnerships; recapture; Section 1231 assets; tax straddles.**

capital expenditures These are expenditures to acquire or make permanent improvements to property the benefits of which extend beyond the end of the taxable year in which they are made; they are generally nondeductible for tax purposes. Instead, they are deducted through depreciation or cost recovery over the property's useful life or recovery period.

(Code § 263; CCH ¶ 13,709; YPG 2.11)

See also **accelerated cost recovery system (ACRS); basis; depreciation; modified accelerated cost recovery system (MACRS).**

capital gains and losses Sales or exchanges of capital assets result in capital gain or loss. These gains or losses are either long-term or short-term. In general, gains and losses on capital assets held for less than one year are short-term, and those held for more than one year are long-term under current law. If capital losses exceed the statutory limit of $3,000, the excess amount can be carried forward until it is deducted in full.

The treatment of śuch gains and losses was significantly changed by the 1986 Tax Reform Act. For taxable years after 1986, the deduction of 60 percent of long-term capital gains was eliminated. Also, beginning in 1987, long-term and short-term capital losses can offset up to $3,000 of ordinary income on a dollar-for-dollar basis.

RRA '93. RRA '93 does not change the 28 percent top tax rate on long-term capital gains. However, as a result of the increase in the top tax rates on ordinary income, RRA '93 provides anti-conversion provisions designed to prevent the conversion of ordinary income into lower taxed capital gains. See the discussion in the Foreword on RRA '93.

(Code §§ 1211, 1212, 1222, 1223; CCH ¶ 32,190, ¶ 32,200, ¶ 32,240, ¶ 32,260; YPG 2.02)

See also **basis; capital asset; Section 1231 assets.**

carrybacks A carryback of certain items may be allowed to offset income, and thus reduce tax, of prior taxable years. Carrybacks are allowable to individuals with respect to the following:

* *Foreign tax credit.* If taxes paid or accrued to foreign countries exceed a statutory limit, the excess may be carried back and taken as a credit in each of the two preceding years (Code § 904(c); CCH ¶ 28,520).
* *General business credit* may be carried back three years (Code § 38; CCH ¶ 4,250).
* *Net operating losses* are allowed a three-year carryback (Code § 172; CCH ¶ 12,001).

carrying charges Taxpayers generally may elect to capitalize carrying charges, adding them to the basis of property to which they relate. Such charges include mortgage interest and other charges on unimproved, unproductive real property; loan interest relating to construction on or improvement of real property; and loan interest relating to the purchase and installation of personal property. The election is also generally available for taxes (other than sales taxes, which must be capitalized) relating to the property. Carrying charges allocable to property or positions related to a tax straddle must also be capitalized.

(Code §§ 263(g), 266; CCH ¶ 13,709, ¶ 2236)

See also **tax straddles.**

carryovers (carryforwards) Taxpayers are permitted to carry over (carry forward) certain items into future years for tax purposes. Carryover items common for individual investors include:

- *Capital losses.* Capital losses exceeding the $3,000 yearly deduction limit can be carried over until the excess amount is deducted in full. See **capital gains and losses.**

- *Charitable contributions.* A five-year carryover is permitted for charitable contributions exceeding statutory limits in a taxable year. See **charitable contributions.**

- *Net operating losses.* A carryover of up to 15 years is allowed for these losses.

- *Foreign tax credit.* A five-year carryforward is allowed a taxpayer when taxes paid (or accrued) to foreign countries exceed a statutory limit in a taxable year.

cash and carry transactions See **commodity futures.**

cash basis The cash basis is an accounting method that is also commonly referred to as the "cash receipts and disbursements method." Taxpayers using the cash basis, including most individual taxpayers, must include in gross (total) income *all* taxable income that is received during the taxable year in cash or its equivalent. Allowable deductions are taken by such taxpayers in the taxable year in which the related disbursement in cash or its equivalent is made. A cash-basis taxpayer may also be required to include income constructively received (i.e., income not actually possessed by the taxpayer but within the taxpayer's control).

The Internal Revenue Code limits the types of business entities that can use the cash basis. In general, for taxable years beginning after 1986, use of the cash basis is limited to corporations and partnerships having annual gross receipts of $5 million or less, partnerships having no C (regular) corporation partners, S corporations, and sole proprietorships. Qualified personal service corporations (PSCs) may also use the cash basis if they are substantially involved in performing services in the areas of health care, engineering, architecture, actuarial science, consulting, or the performing arts. The stock of the qualified PSC must also be substantially owned (i.e., 95 percent in value) by employees performing such services, by their estates, or by an acquirer of such an employee's ownership interest within the preceding 24 months as a result of that employee's death. (Code § 448, 451; CCH ¶ 20,800, ¶ 21,001)

See also **accounting methods.**

cash receipts and disbursements method   See **cash basis.**

cash surrender value   See **life insurance.**

casualty losses   A *casualty* is an event resulting from a sudden, unexpected, or unusual cause, not necessarily natural. Examples of casualties are fires, floods, severe droughts, severe storms, and vandalism.

The amount of a casualty loss on property deductible for tax purposes is the lesser of:

- The actual loss incurred, as measured by the value of the property immediately before the casualty minus its value immediately after the casualty; or

- The property's adjusted basis for purposes of determining a loss on its sale.

The lesser figure is then reduced by:

- $100.

- Insurance proceeds.

- Amounts received with respect to the property sustaining the casualty from disaster relief agencies or an employer.

- Any other compensation received with respect to the property sustaining the casualty.

The total of net casualty losses so determined can be deducted only to the extent that it exceeds 10 percent of the taxpayer's adjusted gross income. Also, for casualty losses on personal property in taxable years beginning after 1986, deduction is permitted only to the extent that the damages are not covered by insurance and the taxpayer has timely filed an insurance claim.

A loss from damage to personal-use property must qualify as a casualty loss to be deductible. A loss from damage to business or investment property, however, may be deductible even if the loss does not qualify as a casualty loss. (Code § 165; CCH ¶ 10,500)

CDs   See **certificates of deposit.**

certificates of deposit   These are certificates representing investments of funds at specified rates of interest, typically with financial institutions, such as banks, savings and loan associations, and investment firms. Interest on such certificates often is includable in the holder's gross income as earned, but the taxability of interest may be deferred to the following taxable year, depending on certificate terms. (Code § 61; CCH ¶ 5501)

charitable contributions   Taxpayers itemizing deductions are allowed to deduct contributions made to, or for the use of, qualified charitable organizations, which may be governmental, public, or private. The Internal Revenue Service provides a list of qualified charitable organizations in *Publication 78*. A charity need not be on this list for contributions to qualify for deduction, however. Such contributions may be in the form of cash or property and are subject to deduction limitations. Any contributions not deductible in the year they are made may be carried over to future taxable years.

The deductible amount of an individual taxpayer's charitable contribution is generally based on the fair market value of the property contributed. That value may be reduced, however, if the property contributed is appreciated property, or if it secured a loan on which the taxpayer has deductible interest after the contribution.

Charitable contributions of a taxpayer are limited to the individual's "contribution base" for the taxable year. In general, this is based on percentages of the taxpayer's adjusted gross income (AGI), without taking into account any net operating loss carryback. A deduction is generally limited to 50 percent of the taxpayer's AGI for contributions to public charities. A limitation of 30 percent of AGI applies to contributions of appreciated capital gain property to public charities and contributions of cash or ordinary income property to private nonoperating foundations. A 20 percent limitation applies to contributions of capital gain property (including certain appreciated stock) to nonoperating foundations. A five-year carryover is available for contributions exceeding the 50 percent and 30 percent limitations, and also to excess contributions to private nonoperating foundations (Code § 170; CCH ¶ 11,675; YPG 2.02).

The taxpayer must usually attach to his or her tax return for the taxable year of the contribution a description of the contributed property and how it was valued. If the contribution was appreciated property, its cost and the determination of the deductible amount must be shown. If a deduction of more than $500 is claimed for a contribution of property, written information regarding the contributed property must be retained by the taxpayer and supplied with the tax return on which the deduction is claimed. Such information includes the manner in which the property was acquired and its cost or other basis. If the total value of noncash charitable contributions exceeds $500, the taxpayer must file Form 8283 with the tax return for that year.

If the value of a contribution exceeds $5,000, or $10,000 for nonpublicly traded stock, individuals and certain other taxpayers claiming the deduction must usually obtain a receipt and attach a qualified appraisal of the property's fair market value to the tax return for the contribution year.

A contribution of appreciated capital gain property may result in a preference for purposes of the alternative minimum tax (AMT). In general, the AMT preference is equal to the amount of the deduction claimed for regular income tax purposes exceeding the taxpayer's adjusted basis for the property contributed.

RRA '93. RRA '93 generally repeals the AMT preference for charitable contributions of appreciated property made after December 31, 1992. The AMT preference for contributions of tangible personal property is retroactively repealed for contributions made after June 30, 1992. For more detail on RRA '93 AMT changes, see the Foreword on RRA '93.

(Code § 57(a)(6); CCH ¶ 5300; YPG 6.03B)

See also **adjusted gross income; alternative minimum tax; AMT preferences; basis; capital asset; capital gains and losses.**

charitable remainder trusts   Under this type of arrangement, an individual places property into an irrevocable trust and provides that its income is to be distributed to the beneficiaries and that, on the death of the last such beneficiary, the property will be distributed to a qualified charity for its unrestricted use. When the trust commences, the individual creating it is generally entitled to a deduction for income tax purposes for the value of the property to be distributed to the charity. His or her estate taxes will also be reduced, since the property will not be included in the estate.

(Code § 164; Reg. § 20.2034–10; CCH ¶ 9500A)

See also **estate tax; irrevocable trust.**

Clifford trust   This type of trust takes its name from a court case and is also frequently referred to as a *10-year* trust. If a transfer in trust was made before March 2, 1986, and the trust grantor retained a reversionary interest in the trust corpus or income that could become effective within 10 years after the last transfer to the trust, the grantor is taxed on the trust income from the transferred property. If an interest in the trust corpus would revert to the grantor's estate at the grantor's death, the trust income would be taxable to the grantor if his or her life expectancy were less than 10 years (Code § 673; CCH ¶ 25,110; YPG 10.02). This provision was *repealed* by the 1986 Tax Reform Act, and different rules apply to grantor trusts with respect to transfers in trust made after March 1, 1986.

collateral mortgage obligations (CMOs)   See **mortgages.**

collectibles   This term covers a wide range of investment items, such as antiques, oriental rugs, rare books, and rare coins. If a taxpayer acquires such items in the course of conducting a business (e.g., as an antiques dealer or as a rare coin dealer), gain or loss on their disposition is generally ordinary income or loss. Expenses incurred with respect to such acquisitions and sales are usually deductible.

However, such items acquired for personal pleasure and subsequently sold generally give rise to capital gain or loss. Most expenses incurred under this status are reflected in determining gain or loss on disposition of the property.

Also, most collectibles are not eligible individual retirement account (IRA) investments. Certain coins are eligible as IRA investments, however.

(YPG 2.02)

See also **capital assets; capital gains and losses; dealer; individual retirement account (IRA).**

commercial paper Commercial paper represents high-yield, short-term unsecured promissory notes issued by major corporations to meet short-term financing needs. These notes, which are not registered with the federal Securities and Exchange Commission (SEC) since they are short-term, are issued for varying periods of up to 270 days.

(YPG 2.02)

commissions There are several types of commissions. For example, brokers charge commissions to execute securities transactions and purchase and sale transactions. Also, a real estate broker charges a commission to a seller, based on a percentage of the property's purchase price. Commissions in these cases generally reduce the gain recognized on the sale of the property.

(Code § 263; CCH ¶ 14,000; YPG 2.02; 2.05)

commodity futures These are contracts to buy or sell a specified amount of a commodity (e.g., gold, pork bellies, heating oil) at a future date at a set price. These contracts are of two general types:

- Regulated futures contracts, which are subject to rules of a board of trade or a commodity exchange (e.g., the Chicago Board of Trade or Chicago Mercantile Exchange) and for which values are listed daily.
- Forward contracts, which are not so regulated.

In general, transactions in such contracts are of four types:

- *Hedges,* which are used to avoid losses from price changes in the related commodity. Hedging transactions generally result in ordinary income or loss and are typically used by processors of commodities.
- *Investment or speculative transactions,* which generally result in capital gain or loss.
- *Straddles,* which involve the simultaneous purchase and sale of two commodity futures contracts on the same exchange and call for the delivery of the commodity in different months. Investors typically expect to realize gain on such investments as a result of commodity market fluctuations. Such transactions may give rise to capital gain or loss, but special rules apply to tax straddles.
- *Cash and carry transactions,* involving the simultaneous purchase and sale of a spot commodity contract calling for (1) the present delivery of the related commodity; or (2) the purchase of the nearest month's futures contract, with delivery to be sought under that contract, and the sale of a futures contract in the expectation of a gain on delivery of the commodity on the closing of the contract due to market forces. Capital gain is generally realized on such contracts, offset by any storage costs incurred with respect to the commodity.

(Code §§ 1092, 1256; CCH ¶ 32,100, ¶ 32,700, YPG 2.02)

See also **capital gains and losses; tax straddles.**

common stock This is a popular equity investment that gives the investor an equity interest in the issuing corporation. Sales of such stock generally give rise to capital gain or loss, long-term if held for more than one year or short-term if held for a shorter period. The holder may or may not be entitled to dividend payments, depending on the issuing corporation's dividend policy. On liquidation or other termination of the corporation, common stockholders' interests generally are satisfied after those of preferred stockholders and bondholders and other creditors.
(YPG 2.02)
See also **blue-chip stocks; capital asset; capital gains and losses; preferred stock.**

community property Under the laws of a number of states, spouses co-own property that either partner acquires during the marriage. States with such laws include Arizona, California, Idaho, Louisiana, Nevada, New Mexico, Texas, and Washington.

complex trusts See **trust.**

condominiums The ownership of a condominium involves individual and concurrent ownership of a unit of real property under state laws. Such an owner has separate ownership of a particular residential unit and is also a tenant in common with the other unit owners with respect to the property's common elements. The common elements include the underlying land, recreational facilities such as a swimming pool, hallways, parking areas, and other features. A transfer of the condominium unit also transfers an undivided interest in the common elements.
(YPG 2.05)

contributions See **charitable contributions; partnerships.**

convertible bonds These are bonds that can be converted into the issuing corporation's stock at a specified price. This conversion right generally results in a lower yield than on a debenture bond. Such bonds also are generally callable, that is, the corporation can compel the investor to convert the bond into stock. The call typically is made when the market value of the stock exceeds the call price of the bonds.
(YPG 2.02)

cooperatives A cooperative involves an indirect form of ownership of real property. In general, it is a corporate entity that buys or constructs real property. As an owner of the corporation's stock, an investor has the legal right to occupy a specific portion of the property (typically an apartment). The tax law permits the investor to claim deductions for the allocable share of the mortgage interest and real estate taxes of the corporation.
(Code § 216; CCH ¶ 12,600; YPG 2.05)

cost (as basis for property) See **basis.**

cost depletion See **depletion.**

Crummey trusts Such a trust, named after a court case, allows trust funds to be kept out of the hands of beneficiaries at the trust grantor's discretion. Nevertheless, such a trust qualifies for the annual gift tax exclusion under the Internal Revenue Code, since a beneficiary may withdraw a fixed yearly sum (i.e., a present interest) equal to the lesser of (1) the annual gift tax exclusion limit of $10,000, or $20,000 with spousal consent, or (2) the grantor's annual contribution to the trust fund. The beneficiary is required to be informed of this withdrawal right, and the funds must be available to the beneficiary on demand. In general, however, this right is not expected to be exercised.
(YPG 5.09; 10.02.E)

D

dealer If an individual is deemed a dealer in real or personal property, the tax consequences of his or her sale of such property will differ from those for a casual seller. A dealer's activities will generally result in ordinary income or loss, whereas the casual seller will generally have capital gain or loss. Installment sale rules also employ the dealer–nondealer distinction.
(YPG 2.02)
See also **capital gains and losses; installment and deferred-payment sales.**

debenture bonds These are unsecured bonds that are not backed by any specified collateral but by the good faith of the issuing corporation.
(YPG 2.02)

debt See **bad debts; bankruptcy; bond.**

deep discount bonds These are bonds sold at a price considerably below their face values. An example is a zero-coupon bond.
(YPG 2.02)
See also **original issue discount; zero-coupon bonds.**

deferred annuities See **annuities.**

depletion This is the gradual reduction of the source of wasting assets through their removal from real property. To compensate for this reduction, a deduction for this annual depletion is allowed, through cost depletion or percentage depletion. The taxpayer uses the method that results in the larger tax deduction. Depletion and applicable depreciation deductions are designed to return the cost or other basis of the property to the taxpayer (Code §§ 611, 613, 613A, 614; CCH ¶ 24,501).

Cost Depletion

This is the usual method for computing depletion deductions on all types of property subject to depletion. The depletable property's capitalized cost is allocated equally to units of material extracted, and costs are deducted ratably as the units are sold. A depletion deduction for the taxable year is determined by dividing units remaining at year end minus units sold during the year by the property's adjusted basis, and multiplying the result by the number of units sold (Code § 611).

Percentage Depletion

Under current tax law, this depletion method is available only for certain types of gas production, geothermal production, and limited amounts of other gas and oil production. Depletion rates and qualified production properties are specified in Code §§ 613 and 613A.

A tax preference also arises for purposes of the alternative minimum tax (AMT), for depletion taken after a taxpayer's aggregate depletion deductions with respect to a property exceed that property's adjusted basis. See **AMT preferences.**

depreciation This represents the deduction from gross income, allowed yearly, of a reasonable allowance for exhaustion, wear and tear, and normal obsolescence of property held for the production of income or used in a trade or business. Depreciation is computed using the straight-line method, under which the depreciation is rated over the property's life, or an accelerated method, such as declining balance or sum of the years' digits. The availability of accelerated methods is subject to certain restrictions specified in the Internal Revenue Code.

For property placed in service after 1986, depreciation is generally taken under the modified accelerated cost recovery system (MACRS). For property placed in service after 1980 and before 1987, depreciation is generally taken under the accelerated cost recovery system (ACRS). For property placed in service before 1981, and other property placed in service at a later date to which ACRS and MACRS do not apply, depreciation is taken under pre-ACRS rules. A taxpayer generally may elect, subject to certain limitations, to deduct the cost of up to $10,000 of qualifying property for the taxable year in which the property is placed in service, in lieu of depreciating such property. For this purpose, qualifying property is generally defined as depreciable tangible property that is purchased for use in the active conduct of a trade or business.

(Code §§ 167, 168, 179; CCH ¶ 11,001, ¶ 12,120, YPG 2.04.F; Appendix B)
See also **accelerated cost recovery system (ACRS); alternative depreciation system (ADS); anti-churning rules; basis; modified accelerated cost recovery system (MACRS).**

discount In general, this term refers to the difference between the face value and the purchase price of a bond, when the purchase price is below the face value. The tax law provides specific rules for certain types of discount, such as acquisition discount, market discount, and original issue discount (OID). See **acquisition discount; market discount, original issue discount (OID).**

(YPG 2.04)

dividend reinvestment plans   Many large corporations with publicly traded stock offer dividend reinvestment plans to their shareholders. Under these plans, shareholders can reinvest dividends by buying more stock in the corporation in lieu of receiving cash. The advantage of such plans is that they offer a reduced cost of investment, in that they involve little or no purchase and sale commissions or administrative costs, may offer a reduced share purchase price (typically 5 percent below market), and may also provide for optional cash purchases with respect to which no commission is charged and/or the purchase cost is below market price.

dividends   In general, dividends are distributions made by a corporation in cash or property to its shareholders from its current earnings and profits or from earnings and profits accumulated after February 28, 1913. These distributions generally constitute taxable income to the shareholders when paid, with certain exceptions.

Certain other distributions made by a corporation also constitute taxable dividends. These include liquidating distributions, property distributions, stock dividends, stock and bond rights, and stock redemptions. Special rules apply to dividends paid by mutual funds (regulated investment companies). Also, certain payments made by a corporation, typically a closely held corporation, to shareholders in the form of excessive compensation, for example, may be treated as taxable constructive dividends.

If a corporation's distributions to shareholders are not made from current or accumulated earnings and profits, they are treated as a return of capital to the shareholders. Such distributions reduce each shareholder's stock basis and are taxable only in excess of that basis.

(Code § 316; CCH ¶ 15,601)

E

equity investments   There are a number of equity investments. The most popular types are:

- Collectibles.
- Common stock.
- Commodity futures.
- Foreign securities (see also **American depositary receipts**).

- Mutual funds.
- New stock issues.
- Precious metals.
- Stock-index futures.
- Warrants.

See also related Encyclopedia listings.

estate   This represents the assets and liabilities of a deceased or bankrupt person. In general, a decedent's estate is a taxable entity that may be subject to income tax and estate tax.

For income tax purposes, a decedent's estate is an entity that is required to file tax returns and remit tax. It is a taxable entity during the period of its administration, with the executor (or administrator, if the decedent died intestate) filing the returns and paying the tax.

The estate's income is taxed to the estate, its beneficiaries, or both. The taxation of these parties is determined on the basis of how the estate's income is distributed under the terms of the decedent's will and/or state law.

In general, the beneficiaries are taxed on distributions from the estate that are actually made or that they are entitled to receive, to the extent of their respective shares of the estate's distributable net income. The estate (through its executor or administrator) is taxed on its taxable income, which is its gross income less certain allowable deductions.

(Code § 641; CCH ¶ 24,751; YPG 2.02)

See also **bankruptcy; estate tax.**

estate tax   This tax is imposed on the transfer of an individual's property upon his or her death and in certain other cases representing the equivalent of such a transfer. It is imposed on the decedent's taxable estate. The *taxable estate* represents the value of the decedent's gross estate, that is, the value of the total property actually transferred or considered transferred, minus allowable deductions. This tax is computed based on a unified rate schedule. Under this schedule, taxable gifts made during the decedent's life and transfers at death are taxed on a cumulative basis.

For transfers made during the years 1984 through 1992, under the unified rate schedule, a maximum tax rate of 55 percent applies to transfers over $3,000,000. For transfers of $2,500,000 to $3,000,000, a 53 percent rate applies.

Although the unified rate schedule prescribes a minimum tax rate of 18 percent, the effective minimum rate for 1987 and later years is 37 percent as a result of the unified estate and gift tax credit. The unified rate schedule also applies in computing tax on generation-skipping transfers.

Tax Computation

A tentative tax is calculated by applying the unified tax rate schedule to cumulative (lifetime and at-death) transfers. The transfers to which this tax applies are

- The taxable estate.
- Taxable gifts made after 1976 (other than gifts includable in the decedent's gross estate).

The tentative tax computed is then reduced by the gift tax payable on gifts made after 1976. Gift taxes paid after 1976 are determined as if the rate schedule in effect in the year of the decedent's death was in effect in the year the gift was made. The estate tax before credits is the result.

Credits. The unified estate and gift tax credit is used first to offset any gift tax on the decedent's lifetime transfers. The federal estate tax may also be reduced by credits for state inheritance, estate and gift taxes, federal gift taxes paid by the decedent on pre-1977 lifetime transfers, foreign estate taxes or duties, and federal estate taxes paid by other estates on earlier transfers made by the decedent.

RRA '93. RRA '93 restores the top estate and gift tax and generation-skipping tax rates of 53 percent and 55 percent, applicable to transfers of more than $2.5 million and $3 million, respectively. It also modifies the income tax rates applicable to estates and trusts. The estate and gift tax rate change is effective for decedents dying and gifts made after December 31, 1992. The income tax rate changes for estates and trusts are effective for taxable years beginning after 1992. See the discussion in the Foreword on RRA '93.

(Code § 2001; YPG ¶ 402K; 5.03; 5.06;507)

See also **estate; generation-skipping tax; gift tax.**

estimated tax If withholding is insufficient to satisfy an individual's federal income tax liability, he or she must pay estimated tax. The estimated tax is based on the amount of federal income tax, including alternative minimum tax, that the individual expects to pay for the taxable year. Any self-employment tax owed is added to this amount, and any allowable credits are subtracted. Individuals pay this tax by using Form 1040ES tax vouchers on a quarterly basis.

Individuals are required to pay estimated tax if they expect to owe at least $500 of federal income tax for the year, and they expect the required annual federal income tax withholding to be less than 90 percent of current-year tax, or 100 percent of the preceding (12-month) year's tax. If estimated tax is owed by an individual, the required estimated tax payment for each of the four quarterly payment periods should be 25 percent of the total estimated amount.

Estates and Trusts

A fiduciary of an estate or trust (e.g., an estate's executor or administrator) or the trustee of a trust is required to make estimated federal income tax payments in the same manner as individuals. Form 1041ES is used to make these estimated tax payments. However, an estate is not required to pay estimated tax in the first two years of its existence. Also, a fiduciary may elect to assign portions of a trust's estimated tax payments to trust beneficiaries.

(Code § 6654; CCH ¶ 40,450)

See also **withholding.**

exchange This is a reciprocal transfer of property, as distinguished from a transfer solely for cash, which generally constitutes a sale. Such transactions may qualify for nonrecognition-of-gain treatment if conditions specified in the Internal Revenue Code are met. However, if a cash payment is made in such a transfer, usually referred to as boot, it will not necessarily prevent the transfer from qualifying for nonrecognition treatment.

(YPG 2.02)

See also **boot; capital assets; tax-free exchanges.**

F

fair market value This is the price that a willing buyer and a willing seller would agree to with respect to a transfer of property, assuming neither is under compulsion to buy or sell. Property may have a fair market value even though it does not have a willing buyer.

However, fair market value cannot be based on assumptions or on a forced sale of property. In general, actual sales of property on the open market are considered reliable and the best evidence of a property's fair market value.

Fannie Mae securities These are privately issued, long-term bonds that are guaranteed by the Federal National Mortgage Association (FNMA). They are general-obligation debentures requiring a minimum $10,000 investment. Principal on these obligations is usually paid monthly along with interest.

(YPG 2.02)

federal obligations. See specific type (e.g., **Treasury bills, Treasury bonds and notes, US savings bonds**).

FHLMC securities See **"Freddie Mac" securities.**

fiduciary This term refers to the trustee of a trust or the executor or administrator of an estate.

See also **estate; trust.**

fixed-income investments See **bond; federal obligations.**

flower bonds These are a special type of US Treasury bonds issued in a limited amount at a deep discount from par (face) value. On the death of the holder of these bonds, they can be redeemed at par value plus accrued interest, but only if the proceeds are applied toward payment of the holder's federal estate taxes. The value of such bonds generally must be included in the holder's taxable estate.

See also **estate.**

FNMA securities See **Fannie Mae securities.**

foreign tax credit This is a credit available to US taxpayers, subject to certain limitations and adjustments prescribed in the tax law, for income tax (or amounts paid in lieu of income tax) paid or accrued during a year to a foreign country or US possession (Code §§ 901 et seq.; CCH ¶ 28,441). A foreign tax credit is also available for purposes of the alternative minimum tax (AMT).

See **alternative minimum tax (AMT).**

Freddie Mac securities These are pass-through bonds that are privately insured by the Federal Home Loan Mortgage Corporation (FHLMC) and not guaranteed by the US government. In general, these securities involve a $25,000 minimum purchase price and guarantee the payment of interest, but not necessarily the payment of principal.

(YPG 2.02)

G

gain or loss See **basis; capital gains and losses.**

general business credit Under current tax law, business-related tax credits are combined in a general business credit. Among the credits included in the general business credit are the low-income housing credit and the investment tax credit, to the extent that it is still available to a taxpayer. The investment credit, applicable to a taxpayer's qualified investments in eligible business property, was repealed for most property placed in service after 1985.

Credit Computation

Computation of this credit involves combining the separate business credits, including any available carrybacks and carryovers, into the combined credit; applying the combined credit on a dollar-for-dollar basis up to the limit specified in the Internal Revenue Code; and carrying back any unused combined credit back 3 years and, if necessary, carrying forward such unused credit for 15 years, applying it on a first-in, first-out (FIFO) basis.

Credit Limit

Only a limited amount of a taxpayer's federal income tax liability can be offset by the general business credit. For post-1986 taxable years, the credit limit for individuals and S corporations is the lesser of the taxpayer's first $25,000 in net regular tax liability plus 75 percent of the excess of that liability over $25,000, or the amount by which that liability exceeds the taxpayer's tentative minimum tax under the alternative minimum tax (AMT) rules.

(Code §§ 38, 39; CCH ¶ 4200, ¶ 4300)

generation-skipping tax   This is a tax generally applicable to a trust having more than one generation of beneficiaries. It applies to generation-skipping transfers, which involve taxable distributions and/or taxable terminations, with respect to a generation-skipping trust or equivalent arrangement. The unified rate schedule applicable for estate and gift tax purposes also applies in computing this tax.

RRA '93.   RRA '93 restores the top estate and gift tax and generation-skipping tax rates of 53 percent and 55 percent, applicable to transfers of more than $2.5 million and $3 million, respectively. The restoration is effective for decedents dying and gifts made after December 31, 1992. See the discussion in the Foreword on RRA '93.

(Code § 2613; YPG 5.03; 5.04.E)

See also **trust.**

gift property, basis.   See **basis.**

gift tax   This is an excise tax on transfers of property (generally, anything of value) by an individual (donor) during his or her life. The tax is generally imposed on the donor and determined by reference to all gifts made. A donee may, however, be liable for gift tax on a gift received, if the donor did not pay the tax. The gift tax is determined under the unified estate and gift tax schedule.

(Code §§ 2501–2505; YPG 5.03; 5.08; 10.02)

See also **estate tax.**

"Ginnie Mae" securities.   See **Government National Mortgage Association (GNMA) securities.**

government bonds and securities   See **federal obligations.**

Government National Mortgage Association (GNMA) securities   These are mortgage-backed pass-through securities, referred to as "Ginnie Maes," guaranteed by the Government National Mortgage Association (GNMA), an agency of the federal government. In general, the underlying mortgages are insured by the Federal Housing Administration (FHA) or the Veterans Administration (VA), and the cash flow for investors is backed by the taxing power and the full faith and credit of the federal government.

$25,000 is the minimum investment in these securities, which offer liquidity in that they can readily be sold on the secondary market. Their prices fluctuate and may drop sharply as interest rates rise, since rates paid on alternative investments are then generally more attractive. Also, if interest rates fall, many of the underlying mortgages are likely to be prepaid, cutting the Ginnie Mae investor's interest income. Prices also are unlikely to rise as sharply on Ginnie Maes compared to other types of security investments, since many investors will not pay a premium for a security that returns a portion of principal monthly.

(YPG 2.02)

grantor trust See **Clifford trust; trust.**

gross income The Internal Revenue Code specifies that gross income is income from whatever source derived, unless a specific exclusion (under Code Sections 101–34) applies.

(Code § 61; CCH ¶ 5502)

guarantor An individual who guarantees a debt of another party is treated for income tax purposes as if he or she is making that loan directly. Accordingly, on the guarantor's payment of the debt the loss resulting is an ordinary loss if incurred in connection with his or her trade or business. Otherwise, the loss is treated as a short-term capital loss.

(Code § 166; CCH ¶ 10,502)

H

hedging transactions These are transactions used to protect against losses due to changes in the price of a commodity used in a taxpayer's trade or business, which is in inventory or to be delivered in the future. Such transactions generally result in ordinary income or loss for the taxpayer.

(Code § 1233; CCH ¶ 32,290)

See also **capital gains and losses; commodity futures.**

hobby losses The hobby loss rules apply to individual taxpayers and S corporations. These rules prohibit such taxpayers from taking deductions attributable to an activity not engaged in for profit, with certain exceptions. The exceptions are deductions otherwise allowable, such as interest and property taxes, which are allowable if the activity was conducted for profit, to the extent that the activity's gross income for the taxable year exceeds the otherwise allowable deductions.

For taxable years after 1986, a taxpayer's activity is presumed to be engaged in for profit when a profit is realized in at least three out of five consecutive taxable years ending with the current taxable year. For activities related to horses, a profit must be shown in two out of seven consecutive years.

A taxpayer may elect to suspend this presumption and thus may generally extend the statute of limitations on any related deficiency for at least two years after the due date of the last year in the 5-year or 7-year period. In general, a taxpayer makes this election by filing a statement with the Internal Revenue Service no later than three years after the taxable year in which the activity began. (Code § 183; CCH ¶ 12, 170; YPG 7.01 et seq.)

holding period See **capital gains and losses.**

home equity debt See **qualified residence interest.**

home, purchase of See **mortgage.**

I

IDCs See **intangible drilling and developmental costs.**

improvements See **basis.**

income tax deductions See **adjusted gross income.**

indemnitor See **guarantor**

individual retirement account (IRA) In general, this is a trust established in writing for the exclusive benefit of an individual and his or her beneficiaries. Financial institutions, such as banks, generally serve as trustees for these accounts. Self-employed individuals are allowed to establish IRA accounts referred to as simplified employee plans (SEPs).

Under IRA arrangements, the individual must be 100 percent vested in the account, and his or her contributions must be in cash and limited to a maximum of $2,000 for a taxable year, except in the case of a rollover. The trust's assets cannot be invested in life insurance contracts and usually cannot be commingled with other assets.

If the individual's entire interest in the account is not distributed to him or her by April 1 of the calendar year immediately following the calendar year in which he or she reaches age 70 ½, he or she must then begin to receive distributions. In general, these distributions must be payable over the life of the individual, the joint lives of the individual and a designated beneficiary, or over a specified period that does not exceed the individual's life expectancy or the joint life expectancies of the individual and the designated beneficiary. If an individual dies after payments have begun under these rules, his or her account balance must be paid out on at least the same schedule as the payment method selected by the decedent. If the individual dies before payouts from the account begin, the account balance must be distributed within five years, unless one of the following is true:

- Payments begin within one year of death to the decedent's designated beneficiary over that beneficiary's life or a period up to that beneficiary's life expectancy.
- The beneficiary is the individual's surviving spouse, and payments begin by the date that the decedent would have reached age 70 ½ and are payable over the surviving spouse's life or over a period up to that spouse's life expectancy.

In general, IRA investments in collectibles such as art and antiques are treated as taxable distributions from the IRA. Also, IRA account funds are included in the estate of a participant for estate tax purposes.

IRA Contributions

An eligible individual may make a contribution to an IRA equal to the lesser of $2,000 or 100 percent of his or her compensation. For taxable years beginning after 1986, the full annual deduction for IRA contributions is available if either of the following conditions holds:

- Neither the individual nor his or her spouse (for married individuals filing a joint tax return) is an active participant in a qualified retirement plan, qualified annuity plan, tax-sheltered annuity, governmental plan, or simplified employee pension (SEP) plan.
- The individual's adjusted gross income (AGI) is not more than
  - $25,000 for single individuals.
  - $40,000 for married couples filing joint returns.
  - $0 for married individuals filing separate returns.

If an individual or his or her spouse is an active participant in a qualified plan and his or her AGI exceeds the applicable amount, the $2,000 deduction is phased out. Under the phaseout, no deduction for IRA contributions is available if the AGI is:

- $50,000 for joint return filers.
- $35,000 for single individuals.
- $10,000 for married individuals filing separate returns.

An individual who is not eligible to take the maximum $2,000 IRA deduction may still make IRA contributions on a nondeductible basis. Any nondeductible contributions made are generally not taxed when recovered in a distribution from the IRA.

An IRA contribution for a given taxable year may be made until the due date of the individual's tax return for that year, not including filing extensions. The maximum tax-deductible IRA contribution may be increased if the individual also contributes to an IRA for a nonworking spouse with whom he or she files a joint tax return. Subject to the deduction limitations described, the maximum deductible annual contribution to IRAs for an individual and his or her spouse is the lesser of 100 percent of compensation or $2,250. The IRA contribution under these circumstances can be divided between the spousal accounts as desired, except that the maximum contribution to either account cannot exceed $2,000.

IRA rollovers. An IRA participant may avoid income tax on certain distributions from qualified retirement plans by rolling over all or part of such a distribution to an IRA within 60 days of the date of the distribution. Except for nondeductible employee contributions, the rollover amount is unlimited. Also, a rollover may be made even if the participant can make tax-deductible IRA contributions.

Excess IRA contributions. If an individual makes a contribution to an IRA, other than a qualifying rollover, that exceeds the statutory contribution limits, a penalty tax applies. The penalty tax is 6 percent of the amount of the excess contribution, unless such excess is returned to the individual by the income tax return due date (including filing extensions) for the taxable year in which such excess contribution is made. Unless the excess contribution is returned by this date, the IRA contributor is liable for the penalty tax for the year in which the excess contribution is made, and also for later taxable years until the contribution is corrected.

Correction is made through repayment of the excess contribution or the making of contributions less than the maximum deductible amount in later taxable years. The 6 percent penalty tax does not apply to nondeductible after-tax IRA contributions, however.

Taxation of IRAs

In general, like other qualified retirement plans, an IRA is not taxable on its earnings. IRA distributions to the participant are subject to tax. The full amount of such a distribution must be included in the participant's gross income, except for any part of such distribution representing a return of nondeductible after-tax IRA contributions.

A receipt of an IRA distribution may avoid being taxed on that distribution if its full amount is rolled over into another IRA, or if the distribution is the full amount of the IRA account and represents only amounts rolled over from a qualified plan. A tax-free rollover is also available for part of a taxpayer's IRA distribution.

Premature IRA Distributions

Premature distributions are subject to a penalty tax of 10 percent of the amount distributed. An IRA distribution is premature if it is made before the participant reaches age 59 ½, unless it is made due to his or her death or disability, or it is made as part of a series of substantially equal periodic payments over the life or life expectancy of the participant and his or her designated beneficiary, or joint life and last survivor life expectancy.

Required IRA Distributions

A 15 percent penalty tax applies if required distributions are not made from a qualified retirement plan, including an IRA. In general, distributions are required to begin by April 1 of the calendar year following the year in which the participant reaches age 70 ½, and, in the event of the participant's death, the remaining IRA account balance must be distributed within a specified time period. Unless such distributions are made, a penalty tax of 50 percent of the difference between the amount distributed and the required distribution must be paid. The penalty tax may be waived, however, if the Internal Revenue Service is satisfied that there is reasonable cause for the failure to make the required distribution.

(Code § 408; CCH ¶ 18,902; YPG 4.01)

See also **individual retirement annuity; qualified retirement, profit-sharing, etc., plans.**

individual retirement annuity This individual retirement arrangement involves a policy or endowment contract issued by an insurance company. The annual premium under such a policy or contract cannot exceed $2,000. The distribution rules applicable to individual retirement accounts (IRAs) also apply to these arrangements. See **individual retirement account (IRA).**

inflation This can be defined as an increase in available money and credit in excess of available goods, resulting in sharp and continuing price rises.

The effects of inflation usually include an increase in the values of hard assets, such as real estate and precious metals, a decrease in the values of inflation-sensitive investments, such as fixed-rate bonds and mortgage-backed securities (e.g., Ginnie Mae securities), and a decline in the purchasing power of currency. Tax bracket "creep" also results, with taxpayers pushed into higher tax brackets as the dollar amounts of income received increase with inflation. An inflation adjustment is allowed under the Internal Revenue Code with respect to certain items; the personal exemption after 1989 is an example.

See also **bond; federal obligations; Government National Mortgage Association (GNMA) securities.**

inheritance This represents a legacy or bequest in money or property from a decedent.

See also **estate; estate tax; gift tax.**

initial public offering (IPO) This is an offering of newly issued stock of a corporation that previously was privately held or is starting up, designed to raise capital from the public. Such an offering generally appeals to growth-oriented investors and is a speculative investment that involves a high degree of risk.

installment and deferred-payment sales When property is sold, a taxpayer usually must recognize gain or loss at the time of sale. However, if a taxpayer is eligible to use the installment method, tax on the sale can be deferred, and gain is recognized in proportion to the installment payments received. Eligible taxpayers are dealers in personal property who regularly use the installment method and taxpayers who sell other property with at least one payment due after the taxable year during which the sale occurs.

The installment method is not available for sales of publicly traded property, such as stocks and bonds, and sales made under a revolving credit plan.

The rules governing installment sales have been changed several times under recent tax legislation. Under the 1986 Tax Reform Act (TRA '86), Internal Revenue Code § 453C was enacted, providing a "proportionate disallowance" rule. The 1987 Revenue Act (RA '87) generally repealed this rule, and further changes were made by the 1988 Technical and Miscellaneous Revenue Act ('88 TAMRA).

Code § 453C was a timing provision designed to accelerate gain on such sales under certain circumstances. Under its proportionate disallowance rule, a taxpayer's annual installment sale gross profit depended on the taxpayer's outstanding debt. The purpose of this provision was to discourage tax deferral through the use of installment sales. It denied installment sale reporting for gains on sales of property to the extent that the taxpayer had a certain ratio of debt to assets in the sale year and subsequent years. This provision was repeated by RA '87, but still applies to nondealer real-property installment obligations from dispositions after August 16, 1986, in taxable years beginning before January 1, 1988, where a taxpayer has "allocable installment indebtedness" after such date. This provision does not apply to nondealer real-property installment obligations from dispositions in taxable years beginning after December 31, 1987. A taxpayer may avoid the § 453C rules by electing to have the RA '87 rules apply.

The rules concerning applicable installment obligations (AIOs) for sales after February 28, 1986, made in a taxable year before the first taxable year ending after December 31, 1986, were changed by '88 TAMRA. These AIOs are deemed created on the first day of the taxpayer's first taxable year ending after December 31, 1986. The TAMRA changes apply as if they were enacted immediately before RA '87.

AIOs Defined

AIOs are obligations, that is, installment sale receivables, from installment sales of the following property:

1. Personal property that a taxpayer regularly sells or disposes of on the installment method.
2. Real property held by a taxpayer for sale to customers in the ordinary course of a trade or business under the installment method.
3. Real property used in taxpayer's trade or business, or held for the production of rental income, if the property's sale price exceeds $150,000.

Summary of Section 453C Rules

If a taxpayer has entered into an installment sale transaction, since the sale constitutes a gain and a portion of the sale price is to be received in a later taxable year, the taxpayer may defer recognition of part of the gain by determining a contract price and a gross profit percentage. The *gross profit percentage* is the ratio of the gain on the sale to the contract price and is applied to the amount of principal in each payment to arrive at the taxable gain in each payment.

The taxpayer next determines *average quarterly indebtedness* (AQI), a term that will be defined in regulations to be issued by the Internal Revenue Service. This determination generally involves all of the taxpayer's indebtedness, except for indebtedness with respect to which personal-use property is the security.

The face amount of all installment obligations outstanding at the end of the taxable year is then determined, excluding installment obligations from the sale of personal-use property. Then the sum of the adjusted basis of all the taxpayer's assets other than installment obligations and personal-use property is determined.

AII Calculation

After the preceding steps have been completed, the taxpayer can calculate "allocable installment indebtedness" (AII). AII is the portion of AIOs treated as payments received with respect to installment sales at the end of the taxable year. This calculation involves dividing the face amount of AIOs outstanding at year end by the sum of the face amount of all installment obligations and the adjusted basis of all of the taxpayer's assets other than installment obligations, multiplying by AQI, and subtracting the amount of AIOs deemed received in earlier taxable years.

Dealer Disposition Rules

Under current law, these rules apply to dispositions of property by dealers after December 31, 1987. They provide that the installment method is not available for dealer dispositions, except for farm property and sales to individuals of time-shares and residential lots.

A dealer disposition is defined as any disposition of personal property by an individual regularly selling or otherwise disposing of personal property of the same type using the installment method, and real property held by the taxpayer for sale to customers in the ordinary course of the taxpayer's trade or business.

Nondealer Real-Property Installment Obligations

Rules are provided for these obligations, arising from dispositions of real property used in the taxpayer's trade or business or held for the production of rental income, if the sale price of such property is more than $150,000. After December 31, 1988, these rules apply to dispositions of any property if the sale price exceeds $150,000. Excepted from these rules are installment obligations from dispositions of personal property, of personal-use property by individuals, of property used in the trade or business of farming, and of time-shares and residential lots.

Part of such an obligation is treated under "pledge" rules as payments received when the obligation secures an indebtedness. Thus, if a taxpayer pledges such an obligation to secure a debt, the taxpayer is considered to have been paid and to have received the amount of that debt.

Also, interest is required to be paid on the deferred tax liability relation to such an obligation under certain circumstances. If such an obligation is outstanding at the close of the taxpayer's taxable year, and the face amount of all such obligations of the taxpayer arising during and outstanding at the end of that year are more than $5,000,000, the taxpayer must add interest on the deferred tax liability to the tax payable for that year.

(Code § § 453, 453A, 453C; CCH ¶ 21,402, ¶ 21,450, ¶ 21,492)

installment loans These are typically consumer loans, such as for the purchase of an automobile, that are repaid through equal monthly payments over the loan term. They may be either secured or unsecured, and a typical term is 12, 24, 36, 48, or 60 months.

insurance In general, this is a contract in which one party (typically an insurance company) agrees to guarantee or indemnify another party against loss arising from a specified event, such as death in the case of life insurance, or

destruction of property in the case of property and casualty insurance. Premiums for insurance policies may be deductible for tax purposes if they are paid in connection with a trade or business activity of the taxpayer.
(Code § 162; CCH ¶ 8450; YPG 5.01 et seq.)
See also **casualty losses; involuntary conversion; life insurance.**

intangible drilling and development costs (IDCs) Costs of developing properties on which oil, gas, or geothermal production activities occur are generally added to their adjusted bases. A deduction is available for such costs, referred to as intangible drilling and development costs (IDCs).

In general, the taxpayer-producer may elect to deduct IDCs currently rather than adding them to a property's basis. This election is made by deducting such costs on the tax return for the first taxable year in which they are paid or incurred. An election to capitalize IDCs is deemed made if the deduction election is not made with respect to such costs. Either election is binding on a taxpayer for all subsequent taxable years.
(Code § 612; CCH ¶ 24,540; YPG ¶ 2.04F)

AMT Preference

For post-1986 taxable years, US IDCs constitute a preference for individuals and corporations for purposes of the alternative minimum tax (AMT). This preference is, in general, equal to the amount by which excess IDCs exceed 65 percent of a property's net income. *Excess* IDCs are an amount by which the IDCs deducted for the taxable year exceed the amount deductible if the IDCs had been capitalized and deducted ratably over a 120-month period.
(Code § 57(a); CCH ¶ 5300; YPG 6.01.C; 6.03.B)
See also **AMT preferences; tax shelters.**

interest This is a charge for borrowing money and generally is a percentage of the amount borrowed. Its tax deductibility depends on the purpose for the borrowing (i.e., business, investment, or personal reasons). Statutory limits apply to the deduction of investment and personal (consumer) interest.

Tracing Rules

In temporary and proposed regulations, the Internal Revenue Service has provided tracing rules relating to the deductibility of interest expense incurred by taxpayers. These rules are generally effective with respect to interest paid or accrued in taxable years beginning after 1986. Under these rules, deductibility is determined on the basis of how the proceeds of a taxpayer's borrowings are used; the source of such borrowings is usually irrelevant. Qualified residence interest, which relates to mortgages on a taxpayer's principal residence or home equity loans (subject to statutory limits), is exempt from these rules.

Proceeds of borrowings are traced to specific expenditures made by the taxpayer under these rules. For example, if a taxpayer obtains a loan to purchase an auto to be used for personal purposes, the loan interest is treated as personal interest subject to deduction limits. If a taxpayer obtains a loan to finance an investment, such as a purchase of securities, the loan interest is treated as investment interest, which also is subject to deduction limits.

(Code § 163; Temp. Reg. § 1.163-8T; CCH ¶ 9102; YPG 3.01 et seq.)

See also **investment interest.**

interest-free loans   Lenders must include in gross income interest that is forgone on certain loans during a taxable year, if no interest is charged or interest is charged at a below-market rate with respect to such loans. Borrowers are entitled to a deduction for the interest forgone or the below-market interest. Deductibility of such interest, however, may be limited if it constitutes consumer interest or investment interest. The income and deduction amounts are generally governed by the original issue discount (OID) rules.

In general, these rules apply to term loans made after June 6, 1984, and demand loans outstanding after June 6, 1984, that are taxable gifts, compensation, dividends, or motivated by tax avoidance. They are not applicable to gift loans of less than $100,000 or to outstanding loans that, in the aggregate, are less than $10,000, unless they are motivated by tax avoidance. If such loans are renegotiated, extended, or revised after June 6, 1984, they are treated as new loans subject to these rules.

A demand loan is a below-market loan under these rules if no interest is charged or the rate is lower than the applicable federal rate (AFR). A term loan is a below-market loan if the loan amount is more than the present value of all loan payments as determined on the loan date using the AFR.

(Code § § 7872, 163; CCH ¶ 44.856, ¶ 9102; YPG 3.08)

internal rate of return   This is a method that can be used by an investor to determine the return on an investment. It is typically used in evaluating real estate investments and represents the effect of discounting. To arrive at this rate, the investor identifies the date of an investment in which he or she has equity and the dates that income amounts, such as sale proceeds, tax benefits, and cash flow, are expected from the investment. The investor then estimates a rate of return from the investment and uses that rate to determine the present values of the funds invested and the future income. Through calculations using different rates of return, the investor arrives at equal present values for the invested funds and future income. The rate ultimately determined through these calculations is the actual rate of return for the investment.

inter vivos trust This is a trust created during the grantor's (maker's) lifetime.
See also **trust.**

intestacy If a decedent dies *intestate,* he or she has no will. In such a case, the probate court appoints a personal representative to oversee the payment of creditors' claims, estate and income taxes, and the distribution of the estate's assets. The court may also appoint other individuals in administering the estate, such as attorneys, accountants, and appraisers. The attendant costs incurred may greatly deplete the estate's assets.
See also **estate.**

investment interest Except for corporations, taxpayers are allowed to deduct interest paid on funds borrowed for investment purposes. Such interest may be deducted, however, only to the extent of the taxpayer's net investment income for the year. Any investment interest exceeding the deduction limit is subject to a phased-in disallowance and may be carried forward indefinitely.

From 1987 to 1990, the investment interest disallowance is:

* The excess of investment income over the $10,000 allowance (or $5,000 for married persons filing separate tax returns) granted under prior law.
* The "applicable percentage" (80 percent for 1989 and 90 percent for 1990) of investment interest up to the $10,000 (or $5,000) allowance.

If interest is incurred in a trade or business activity in which the taxpayer does not materially participate, interest expense allocable to that activity constitutes investment interest if the activity is not a passive activity under the passive loss rules (Code § 469). If a loan is obtained to buy or carry an interest in passive activity, the loan interest expense qualifies as investment interest to the extent that it is related to portfolio income.

Net Investment Income

This represents the excess of investment income over investment expenses.
Investment income is

* Interest, dividends, rental, and royalty gross income.
* Portfolio income for purposes of the passive loss rules.
* Gains on disposition of investment property
* Income from a trade or business activity, not constituting a passive activity under the passive loss rules, in which the taxpayer does not materially participate.

Investment expenses are deductible expenses other than interest directly connected with net investment income. Such expenses are those exceeding the limit of 2 percent of adjusted gross income applicable to miscellaneous expenses of individuals.

For purposes of the investment interest deduction limit, net investment income is reduced by passive activity losses allowable under the passive loss rules, except for net losses from rental real estate activities in which the taxpayer actively participates.

RRA '93. Effective for taxable years beginning after December 31, 1992, RRA '93 excludes net capital gain from the definition of investment income for purposes of the computation of a taxpayer's net investment income. Taxpayers are, however, permitted to elect to include net capital gain in investment income and forgo the benefit of the 28 percent top tax rate on capital gains with respect to the amount included.

(Code § 163(d); CCH ¶ 9102; YPG 3.06)

See also **adjusted gross income; passive loss rules.**

investment tax credit (ITC) A credit was available for a taxpayer's qualified investments in eligible business property (Code § 46). This credit was repealed, with certain exceptions, for property placed in service after 1985 (Code § 49). Exceptions are provided for amortizable reforestation costs and for elected qualified progress payments for periods before January 1, 1986. Transition rules were also provided for certain property under construction or reconstruction under contract or on which work began before 1986. To the extent that this credit is still available to a taxpayer, it is combined into a general business credit. The disallowed amount of ITC can no longer be carried forward.

ITC Amount

If a regular 10 percent ITC was taken in a taxable year beginning after June 30, 1987, that credit must be reduced by 35 percent. Any credit carryforwards taken in such taxable years must also be reduced by 35 percent. Thus, the regular 10 percent credit is reduced to 6.5 percent.

Qualified Property

In general, the credit applies to tangible depreciable personal property and to depreciable real property, except buildings and their structural components. Other specific types of qualified property are enumerated in Code § § 46 and 48. The basis of qualified property is cost. For used property, the cost basis is limited to $125,000, or $150,000 for post-1987 taxable years.

Leased Property

Individual taxpayers may claim ITC on qualified leased property if they are in the business of making short-term leases or if they produce or manufacture the

property. The lessor can, however, elect to waive the ITC for new qualified property and allow the lessee to claim it.
(Code § § 46, 47, 48, 49; CCH ¶ 4502 et seq.)

Qualified Investment

ITC is based on qualified investment in property. The *qualified investment* is determined by multiplying the property's basis by an *applicable percentage*. For qualifying property placed in service after 1980, this percentage is 60 percent for three-year property and 100 percent in other classes, as specified in Code § 46(c). Qualified investment is measured prior to the 35 percent reduction required in taxable years beginning after June 30, 1987.

ITC Recapture

When qualified property ceases to be such or is prematurely disposed (or prematurely becomes public utility property), ITC taken with respect to the property may be recaptured in whole or in part. The difference between the ITC originally claimed, including any carryforwards and carrybacks, and the ITC allowed is added to the taxpayer's tax liability for the year in which the property is disposed.

involuntary conversion This occurs when a taxpayer's property is stolen, accidentally destroyed, or taken in condemnation, and the taxpayer receives a payment for the condemnation or insurance proceeds. Property transferred under imminence of condemnation by a governmental unit or threat may also qualify for involuntary conversion treatment. Even if property is sold or transferred voluntarily, it may qualify for involuntary conversion treatment if that property and a condemned property owned by the same taxpayer have a "substantial economic relationship," constituting a single economic unit. The sale, exchange, or destruction of livestock as a result of disease also qualifies for involuntary conversion treatment.

The following rules apply where payment is made for property condemned or destroyed by casualty, and the taxpayer replaces it with property that is similar or related in use or service (i.e., functionally the same as the original property):

- If the proceeds received by the taxpayer are less than or equal to the cost of the replacement property, gain is not recognized.
- If the proceeds exceed the replacement property's cost, gain is only partially recognized, (i.e., only to the extent of the excess proceeds).
- Any loss on an involuntary conversion is recognized.

These rules providing for nonrecognition of gain in whole or part apply only if all the following conditions hold:

* The replacement of the involuntarily converted property takes place within a specified time limit.
* The replacement property qualifies as replacement property.
* The taxpayer elects to have involuntary conversion treatment apply.

Also, if property is converted *directly* into replacement property similar or related in use or service, no gain is recognized.

Time Limit

For the nonrecognition-of-gain rules to apply, where property is converted into money or property not similar or related in use or service, a replacement with qualified property must be made during a period:

1. Beginning on the earlier of
   * The date on which the involuntarily converted property was destroyed, condemned, or seized.
   * The earliest date of imminence or threat of condemnation or seizure.
2. Ending on one of the following:
   * Two years after the end of the first taxable year in which any gain is realized.
   * A later date approved by the Internal Revenue Service on the application of the taxpayer, based on reasonable cause.

This time limit does not apply, however, if property is converted *directly* into similar property or property related in service or use. Also, a three-year replacement rule applies with respect to condemnation of real property held for productive use in a trade or business or for investment.

Qualified Property

To qualify for involuntary conversion treatment, replacement property must be:

1. Similar or related in use or service to the property converted, except for condemned real property held for investment or for use in a trade or business.
2. Held on the date of the conversion of the original property, if acquired before that date.

3. Purchased as a replacement for the original property.

4. Acquired other than by gift.

(Code § 1033; CCH ¶ 31,540)

See also **insurance.**

irrevocable trust   This trust arrangement involves a completed gift at the time the grantor (maker) transfers property into the trust. Once the transfer is completed, the grantor's powers and ability to act with respect to the property are limited, as the grantor has no reversionary interest and has minimal power with respect to the operation of the trust.

Such a trust may be desirable if the grantor is concerned with minimizing estate taxes by transferring a portion of his or her assets before death. The appreciation on such assets when in the trust usually escapes estate and gift taxes.

(YPG 10.02)

See also **estate tax; gift tax; trust.**

J

joint-and-survivor arrangements   There are a number of joint-and-survivor arrangements.

Joint-and-Survivor Annuities

These annuities provide for smaller regular payments than straight-life annuities (for one annuitant), since the payout is over a longer period of time. When the annuitant dies, payments continue at a reduced level to the spouse or other party selected by the annuitant.

(YPG 5.04.B.4)

See also **annuities.**

Joint-and-Survivor Life Insurance

Under this type of life insurance policy, marriage partners can both be insured. The payment on the insurance policy is made on the death of the surviving spouse. This type of policy was prompted by the unlimited martial deduction allowed for estate tax purposes. This is because the estate of the spouse who dies first can pass tax-free to the surviving spouse. Accordingly, insurance covering an estate's tax and expenses is not necessary until the surviving spouse dies.

(YPG 5.01)

See also **life insurance.**

Joint-and-Survivor Retirement Plan Benefits

The Employee Retirement Income Security Act of 1974 (ERISA) requires employer plans to cover married employees under a joint-and-survivor pension. Thus, after the death of an employee covered under a plan, plan benefits are paid to his or her spouse or other beneficiary. These post-death payments cause the benefits of this annuity to be less than those of a simple life annuity.

If a covered employee dies before retirement, ERISA requires that the employee's surviving spouse be covered under the employer's plan, as long as the employee and his or her spouse were married for at least 12 months before the employee's death.

(YPG 4.03)

See also **annuities.**

joint tenancies   Joint tenants hold an undivided interest in any asset, usually bank accounts, real estate, or securities, and each such tenant is entitled to his or her share of income produced by the asset and to its full use and disposition. This undivided interest exists whether or not the tenants made equal contributions toward the acquisition of the asset.

This form of ownership of property is most frequently used by married couples. The principal reason for this is that, when one joint tenant (e.g., a spouse) dies, the decedent's interest in the property passes to the other joint tenant(s) (e.g., the surviving spouse) without inclusion in the decedent's estate in probate.

Despite the fact that this form of ownership is very popular, it offers no federal income, estate, gift, or state tax advantages. How and when tax is imposed with respect to such arrangements depends on the type of asset involved. For example, gift tax is due on the establishment of a joint tenancy in registered marketable securities, but gift tax is not due with respect to US savings bonds held in joint tenancy until the joint tenancy is ended. A significant tax disadvantage is that multiple-estate taxation can result from a joint tenancy, since all property subject to the joint tenancy is included in the estate of each joint tenant upon his or her death. However, a surviving spouse may be able to obtain an exclusion for property held by a deceased spouse as a joint tenant.

When an individual disposes of his or her interest in property held in joint tenancy by sale or gift, his or her joint tenants still hold the property as joint tenants. The new owner of the interest acquired by purchase or gift, however, is not a joint tenant, but a tenant in common, with respect to the property.

It can be difficult for a joint tenant to alter or end a joint tenancy and recover his or her initial contribution to the arrangement. Such an alteration or termination can be accomplished through a court action brought by one or more joint tenants, a court order in a divorce proceeding, or through the agreement of the joint tenants. The inherent difficulty in such an arrangement is that, typically, a joint tenant making a larger contribution to the joint tenancy makes an irrevocable gift to joint tenant(s) who made smaller contributions. *See also* **estate tax; tenancy by the entirety; tenancy in common.**

junk bonds These bonds, also commonly referred to as "high-yield" bonds, offer higher yields (i.e., interest payments) than higher-quality, investment-grade bonds as rated by the major bond rating services, Moody's and Standard & Poor's. As a rule of thumb, they are bonds that have a Moody's rating of BB or lower or a Standard & Poor's rating of Bb or lower. Many of these bonds have been issued in corporate leveraged buyouts, and many are also components of "high-yield" bond mutual funds.

(YPG 2.01)

See also **bond funds; mutual funds.**

K

Keogh (HR 10) plans A self-employed person is permitted to make tax-deductible contributions to qualified retirement and profit-sharing plans, referred to as Keogh or HR 10 plans, established for himself or herself and his or her employees. The tax on the income earned on the assets of such plans is deferred, as it is not taxed until it is withdrawn.

For purposes of such plans, a *self-employed* person is any person conducting a trade or business, including sole proprietors, independent contractors, and partners.

Coverage is restricted for *owner-employees,* defined as 100 percent owners of an unincorporated business, or partners having a capital or profits interest in a partnership of over 100 percent. These individuals cannot be covered under such plans unless all of the full-time employees of the business or partnership who are at least 21 years old or who have completed one year of service are covered.

Contribution Limit

Contributions to such plans are limited by statute. The applicable limit depends on whether the plan is a defined benefit plan or a defined contribution plan.

In a defined benefit plan, the participant's benefits are set at a certain amount. In a defined contribution plan, benefits are based on amounts paid into each participant's plan account, plus any allocable income or gains and forfeitures of other participants' accounts, minus allocable expenses and losses.

For defined contribution plans, owner-employees are allowed to contribute the lesser of $30,000 or an effective rate of 20 percent of earned income for the year for themselves. For this purpose, *earned income* is net self-employment earnings from a business or profession in which personal services are performed. In the case of a creator of property, such as an author, net earnings from the property and ordinary gain are taken into account.

For defined benefit plans, contributions are limited to the lesser of $90,000, adjusted for inflation, or the average compensation of the participant for his or her three highest-paid consecutive years.

Deduction Limit

Contributions made by self-employed persons on behalf of their employees are fully deductible within the deduction limits applicable to qualified plans. In determining the amount of that deduction, the self-employed person determines his or her own allowable contribution deduction and subtracts this amount to arrive at adjusted gross income. The resulting contribution amount for the employees is then treated as a deductible business expense.

(Code § § 401, 415; CCH ¶ 17,502 et seq.; YPG 4.02)

See also **adjusted gross income.**

kiddie tax Unearned income, from whatever source (such as interest and dividends), of a minor child under age 14 can be taxed at the top marginal tax rate of his or her parents. It will be so taxed if that unearned income exceeds the sum of the basic $600 standard deduction allowable for dependents and the greater of $600 or any itemized deductions directly related to that income. This $600 standard deduction is adjusted for inflation. (The $600 figures apply for 1993.)

For married individuals filing separate tax returns, the marginal tax rate with the greater amount of taxable income applies. The kiddie tax is computed on Form 8615.

"Allocable Parental Tax"

The determination of such a child's tax requires the parents to compute the "allocable parental tax." In summary, this tax is the excess of (1) the tax imposed on the parent's taxable income if that income included the net unearned income of all of that parent's children, over (2) the income otherwise taxable to the parent.

Parental Election

For taxable years after 1988, a parent may elect to include on the parental tax return the income of a child under age 14 if it is between $500 and $5,000 and made up of only interest and/or dividends (including Alaska Permanent Fund Dividends). For this election to be made, estimated tax payments cannot have been made in the child's name and in the child's taxpayer identification number (TIN), and the child cannot be subject to backup withholding. The election is made by completing Form 8814 and including this form in the parental return.

(Code § 1(i); CCH ¶ 3175 et seq.; YPG 10.01)

L

land If not held for use in trade or business, land qualifies as a capital asset. If used in a trade or business, it qualifies as a § 1231 asset. If it is a § 1231 asset, it may qualify for long-term capital gain treatment, if held for more than one year, or ordinary loss treatment. If held for sale to customers by a dealer in the ordinary course of business, its sale produces ordinary income.

Taxes, mortgage interest, and other charges incurred with respect to unimproved land may be capitalized or deducted at the taxpayer's election. Expenses incurred in clearing land may also be deductible.

Farmers may also deduct expenses for soil and water conservation and erosion prevention costs when paid or incurred with respect to land used in the business of farming. If such expenses are not deducted, they must be capitalized and added to the taxpayer's tax basis for the land.

As a general rule, land does not qualify for depreciation or an allowance for cost recovery. The cost of work such as excavation and grading with respect to roadways placed on land may qualify, however. Costs of landscaping in connection with structures built on land may also qualify.

(Code § § 167, 168, 175, 266, 1221, 1231; CCH ¶ 11,002, ¶ 11,250; YPG 2.01)

See also **accelerated cost recovery system (ACRS); capital gains and losses; capital expenditures; depreciation; modified accelerated cost recovery system (MACRS).**

lease A lease may qualify as a capital asset, a § 1231 asset, or as an ordinary income–producing asset. It qualifies as a capital asset if the property involved is nondepreciable property. It qualifies as a § 1231 asset if the property involved is depreciable property used in a trade or business and held for more than one year. If the taxpayer is in the business of selling leases in the ordinary course of business, a sale of a lease produces ordinary income.

Payments made to a lessee for the reduction of a lease's term or its cancellation generally qualify for capital gain treatment, except to the extent that the depreciation recapture or cost recovery (ACRS or MACRS) rules apply. If a lessor is paid an amount to cancel or alter a lease, the payment constitutes ordinary income.

leasehold improvements Improvements to leased property made by a lessee generally do not produce income for the lessor when the improvement is made or at the end of the lease term. However, leasehold improvements will produce income for the lessor if they are made by the lessee in lieu of the payment of rent. Under these circumstances, the lessor receives income in the amount of the fair market value of the improvements at the time they are made. The lessor, however, is not required to adjust his or her basis for the property as a result of the improvements.

The lessee making leasehold improvements can recover their cost. Under the accelerated cost recovery system (ACRS) (generally applicable to property placed in service after 1980 and before 1987), the lessee recovers the cost of the improvements over the shorter of the applicable ACRS recovery period or the remainder of the lease term on the date the improvement was acquired or completed. Under the modified accelerated cost recovery system (MACRS) (generally applicable to property placed in service after 1986), the cost of leasehold improvements is recovered in the same way as the recovery deduction for the leased property as if it had been placed in service at the same time as the improvements. For this purpose, the MACRS class of the leased property applies. In general, under MACRS, the applicable recovery periods are 27.5 years for residential rental property and 31.5 years for nonresidential real property.

(Code § § 109, 167, 168, 1221, 1231; CCH ¶ 7020, ¶ 11,002, ¶ 11,250, ¶ 12,060, ¶ 32,220, ¶ 32,272)

See also **accelerated cost recovery system (ACRS); capital gains and losses; depreciation; lease; modified accelerated cost recovery system (MACRS); section 1231 assets.**

legacies See **inheritance.**

legal expenses Legal expenses may be deducted for income tax purposes when incurred in connection with a taxpayer's trade, business, or profession. They may also be deductible if they are related to a nonbusiness activity that produces rental or royalty income.

Legal expenses incurred in defending a civil suit related to a taxpayer's business can qualify as a deductible business expense. Legal expenses are deductible as expenses incurred with respect to the production of income when they are incurred in connection with a taxpayer's efforts to obtain an adjustment of property taxes on income-producing real property and securities. Similarly deductible are legal expenses incurred:

- For tax advice with respect to a divorce action.

- In connection with the administration of an estate or trust (unless they are related to tax-exempt income or have been deducted in determining the estate tax).

- In terminating a trust or with respect to trust distributions.

- With respect to a specific income-producing property, such as the recovery of that property or conserving and/or managing that property when it is owned by a minor child.

Nondeductible legal expenses include those incurred in defending title to income-producing property and those incurred in connection with a will contest.

Legal expenses sometimes may constitute capital expenditures that cannot be deducted currently, such as those incurred in obtaining a long-term lease on real property or in seeking a reduction of a property tax assessment.

life annuities See **annuities.**

life estates A life estate is an interest in property that exists during the holder's lifetime and qualifies as a capital asset. If such an interest is acquired by the holder by gift or as a bequest from a decedent, his or her basis for that interest is zero. Consequently, any gain on its sale or exchange is fully taxable to the holder. In the case of a life tenancy in real property, depreciation on such property is deducted over the *property's* useful life, *not* the holder's life expectancy. (Code § § 1001, 1221; CCH ¶ 29,620, ¶ 32,220)

life insurance An individual purchases life insurance to protect his or her dependents or beneficiaries by providing them with income in the event of his or her death. Life insurance is also used to create liquidity in the insured's estate. There are a number of types of life insurance, and certain policies offer income tax advantages, which will be described.

Term Insurance

This is insurance coverage for a specific period of time, and benefits will be paid under such coverage if the insured dies within that period. In general, this is the least expensive form of life insurance and is popular among young persons, enabling them to provide for family needs in the event of their deaths.

Because of its relatively low cost, such insurance offers flexibility to the insured, in that he or she can increase coverage to meet changing needs without a substantial financial burden. A disadvantage of term insurance for some individuals is that, unlike some other types of life insurance, no savings element is present.

Whole Life Insurance

Under this type of insurance coverage, the insured pays a fixed insurance premium during life, and a fixed amount is payable under the policy upon the insured's death. Unlike term insurance, this coverage offers a savings feature.

This feature forces the insured to save, in that the part of the premium paid that is not for straight insurance protection is invested by the insurer. The capital portion of the premiums and the interest earned thereon constitute cash surrender value for the insured. The insured may obtain a loan of this amount from the insurer, or it may be added to the death benefit payable under the policy.

The chief disadvantages of this type of insurance coverage are that the returns on the capital invested are generally much lower than those offered by alternative investments, the cost of this coverage is much higher than for the straight insurance protection of term insurance, and the investment returns and death benefit do not change in response to economic factors such as inflation. The chief advantage of this type of coverage is that premiums are typically at a fixed rate.

Single-Premium Life Insurance

This type of insurance coverage was introduced as an alternative to single-payment annuities, as a result of tax law changes that eliminated the tax advantages of such annuities. Under such coverage, the insured invests a lump sum to finance the policy death benefit and a tax-deferred investment. With respect to such policies, the insured generally can obtain a policy loan at below-market interest rates, tax-free. The tax-advantage aspect of such coverage has been restricted by the Technical and Miscellaneous Revenue Act of 1988 and by the Revenue Reconciliation Act of 1989 (see below).

Variable Life Insurance

This type of life insurance coverage is similar to whole life insurance in that part of the premium paid by the insured is for straight life insurance coverage and the remainder is invested to build up cash surrender value. The difference between these types of policies is that, under a variable life insurance policy, the investment (capital) part of the premium is invested in accordance with the insured's wishes—typically in stocks, bonds, money market funds, or a combination thereof. Depending on the policy terms, the insured may be able to shift his or her investment several times during a year among the investment options offered. This investment flexibility is not available with whole life policies, for which investment returns are based on the insurer's general investment portfolio.

The advantages of such insurance coverage are the investment flexibility, with the opportunity to exceed the investment returns on whole life policies, and tax advantages. The disadvantages of such insurance coverage are its cost, which includes sales commissions, and the amount of the policy's cash surrender value, which can be substantially reduced if losses are incurred with respect to funds invested.

Hybrid Policies

There are a number of types of hybrid life insurance policies. Among these are credit life insurance, modified life insurance, and universal life insurance.

Credit life insurance. When a borrower obtains a loan, this type of coverage may be required to cover the loan balance. This form of life insurance is generally more costly than other forms of life insurance coverage.

Modified life insurance. This type of coverage involves a whole life insurance policy providing for low premiums over the initial term, which may be 5 or 10 years, and an increased premium thereafter.

Universal life insurance. This is a variation on a whole life policy that offers a money market rate based on a specified financial index, such as US Treasury bill rates. Advantages of this type of insurance coverage are superior cash flow, in that the insured can withdraw some of the policy's cash surrender value in the form of dividends, and flexibility, in that additional life insurance coverage may usually be purchased through increased cash surrender value. The disadvantages of this insurance coverage are that it typically offers a low investment return, and the amount of fees charged by insurers are typically higher than those charged on whole life policies or other investment-oriented policies.

Tax Consequences

The Technical and Miscellaneous Revenue Act of 1988 ('88 TAMRA) made significant tax law changes with respect to investment-oriented life insurance policies. The tax consequences with respect to the most popular types of life insurance are as follows:

Term insurance. As noted earlier, term insurance does not involve cash surrender value. Accordingly, a transfer of such a policy to a trust or another person generally is not a taxable event and therefore may be a useful estate planning tool, as in the case of a transfer to a Crummey trust. The policy proceeds are exempt from income tax but are included in the estate of the insured upon the insured's death. (See **Crummey trust.**)

Whole life insurance. Tax deferral on investment income is a key reason for the popularity of whole life insurance coverage. The income earned (i.e., the cash surrender value of the policy over the premium paid by the insured) is taxable upon the insured's surrender of the policy. As is the case with term insurance, policy proceeds are not taxable for income tax purposes but are includable in the insured's estate for estate tax purposes. Gift tax may be incurred if the policy is transferred.

Interest on whole life policy loans may be deductible for tax purposes. Certain limits apply to business-related policy loans. In general, with respect to policy loans over $100, interest paid is deductible under a four-of-seven test (i.e., premiums for the first four of seven policy years are paid by other means than through a policy loan). Also, for individuals, interest on such loans is treated as personal interest, the deductibility of which is limited and totally phased out after 1990.

Single premium life insurance. The tax treatment of investment-oriented life insurance—specifically, single-premium life insurance—was changed by the '88 TAMRA. (See below.)

Universal life insurance. As is the case with other types of life insurance coverage, death benefits under universal policies are not subject to income tax. These benefits are includable in the insured's estate for estate tax purposes. Dividend income on these policies is nontaxable, although interest earned on any reinvested dividends is subject to tax when withdrawn. Interest on a loan against such a policy is deductible if the four-of-seven test is met, or if the loan is a business loan or is made as a result of an unexpected financial emergency.

Variable life insurance. The tax consequences with respect to such insurance policies are similar to those of whole life policies.

Living benefits policies. Some life insurance companies offer policies that allow for the payout of policy face value before the insured's death under certain circumstances. These policies provide the typical death benefit as well as living benefits. The living benefits would cover the costs of medical care and long-time care, usually in cases where the insured develops a terminal or catastrophic illness.

As there has been uncertainty as to the tax treatment of such benefits, the IRS issued proposed regulations dealing with their tax treatment. (See Prop. Reg. § 1.7702–2.) The proposed regulations cover two categories of benefits: "qualified accelerated death benefits" (QADBs), and "additional benefits" (ABs). QADBs are excluded from a recipient's income as they are treated as paid by reason of the insured's death. Also set forth in the proposed regulations are conditions under which ABs can be excluded from a recipient's income.

Life Insurance Policy Provisions of the 1988 Technical and Miscellaneous Revenue Act

Under '88 TAMRA, tax advantages of investment-oriented life insurance policies—specifically single-premium life insurance policies—were restricted. TAMRA focuses on modified endowment contracts.

A *modified endowment contract* is a life insurance contract (under Code § 7702) that does not satisfy a "seven-pay" test. This test is not met if the cumulative amount to be paid under the contract at any time during the first seven contract years is more than the net level premiums payable before that time at which the contract provides for paid-up future benefits after seven level annual premiums are paid. The amount paid under the contract is the total of premiums paid less any amounts received (other than annuity payments) excludable from income. For this purpose, loans or loan repayments are not taken into account. The seven-pay test rules apply only to distributions in the contract year in which the test is not met and later contract years.

If an insurance contract is a modified endowment contract, amounts received are first treated as income and then as a recovery of the basis in the contract, unlike the basis ordering rule otherwise applicable to life insurance contracts. Loans under, or secured by, such contracts are considered amounts received under the contracts according to these rules.

Provisions of the Revenue Reconciliation Act of 1989

The Revenue Reconciliation Act of 1989 provides rules applicable to second-to-die policies, which are also commonly referred to as last-to-die or last survivor policies. Under these rules, if the death benefit is reduced below the lowest death benefit level provided for the first seven years under the insurance contract, the seven-pay test (discussed earlier) is applied as though the contract were originally issued with the reduced death benefit. If the contract fails the seven-pay test, it is treated as a modified endowment contract with respect to distributions made during the contract year in which the death benefit reduction takes place and later years, and also distributions made in anticipation of a reduction in the death benefit (as provided in regulations). These rules apply to life insurance contracts entered into on or after September 14, 1989 (Act § 7647 (b)).

(Code § § 72, 264, 7702; CCH ¶ 6100, ¶ 14,002, ¶ 43,950; YPG 5.01 et seq.)
See also **life insurance loans.**

life insurance loans   Interest on a loan made against a life insurance policy that is added to principal under the contract terms if unpaid when due is nondeductible by a taxpayer on the cash basis.

Interest paid or accrued on a loan made or continued to buy or carry a single-premium life insurance policy, endowment contract, or single-premium annuity contract is nondeductible. Also nondeductible is interest on a loan made to buy or carry life insurance, endowment, or annuity contracts after August 5, 1963, if a systematic plan exists for borrowing the contract's cash surrender value and if the yearly interest payable exceeds $100. However, the interest is deductible if the loan was entered into for business purposes (other than for business life insurance), if the loan was prompted by unexpected financial circumstances, or if four of the first seven annual payments are not paid through use of the loan proceeds.

(Code § 264; CCH ¶ 14,002; YPG 5.02)
See also **cash basis; life insurance.**

limited partnerships See **partnership.**

livestock Sales or involuntary conversions of livestock qualify for capital gain/ordinary loss treatment under Code § 1231 if the livestock, other than cattle and horses, were held for dairy, draft, breeding, or sporting purposes for at least 12 months. For cattle and horses, the holding period must be at least 24 months for § 1231 treatment to apply. The holding period commences on the date that the livestock are acquired, not the date that the livestock are actually placed in service. Livestock are involuntarily converted if their destruction, sale, or exchange is necessitated by disease.

  (Code § § 1033, 1231; CCH ¶ 31,540, ¶ 32,272; YPG 2.01)

living trusts See **inter vivos trust.**

load mutual funds See **mutual funds.**

loans There are a number of types of loans that individuals can enter into. Included among these are home equity loans, installment loans, interest-free loans, life insurance loans, margin loans, mortgage loans, and qualified plan loans. Loan interest paid may be fully or partially deductible, depending on the type of loan involved.

  The most common type of loan entered into by individuals is a consumer loan. Bank account automatic overdrafts, lines of credit, and credit card loans are examples. The deductibility of interest on these loans is limited and totally phased out after 1990. See **interest.**

  There are two basic categories of consumer loans: secured loans and unsecured loans. *Secured loans* are collateralized loans having property as security, such as auto loans and bank savings passbook loans, and are typically paid in monthly installments over 12, 24, 36, or 48-month terms. *Unsecured loans* are not collateralized, with repayment based on the borrower's full faith and credit. These loans typically are also paid in monthly installments.

  (YPG 3.01)

long-term capital gains and losses See **capital gains and losses.**

low-income housing credit This is part of the general business credit allowed under Code § 38. It can be claimed by taxpayers with respect to qualified low-income housing projects that they acquire, construct, or rehabilitate. The credit claimed does not reduce the depreciable basis of qualified low-income housing. Carryforwards and carrybacks of the credit are subject to rules provided in Code § 89. (*Note:* This credit was extended by the Revenue Reconciliation Act of 1989, as will be discussed.)

  If such qualified housing is placed in service after 1987, the rate of credit allowed is the applicable percentage set by the Internal Revenue Service for the month in which it is placed in service. If construction or rehabilitation expenses are more than minimum amounts set for non-federally subsidized low-income housing units, the rate of credit is determined as follows. Under the rate computation, the present value of the 10 annual credit amounts at the start of the credit period is equal to the qualified basis of the low-income housing involved.

A 30 percent rate applies to low-income housing subsidized by the federal government and is applicable in determining the credit rate for existing low-income housing units acquired. This rate also applies to rehabilitation expenses below the minimum rehabilitation requirements for low-income housing incurred before the credit period's initial year.

Claiming the Credit

A taxpayer claims the credit over a 10-year-period that begins with the taxable year in which the qualified housing is placed in service. Alternatively, a taxpayer may elect to have the 10-year period begin in the taxable year following the placed-in-service year. This alternative election is available, however, only if the housing is qualified low-income housing as of the initial year of the 10-year credit period.

The credit for the initial year is reduced to take into account any period during that year in which any units of such qualified low-income housing are not occupied. If the reduction applies, the taxpayer is entitled to a credit in the amount of the reduction in the year following the 10-year credit period (year 11).

Rehabilitation Expenses

For rehabilitation expenses, the low-income housing credit is available only if all expenses incurred during any period of 24 months are at least $2,000 for each low-income housing unit as of the end of the initial year in the credit period.

Interplay with Passive Activity Credit Rules

The low-income housing credit is considered to relate to real estate activities in which the taxpayer materially participates for purposes of the passive activity credit rules. Limitations on passive activity credits from such activities apply to the low-income housing credit.

Qualified Low-Income Housing

To qualify for the low-income housing credit, residential rental property must meet certain requirements. These requirements include certification of the housing project by the Internal Revenue Service, specified low-income tenant occupancy levels, specified gross rent levels, and credit authority from the state in which the project is located.

Credit recapture. The low-income housing credit can be partially recaptured if the housing for which it is claimed fails to meet the qualification requirements for a 15-year period.

RRA '89. The Revenue Reconciliation Act of 1989 extended the low-income housing credit through December 31, 1990, and made miscellaneous changes to the credit. In general, under the Act, the credit is allowed with respect to property financed by tax-exempt bonds issued before 1990 if the property is placed before 1992 and over 10 percent of estimated costs for the project are incurred before January 1, 1990. Some additional costs may be incurred after 1989. For substantial rehabilitation of property, the minimum qualifying expenditure was raised from $2,000 to $3,000 of qualified basis for each low-income housing unit, or 10 percent of adjusted basis, whichever is greater. Also, the credit can be used to offset tax on passive activity income without regard to the phaseout applicable when adjusted gross income exceeds $200,000 (Act § § 7108, 7109).

RRA '93. RRA '93 retroactively extends and makes permanent the low-income housing tax credit, which expired after June 30, 1992. It also makes certain other modifications with respect to the credit. See the Foreword on RRA '93.
(Code § 42; CCH ¶ 4380; YPG 2.04.F)
See also **basis; general business credit; passive loss rules.**

low-interest loans These loans are also referred to as "below-market interest loans." Under Code § 7872, loans with terms providing for no payment of interest or for interest payments below-market rates are recharacterized. Under this provision, such loans are deemed to bear a statutory federal interest rate.
Such loans are considered to involve some form of payment, such as compensation, a contribution to corporate capital, a dividend from a corporation, or a gift (e.g., from the lender to the borrower). Such a payment is then considered to be transferred back from the borrower to the lender as loan interest.
This provision is applicable to

1. Loans having a tax-avoidance purpose.
2. Gift loans.

3. Loans from a corporation to a shareholder.
4. Loans representing compensation:
   a. From party engaging an independent contractor.
   b. Between an employer and an employee.
5. Any loan having a below-market rate of interest where the interest terms have a significant effect on the tax liability of the borrower or the lender.

Gift and Demand Loans

Interest for gift and demand loans is imputed in an amount considered to be transferred from the lender to the borrower on the final day of a calendar year with respect to the loan. With respect to term loans other than gift loans, interest is imputed in an amount equal to the amount of the loan over the present value of all loan payments, as of the date the loan was made.

Special Rules

Special rules apply to employer loans to employees purchasing a new principal place of residence. With respect to such loans, the applicable federal rate as of the purchase contract date controls. Loans by elderly individuals to continuing care facilities under continuing care contracts are also subject to special rules.

Exceptions

Certain de minimis exceptions apply to these rules. With respect to gift loans, there is a $10,000 exception for loans in the nature of compensation or related to a corporate stockholder's holding. Another de minimis rule applies with respect to gift loans between individuals with a total outstanding amount of no more than $100,000. In such cases, the amount considered to be transferred from the borrower to the lender at year end is imputed to the lender, but only up to the amount of the borrower's net investment income for that year. If such income of the borrower is under $1,000, the lender will have no imputed interest income.

A separate set of rules applies under the Internal Revenue Code with respect to unstated interest on deferred payment sales.

(Code § 7872; CCH ¶ 44.856 et seq.; YPG 3.08)

lump-sum distributions (LSDs) A distribution from a qualified plan (e.g., pension or profit-sharing plan) is a lump-sum distribution (LSD) if it involves the full balance in a plan participant's account or, if the participant has accounts in multiple plans of a single employer, the full balance in all accounts of the same type of employer plan.

Withholding on LSDs. Effective for LSDs made after 1992, withholding is required at the rate of 20 percent on any LSD eligible to be rolled over but is not transferred directly (i.e., trustee-to-trustee transfer) to another plan (P.L. 102–318, 7/3/92).

Tax Treatment

In general, for post-1986 taxable years, 10-year averaging is no longer available for LSDs from qualified plans. A phaseout provision applies to pre-1974 capital gains with respect to LSDs. Under the phaseout, a plan participant who is at least age 59 ½ and receives an LSD can elect to have a portion of the LSD constituting pre-1974 plan participation subject to tax at a maximum of 20 percent rate as a capital gain. The applicable phaseout percentages for calendar years 1989, 1990, and 1991 are 75 percent, 50 percent, and 25 percent, respectively.

This is a one-time election concerning taxpayers receiving LSDs from more than one plan. This election applies in determining whether a later plan distribution is eligible for averaging and also for all purposes under the Internal Revenue Code.

Five-year averaging. This averaging is available for a plan participant who is at least age 59 ½ and also to a distributee of a plan participant who is at least age 59 ½ when the distribution is made. The method of computation under this five-year averaging method is the same as under the 10-year averaging method permitted under prior law. If five-year averaging is elected by a plan participant with respect to an LSD, his or her tax is determined as if the LSD has been earned over a five-year period.

A special rule applies to plan participants who attain age 50 before 1986. Under this rule, such a participant can make a one-time election to use five-year averaging, applying current-law tax rates. Such a participant can make a one-time election to use 10-year averaging, even though the participant has not attained age 59 ½, using prior-law tax rates.

These plan participants can also elect capital gain treatment with respect to the LSD portion relating to pre-1974 plan participation, and the five-year phaseout will not apply.

The special rule applies to individuals and estates or trusts receiving an LSD with respect to plan participants attaining age 50 before 1986.

Note: An election to use income averaging with respect to an LSD received before a participant attains age 59 ½ precludes an election otherwise available after the participant attains age 59 ½.

When 10-year averaging is used, the plan participant has to compute tax on post-1986 LSDs at 1986 rates. This means that the pre-1986 zero-bracket amount is applicable.

Under the five-year averaging, tax rates applicable to single individuals must be used. For post-1987 taxable years, the five percent surtax applicable to specified income levels applies in computing the tax on the LSD.

Benefits and elections applicable to LSDs. The amount exempt from tax is:

- The portion of the LSD contributed by the participant.
- If securities are distributed, their unrealized appreciation, unless the plan participant elects, on the tax return on which the LSD is reported, to include such appreciation as part of the LSD and also in the basis of those securities.

Capital gain treatment applies to the portion of the LSD relating to the participant's pre-1974 plan participation. However, effective in 1988, the tax rate advantage applicable to capital gains was phased out. Beginning in 1988, the same tax rates applicable to ordinary income apply to capital gains, with certain exceptions.

The capital gain portion of an LSD is determined using the following formula:

$$\frac{\text{Taxable amount of LSD X Months of pre-1974 plan participation}}{\text{Total months of plan participation}}$$

The ordinary income portion of an LSD is determined using the following formula:

$$\frac{\text{Taxable amount of LSD X Months of post-1973 plan participation}}{\text{Total months of plan participation}}$$

Five-year averaging applies to the portion of an LSD other than the participant's own contributions and amounts relating to pre-1974 plan participation subject to capital gain treatment. However, it also applies to the pre-1974 plan participation amount, and the capital gain treatment of such amount does not apply if the ordinary income election is made. A five-year averaging election can be made only once during a plan participant's lifetime. This election also is *irrevocable.*

A minimum distribution allowance applies to the balance of an LSD, after deduction of the plan participant's contributions and the pre-1974 plan participation amount, but only if that balance is less than $70,000. The minimum distribution allowance is $10,000 less 20 percent of the excess of the taxable amount of the LSD over $20,000, with the following exceptions:

- If the taxable amount of the LSD is less than $20,000, the allowance is 50 percent of that taxable amount.
- The allowance can never go below zero.

The top minimum distribution allowance is 50 percent of the total taxable amount of the LSD, with a ceiling of $10,000. For LSDs of $20,000 or less, only 50 percent is taxable. For taxable LSD amounts over $20,000, this allowance is reduced by $1 for every $5, and no allowance is available if the taxable amount of the LSD is $70,000 or over.

The ordinary income election is a one-time election that applies to the pre-1974 plan participation amount of an LSD. It may provide a tax benefit to a plan participant if the five-year averaging election is made. If this election is not, or cannot, be made, regular tax rules will apply. Typically, this election would be made by a plan participant of at least age 59 ½ if the distribution is large or if the participant is in a high tax bracket.

If an individual was a plan participant before 1974, he or she should compute income tax liability under the available alternatives. This involves computations with and without capital gain treatment, taking into account the potential application of the alternative minimum tax.

Distributions to beneficiaries of participants.   The provisions set forth apply to LSDs received by the beneficiaries of a plan participant. However, the beneficiaries have an additional tax break. This is because such an LSD is tax-exempt up to $5,000 under the death benefit exclusion allowed under the Internal Revenue Code.

Qualified domestic relations order (QDROs).   A distribution from a qualified plan made under a qualified domestic relations order (QDRO) with respect to a plan participant, to the credit of a spouse or former spouse of that participant, qualifies as an LSD.

(Code § 402; CCH ¶ 18,202 et seq.; YPG 4.01 et seq.)

M

margin account This is an account maintained with an investment firm that allows the investor to purchase securities on credit. In effect, use of such an account involves a down payment on a securities purchase. This down payment is the margin amount required to be deposited in the investor's account with the firm. Investment firms typically set minimum margin account balances and required margin percentages to discourage the use of such accounts by small investors. With respect to the balance of the purchase price of a security purchase, the margin requirement can be satisfied by depositing the security so purchased in the investor's account as collateral.

The use of a margin account creates the possibility of magnified gains and losses on securities purchased, as opposed to purchases of securities through standard investment accounts.

(YPG 3.06)

market discount This is the amount by which a bond's stated redemption price exceeds its basis immediately after it is acquired. For bonds issued after July 18, 1984, gain on disposition is ordinary interest income to the extent that there is *accrued market discount,* which is an amount bearing the same ratio to the bond's market discount as the number of days the investor held the bond bears to the number of days from the bond's acquisition date to its maturity date. An investor may, however, elect to include accrued market discount in income for tax purposes in the year in which it arises on a ratable or constant interest basis. The market discount rules apply to any bond, note, certificate, or evidence of indebtedness with respect to which there is market discount.

The IRS provided new procedures for taxpayers for electing to include market discount in current income, requesting IRS consent to revoke such an election, and when electing to use a constant interest rate to compute accrued market discount on a bond before its disposition. If a taxpayer follows these procedures after September 22, 1992, IRS consent to the change is automatic (Rev. Proc. 92–67).

RRA '93. RRA '93 provides anti-conversion rules designed to prevent the conversion of ordinary income to lower taxed capital gains. One of these rules extends the market discount rules to acquisitions after April 30, 1993, of tax-exempt bonds and bonds that were issued on or before July 18, 1984 (previously grandfathered under the rules). See the Foreword on RRA '93.

(Code § 1278; CCH ¶ 32,900)

See **bond.**

minimum tax See **alternative minimum tax (AMT).**

minors See **kiddie tax.**

modified accelerated cost recovery system (MACRS) This cost recovery system applies to tangible depreciable property placed in service after December 1, 1986, except for property subject to transition rules. Under this system, the cost of property, depending on its type, is recovered over 3, 5, 7, 10, 15, 20, 27 ½, or 31 ½ years. Cost recovery or depreciation on property placed in service before 1987 is claimed under the method employed when that property was placed in service.

MACRS coverage was subject to an election by a taxpayer, if such property was placed in service after July 31, 1986, and before January 1, 1987.

RRA '93. RRA '93 increases the depreciation period for non-residential real property from 31.5 to 39 years. See the Foreword to RRA '93.

Property Eligible for MACRS

In general, property placed in service after 1986 used in a trade or business or for the production of income is subject to cost recovery under this system. Excluded is property subject to a cost recovery method not involving a term of years (e.g., property not covered under the anti-churning provisions of the MACRS rules, the unit-of-production method, or the income forecast method); public utility property (unless it involves a normalization method of accounting); motion picture films and video tapes; sound recordings; intangible assets; and, in general, property excluded from MACRS under anti-churning rules and placed in service before 1987. Listed property also is subject to MACRS. For a description of listed property, see **accelerated cost recovery system (ACRS).**

Classes of Depreciable Property

Classes of depreciable property generally include property under Code §§ 1245, 1250, and the Asset Depreciation Range as of January 1, 1986. After 1986, Code §§ 1245 and 1250 are used to define depreciable property.

The class life of property determines its applicable recovery period, the applicable cost recovery method, and the applicable convention.

MACRS class lives. Under MACRS, property is classified according to the following class lives:

- *3-year property:* This is property having a class life of 4 years or less, including, at the placed-in-service date, racehorses over 2 years old and other horses over 12 years old.

- *5-year property:* In general, this includes property having a class life over 4 years and less than 10 years. Specific types of property are included in this class life under the Internal Revenue Code, the most important of which are automobiles and light-duty trucks.

- *7-year property:* This is property with an ADR class life of at least 10 years but less than 16 years, railroad track, single-purpose agricultural or horticultural structures generally placed in service prior to 1989, office furniture and fixtures, and other property not having a class life and not otherwise classified.

- *10-year property:* This is property having a class life of 16 or more years and less than 20 years. This property generally includes barges, tugboats, and other vessels, and certain single-purpose agricultural or horticultural structures.

- *15-year property:* This is property having a class life of more than 20 years but less than 25 years.

- *20-year property:* This is property having a class life of 25 years and over, other than real property specified under Code § 1250 having a class life of 27.5 years.

- *27.5-year residential real property:* This is residential real property, including, in general, dwelling units producing at least 80 percent of the property's gross rental income.

- *31.5-year nonresidential real property:* This is real property, as specified under Code § 1250, that is not residential real property or real property having a class life of less than 27.5 years.

Recovery Methods

Under this system, the cost of property is recovered by use of:

- The applicable depreciation method.
- The applicable recovery period.
- The applicable convention.

Alternative election.   Taxpayers are permitted to elect, as an alternative with respect to the applicable depreciation method, straight-line MACRS over the applicable recovery period. Unlike the regular straight-line depreciation method, salvage value is not taken into account when this method is elected. This election is applicable to all MACRS class property placed in service in the taxable year and is made on the tax return for the placed-in-service year.

Applicable methods. For 3-, 5-, 7-, and 10-year property classes, the 200 percent declining-balance method is used for recovery over the applicable term of the class. The half-year convention and a switch to the straight-line method apply.

For 15- and 20-year property classes, the 150 percent declining-balance method is used. The half-year convention and a switch to the straight-line method apply.

The straight-line method and the mid-month convention (to be discussed) apply with respect to residential rental and nonresidential real property.

A taxpayer may elect to recover the cost of certain property to which MACRS would otherwise apply using the 150 percent declining-balance method over the applicable class life. This election is available for property covered under MACRS other than 15-year property, 20-year property, nonresidential real property, residential rental property, and property with respect to which straight-line recovery over the applicable recovery period is elected. For personal property to which no class life applies, a 12-year life is used if this election is made. The 150 percent declining-balance method is generally used with depreciable property used in farming.

Computing MACRS Deductions

The cost recovery deduction available to a taxpayer with respect to eligible property is determined as follows:

1. Determine the applicable depreciation rate. This is done by dividing 1 by the applicable recovery period.
2. Multiply the rate determined under step 1 by the cost recovery percentage applicable to the property. Thus, 1.5 or 2 would be used for property subject to the 150 percent or 200 percent declining-balance method, respectively.

In the first recovery year, the applicable declining-balance recovery rate and the half-year convention apply. Cost recovery claimed in the first year is subtracted from the property's adjusted basis in the second year when the applicable declining-balance recovery rate is applied in determining the cost recovery deduction for that year.

The cost recovery rate can also be determined by dividing the applicable declining-balance rate, either 150 percent or 200 percent, by the applicable recovery period.

General asset accounts. Under MACRS, there is an exception to the general rule that a gain or loss is required to be determined on disposition of property depreciated under this system. This exception applies to mass asset accounts, with respect to which a taxpayer is allowed to elect to claim depreciation on all assets in such an account as if they were a single asset.

According to proposed IRS regulations, items that can be included in such accounts include those whose value is small with respect to the value of all assets included therein, which are numerous in quantity, which are typically accounted for on a quantity or total dollar basis, and which have the same present class life.

The proposed regulations also allow taxpayers to elect to place assets in one or more general asset accounts, each of which is depreciated as a single asset. Each general asset account can include only assets having the same asset class, depreciation method, recovery period, convention (i.e., half-year or mid-quarter), and taxable year in which placed in service.

Taxpayers determine the deductible depreciation with respect to each general asset account using the applicable depreciation method, recovery period, and convention for all assets in each account. The taxpayer then records the annual allowable depreciation in a depreciation reserve account with respect to each general asset account.

MACRS tables. Alternatively, MACRS depreciation tables may be used to determine the cost recovery allowance. The MACRS tables (provided in Appendix B) provide the applicable convention and the conversion from the applicable declining-balance cost recovery method to the straight-line method in the taxable year in which the straight-line method provides a larger deduction.

These tables may be used by a taxpayer with respect to property eligible for MACRS that is placed in service during a taxable year. If a table is used, that table must also be used to determine the cost recovery allowance with respect to the subject property for its full recovery period. When a table is used, it must be used during the full recovery of the subject property. Use of a table cannot be continued by a taxpayer, however, if the basis of the subject property is adjusted, except for adjustments due to cost recovery allowances or an addition or improvement to subject property that is also subject to an allowance for cost recovery.

Straight-line MACRS. Under the straight-line method, each taxable year in the applicable cost recovery period has a new cost recovery rate. In general, for each such year, the applicable cost recovery rate is determined by dividing 1 by the remainder of the applicable recovery period as of the beginning of that year. The resulting rate is applied to the basis of such property, for cost recovery purposes, after application of the relevant convention.

Amount deductible without the use of tables. If the tables provided by the IRS are not used, cost recovery with respect to the unrecovered basis of subject property is determined by use of the declining-balance method. When the straight-line rate equals or exceeds the declining-balance rate, the straight-line method is used.

Alternative MACRS method.   The Internal Revenue Code provides an alternative MACRS cost recovery method whereby deductions that would be allowed under MACRS are reduced. This is because this method involves the use of Asset Depreciation Range (ADR) lives.

Under this method, the deductible amount is determined using the straight-line method, as well as the applicable convention and recovery period. For purposes of this method, the applicable recovery period is the class life for all property, except for personal property having no class life, to which a 12-year life applies, and real property, to which a 40-year life applies. This method is also used in determining cost recovery deductions with respect to luxury automobiles and other listed property (under Code § 280F).

This alternative MACRS method may be irrevocably elected with respect to any class of property for any taxable year. This election can be made with respect to specific residential rental and nonresidential real properties.

Applicable Averaging Conventions

In computing cost recovery deductions under MACRS, straight-line MACRS, and alternative MACRS, the following averaging conventions apply. The cost recovery deduction is available as of the date on which the subject property is placed in service using the applicable convention.

Half-year convention.   Under this convention, eligible property is considered to have been placed in service or disposed of in the middle of the taxable year in which it was disposed of or placed in service. As a result, a half-year's cost recovery is allowed with respect to such property in that year, even in the case of a short taxable year. This convention applies to property other than nonresidential real property and residential rental property.

Mid-month convention.   Under this convention, property is considered to be placed in service or disposed of during the middle of a month. The number of months eligible property is in service determines the allowable deduction. As a result, a half-month's cost recovery is allowed with respect to such property. This convention applies to nonresidential real property and residential rental property.

Mid-quarter convention. This convention generally applies to eligible property when 40 percent of the aggregate tax bases of such property are placed in service in the last quarter of the taxable year. Under this convention, all eligible property placed in service during any quarter of a taxable year is considered to be placed in service at that quarter's midpoint. In the year such property is initially placed in service, the allowable cost recovery deduction is determined by computing the allowable amount for the entire taxable year and multiplying that amount by the percentage applicable to the placed-in-service quarter, as follows:

- First quarter: 87.5 percent.
- Second quarter: 62.5 percent.
- Third quarter: 37.5 percent.
- Fourth quarter: 12.5 percent.

The allowable cost recovery deduction may also be determined using tables provided by the Internal Revenue Service (see Appendix B).

Recapture of MACRS Deductions

When MACRS deductions have been claimed on tangible personal property, gain on the disposition of such property is recaptured to the extent of such deductions. Such recapture does not apply with respect to gain on the disposition of nonresidential real property and residential rental property with respect to which cost recovery under straight-line MACRS is recovered.

(Code § 168; CCH ¶ 11,250; YPG 2.04F; Appendix B)

mortgage This is a debt arrangement between a borrower, called a mortgagor, and a lender, called a mortgagee. Under such an arrangement, the mortgagee receives the right to look to the mortgaged property, usually real property, for repayment of the debt in the event of default on the loan by the mortgagor.

The following are types of mortgages that are currently popular.

Fixed-Rate Mortgages (FRMs)

Under this type of mortgage, the mortgagor is assured of a fixed loan interest rate and monthly mortgage payments that will not change over the loan term. In the initial years of the loan term, most of the mortgage payment is applied to the interest owed, and, as the loan matures, larger amounts are applied to reduce its principal amount.

The fixed interest rate offered by such mortgages can be either an advantage or disadvantage. It is advantageous when prevailing interest rates rise, and is disadvantageous when those rates fall. If rates fall substantially—2 percent or more, as a rule of thumb—mortgagors usually should consider refinancing. Typically, however, refinancing involves significant costs for the mortgagor. These costs should be taken into account in determining whether a drop in prevailing interest rates justifies a refinancing.

Adjustable-Rate Mortgages (ARMs)

Under this type of mortgage, loan interest can rise or fall depending on prevailing interest rates. The interest rate charged on an ARM may be related to the prevailing rate on 6-month US Treasury bills, the average cost of funds for the lending institution making the loan, or indices of average rates charged on mortgages.

Typically, the first-year interest rate on ARMs is lower than the first-year rate charged on FRMs. This is because the lender's risk is reduced by the ability to adjust the interest rate in accordance with market conditions. The interest rate initially charged, usually for the first year or a shorter period, is considerably lower than the interest rate charged on a FRM—perhaps as much as 3 percent—and is often referred to as a "teaser" rate.

ARMs, however, do provide an interest rate cap. Under this cap, the variation in loan interest cannot exceed a specified percentage, typically 2 percent to 3 percent within an adjustment period, which usually is one year or six months. Also, the interest rate cannot exceed a specified ceiling rate over the term of the loan. This ceiling rate can be as high as five or more percentage points over the initial rate.

Such mortgages may also place a cap on the amount of the mortgagor's monthly payment. However, if such monthly payments are insufficient to cover the applicable interest rate over the loan term, *negative amortization* is the result. When this is the case, the loan amount increases, as the applicable rate is paid in larger or extended payments and the interest payable is increased.

In a ruling, IRS treated as deductible qualified residence interest when paid an interest overcharge resulting from a bank's incorrect interest calculation on an ARM. The taxpayer is required to include in gross income a recovery of the interest overcharge in the year of recovery. The income inclusion is required to the extent that the deduction of the amount overcharged reduced the taxpayer's federal income tax in a prior year (Rev. Rul. 92–91).

Shared-Appreciation Mortgages (SAMs)

Under this type of mortgage, available for personal residences, the monthly payments are usually lower than for other types of mortgages. The reason is that, on the sale of the property, the mortgagee is entitled to part of any appreciation, typically up to 50 percent. However, if the mortgage term ends before the property is sold, the mortgagor must pay the specified percentage of any appreciation to the mortgagee. The availability of funds for such a payment may present a serious problem for a mortgagor.

Graduated-Payment Mortgages (GPMs)

This type of mortgage is available only for residential real property. The monthly payments on such a mortgage are fixed at a relatively low rate during the initial years of its term. Thereafter, the payments increase so that the mortgage will be fully repaid at the end of its term. As is the case with fixed-rate and variable-rate mortgages, a drop in prevailing market interest rates may make refinancing desirable. The costs of refinancing, however, must be taken into account in determining whether it would be advantageous.

Balloon Mortgages

These mortgages involve payments determined under the regular full term of a mortgage loan—typically 30 years—with the balance due, however, after a short period—typically three to five years. The monthly payments are applied only to loan interest, which usually is set at a fixed rate. These mortgages can work to a mortgagor's advantage if prevailing market interest rates have fallen when the balloon payment is due. When this is the case, the mortgagee can finance the balloon payment, or refinance the loan, at a lower cost.

The effect is the opposite if prevailing market interest rates have risen when the balloon payment is due. Financing the balloon payment or refinancing the loan is then more expensive, and such financing or refinancing may be more difficult, depending on the mortgagee's creditworthiness and the amount of the loan.

Other Types of Mortgages

Second mortgages. These are mortgages that are junior (secondary) to the primary mortgage on real property. Property owners often provide these loans to enable buyers to meet the full purchase price. They may also be made by financial institutions, such as banks and insurance companies, and by other entities, such as mortgage and finance companies.

The interest rates set on such mortgages are usually considerably higher than those on primary mortgages—typically as much as 4 percentage points higher. The higher rate is due to the lender's risk with respect to a second mortgage, as the primary mortgage is satisfied first.

Reverse mortgages. These mortgages are typically taken out by older persons who wish to cash in on the appreciation of their personal residences. Basically, they involve monthly payments to the mortgagor at a specified rate designed to cover the full loan amount at the end of its term. The full amount of the mortgage is then to be repaid to the mortgagee (or the amount due on the mortgagor's death). Mortgagors sometimes buy insurance in an amount sufficient to cover the amount required to be repaid.

Wrap-around mortgages. This type of mortgage provides a seller of property with an installment note in the amount of the seller's outstanding mortgage or other debt on the property. The seller typically uses the payments received from the buyer to pay down the wrapped debt.

For tax purposes, the installment sale of property involving a wrap-around mortgage, the buyer is not considered to have acquired such property subject to or assuming the seller's mortgage.

Mortgage Assumptions

Some mortgages provide for assumption by the buyer of the seller's mortgage on the property sold. When the mortgage is assumed, the seller remains liable to the mortgagee for repayment, while the buyer is required to make loan payments and is also liable for applicable penalties on default. Most mortgages, however, provide that the current balance must be repaid when the mortgaged property is sold.

Tax Deductibility of Interest

In general, interest paid or incurred in connection with a trade or business is fully deductible, whereas interest paid or incurred with respect to investments is subject to a deduction limit. The deductibility of personal (consumer) interest is subject to a phaseout, under which 10 percent is deductible in 1990 and none is deductible thereafter.

With respect to personal residences, mortgage interest is fully deductible within statutory limits. A limited amount of interest on home equity loans also is deductible (see **qualified residence interest**).

(Code §§ 162, 163; CCH ¶ 8402, ¶ 9402; YPG 3.07)

mortgage-backed bonds See **mortgage-backed securities.**

mortgage-backed securities These securities are of two principal types:

- Mortgage-backed bonds.
- Mortgage-backed pass-through securities.

Mortgage-Backed Bonds

These bonds, when issued by state and local governmental agencies, may be tax-exempt but may be called by the issuer if financing costs decline. [*Note:* The alternative minimum tax may apply to certain private activity bonds. See **alternative minimum tax (AMT)**.]

These bonds may also be issued by mortgage lenders, with a mortgage pool as collateral. To provide security, the mortgage pool's value exceeds the value of the bond issue, typically by at least 25 percent.

In general, the minimum investment amount with respect to these bonds is $10,000; above that amount, bond values increase in units of $1,000. These bonds typically have maturities of five or more years, with bond principal paid at maturity and bond interest paid semiannually. Their sale produces capital gain or loss.

Mortgage-Backed Pass-Through Securities

These include the following types of securities:

- Collateralized mortgage obligations.
- Fannie Maes.
- Freddie Macs.
- Ginnie Maes.

Private mortgage lenders may also issue mortgage-backed pass-through securities.

Collateralized mortgage obligations (CMOs). These are mortgage-backed pass-through securities issued by the Federal Home Loan Mortgage Corporation (FHLMC). In general, these securities consist of four groups having four different maturity lengths between 5 and 20 years. Investors receive semiannual interest payments, except for those holding the securities having the longest maturity. All principal payments are made to the holders of securities with the shortest maturity. When investments in this group expire, principal payments go to the next group, and when those investments expire, payments go to the next group. Holders of securities in the group having the longest maturity are paid principal and interest in a lump sum.

To invest in all but the group of securities having the longest maturity, a $25,000 minimum payment is required. For securities in the group having the longest maturity, an investment may be made for as little as $1,000.

(YPG 2.01)

See also **"Fannie Mae" securities; "Freddie Mac" securities; Government National Mortgage Association (GNMA) securities.**

mortgage refinancing See **mortgage.**

municipal bonds These are bonds issued by local governmental units having maturities from 1 to 30 years and, in general, paying interest through coupons to be redeemed by the holder semiannually. There are two basic types of municipal bonds: general obligation bonds (typically referred to as "GOs") and revenue bonds.

GOs are considered to provide more safety to an investor in that they are backed by the full faith and credit of the issuing governmental unit and are also secured by its taxing power and the revenues it receives. Revenue bonds are issued to finance specific projects of the issuing governmental unit (e.g., sports stadiums and toll highways). They are considered to involve more risk for the investor than GOs, since interest payments are made from the revenues generated from the related project and they are not backed by the full faith and credit of the issuing governmental unit.

Tax Advantages

Many of these bonds are free from federal income tax. Some are also free from state and local taxation. For example, a New York City bond issue is typically exempt from federal, New York state, and New York City income taxes. Because of their tax-advantaged aspect, these bonds generally have lower interest yields than US Treasury or good-quality (i.e., according to ratings of Standard & Poor's or Moody's investors services) corporate bonds.

Municipal bond investments may also be made through purchases of units in municipal bond funds or unit trusts offered by securities brokers. [*Note:* Some municipal bonds are private activity bonds for purposes of the alternative minimum tax. See **alternative minimum tax (AMT.)**]

(Code § 61; CCH ¶ 5501; YPG 2.04)

See also **alternative minimum tax (AMT); capital gains and losses.**

municipal notes These notes are short-term investments typically issued by local governmental units for cash flow purposes. They may have maturities of as little as one month or as long as three years, although most mature within one year of issuance. They are sold at a discount and are redeemed at face value on maturity. The difference between the purchase and redemption prices represents interest to the holder. This interest is usually exempt from federal income tax and from tax in the issuing jurisdiction.

These notes are of several types, based on their underlying financing:

- *Bond anticipation notes.* These are redeemed through use of the proceeds of new bond issues.

- *Project notes.* These are generally issued by local housing units to finance housing projects. They represent a safe investment, in that they are typically backed by the US government's full faith and credit and taxing power.

- *Revenue anticipation notes.* These are backed by nontax revenues received by the issuing governmental unit, such as federal or state aid.
- *Tax anticipation notes.* These are financed by the issuing governmental unit's anticipated tax revenues and other unrestricted revenues.

(Reg. § 1.61–7; CCH ¶ 5501; YPG 2.04)

mutual funds These funds involve pooled investments, typically by small investors wishing to diversify. They are managed by investment professionals in accordance with stated fund investment objectives. Fund objectives are designed to take into account specific investment goals of shareholders, such as current income, preservation of capital, and long-term or short-term growth.

Investments by these funds may include stocks, bonds, options, money market investments, precious metals, and foreign securities. Stock and bond funds may invest in specific types of stocks and bonds. Stock fund investments may, for example, include over-the-counter stocks and stocks in industry sectors, such as high technology, forest products, and natural resources. Bond fund investments may, for example, include junk (high-yield) bonds, US government bonds, tax-exempt bonds issued within a particular state, and zero-coupon bonds.

The value of investments in these funds, like the value of straight investments in stocks and bonds, fluctuates in accordance with market forces, such as market interest rate levels. The relative risks and returns of these funds are generally a function of the quality of the assets in their portfolios. Expenses charged to investors may vary depending on the classification of the particular fund involved.

For federal income tax purposes, mutual funds are classified as, and are taxed under rules applicable to, regulated investment companies.

Mutual Fund Distributions

Mutual funds distribute income to investors in the form of income dividends and capital gains. Dividends are distributed from portfolio income, and capital gains are distributed from the proceeds of sales of portfolio assets. Dividend payments are often made to fund shareholders on a monthly basis, and capital gain payments generally are not made on a fixed schedule but are related to the timing of portfolio asset sales.

Dividend distributions generally constitute ordinary income to a mutual fund investor, unless the fund's portfolio consists of tax-exempt assets. However, some state and cities (e.g., Connecticut and New York) that impose a personal income tax treat dividends from funds having tax-exempt portfolio assets as fully taxable. These jurisdictions tax such dividend distributions on the theory that the income earned on the fund's portfolio nullifies its tax-exempt character when it is passed through to the shareholders.

Mutual Fund Classifications

With respect to expenses charged to investors, mutual funds are classified as no-load, low-load, and load funds.

No-load funds. Currently, this is the most popular group of mutual funds. Investors are not charged any sales commissions, referred to as loads, to invest in these funds. This is because they purchase shares in the funds directly from the fund sponsors.

Management fees associated with these funds are charged to investors through deductions from fund portfolio assets. This charge typically amounts to as much as 1 percent of the average daily assets of the particular fund. Management fees are deducted before the market price of shares is established.

Some no-load funds charge additional fees to investors. These charges may include redemption fees and contingent deferred sales charges. The former are charged against the net asset value of an investor's fund shares at the time of sale, and the latter are charged against the investor's fund balance if his or her shares are redeemed within a specified period after purchase.

Low-load funds. These funds typically charge lower commissions than load funds. These charges may range as high as 2 percent of the dollar amount of the investor's purchase or sale of fund shares.

Load funds. These mutual funds charge a commission on an initial investment. This charge may be as high as 8.5 percent and is paid either to the fund marketer or to the securities broker/dealer marketing the fund.

Shares in load and low-load funds may be purchased through financial institutions, securities broker/dealers, and, with respect to some funds of this type, directly from mutual fund sponsors. As noted, shares in no-load mutual funds are usually purchased by investors directly from the fund sponsors.

Mutual fund sponsors typically maintain a "family" of mutual funds. Investors who purchase shares in a fund maintained by such a sponsor may be offered the opportunity to move their investment to other funds in the "family" at little or no cost.

Mutual funds are also categorized as either closed-end or open-end.

Closed-end funds. These are publicly traded mutual funds having a fixed number of shares. Investors who buy and sell shares in these funds buy from and sell to other investors, not the fund sponsors.

These are not as popular with investors as open-end funds. Share prices of closed-end funds vary in relation to market forces, and there are fewer closed-end fund offerings than open-end fund offerings. Shares in closed-end funds often may be purchased at a significant discount to the per-share net asset value.

Open-end funds. These funds issue new shares for purchase by investors. They typically have distributors that engage securities broker/dealers for the purchase and sale of fund shares. Purchases and sales of open-end fund shares are made between the investor and the fund sponsor, unlike purchases and sales of closed-end fund shares. Share prices are based on the fund's net asset value. That value is divided by the number of outstanding fund shares to derive the per-share net asset value.
(YPG 2.04.A)

N

notes See **capital gains and losses; municipal notes.**

O

options There are a variety of options available to investors, including:

- *Call options.* These options provide the holder with a right, but not an obligation, to buy 100 shares (per option) of a publicly held, actively traded common stock at a fixed price during the option's term.
- *Put options.* These options provide the holder with a right, but not an obligation, to sell 100 shares (per option) of a publicly held, actively traded common stock at a fixed price during the option's term.

These options generally are written on highly capitalized, actively traded common stocks but are not available on all common stocks, even if traded on the New York Stock Exchange (commonly referred to as the "Big Board"). In exchange for the right to buy or sell the underlying stock under a call or put option, the buyer of the option pays a premium to the writer of the option. The option premium price bears a relation to the market price of the underlying stock. A commission is also charged by the securities broker/dealer executing the purchase or sale transaction. The premium and commission are payable even if the option purchaser does not exercise the option.
(YPG 2.03)
See also **capital gains and losses.**

original issue discount *Note:* This description of the tax treatment of original issue discount (OID) relates only to bondholders, and not to bond issuers.

OID on corporate bonds issued before July 2, 1982—or issued after July 1, 1982, under a binding agreement entered into before July 2, 1982—is included in the income of the bondholder, holding the bonds as capital assets, over the bond's term. For bonds issued after July 1, 1982, OID is included in the bondholder's income in the same way as the actual economic accrual of the bond interest.

The OID rules apply to obligations issued by natural persons after March 1, 1984, with certain exceptions. The exceptions apply when:

- The borrower and lender are natural persons. (A husband and wife are considered one person, unless they lived apart during the entire taxable year.)
- All loans between borrower and lender total no more than $10,000.
- Federal income tax avoidance is not a principal objective of the loan.
- The loan is not made in the course of the lender's trade or business.

These rules also generally apply to privately placed debt instruments issued as consideration for the sale or exchange of property after 1984, with an exception. This statutory exception applies to certain debt instruments issued under a written contract binding on March 1, 1984, and which remains binding until the sale or exchange occurs.

These rules do not apply to certain privately placed debt instruments, including

- Those issued in connection with the sale of a farm for $1 million or less by an individual, testamentary trust, estate, small business corporation (Code § 1244), or a certain type of partnership (meeting requirements similar to the small business corporation rules).
- Those issued in connection with an individual's sale of a personal residence.
- Those whose combined value, and any additional consideration to be received with respect to a sale, is not more than $250,000.
- Those that are part of a publicly traded debt issue or are exchanged for publicly traded stock or securities.
- Those exempt under the deferred payment interest (Code § 483) rules.
- Those exchanged for a patent (under Code § 1235) where amounts received are contingent on productivity, use, or disposition.

The OID rules employ the applicable federal rate (AFR). The AFR is related to the term length of a privately placed debt instrument, including any renewal options. Term lengths of debt instruments correspond to term lengths of US Treasury obligations, as set forth below. The US Treasury sets the AFR for six-month periods, and this rate is based on the average six-month market yield of securities issued by the Treasury.

- *Short-term securities:* Securities with terms of up to three years.
- *Mid-term securities:* Securities with terms of more than three years but less than nine years.
- *Long-term securities:* Securities with terms of over nine years.

The OID income accrual rules are also applicable to cash-basis holders (generally, individuals) of debt instruments that are not held as capital assets. In addition, the OID rules apply to debt instruments issued in connection with services rendered or the use of property.

The OID rules are also related to obligations having unstated interest and to stripped bonds.

(Code §§ 1274, 483; CCH ¶ 32,800, ¶ 22,290; YPG 3.04.F)

See also **capital gains and losses; stripped bonds.**

over-the-counter stocks These are stocks, primarily common stocks, that are not traded on a major US securities exchange, such as the New York Stock Exchange or American Stock Exchange. There are other, smaller exchanges on which there is trading of publicly held shares, such as the Honolulu, Intermountain, Midwest, Pacific, Philadelphia, and Spokane exchanges.

Dealers in over-the-counter stocks use the National Association of Securities Dealers Automated Quotation (NASDAQ) system. In general, corporations whose stocks are traded over the counter are not as well capitalized as those whose stocks are traded on major securities exchanges. Accordingly, the share prices of over-the-counter stocks tend to move upward and downward with more volatility, and thus they involve greater potential risk and greater potential reward for the investor.

(YPG 2.01)

P

participation certificates See **Freddie Mac securities.**

partnership In a partnership, investors pool their funds for a specific investment purpose, such as the construction or acquisition and operation of residential or commercial real property. Most investors purchase interests (typically called *units*) in limited partnerships. The liability of a limited partner with respect to the partnership is limited to the amount of that partner's investment in it. Management of such a partnership is the responsibility of general partners, whose liability is not so limited.

Advantages and Disadvantages of Partnerships

The following are advantages characteristic of limited partnerships.

- *Tax advantages.* (See the following discussion of tax treatment.)
- *Limited liability with respect to the partnership.* As noted, the investor's liability is limited to the amount he or she invests in the partnership.
- *Simplicity of investment.* An investor need only make one payment to acquire a limited partnership interest. Also, such an interest can be acquired for a relatively small amount, usually as little as $5,000. Thus, with a relatively small investment, an investor can acquire an interest in a highly valuable property having the potential for future appreciation and tax benefits.

- *Lack of management responsibility.*
- *Relative risk.* An investment in a limited partnership offers investment diversification, and professional management of the partnership venture typically reduces an investor's risk.

The following are disadvantages characteristic of limited partnerships:

- *Potential tax liabilities.* (See the following discussion of tax treatment.)
- *Liquidity of investment.* Not all limited partnership interests are traded on an established securities exchange. The financial strength of a partnership is a key factor in an investor's ability to sell a limited partnership interest. An investor may not be able to sell such an interest if that interest is not publicly traded or the partnership in which that interest is held is financially troubled.
- *Lack of control over management.* As previously noted, a limited partner has no opportunity to participate in the management of the partnership venture. Most limited partners lack familiarity with general partners and management installed by general partners.
- *Relative risk.* Although limited partnerships are required to issue detailed prospectuses, it usually is difficult for an investor to assess the quality of and potential income from the underlying partnership assets. This can be particularly difficult when a limited partnership is highly leveraged, that is, incurs substantial debt, or involves a "blind pool," that is, does not specify the partnership's investment property. Also, there may be unexpected tax liabilities for investors in limited partnerships.
- *Fees.* Limited partners frequently charge substantial fees to investors. These fees reduce the overall return on the investment and should be carefully considered before the limited partnership interest is purchased.

Summary of Tax Rules Applicable to Partners and Partnerships

The following is a brief summary of the key federal income tax rules applicable to partners and partnerships. These rules, as set forth in the Internal Revenue Code and federal income tax regulations, are extensive and complex. For convenience in researching tax issues regulated to partners and partnerships, references to the Code and Regulations and to the relevant paragraph in the Commerce Clearing House *Standard Federal Tax Reporter,* as applicable, are provided with respect to specific points discussed. A discussion of tax implications and tax planning opportunities relating to partnerships is presented in detail in the Year-Round Planning Guide.

Under the federal income tax law, a *partnership* is a syndicate, pool, joint venture, or other unincorporated organization conducting any business, financial operation, or venture, that does not fall under the Internal Revenue Code classification of a corporation, trust, or estate (Code § 761; CCH ¶ 25,900).

A partnership is not a separate, taxable entity; it is commonly referred to as a pass-through entity. Tax is imposed on the partners' shares of the partnership's taxable income, whether or not actually distributed (Code § 701; CCH ¶ 23,560 et seq.).

Partnership taxable income. A partnership's taxable income is determined in the same manner as an individual's taxable income, with certain exceptions. Also, the following items taken into account in the tax computation of individuals are not available to partnerships:

- Deduction for personal exemptions.
- Deduction for foreign taxes.
- Deduction for net operating loss.
- Deduction for charitable contributions.
- Itemized deductions allowed for individuals.
- Capital loss carryover.
- Deduction for depletion (for oil and gas wells).

Exceptions: A partner's share of certain partnership items, whether or not actually distributed, must be included in the partner's taxable income for his or her taxable year within which or with which the partnership's taxable year ends, as set forth under Code § 702 (CCH ¶ 3904):

- Long-term and short-term capital gains and losses.
- Section 1231 gains and losses.
- Charitable contributions.
- Dividends subject to a "statutory dividends received" deduction (under Code §§ 243–47).
- Taxes paid or accrued to foreign countries and US possessions.
- Income, gain, loss, deduction, and credit items as required under the regulations, which included nonbusiness expenses; bad debt recoveries; prior taxes; income, gain, or loss to the partnership from transactions with partners in connection with unrealized partnership receivables (§ 751 assets) or inventory items; and other items specified in the regulations (Reg. § 1.702–1; CCH ¶ 3905).
- Taxable income or loss, other than the items described above, which must be separately computed.

Section 751 assets. These represent unrealized receivables, which, in general, are rights to income not included in a partnership's gross income under its accounting method. These also include inventory items, which are items that would not be treated as capital or § 1231 (capital gain or ordinary loss) assets when sold by the partnership or by a partner, if held by the partner (Code § 751; Reg. § 1.751–1; CCH ¶ 25,800).

Partnership taxable year. Partnerships generally are required to use a majority-interest taxable year. The tax law provides that this is the taxable year of one or more partners who have, as of the testing day, a more than 50 percent aggregate interest in partnership profits and capital. In general, the *testing day* is the first day of the partnership's taxable year.

Where partners owning a majority interest in a partnership have different taxable years, the partnership is required to have the same taxable year as its principal partners. For this purpose, "principal partners" are partners who individually own 5 percent of partnership profits or capital.

If a partnership cannot establish a taxable year in accordance with the preceding rules, it is required to use the calendar year (or other taxable year if requirements prescribed in the regulations are met) (Code § 706; CCH ¶ 25,460).

Some partnerships may elect to have a taxable year other than the one required by statute, which, for most partnerships, is the calendar year. When such an election is in effect, the electing partnership generally is required to make a required payment. This payment is intended to cover the tax otherwise payable as the result of the partnership's use of a taxable year other than the one generally required by statute (Code §§ 444, 7519; CCH ¶ 43,600, ¶ 20,600).

Effect of changes in partnership. A partnership's taxable year will not end as a result of death, retirement, or withdrawal of a partner from a partnership. However, a partnership's taxable year closes *with respect to a partner* when that partner sells or exchanges his or her full partnership interest or that interest is liquidated, unless the partner dies (Code § 706; CCH ¶ 25,460).

Partnership elections. Any election pertaining to a partnership's taxable income is required to be made at the partnership level. Such elections, for example, are to be made with respect to depreciation methods and accounting methods. Such an election, once made, applies to all partners (Code § 703; Reg. § 1.703–1; CCH ¶ 25,400).

Interplay with at-risk rules. Partnerships and their partners are subject to the at-risk rules provided under the Internal Revenue Code. Under these rules, a partner's deductible losses are limited to amounts at risk with respect to the partnership activity. An at-risk amount does not include any partnership liability, or any portion thereof, with respect to which the partner has no personal liability. (See **at-risk rules.**)

Interplay with passive loss rules. The passive loss rules prescribed under the Internal Revenue Code apply at the *partner* level, not the partnership level, to every partner's share of a loss or credit related to a passive activity of the partnership. In general, under the passive loss rules, a *passive activity* is a trade or business activity in which a partner does not materially participate. Also, in general, a limited partner's interest in a limited partnership does not involve material participation. (See **passive loss rules.**)

Basis of partnership interest. When a partner purchases his or her interest in a partnership for cash (or its equivalent), the basis for that interest (subject to adjustment) is the purchase price. If the partner contributes property to the partnership, the basis of that partner's interest in the partnership is increased by the adjusted basis of that property when the contribution is made.

A partner's basis for his or her partnership interest is increased by the distributive share of partnership taxable income, tax-exempt income, and also excess deductions for depletion over its basis in the depletable property. A partner's basis for his or her partnership interest is decreased by distributions by the partnership, but not below zero, by his or her share of partnership losses, by his or her share of expenses that are nondeductible at the partnership level and not chargeable to capital account, and by any oil and gas depletion deduction (Code §§ 705, 722; CCH ¶ 25,440, ¶ 25,560).

Holding period. For a partner, the holding period of a partnership interest is measured from the date that the interest was acquired. This holding period is *not* measured by the acquisition date(s) of specific partnership property.

Purchase and sale of partnership interest. In general, a partnership interest constitutes a capital asset in the hands of an investor. However, limitations apply with respect to capital gain treatment under which amounts received by partners relating to their respective shares of unrealized partnership receivables or substantially appreciated partnership property, as previously discussed, constitutes *ordinary* and not capital gain or loss (Code §§ 741, 751; CCH ¶ 25,740, ¶ 25,800).

Partners' loss limitations. A partner's allowable share of a partnership's loss, including the partnership's capital loss, is limited to the adjusted basis of his or her partnership interest at the end of the loss year of the partnership (Reg. § 1.704–1; CCH ¶ 25,420).

RRA '93. Under RRA '93, for partnerships that are not service providers, a limit is placed on the deductibility of the part of a payment made for goodwill and unrealized receivables, including depreciation recapture, from payments made in liquidating the partnership interest of a retiring or deceased partner. See the Foreword on RRA '93.

passive activity credits See **passive loss rules.**

passive activity losses See **passive loss rules.**

passive loss rules For post-1986 taxable years, taxpayers generally must net income against losses from passive activities during a taxable year. For taxpayers acquiring interests in passive activities before October 23, 1986, a five-year phase-in rule applies, whereby passive activity losses and credits are 90 percent disallowed for taxable years beginning in 1990 and totally disallowed thereafter. Also, under a transition rule, certain post-1983 investments in low-income housing projects do not involve passive losses for up to seven years after the taxpayer's initial investment.

Treatment of Losses

Excess passive losses cannot offset active income or portfolio income. *Active* income includes wages, salaries, self-employment, or trade or business income. *Portfolio* income includes interest, dividends, royalties, annuities, and gain from the sale of investment property.

Excess passive activity losses that cannot currently be deducted are suspended. Such losses are carried over to future taxable years and can only offset passive income of the future year. But when there is a disposition of an activity producing suspended losses, the suspended losses related to that activity are freed up and can be used to offset active income as well.

Treatment of Credits

Credits arising from passive activities are generally subject to the same rules applicable to passive losses. Accordingly, they can offset tax arising from net passive income, and, in general, they can be carried forward indefinitely.

Participation Rules

An activity is not considered passive if a taxpayer materially participates in that activity by spending a minimum of 500 hours in it during the taxable year. If 100 to 500 hours are spent by a taxpayer during a taxable year, there is an unfavorable result. This is because income from the activity is treated as nonpassive, but any losses are treated as passive losses.

If a taxpayer participates in a personal service activity (e.g., accounting, law, or medicine), participation is not treated as participation in a nonpassive activity if that participation has been active for any three preceding taxable years. This is the case even if the taxpayer does not currently participate in such activity.

Special rule for rental real estate activities. With respect to rental real estate, a separate special loss deduction of $25,000 is allowed against active income of taxpayers having adjusted gross income (AGI) of less than $100,000 (or, if less than $150,000, taxpayers are subject to a deduction phaseout). This special deduction is allowed only if the taxpayer *actively participates* in the rental real estate activity. In general, to actively participate, a taxpayer must own a minimum interest of 10 percent in the rental real estate activity and have some involvement in the management of the activity. This level of participation is less than *material participation,* and a fixed-hour requirement need not be met.

RRA '93. RRA '93 provides relief from the passive activity loss rules for certain real estate professionals who materially participate in rental real estate activities if certain requirements are met. See the Foreword on RRA '93.

Definition of Activity

Definition of the term *activity* is key under the passive loss rules. The term was initially defined in temporary IRS regulations that generally applied to taxable years ending after August 9, 1989. New proposed regulations were issued by the IRS on May 15, 1992, and are discussed below.

For purposes of the passive loss rules, a taxpayer is required to categorize the activities in which he or she participated. Classification and the definition of each activity are important under these rules in that their limitations are based on an activity-by-activity analysis. Also, many determinations that must be made for purposes of applying the limitations, such as the material participation test, the active participation standard in connection with rental real estate activities, and the disposition of an entire interest in a property test, are made on the basis of how an activity is defined.

The determination of the time when suspended passive losses can be freed up and deducted against active income depends on whether the taxpayer's business ventures constitute a single activity under the applicable rules. The sale of part of an activity does not free up suspended passive losses. Such losses are freed up only when there is a disposition of the taxpayer's full interest in the passive activity.

An *undertaking* is the smallest unit constituting an activity under the passive loss rules. This is, in general, any business operation owned by the same person and conducted at the same location.

Federal income tax regulations provide that a rental business and a nonrental business cannot be a single undertaking. This is so even if such businesses have the same owner and they are in the same location. Such operations are separated because a rental activity is automatically treated as a passive activity. Accordingly, a combination of two such operations into a single undertaking could result in a combination of a passive activity with a trade or business activity.

Aggregation Rules

When an undertaking is identified and established, the taxpayer is required to determine whether it is a separate activity or required to be aggregated with other undertakings conducted in a single activity. In addition, undertakings in the same line of business or vertically integrated are generally required to be aggregated into a single activity. There is vertical integration between undertakings when a single business unit constituting such an undertaking sells or receives over 50 percent of its product to or from another such unit.

Undertakings are required to be aggregated into a single activity *only* in determining a taxpayer's level of participation in an activity. Such aggregation is a key factor in determining whether the taxpayer participates in the activity in question for 100 to 500 hours. However, a taxpayer may divide different undertakings to free up a suspended loss when one particular undertaking is sold. Accordingly, even where a taxpayer must aggregate multiple undertakings into a single activity in determining his or her level of participation, such aggregation is *not* required in determining whether any suspended losses can be freed up and deducted from the taxpayer's active income.

Special rules apply to rental real estate, with respect to which the aggregation rules described generally do not apply, and also to personal service activities.

Discussion of May 15, 1992, proposed PAL regulations. These proposed regulations generally take a facts-and-circumstances approach under which one or more business activities or rental activities are treated as a single activity if the activities represent an appropriate economic unit for the purpose of measuring gain or loss under the passive activity loss rules.

A taxpayer is allowed to use any reasonable method of applying the relevant facts and circumstances when grouping activities. In general, the following factors are the most important:

- Similarities and differences in types of business.
- The extent of common control.

- The extent of common ownership.
- Geographic location.
- Interdependence between activities.

Observation. The prior temporary regulations were less flexible in their approach, providing for a mechanical grouping of undertakings, initially by geographical location.
(Code § 469; CCH ¶ 21,960 et seq.; YPG 8.01 et seq.)

pensions See **qualified retirement, profit-sharing, etc., plans.**

percentage depletion See **depletion.**

personal holding company A personal holding company (PHC) is any corporation, with certain exceptions, having both the following:

- PHC income (to be discussed) for the taxable year constituting at least 60 percent of its adjusted ordinary gross income.
- Over 50 percent in value of its stock owned, directly or indirectly, by or for no more than five individuals, at any time during the second half of its taxable year.

Exceptions

The following are not PHCs:

- A tax-exempt corporation (under Code § 501).
- A bank or a US building and loan association.
- A life insurance or surety company.
- Certain finance companies, as long as they meet certain statutory requirements regarding interest income and stockholder loans.
- A foreign corporation, all outstanding shares of which are owned by nonresident alien individuals or foreign entities in the second half of its taxable year.
- A small business investment company, unless it has a shareholder directly or indirectly owning at least 5 percent of an entity to which this company provides funds.
- A corporation involved in a bankruptcy or similar proceeding, unless the proceeding was motivated by tax avoidance.
- A passive foreign investment company (under Code § 1296).

Tax Treatment

A 39.6 percent special PHC tax is imposed on the undistributed income of a PHC. This tax is imposed on the PHC in addition to the regular federal corporation income tax. It applies only to the undistributed income of a PHC. Such income is, in general, taxable income, less federal income tax and dividends paid.
(Code §§ 541–44; CCH ¶¶ 23,401 et seq.)

personal property This is property other than real property—for example, stocks, bonds, collectibles, and antiques. Such property may be subject to an allowance for cost recovery or depreciation and may also give rise to a capital gain or loss upon disposition.
(YPG 2.01)

See also **accelerated cost recovery system (ACRS); capital gains and losses; depreciation; modified accelerated cost recovery system (MACRS); Section 1231 assets.**

personal residence See **qualified residence interest; residence, personal, sale of.**

points Many taxpayers are required to pay points in connection with obtaining a mortgage on real property. Special tax rules apply with respect to points, which constitute prepaid interest. In general, prepaid interest is deductible over the term of the loan to which it relates. However, certain points paid by taxpayers are excepted from this general rule.

Excepted are points paid in connection with debt incurred by a taxpayer to purchase or improve his or her personal residence, when the residence secures that debt. Also, to qualify for this exception, the payment of points must be an established business practice in the area in which the debt is incurred, and the amount paid does not exceed the amount generally charged there.

Note. The IRS treats points as deductible only when paid with respect to the taxpayer's personal residence, not with respect to a second residence, or a home equity loan, or a line of credit. According to the IRS, points paid with respect to the refinancing of a mortgage loan on a principal residence are only deductible ratably over the loan term. However, a Federal Circuit Court of Appeals reached a different holding in a case where taxpayers acquired a personal residence with short-term financing secured by the residence. The taxpayers subsequently obtained refinancing within the period of the short-term loan, paying points. The court held that the points were deductible when paid under the above exception (*Huntsman*, 8th Cir.).

Further note. The IRS disagrees with the decision in *Huntsman*, and is bound by it only within the Eighth Circuit.

Safe harbor. The IRS has provided a safe harbor with respect to the deductibility of points paid by cash-basis taxpayers during taxable years beginning after December 31, 1991. To be deductible under this safe harbor procedure, points must be paid directly by a taxpayer with respect to the purchase of a personal residence and are designated as such on the settlement statement, computed as a percentage of the amount borrowed, and conform with business practices where the residence is situated (Rev. Proc. 92–12).

See also **mortgage; qualified residence interest.**

preferred stock This type of stock has characteristics similar to bonds. This is because it provides an investor with dividends set at a fixed rate. However, as is the case with common stock, a dividend cannot be paid until it is earned and paid by the issuing corporation. Also, as is the case with bonds, the price of publicly traded shares of preferred stock varies with interest rate trends. Thus, if interest rates decline, preferred share prices typically rise; and, if rates rise, those prices typically decline.

However, by purchasing shares of preferred stock, an investor may acquire a fixed-rate investment at a lower cost than the purchase of many bonds. This is because an investment in bonds typically requires a minimum investment of $5,000, although prices of such bonds in the secondary market may vary.

Features

The following features may be present with respect to a particular issue of preferred stock. These features are not present in all such issues. Some issues have none of these features and merely provide a fixed dividend.

Callability. This feature enables the corporate issuer to redeem the preferred shares issued at a specified price and retire them. Typically, if lower-cost financing is available to the issuer, it will redeem the preferred shares if this feature is present.

Convertibility. This feature allows the holders of preferred shares to convert them into shares of common stock of the issuing corporation. The holders of such shares would generally benefit from this feature when the per-share price of the issuing corporation's common stock exceeds the price of its preferred stock.

Cumulative dividends. If a preferred stock issue provides this feature, investors are entitled to any unpaid dividends on these shares on a cumulative basis. Also, cumulative preferred dividends must be paid before any dividends are paid on the issuing corporation's common stock.

Participation. This feature permits holders of preferred shares to participate in any special benefits provided by the issuing corporation to its other shareholders (e.g., dividend increases).

Voting rights. Some preferred stock issues, like common stock issues, provide voting rights. These voting rights enable holders of such preferred shares to have an interest in the affairs and management of the issuing corporation. (YPG 2.01)

premium See **bond premium; insurance.**

private activity bonds These are bonds, as defined in Internal Revenue Code § 142, issued after August 7, 1986, and subject to certain exceptions under transition rules. They include bonds issued to finance mass commuting facilities, certain water and sewage disposal projects, and certain multifamily residential rental projects. The interest on these bonds is a preference for purposes of the alternative minimum tax (AMT).

RRA '93. RRA '93 exempts from the private activity bond limitations high-speed intercity rail facility bonds issued with respect to government-owned property. See the Foreword on RRA '93.

[Code § 57(a)(5); CCH ¶ 5300; YPG 6.03.B]

See also **alternative minimum tax (AMT); AMT preferences; bond.**

probate This is a legal process under which the estate of a deceased person is settled. It generally involves the orderly distribution of the decedent's assets to his or her heirs.

This process is simplified if the decedent has a will that is valid under the laws of the jurisdiction in which he or she lived. Such a decedent dies *testate.* If the decedent dies without a will, he or she dies *intestate.*

If the decedent has a will, it specifies an executor of the estate. The executor is empowered to see to the orderly settlement of the decedent's estate, that is, payment of the decedent's debts and distribution of his or her assets, in accordance with applicable law. If the decedent does not have a will, the probate court having jurisdiction will appoint an administrator for the estate. If an administrator is appointed, expenses involved in settling the decedent's estate may be increased. This is because the administrator is generally required to employ professionals, such as accountants, appraisers, attorneys, and realtors, to assist in settling the estate. Generally, if a decedent dies testate, many potential problems requiring the services of such professionals are resolved.

See also **estate; estate tax; gift tax.**

Q

qualified residence interest This is interest paid or accrued in a taxable year in connection with acquisition or home equity indebtedness incurred with respect to a qualified residence. A *qualified* residence is the principal residence of a taxpayer and one other residence, such as a vacation home. To be qualified, such a residence must be used by the taxpayer for the greater of 14 days or 10 percent of the days that it is rented during the taxable year. The residence may still be qualified, however, even if it is not rented or used as a dwelling unit at any time during the taxable year. If owners of the residence are married and do not file a joint tax return, they are treated as one taxpayer unless they otherwise provide in writing.

Acquisition Indebtedness

This is indebtedness incurred in acquiring, constructing, or substantially improving a qualified residence that is secured by that residence. If this indebtedness is refinanced, it still qualifies as acquisition indebtedness as long as it does not exceed the principal amount existing before the refinancing.

Home Equity Indebtedness

This is all indebtedness, other than acquisition indebtedness, secured by a qualified residence, as long as that indebtedness does not exceed the residence's fair market value, reduced by applicable acquisition indebtedness. Interest arising from this indebtedness is deductible for tax purposes even if the debt proceeds are used for personal purposes.

Deduction Limits

There are deduction limits on interest paid or accrued with respect to indebtedness on a qualified residence. Acquisition indebtedness that gives rise to deductible interest cannot exceed an aggregate amount of $1 million. Home equity indebtedness that gives rise to deductible interest cannot exceed an aggregate amount of $100,000. These amounts are reduced by 50 percent for married individuals filing separate tax returns. Any interest not deductible under these rules is deductible, subject to limits, as personal (consumer) interest before 1991.

Special Rules for Indebtedness Incurred before October 13, 1987

If indebtedness is incurred by a taxpayer with respect to a residence on or before October 13, 1987, that indebtedness is treated as acquisition indebtedness but is not subject to the $1 million limit. Such indebtedness reduces the amount of that limit, but not below zero. It also generally includes indebtedness secured by a qualified residence to refinance indebtedness existing before October 13, 1987, as long as the principal amount refinanced does not exceed the principal amount of the indebtedness originally incurred.

(Code § 163(h); CCH ¶ 1210; YPG 3.07 et seq.)

qualified retirement, profit-sharing, etc., plans Special tax treatment applies to certain pension, profit-sharing, and stock bonus plans, as long as those plans meet statutory requirements specified under Code § 401. Although participation in some qualified plans is automatic upon an individual's employment, participation or investment in some qualified plans may be optional. Also, the levels of contributions to and withdrawals from qualified plans involve investment decisions on the part of participants. This Encyclopedia listing covers investments in such plans by individual participants, rather than the tax treatment applicable to employer sponsors of such plans, which is beyond the scope of this book.

Retirement Plans

These plans are of two basic types: defined benefit plans and defined contribution plans.

Defined benefit plans. This type of plan provides for specified retirement benefits. Under most plans of this type, monthly benefits are provided to retired participants, and these benefits are typically based on the compensation received by the participant and the length of the participant's service to the employer. Contributions to such plans are not made to separate accounts of participants, and they are actuarially determined. Such a plan can include an annuity plan, which is funded through an employer purchase of one or more annuity contracts.

Defined contribution plans. This type of plan is also commonly referred to as a "money purchase" plan. Under this type of plan, the employer provides for a specified contribution to a participant's account, typically based on a percentage of the participant's compensation from the employer. Unlike defined benefit plans, contributions are allocated among participants' accounts based on a specified formula. The benefits received by participants from these plans are based on plan contributions, plan asset appreciation or depreciation, and account forfeitures of other plan participants. Profit-sharing plans and stock bonus plans [including employee stock ownership plans (ESOPs)] are classified as defined contribution plans.

Profit-sharing plans. Under these plans, classified as defined contribution plans, employers contribute a percentage of profits. There is no required contribution percentage, but the employer contributions are substantial and recurring.

Qualification Rules

Qualified plans must comply with a number of statutory rules, including the following.

Nondiscrimination rules. For a plan to be qualified under statutory rules, it cannot discriminate in plan benefits, contributions, or coverage to the benefit of employees who are highly compensated. Also, strict requirements apply to "top-heavy" plans, which are plans designed to benefit key employees of the employer sponsoring the plan.

Special nondiscrimination rules apply to contributions of qualified plan participants and employer contributions that match those contributions.

Benefit and contribution limits. Limits on participant benefits and contributions apply with respect to qualified plans. For defined benefit plans, a participant's annual normal retirement benefit cannot exceed the lesser of 100 percent of a participant's average compensation for his or her three consecutive years of highest compensation, limited to $200,000 for benefits accruing in post-1987 years, or an amount indexed for inflation. There may be limits to the 3-year provision. The compensation and dollar limits are reduced for participants with less than 10 years of plan participation.

The applicable dollar amount is actuarially reduced when a participant retires before reaching the statutory Social Security retirement age. However, that amount is actuarially increased when a participant retires after the statutory Social Security retirement age.

For defined contribution plans, the limit on an annual increase to a participant's account is generally the lesser of 25 percent of the participant's yearly compensation, limited to $200,000 for post-1987 years, or $30,000.

Complex special rules apply to individuals who are participants in a defined benefit plan and a defined contribution plan.

RRA '93. RRA '93 reduces to $150,000 the maximum amount that can be considered for purposes of calculating benefits from and contributions to a qualified plan. For 1993, $235,840 is the maximum amount. The reduction applies for plan years beginning after December 31, 1993, and the lower limit will be indexed for inflation in later years. See the Foreword on RRA '93.

Payment of benefits. In general, the payment of benefits in a qualified plan must begin (subject to an exception, to be described) no later than the 60th day after the end of the latest plan year in which:

- The participant reaches age 65 or normal retirement age under the plan, whichever is earlier;
- The participant completes 10 years' participation in the plan; or
- The participant's service with the employer is terminated.

A participant may elect to have the payment of plan benefits begin after the date of his or her retirement. However, the payment of benefits generally must begin by April 1 of the calendar year after the year in which the retired participant reaches age 70 ½.

A special provision applies in cases where the participant is not a 5 percent owner of the employer sponsoring the plan in the plan year that ends with or within the calendar year the participant reaches age 66 ½ or any later year, and the participant reached age 70 ½ by January 1, 1988. Under this provision, the date on which the payment of benefits is required to begin may be deferred as long as April 1 of the year after the calendar year in which the participant separates from the sponsoring employer's service.

Note: For purposes of the preceding rules, a participant reaches age 70 ½ on the day of the sixth month following the month in which he or she reaches age 70 corresponding numerically to his or her birthdate.

Minimum distribution requirements. Plan benefits are required to be paid out to an eligible participant over a period not longer than the participant's life or life expectancy, or the combined lives or life expectancies of the participant and a beneficiary designated by the participant. When distributions are made to a participant before death, the undistributed amount, if any, payable to the participant's beneficiary must be distributed no less rapidly than for the predeath distribution method. If no predeath distribution is made, the participant's full plan interest must generally be distributed to the designated beneficiary within five years after the participant's death.

There are several exceptions to this five-year distribution rule. This rules does not apply where any part of the participant's interest may be paid to, or for the benefit of, his or her designated beneficiary; the part of the participant's interest to which the surviving spouse as designated beneficiary is entitled is to be distributed over the beneficiary's life or up to his or her life expectancy; and distributions begin no later than one year after the participant's death. With respect to the exception for the participant's surviving spouse, the five-year distribution rule does not apply if the surviving spouse's interest is distributed over his or her life or up to his or her life expectancy, and the distributions begin no later than the date on which the participant would have reached age 70 ½. Should the surviving spouse die before benefit payments begin, the spouse is treated in the same manner as the plan participant. For this purpose, annual recalculation of life expectancies is permitted. Also, in general, for purposes of the rules described, payments made over participant or beneficiary lives or life expectancies are required to be made in level, nonincreasing amounts.

Key Legislative Changes Affecting Qualified Plans

The following are key tax law changes made under recent legislation, effective, except as otherwise noted, for post-1986 plan distributions.

Five-year forward averaging. This averaging, as provided by the Tax Reform Act of 1986 (TRA '86), is limited to a taxpayer who is at least age 59½ when a distribution is made from a qualified plan. Under the 1988 Technical and Miscellaneous Revenue Act ('88 TAMRA), this averaging applies to distributions received by a plan participant who was at least age 59½ at the time of distribution.

Capital gain treatment. This treatment may be elected, under TRA '86, with respect to pre-1974 participation. Under a transition rule, it may be elected by individuals reaching age 50 before 1986, with a flat 20 percent tax rate applicable. Under '88 TAMRA, this treatment is available to plan participants who reach age 50 before 1986 or individuals, estates, or trusts that receive a lump-sum distribution from a qualified plan with respect to plan participants who reach age 50 before 1986.

Lump-sum distributions. Tax averaging with respect to lump-sum distributions from qualified plans made after 1986 was reduced from 10 years to 5 years by TRA '86. Individuals reaching age 50 before 1986 could elect, under a transition rule, to use 10-year averaging under tax rates applicable in 1986. This election is also available, under '88 TAMRA, to plan participants who reach age 50 before 1986 or individuals, estates, or trusts receiving a lump-sum distribution from a qualified plan with respect to plan participants who reach age 50 before 1986.

Note: TAMRA also requires taxpayers, for purposes of computing tax on a lump-sum distribution under 10-year averaging, to reflect the zero bracket amount applicable for pre-1986 taxable years.

Tax rates applicable to single individuals are used in connection with five-year averaging. Also, a taxpayer may make only one election with respect to tax averaging on a lump-sum distribution, and this election applies for all purposes under the Internal Revenue Code.

Capital gains. For qualified plan distributions made after 1986, 10-year averaging was repealed, as noted previously. Capital gains treatment for amounts attributable to pre-1974 plan participation is phased out over a six-year period. Also, as noted earlier, five-year averaging may be elected for a lump-sum distribution received by a plan participant, and a transition rule is also provided. The capital gains phaseout percentages are 50 percent for 1990 and 25 percent for 1991.

Averaging. To elect 5-year averaging, or 10-year averaging under the transition rule, a lump-sum distribution from a qualified plan is required in the amount of the electing employee's plan account balance. Such a distribution, required to be paid within one taxable year, is made on account of the plan participant's death; reaching age 59½; separation from service from the plan sponsor, regardless of cause (except for self-employed persons or owner-employees); or disabilty.

Rollovers. A participant in a qualified plan is allowed to withdraw his or her plan account balance (or a portion thereof, as will be described) and reinvest that amount, tax-free, in another qualified plan or in an IRA. The rollover amount cannot exceed the value of the cash or property received by the plan participant minus the contributions made to the plan by the participant. A tax-free rollover is also available if the qualified plan is terminated or, if the plan is a stock bonus or profit-sharing plan, if plan contributions are totally discontinued. A tax-free rollover is also available to a spouse of a deceased participant in a qualified plan.

A partial distribution from a qualified plan may qualify for tax-free rollover treatment. However, for post-1986 partial distributions from qualified plans, a rollover is available only if made on account of the plan participant's death, separation from the sponsoring employer's service, or disability. In addition, a partial distribution must amount to at least 50 percent of the participant's plan account balance and cannot be part of a series of periodic payments, and the rollover of such amount must be elected.

Death benefit exclusion. A beneficiary who receives a distribution from a qualified plan as a result of a plan participant's death is allowed to exclude up to $5,000 of that amount from income. The exclusion is available as long as the plan participant's right to receive such amount was forfeitable immediately before his or her death. This exclusion is available even if the qualified plan participant was self-employed or an owner-employee.

(Code §§ 101, 401 et seq.; CCH ¶ 6502, ¶ 17,502 et seq.; YPG 4.03 et seq.)

qualified terminable interests Transfers of terminable interests, for example, annuities, life estates, or terms for years, generally cannot qualify for the marital deduction provided for purposes of the federal estate or gift tax. However, for individuals who die after 1981, an exception to the general rule is available for qualified terminable interest property (QTIP).

In general, the marital deduction is allowed to an individual or the individual's estate for the full value of a bequest or gift of property to his or her spouse, although the spouse receives only a qualifying life income interest, and all other interests in that property, including the remainder interest, pass to others.

As long as the applicable QTIP rules are met, a life interest in property granted by an individual to his or her surviving spouse is not treated as a terminable interest. All such property is treated as passing to the surviving spouse. Therefore, the transferred property's full value qualifies for the marital deduction.

QTIP

As noted, the marital deduction is available for the full value of qualified terminable interest property (QTIP) if QTIP treatment is elected by the individual donor or the executor of an individual's estate. QTIP is property passing from a decedent to his or her spouse who is entitled to receive, on an annual or more frequent basis, all or part of the property's income. This spousal income interest is a *qualified income interest* (QII). QIIs do not include income interests granted for a term of years or conditionally terminable life interests.

The power to appoint any interest in the transferred property to another person, except the transferee spouse during his or her life, cannot be given to anyone, including the spouse. But powers may be created or retained with respect to some or all of the property, as long as all such powers are exercisable only upon or after the death of the transferee spouse.

Annuities are, in general, treated similarly to income interests. For joint and survivor annuities in which spouses have the sole right to payments, the marital deduction is available with respect to a transfer of an interest to a spouse before the death of the surviving spouse. However, for decedents who die, and for transfers made, after December 31, 1981, where an individual donor or the individual's executor irrevocably elects not to have QTIP treatment apply, such a transfer does not qualify for an estate or gift tax marital deduction.

Note: In determining the federal estate tax liability of a decedent, a property interest's value cannot be deducted more than once. This rule presumably is designed to prohibit a double deduction from a transfer of property divided between a charity and a spouse.

The irrevocable election of a marital deduction for the value of QTIP is made on the estate tax return of the decedent. The election may be made for all or part of any property qualifying as QTIP.

Where a QII is transferred to a spouse, providing for a charitable remainder trust or unitrust, the property's full value is treated as passing to the surviving spouse and qualifies for the marital deduction.

Transfer taxes. Transfer taxes apply to property subject to a QTIP election at the earlier of the date on which a spouse makes any disposition of all or part of a QII or the date of death of that spouse. If a spouse makes a lifetime transfer of a QII, this constitutes a taxable gift in the amount of the transferred property's full value, reduced by any amount received by that spouse as a result of the transfer. The full value of such QII property otherwise is included in the spouse's gross estate at fair market value at the date of his or her death or on the alternate valuation date, if that date is elected.

Recovery of gift tax paid on a remainder interest with respect to a lifetime transfer of an income interest, or of estate tax paid due to an increase in the spouse's gross estate, may be obtained by the spouse or the spouse's estate, in addition to any penalties or interest related to such additional taxes.

QTIP trusts. These trusts involve bequests of qualified terminable interest property. Three types of trusts are commonly utilized: marital trusts, nonmarital trusts, and QTIP trusts.

(Code § 2056)

R

rabbi trust Many corporations establish deferred compensation plans for key executives as an incentive and to retain their services. Such plans do not qualify for the favorable tax benefits accorded qualified plans because they discriminate in favor of highly compensated employees. However, such plans can be established in a manner so that key employee participants do not:

* Constructively receive payments from the plan, and
* Receive an economic benefit from the plan before payments are actually made to them.

Typically, employees covered under such plans are limited only to contractual rights to receive future payments from the sponsoring employer. A significant potential disadvantage to employees participating in such plans is that their rights to plan payments are dependent on the plan sponsor's economic health. The rabbi trust received its name as a result of a private letter ruling in which a congregation established a similar deferred compensation arrangement for the benefit of its rabbi. According to the IRS, which approved that arrangement, the employer can establish certain trusts to provide for the future payment of benefits without causing participating employees to be immediately taxable on those benefits. Such a trust must be a grantor trust that is subject to the claims of creditors if the sponsoring employer becomes insolvent. For income tax purposes, such a trust would be considered a grantor trust.

The employee would not be entitled to a deduction for amounts transferred to the trust at the time of transfer, but will be entitled to a deduction at such time as a participant is required to include plan benefits in income.

Model trusts. The IRS has issued two revenue procedures prescribing rules for obtaining a private letter ruling with respect to an unfunded deferred compensation plan. In one of these revenue procedures, a model rabbi trust arrangement is provided. In the other, general rules are provided with respect to unfunded plans, whether or not a rabbi trust is included. These revenue procedures apply to ruling requests made after July 28, 1992 (CCH ¶ 18,209.025).

real estate See **accelerated cost recovery system (ACRS); depreciation; modified accelerated cost recovery system (MACRS); mortgage; partnership; personal residence, sale of; real estate investment trusts (REITs); real estate mortgage investment conduits (REMICs)**

real estate investment trusts (REITs) Corporations—except for banks, insurance companies, trusts, or other associations—that invest in real estate and/or mortgages on real estate—that meet statutory requirements with respect to ownership and purpose and that also meet statutory gross income and diversification tests may elect to be treated as real estate investment trusts (REITs) for tax purposes.

Unincorporated trusts or associations may elect REIT status as long as they were not REITs in preceding taxable years. This is the case even if, in the first taxable year in which REIT status is elected, the entity has less than 100 shareholders or meets the stock ownership test applicable to personal holding companies (i.e., 50 percent in value of the entity's stock is owned by five or fewer individuals). The requirements must, however, be met after the first taxable year.

A REIT may hold property for sale to customers in the ordinary course of business. However, such sales are considered prohibited transactions subject to a 100 percent tax on the realized net income.

To qualify as a REIT, a trust or association must meet the following tests during a taxable year:

- At least 95 percent of gross income is composed of dividends; interest; real property rents; gains from sales of stock, securities, or real property; other than inventory or property sold in the ordinary course of the taxpayer's trade or business; abatements and refunds of real property taxes; and foreclosure income.

- At least 75 percent of gross income is composed of rents; mortgage interest; gains from sales of real property and mortgage interests; income derived from other qualified REITs; real property tax refunds and abatements; and foreclosure income.

- No more than 30 percent of gross income is produced by the sale or disposition of stock or securities held for less than the applicable long-term capital gain holding period; property held for sale in the ordinary course of business (e.g., inventory) other than foreclosure property; and real property held less than four years and non-involuntarily converted (under Code § 1033) or foreclosure property.

Also, at least 75 percent of a qualifying REIT's total asset value must be composed of real estate, including mortgage interest, cash and equivalents such as accounts receivable, and government securities. Not more than 25 percent of a qualifying REIT's total asset value can be composed of securities, other than government securities, and it cannot own securities of any one issuer amounting in value to more than 5 percent of its total assets or 10 percent of such an issuer's outstanding voting securities.

Taxation of REITs

A REIT that distributes a minimum of 95 percent of its taxable income for a taxable year is generally taxable at rates applicable to regular US corporations on their retained earnings other than capital gains. Distributed earnings are taxed to shareholders, and the REIT is allowed a dividends-paid deduction.

If a REIT has a net operating loss (NOL), it cannot be carried back to a prior taxable year but may be carried forward to each of the next 15 years. A NOL for a year in which REIT status was not elected cannot be carried back to a year in which REIT status was elected. In determining the maximum amount of capital gain dividends that can be distributed for a taxable year, a REIT cannot offset net capital gain by any part of a current-year or carryover NOL so as to increase the capital gain available. If a REIT elects to distribute capital gain dividends in an amount more than its net income for the taxable year, it must increase any NOL carryover by that amount.

Taxable income distributed by a REIT is taxable to shareholders as ordinary income. Distributed capital gains are long-term capital gains for shareholders.

REIT Distributions

Any loss on a sale of exchange of stock or an interest in a REIT held by a taxpayer for six months or less constitutes a long-term capital loss to the extent that that taxpayer received a long-term capital gain distribution. This rule applies to losses pertaining to REIT stock or interests with respect to which a taxpayer's holding period commenced after July 18, 1984.

A REIT capital gain dividend is treated as a long-term capital gain (i.e., as a gain from the sale or exchange of a capital asset held, under current tax law, for more than 12 months). The rule just given, however, does not apply to losses from the disposition of REIT stock or interests under a plan providing for a periodic liquidation of interests in the REIT. A loss on the sale or exchange of REIT stock or a REIT interest, when held by the taxpayer for 30 days or less and acquired between June 23, 1984, and December 31, 1987, is a long-term capital loss to the extent of capital gain dividends received during that 30-day period.

REIT Deficiency Dividends

Generally, if the amount required to be distributed by a REIT for purposes of the 95 percent test is increased, or dividends distributed for that year are decreased as a result of a court determination, the REIT may distribute a deficiency dividend to avoid disqualification from REIT status.

(Code §§ 856, 857; CCH ¶ 26,760, 26,720)

real estate limited partnership See **partnership.**

real estate mortgage investment conduits (REMICs) These are special entities under the tax law that hold a fixed mortgage pool and issue various classes of interests (regular or residual) to investors. A *regular* interest in a REMIC is generally an interest whose terms are fixed on the REMIC's start-up day (to be defined) and with respect to which payment of a specified principal amount is provided.

REMIC status must be elected by the entity, and that status continues as long as requirements set forth in the Internal Revenue Code are met. In general, under these requirements, substantially all assets of a REMIC at the end of the third month that began after its start-up day, and each succeeding quarter, must be qualified mortgages and permitted investments.

A REMIC's *start-up day* is the day it issues interests to investors. Permitted investments include cash-flow investments (i.e., temporary investments of funds before distribution to investors), qualified reserve assets (i.e., intangible property held for investment in a qualified reserve for expenses and for certain distributions of funds), and foreclosure property.

Tax Treatment

REMICs, in general, are not taxable entities but pass-through entities. They pass through income to interest holders and are not taxed themselves unless they engage in specified prohibited transactions, to which a tax of 100 percent of the resulting income applies.

Holders of regular REMIC interests are taxed on the REMIC's income that would be taxable to an accrual-basis holder of a debt instrument having similar terms. Holders of a residual interest in a REMIC take into account their daily portions of that REMIC's taxable income or net loss for each day in a taxable year that such an interest is held. However, such a holder cannot reduce taxable income below an *excess inclusion* for that year, which is the amount of any excess of net income passed through to the holder by the REMIC over a deemed interest component called the *daily accrual.*

When a regular REMIC interest is disposed of, any gain is treated as ordinary income in the amount of unaccrued original issue discount (OID) calculated at 110 percent of the applicable federal rate (AFR) at the time that the holder acquired the interest in the REMIC.

(Code §§ 860A–F; CCH ¶ 26,800)

See also **original issue discount (OID).**

real estate tax shelters See **partnership; tax shelters.**

recapture There are several recapture rules under the Internal Revenue Code. These provide for the recapture of certain tax benefits allowed under the Code, notably, favorable tax depreciation rates and certain credits, particularly the formerly allowed investment credit. For discussion of specific recapture provisions under the Code, see **accelerated cost recovery system (ACRS); depreciation; investment tax credit (ITC); modified accelerated cost recovery system (MACRS).**

recovery methods See **accelerated cost recovery system (ACRS); modified accelerated cost recovery system (MACRS).**

recovery property See **accelerated cost recovery system (ACRS); modified accelerated cost recovery system (MACRS).**

redemptions In general, this term refers to the purchase of stock, bonds, or other interests by the issuing entity, typically a corporation, from the holders of such interests. For discussion of redemptions of specific interests, see **annuities; bond; common stock; preferred stock.**

regulated futures contracts See **tax straddles.**

regulated investment companies See **mutual funds.**

REITs See **real estate investment trusts (REITs).**

rentals See **rents.**

rents These represent amounts paid or accrued by a lessee of property to the lessor of that property. These amounts are included in gross income by the lessor.

The lessor must also include in gross income any expenses paid by the lessee for the lessor and any payments received in connection with the cancellation of a lease.

(Code § 61; CCH ¶ 5502)

repairs These involve work intended to keep property in efficient operating condition. Expenditures for such work may be deductible as business expenses when incurred in connection with property used in a trade or business.

However, if such expenditures add to the property's value or its useful life, they constitute capital expenditures that must be added to the taxpayer's cost basis for the property and recovered through depreciation.

Special rules apply in connection with repairs made in preparation for the sale of real property—so-called fix-up expenses.

(Code § 162; CCH ¶ 8450; YPG 2.11)

See also **accelerated cost recovery system (ACRS); basis; capital expenditures; modified accelerated cost recovery system (MACRS).**

repossessions Two types of property are subject to repossession by sellers; personal property and real property. The specific tax rules applicable to these two types of property are discussed in the following sections.

Personal Property

Repossession of personal property sold under the installment method is considered to involve a disposition of the underlying installment note. The amount of the resulting gain or loss on that disposition is the difference between the seller's basis for the underlying installment note and the fair market value of the property when it is repossessed. The character of any resulting gain or loss is the same as on the original sale. The seller's basis for the installment note is the note's face amount less the seller's deferred gross profit with respect to the sale on repossession.

Also, a bad-debt deduction may be available to the seller in cases where the installment note balance is not fully satisfied by the repossession of the property and that balance cannot be collected.

Real Property

When a seller (or the beneficiary or estate of a deceased seller) repossesses real property secured by an installment note, no loss can be claimed. Any gain on the repossession is limited. The limit on the seller's gain is the amount of money and the fair market value of other property received before the repossession, other than the buyer's notes, in excess of the gain reported before the repossession. For purposes of figuring this limit, the sale price of the property is reduced by the costs of repossession, such as sales commissions and legal fees.

Personal Residences

Special rules apply if there is an installment sale of an individual's principal residence and, under statutory rules, the individual deferred payment of tax on the resulting gain due to the replacement of that residence or excluded gain from tax under the exclusion available to individuals age 55 and over. In general, under these special rules, if the individual resells the residence within one year after the date of the repossession, the original sale of the residence and its resale are considered to be a single transaction. The seller's gain is determined on the basis of the sale *and* the resale, and any deferrable or excludable gain is then determined. The general rules applicable to repossessions apply if the property is not sold within the one-year statutory period.

Basis of Repossessed Real Property

In general, the basis of real property that has been repossessed is the seller's adjusted basis of the indebtedness secured by that property on repossession, plus any gain then recognized and any repossession costs incurred by the seller. If, as a result of the repossession, the related indebtedness is not discharged, the basis of that indebtedness is zero. If, before repossession, the seller treated the secured indebtedness as worthless, in whole or part, the seller is treated as having received on repossession an amount equal to that treated as worthless. This amount also increases the seller's adjusted basis in the indebtedness.

(Code § 1038; CCH ¶ 31,640)

residence, personal, sale of A taxpayer can postpone or partially recognize gain from the sale of a principal residence for tax purposes if he or she buys or builds a new principal residence within two years before or after the date of sale of the former principal residence. The new principal residence must be used by the taxpayer within this period.

If these requirements are met, gain on the sale of the taxpayer's former principal residence is recognized only to the extent that the adjusted sales price of that residence is greater than the taxpayer's cost for the new principal residence. If the cost of the new principal residence is equal to or greater than the adjusted sales price of the former principal residence, no gain is recognized by the taxpayer. The adjusted basis of the principal residence acquired by the taxpayer is reduced by the gain not recognized on the sale of his or her former principal residence.

Note: An exchange of a taxpayer's principal residence for another residence to be used as the taxpayer's principal residence is treated as a sale. A taxpayer's acquisition of a principal residence in exchange for other property is treated as a purchase of that residence.

Nonrecognition of gain is also available if one spouse dies after the date of sale of the couple's former principal residence and before a replacement residence is purchased, as long as the surviving spouse purchases the replacement residence within the two-year statutory replacement period.

Disposition of a residence due to condemnation or a threat thereof, or a seizure or requisition of the residence, may be treated as a sale of the residence; or, if the taxpayer so elects, the involuntary conversion nonrecognition rules will apply.

The adjusted sales price is the amount realized on the sale of the residence, less the qualified expenses to fix up that property for sale. The amount realized on the sale is the sales price less the expenses incurred with respect to the sale (e.g., broker's commissions, title policy fees, state taxes, and points paid by a seller to a lender with respect to a buyer's mortgage).

Fix-up expenses with respect to the sale of a residence are deducted from the amount realized on the sale as long as such expenses are not otherwise deductible in determining the taxpayer's taxable income, are not capital expenditures required to be added to the basis of the residence, are paid within 30 days of the sale of the residence, and as long as the fix-up work is completed during the 90 days ending on the date of the contract of sale.

A taxpayer need not actually occupy his or her former principal residence on the date of its sale. This is so even if the taxpayer moved into a replacement residence and rented the former residence prior to its sale, or rented out the replacement residence before occupying it. However, the taxpayer must physically occupy the replacement residence before the end of the statutory replacement period.

Ownership of stock in a cooperative housing corporation or ownership of a condominium unit is treated the same as ownership of a personal residence, as long as the purchaser uses the cooperative or condominium housing as his or her principal residence.

Limitations

Three limitations on the nonrecognition rule apply:

- When a new principal residence is purchased and sold before the sale of the taxpayer's former principal residence, gain must be recognized on the sale.
- If, during the statutory two-year replacement period, more than one residence is purchased as a principal residence, the property last acquired is considered a new residence under the nonrecognition rule.

- If, under the statutory two-year replacement rule, the taxpayer made another sale to which the nonrecognition rule applies, nonrecognition treatment generally will not apply to that second sale.

Note: If a taxpayer acquires a new principal residence more than once during the statutory replacement period for employment-related reasons, tax-free rollover treatment may be available.

Exclusion for Taxpayers Age 55 and Over

Taxpayers age 55 and over who sell a principal residence may elect to exclude from tax up to $125,000 of gain on the sale. For married taxpayers filing separate returns, the maximum excludable amount is $62,500.

A second qualification for this exclusion is that the taxpayer must have owned and used the residence as a principal residence for a total of at least three years during the five-year period ending on the date of its sale. A condominium or ownership of stock in a cooperative housing corporation qualifies under the rule. Spouses owning a residence as joint tenants, tenants by the entirety, or as community property owners, and who file a joint tax return for the taxable year in which the residence is sold, are considered a single person for the purposes of this exclusion.

With respect to sales of residences after September 30, 1988, a taxpayer will meet the use rule if, during the prescribed five-year period, he or she becomes physically or mentally incapable of caring for himself or herself, owns and uses the residence for at least one year, and during the five-year period, owns the property and lives in a facility licensed to care for individuals unable to care for themselves.

This election can be used in conjunction with the nonrecognition rules that permit deferral of all or part of the gain not excluded under the $100,000 or $125,000 exclusion available to homeowners.

A single lifetime election is available to a taxpayer, and married taxpayers are allowed a single election *per couple.* If spouses make the election during their marriage and they later divorce, the election is unavailable to them or their new spouses in the future. But, if two unmarried individuals who each made the election to marry, no recapture tax will apply.

A taxpayer over age 55 whose spouse is deceased meets the holding period and use requirements if the taxpayer reaches age 55 before the date of sale of the residence and did not remarry, and the deceased spouse met the holding and use requirements and did not take the exclusion on a different property.

(Code §§ 121, 1034; CCH ¶¶ 7260, 31,560; YPG 2.05 et seq.)

retirement of assets See **accelerated cost recovery system (ACRS); depreciation; investment tax credit (ITC); modified accelerated cost recovery system (MACRS).**

retirement plans See **qualified retirement, profit-sharing, etc., plans.**

revocable trusts. These trusts are not created to obtain tax advantages but solely for non-tax-related reasons. Basically, a grantor of such a trust seeks to retain control of the trust assets, thereby forfeiting tax advantages typically obtained through the use of such an arrangement as an irrevocable trust.

The major benefit of such a trust is that the assets transferred to the trust escape the probate process and its attendant expense and delay. Use of this type of trust can minimize potential claims of creditors and heirs after the grantor's death, since the assets transferred to the trust are not includable in the grantor's estate.

See also **irrevocable trust; probate.**

rollovers See **individual retirement accounts (IRAs); qualified retirement, profit-sharing, etc., plans; residence, personal, sale of.**

royalties Royalty payments are required to be included in the gross income of the recipient. Such payments include those made with respect to copyrights on artistic, literary, musical, and other creative works or patents. They also include payments received with respect to ownership interests in gas, mineral, oil, or timber properties. With respect to the latter types of royalty payments, taxpayers are typically entitled to an allowance for depletion.

(Code § 61; CCH ¶ 5502)
See also **depletion.**

S

S corporations Basically, an S corporation is not a taxpaying entity. The income and expenses of these corporations are generally passed through to shareholders, who report such items on their individual tax returns.

In general, for a corporation to qualify as an S corporation, it can have no more than 35 shareholders. Eligible shareholders include individuals (except for nonresident aliens), estates, and certain trusts, including grantor trusts, voting trusts, qualified Subchapter S trusts, and testamentary trusts (for a 60-day period starting on the day that the stock is transferred to the trust under the decedent shareholder's will). Also, to qualify as an S corporation, a corporation cannot have more than one class of stock issued and outstanding.

The computation of the taxable income of an S corporation for purposes of determining the items to be passed through to shareholders is similar to that for partnerships, with some exceptions. The taxable income of an S corporation is similar to that of an individual, with some exceptions, such as certain items required to be computed separately and certain personal deductions (e.g., charitable contributions, net operating losses).

When an S corporation has earnings and profits from years in which it was a C (regular) corporation, it may be subject to tax at the corporate level on any passive investment income, such as royalties, rents, dividends, interest, annuities, or gains from the sale of stock and securities. Such an S corporation may possibly be subject to the termination of its S corporation election.

Note: The preceding represents only a brief presentation of the S corporation qualification rules; a discussion of the tax rules applicable to an S corporation as an entity, including the election, revocation, or termination of S corporation status, is beyond the scope of this book. The following discussion focuses on the taxation of shareholders of S corporations.

Shareholder Tax Treatment

In general, S corporation shareholders report their respective shares of the corporation's income, deduction, loss, and credit items in their taxable years in which the corporation's taxable year ends. These items are generally computed on a daily basis, and also on the basis of a shareholder's holdings on each day during the corporation's taxable year.

A shareholder's deduction with respect to the S corporation's losses and deductions is limited. This limit is the sum of the shareholder's adjusted bases in stock of the corporation and any debt owed to the shareholder by the corporation. Special rules apply where the S corporation's election is terminated.

A shareholder's deductible loss with respect to an S corporation may further be limited by the at-risk and passive loss rules. See **at-risk rules** and **passive loss rules.**

S Corporation Distributions

An S corporation's distributions of cash or property to shareholders is generally taxed based on whether the corporation has earnings and profits. In general, an S corporation cannot have earnings and profits except for those related to taxable years when the corporation was not an S corporation or to pre-1983 S corporation years. If an S corporation does not have earnings and profits, distributions are treated first as a tax-free return of capital up to the shareholder's basis for the S corporation stock and then as gain on a sale or exchange.

If the corporation has earnings and profits, distributions are deemed made in the following order:

1. Nontaxable return of capital to the extent of an accumulated adjustments account (AAA).
2. Dividends to the extent of the S corporation's accumulated earnings and profits.

3. Nontaxable return of capital to the extent of the remaining basis of the S corporation shareholder's stock.

4. Gain from a sale or exchange.

For purposes of this rule, specific statutory rules apply to an AAA. An AAA, in general, concerns the taxability of distributions by an S corporation with accumulated earnings and profits. A complete discussion of the tax rules applicable to an AAA is beyond the scope of this book. For further coverage, see Code § 1368(e) and CCH ¶ 4846K.

Note: The distribution priority rules just described may be avoided if an election is made to treat the distributions as dividends. All shareholders who receive distributions from the S corporation during the taxable year, however, must consent.

Basis Adjustment

When a corporation has a valid S election in effect, its shareholders make the following adjustments to the basis of their stock in the corporation.

Basis increase. The basis of S corporation stock is increased by the shareholder's respective share of:

• *All* income items of the S corporation that are separately computed and passed through to the shareholders.

• Other income of the S corporation that is not separately computed.

• The amount of the S corporation's depletion deductions over its basis for the depletable property.

Basis decrease. The basis of S corporation stock is decreased by the shareholder's respective share of:

• Distributions that are not includable in shareholder income by statute.

• *All* of the S corporation's loss and deduction items separately stated and passed through to shareholders.

• The S corporation's loss that is not separately computed.

• Expenses of the S corporation that are not deductible in determining its taxable income and not properly chargeable to capital account.

• The shareholder's deduction for depletion of oil and gas wells not in excess of the shareholder's proportionate share of the adjusted basis of such depletable properties.

When a shareholder's basis for S corporation stock is decreased to zero as a result of all but the first of these decrease adjustments, further net decrease would be applied against any debt owed to the shareholder by the S corporation. A later basis increase would be applied to the basis of that debt and then to the basis of the shareholder's stock.

(Code §§ 1361 et seq.; CCH ¶ 33,421 et seq.)

sales and exchanges See basis; capital asset; capital gains and losses; installment and deferred-payment sales; recapture; Section 1231 assets; tax-free exchanges.

salvage value In general, this is the value of depreciable or cost recovery property when it is retired from use.

See also **accelerated cost recovery system (ACRS); depreciation; modified accelerated cost recovery system (MACRS).**

savings bonds See US savings bonds.

Section 401(k) plans These employer-sponsored plans are named after the section of the Internal Revenue Code providing for them, and are also referred to as cash or deferred arrangement (CODAs). Under these plans, an employee can elect to receive a cash payment from his or her employer or to have the employer make a contribution to a profit-sharing plan. The employee may elect to receive part cash and have the balance contributed to the profit-sharing plan. The amount of the contribution to the profit-sharing plan is subject to statutory limits, adjusted for inflation each year. For 1994, the statutory limit is $9,240.

An employee who elects to have the employer contribute to the profit-sharing plan will not be taxed currently on the amount contributed on his or her behalf, as long as the plan meets statutory nondiscrimination rules designed to prevent plan distribution in favor of highly paid employees. When an employee's elective plan deferrals exceed the statutory limit, he or she is taxed currently on the excess amount. The excess amount does not increase the employee's basis in his or her plan account, so the employee will again be taxed on that amount when it is withdrawn from the plan.

Employee withdrawals from such a plan may generally be made when a corporate employer sells all of its business assets to another corporation or, under certain circumstances, sells its entire interest in a subsidiary.

Employees are also permitted to make hardship withdrawals from such plans. After 1988, such withdrawals are limited to all of the employee's elective contributions to the plan, whenever allocated, and any earnings on elective contributions allocable before 1989.

[Code § 401(k); CCH ¶ 18,112]

Section 1231 assets These assets include real estate and other depreciable property used in a trade or business that are excluded from the definition of capital assets for purposes of the capital gain and loss rules. But, under a special rule, all gains and all losses with respect to such assets are grouped separately. When such gains exceed such losses, each gain and each loss is treated as if the related asset was held for the long-term capital gain holding period. When the losses exceed the gains, each gain and loss is treated as if the related asset produced ordinary gain or loss. In determining such gains and losses, the following are taken into account:

- Property used in a trade or business subject to cost recovery or depreciation held for more than the statutory long-term capital gain or loss holding period.
- Business real estate held longer than the statutory long-term capital gain or loss holding period.
- Trade or business property that is involuntarily converted and held longer than the statutory long-term capital gain or loss holding period.
- Capital assets that are involuntarily converted and held longer than the statutory long-term capital gain or loss holding period.
- Crops, where the land on which they are grown was held longer than the statutory long-term capital gain or loss holding period.
- Livestock.
- Certain coal, domestic iron ore, and timber.

If such an asset also qualifies as Section 1245 property or Section 1250 property (or certain mining property), the Section 1231 gain on the sale or exchange of such property is the amount by which the total resulting gain is more than the Section 1245 or Section 1250 gain (or Section 617 gain with respect to mining property). A loss disallowed under another Code section is not taken into account under the preceding rules.

Recapture Rules

If a taxpayer has a net Section 1231 gain for a taxable year, the taxpayer must go back to the five most recent preceding taxable years to determine if any there are net Section 1231 losses to be recaptured. If the taxpayer used any such losses, net Section 1231 gain for the current year must be treated as ordinary income up to the amount of Section 1231 losses not recaptured during that five-year period on a first-in, first-out basis.

Involuntary Conversions

Gain and loss from involuntary conversions of qualified property (as described earlier) are subject to the rules of Section 1231, unless the taxpayer elects to have the nonrecognition rules of Section 1033 apply. The converted property must be held longer than the statutory long-term capital gain holding period.

A special rule applies with respect to casualty or theft losses, depreciable business property, and capital assets held longer than the statutory long-term capital gain holding period and related to the taxpayer's trade or business or a for-profit transaction. The gains and losses from such casualties and thefts are required to be separately grouped. If gains are greater than or equal to losses on such casualties and thefts, the gains and losses are combined with other transactions involving Section 1231 assets in determining whether there is a net gain or loss for purposes of Section 1231. If the losses exceed the gains on such casualties and thefts, the gains and losses are not combined with other transactions involving Section 1231 assets, and the net loss is treated as an ordinary loss.

Livestock

Under Section 1231, sales or involuntary conversions of livestock, except poultry, held for draft, breeding, dairy, or sporting purposes may qualify for capital gain treatment. To qualify, such livestock must be held by the taxpayer for at least 12 months (24 months in the case of horses and cattle). The date of the acquisition of such livestock begins the taxpayer's holding period. An involuntary conversion of livestock, for purposes of this rule, includes destruction or a sale or exchange made as a result of disease.

(Code § 1231; CCH ¶ 33,272; YPG 2.01)

See also **capital gains and losses.**

securities See **bond; options; stock.**

self-employment tax This tax is imposed on self-employed individuals for the purpose of providing Social Security benefits. This tax is assessed on the basis of the self-employment income of such an individual and is added to the income tax reported on his or her individual income tax return.

(Code § 1402; CCH ¶ 33,861)

short sales In basic terms, an investor makes a short sale when selling stock (or other property, such as commodity futures) that is not intended to be delivered by the investor as a result of the sale. There are two types of short sales; a regular short sale, which is made when the investor does not own the stock (or other property) sold, and a short sale "against the box," which is made when the investor does own the stock (or other property) sold.

An investor would make a short sale if he or she anticipates that the value of the stock sold will decline. The investor's securities broker borrows the stock sold so that it can be delivered to its buyer. The cash value of the stock sold is deposited with the party lending the stock involved. Certain restrictions on such sales are prescribed by stock exchange rules and securities law regulations.

The investor who sells short must subsequently cover the short sale by purchasing the amount of stock borrowed from the lender. If the investor can purchase the stock involved at a price lower than the short sale price, he or she has a taxable gain. The amount of the gain is the difference between the short sale and purchase prices, reduced by any related expenses such as commissions. If the investor has to purchase the stock involved at a price higher than the sales price, he or she has a loss for tax purposes.

Tax Rules Applicable to Short Sales

An investor does not recognize gain or loss on a short sale until he or she delivers the related stock for purposes of closing the short sale transaction. Whether the resulting gain or loss is long-term or short-term depends on the holding period of the stock delivered to close the short sale transaction. The date of the short sale is irrelevant in determining whether the gain or loss is long-term or short-term.

Substantially identical stock. Special rules apply when an investor held stock that is substantially identical to the stock sold in the short sale when the short sale was made or closed. One set of rules applies if the "substantially identical" stock was held for less than the long-term capital gain holding period (currently, over one year). Another set of rules applies if the "substantial identical" stock was held longer than the long-term capital gain or loss holding period.

If substantially identical stock is held for less than the long-term holding period, gain resulting from the closing of the short sale is short-term. Also, the holding period for that stock begins on the earlier of the date that the short sale was closed or the date of sale, gift, or any other disposition of the stock.

If "substantially identical" stock is held longer than the long-term holding period, a loss resulting from the closing of the short sale is long-term. The holding period of the stock used to close the short sale is not taken into account.

Note: Statutory "wash sale" rules are also applicable to short sales. As a result, a loss on a sale of "substantially identical" stock, or another short sale of such stock, made within 30 days after a short sale is closed is not allowed for tax purposes. See **wash sales.**

Short sales against the box. A short sale against the box involves stock owned by the investor. Tax deferral on the gain from such a sale from the current year to the following year may prove advantageous to an investor. This deferral is possible because the gain is not taxed until the sale is closed in the following year. The gain is also long-term.

(Code § 1233; CCH ¶ 32,290 et seq.; YPG 2.04.B)

See also **capital gains and losses.**

short sales against the box　See **short sales.**

short-term capital gains and losses　See **capital gains and losses.**

small business corporations　See **S corporations; small business investment companies; small business stock.**

small business investment companies　Such corporations operate under the Small Business Investment Act of 1958. Investors in the stock of such companies are allowed an ordinary loss on such stock on a sale or exchange.

RRA '93.　Under RRA '93, any individual or C (regular) corporation is allowed to elect not to recognize gain realized on the sale of publicly traded securities if the individual or C corporation uses the sale proceeds within 60 days to buy common stock in a specialized small business investment company. See the Foreword on RRA '93.

(Code § 1242; CCH ¶ 32,453)

small business stock　Investors in "small business stock," typically referred to as "Section 1244 stock," have tax advantages when issued by a qualifying corporation. A qualifying corporation is a corporation that receives money and other property as a contribution to its capital not in excess of $1 million. A number of statutory qualification requirements are applicable to such corporations, including a requirement that such a corporation be largely an operating company.

In general, the determination of whether this requirement is met is made when the stock is issued, although all amounts received for stock issued by the corporation are taken into account. Also, non-cash property received by the corporation is taken into account in the amount of its adjusted basis, reduced by any liabilities that the property was subject to or that were assumed by the corporation.

The maximum ordinary loss allowable to a taxpayer is $50,000 for taxpayers filing returns as single individuals, and $100,000 for those filing joint tax returns.

A corporation issuing § 1244 stock should maintain certain records regarding the stock issuance to ensure that shareholders will be allowed ordinary loss treatment. These records are the following:

- The date of issuance.
- The names of the persons to whom the stock was issued.
- The amount and type of consideration received from each person to whom the stock was issued.
- The amount of money and the corporation's basis for property received in exchange for stock, as a contribution to capital and as paid-in surplus.
- When property is received for stock in a tax-free exchange, the transferor's basis for that property and its fair market value on receipt by the corporation.

- Financial statements showing the source of its gross receipts for five years or the period of its existence, if shorter.
- Information on any tax-free stock dividends made by the corporation with respect to § 1244 stock.
- Information on any reorganizations in which stock is transferred for § 1244 stock.

For a shareholder to claim an ordinary loss deduction with respect to § 1244 stock, the regulations require a statement to be attached to the shareholder's return for the year in which the loss occurred. This statement must include the following information:

- The address of the corporation that issued the stock.
- How the shares were acquired.
- The nature and type of the consideration paid for the shares.
- For shares acquired in exchange for property, the basis and fair market value on the transfer date.

Remember this. Corporations, trusts, and estates are not eligible for the benefits of § 1244. Also, if § 1244 shares are transferred in any manner, or they are distributed by a partnership to partners, the transferee or distributee will not be permitted ordinary loss treatment.

Observation. Section 1244 stock is particularly beneficial when the issuing corporation is an S corporation. This is because when losses are passed through to shareholders, the shareholder's basis in the stock is reduced and the possibility arises that the annual § 1244 loss limit will be exceeded if the corporation fails.

RRA '93. RRA '93 permits a noncorporate taxpayer who holds qualified small business stock for over five years to exclude from income 50 percent of any gain from the sale or exchange of the stock. See the Foreword on RRA '93.
(Code § 1244; CCH ¶ 32,490; YPG 2.01)

stock See **capital asset; common stock; options; over-the-counter (OTC) stock; stock rights.**

stock index futures These involve contracts to buy or sell the cash value of a stock index, such as the Standard & Poor's (S&P) index of 500 stocks, by a specified date. The cash value is calculated by multiplying a specified amount by the index number.

stock index options These are options giving the holder a right, but not an obligation, to buy or sell an investment at a specified date and a specified ("strike") price. The related investment is typically a stock index futures contract or the cash value of a stock index.

See also **stock index futures.**

stock rights A corporation may issue such rights, which provide the holder, ordinarily a holder of stock in the corporation, the right to purchase a specified amount of the corporation's stock at a set price. In general, no tax results from the distribution of such rights by a corporation. However, if a corporation issues taxable stock rights, the fair market value of such rights generally must be included in the holder's taxable income at the time they are distributed.

Note: The taxpayer's holding period for stock rights includes the period for which the taxpayer held the stock with respect to which the rights were issued. Also, the holding period for stock acquired by exercise of stock rights includes the period beginning with the date on which the rights were exercised.

(Code § 307; CCH ¶ 15,400 et seq.)

straddles See **tax straddles.**

straight-line depreciation See **accelerated cost recovery system (ACRS); depreciation; modified accelerated cost recovery system (MACRS).**

stripped bonds These are bonds with respect to which the principal and the interest coupons have been separated ("stripped").

T

taxable year See **accounting periods.**

taxable income As a general rule, a taxpayer determines taxable income by subtracting his or her allowances for personal exemptions and standard or itemized deductions from adjusted gross income.

(Code § 63; CCH ¶ 6020)

tax-free exchanges When property is acquired in an exchange on which a taxpayer recognizes no taxable gain or loss, the taxpayer will have the same tax basis for the property acquired in the exchange as for the property exchanged. The taxpayer's basis for the property received in the exchange is referred to as the "substituted basis."

(Code § 1031; CCH ¶ 31,502 et seq.)

tax penalties A number of penalties are provided in the tax law for failure to pay tax due or with respect to certain transactions. (*Note:* The civil tax penalty structure was significantly modified by the Revenue Reconciliation Act of 1989. Many of these modifications apply to tax returns having a due date, without regard to filing extensions, *after December 31, 1989.* Modified penalties affecting individual taxpayers are discussed at the end of this Encyclopedia listing.) Penalties often assessed to individuals include the following.

RRA '93. The Revenue Reconcilitation Act of 1993 raised the standard for preparer and accuracy-related (see below) penalties. See the Foreword on RRA '93.

Failure to pay. This nondeductible penalty is 0.5 percent of the taxpayer's unpaid taxes for each month, or part thereof, that the taxes go unpaid. The penalty rate increases to 1 percent when the IRS issues a notice to levy or a notice or demand for immediate payment of tax. The penalty, in total, cannot exceed 25 percent of the tax owed by the taxpayer.

This penalty is assessed based on the tax reported on the taxpayer's return, reduced by any of the reported tax paid, including tax withholding. However, if the tax actually owed by the taxpayer is less than the tax reported on the return, the penalty is based on the tax actually owed.

This penalty generally does not apply if there is reasonable cause for the failure to pay, if a filing extension was granted (in most cases), or with respect to estimated tax. Also, the penalty does not apply with respect to underpayment of estimated tax where tax reported as owed on the taxpayer's return, after withholding, is not greater than $500. A special waiver of this penalty may apply to taxes owed before April 16, 1989, as a result of provisions of the 1988 Technical and Miscellaneous Revenue Act ('88 TAMRA).

Failure to file. A penalty of 5 percent per month is assessed with respect to a taxpayer's failure to file his or her tax return at the time required by the tax law. The maximum amount of this penalty is 25 percent of the tax required to be reported. (*Note:* If this penalty and the failure-to-pay penalty both apply to the months involved in the penalty assessment period, this penalty is reduced by $1 for each $1 of the failure-to-pay penalty.)

A minimum failure-to-file penalty applies with respect to failure to file within 60 days of the filing date, including extensions allowed, in an amount equal to the lesser of $100 or the amount of the tax underpayment (Code § 6651; CCH ¶ et seq.).

Substantial understatement. A 25 percent penalty applies (for assessments made after October 21, 1986) with respect to any federal income tax understatement, that is, an understatement of greater than 10 percent of the tax owed by the taxpayer or $5,000. This penalty does not apply, with an exception concerning tax shelters, as long as the taxpayer provides substantial authority or adequate disclosure of facts with respect to items on the tax return. It does not apply when the statutory overvaluation penalty applies.

The regulations provide guidance with respect to substantial authority or adequate disclosure of facts regarding a position taken on a tax return. In general, a reasonable interpretation of a statutory provision may constitute substantial authority. Included among items not considered substantial authority are proposed IRS regulations, IRS letter rulings (except those issued directly to a taxpayer), actions on decisions (AODs), IRS general counsel memoranda, post-enactment descriptions of tax statutes (except for statutory explanations prepared by the staff of the Congressional Joint Committee on Taxation), legal treatises, periodicals, or opinions given by other lawyers or tax professionals.

With respect to adequate disclosure, the requirement is usually met if a filled-in Form 8275 is included in the taxpayer's return or disclosure is otherwise made in accordance with regulations under Code § 6661 (Code § 6661; CCH ¶ 5560J).

Negligence. A penalty of 5 percent of the tax on all underpayments resulting from negligence, but not fraud, applies for tax returns due after 1988, without taking filing extensions into account. Interest is charged on the addition to tax attributable to negligence as of the due date of the taxpayer's return, including filing extensions, up to the date that the additional tax is paid. In addition to negligence, this penalty applies to a taxpayer's careless, reckless, or intentional disregard of tax rules and regulations (Code Section 6653(a); CCH ¶ 5528).

Fraud. A penalty of 75 percent applies to the amount of tax underpayment resulting from fraud. Interest is charged on the addition to tax attributable to fraud, as of the due date of the taxpayer's return, including filing extensions, up to the date that the additional tax is paid (Code § 6653(b); CCH ¶ 5528).

Overstatement of valuation of property. A penalty may apply to overvaluation of property on tax returns filed by individuals, closely held corporations, personal service corporations, or individual partners of partnerships, where there is a tax underpayment of at least $1,000 resulting from the overstatement. The following penalty percentages apply to such tax underpayments:

- 30 percent if the overvaluation is more than 250 percent of the proper valuation.
- 20 percent if the overvaluation is between 200 percent and 250 percent of the proper amount.
- 10 percent if the overvaluation is between 150 percent and 200 percent.

(Code § 6659; CCH ¶ 5701 et seq.)

Frivolous return. A $500 penalty applies when a taxpayer files a frivolous tax return, which is a tax return that is patently improper and does not involve a valid dispute between the taxpayer and the IRS (Code § 6702; CCH ¶ 5595F et seq.).

Failure to list Social Security number of dependent. If a taxpayer claims a personal exemption for a dependent who is at least two years old on his or her tax return due after 1989 without providing the dependent's taxpayer identification number (TIN) (i.e., Social Security number), or provides an incorrect TIN, a $5 penalty applies for each failure to report the required TIN. Also, a $50 penalty applies to each failure to furnish a TIN to another person, or to include another person's TIN in any return, statement, or document as required by statute (e.g., to a spouse paying alimony) (Code § 6109; CCH ¶ 5228).

Understatement of estimated tax. For individuals and most trusts and estates, there is an addition to the tax owed in the amount of the interest accruing on an underpayment for the period that the underpayment exists. Interest on tax underpayments, in general, is charged at the applicable federal short-term interest rate (as adjusted quarterly) plus 3 percentage points (Code §§ 6654(a), 6601; CCH ¶ 5501, ¶ 5534).

Modification of Civil Penalty Structure by Revenue Reconciliation Act of 1989

As noted earlier, the Revenue Reconciliation Act of 1989 (RRA '89) significantly modified the civil penalty structure in the tax law. Many of these modifications apply to tax returns having a due date, without regard to filing extensions, *after December 31, 1989*. (See CCH ¶ 40,551 et seq.)

RRA '89 consolidates into a single part of the Internal Revenue Code *all* generally applicable civil penalties relating to the accuracy of a taxpayer's return. These include the negligence penalty, the substantial understatement penalty, and the valuation penalties. These penalties, as consolidated, are also consolidated with the fraud penalty by RRA '89.

RRA '89 repeals these penalties as enacted under previous law. It consolidates these accuracy penalties in a new structure under which they cannot be stacked. The RRA rules on the accuracy penalties generally apply to tax returns having a due date, without regard to filing extensions, after December 31, 1989.

The accuracy-related penalty, imposed at a 20 percent rate, applies to the portion of any tax underpayment due to

• Negligence.

• Any substantial understatement of income tax.

• Any substantial valuation overstatement.

• Any substantial estate of gift tax valuation understatement.

It also applies to any substantial overstatement of pension liabilities, a topic beyond the scope of this book.

Negligence.   When a tax underpayment is due to negligence, this penalty applies only to the portion of the underpayment due to negligence. Under previous law, the negligence penalty applied to the *entire* tax underpayment.

For purposes of this penalty, *negligence* is any careless, reckless, or intentional disregard of rules and regulations, and any failure by a taxpayer to make a reasonable attempt to comply with Internal Revenue Code provisions. Also, RRA '89 repealed the presumption under previous law under which an underpayment is treated as due to a failure to include on an income tax return an amount reported on an information return.

Substantial understatement of income tax.   The accuracy-related penalty applicable to the portion of an underpayment due to a substantial understatement of income tax is the same as the penalty provided under previous law, with three basic changes:

1. The rate is reduced to 20 percent.
2. The list of authorities in Treasury Regulations on which taxpayers are permitted to rely is expanded by the RRA to include proposed regulations: private letter rulings; technical advice memoranda; actions on decisions (AODs); general counsel memoranda (GCMs); and Internal Revenue Service press releases, notices, and similar documents published in the *Internal Revenue Bulletin.* The list of authorities on which taxpayers may rely is also expanded to include general explanations of federal tax legislation ("Blue Book") prepared by the Congressional Joint Committee on Taxation.
3. The RRA requires the Internal Revenue Service to publish, at least annually, a list of tax return positions affecting a significant number of taxpayers with respect to which the IRS believes that there is no substantial authority.

The Revenue Reconciliation Act of 1993 (RRA '93) made additional changes with respect to the substantial understatement penalty. Under RRA '93, effective for tax returns due, without regard to extensions, after December 31, 1993, this penalty cannot be avoided by disclosing a nonfrivolous tax return position unless there is a reasonable basis for that return position. See the Foreword on RRA '93.

Substantial valuation overstatement.   The penalty applicable to the portion of an income tax underpayment due to a substantial valuation overstatement is basically the same as the penalty applicable under previous law, with five basic changes:

1. The penalty is extended to *all* taxpayers.
2. A substantial overstatement exists if the value or adjusted basis of any property claimed on a taxpayer's return is 200 percent or more of the correct value or adjusted basis.

3. The penalty applies only if the amount of the underpayment due to a valuation overstatement is more than $5,000 ($10,000 for most corporations).

4. The amount of the penalty for a substantial valuation overstatement is 20 percent of the related underpayment if the value or adjusted basis claimed is 200 percent or more but less than 400 percent of the correct value or adjusted basis.

5. The rate of this penalty is doubled if the value or adjusted basis claimed is 400 percent or more of the correct value or adjusted basis.

Note: RRA '89 did not modify existing rules applicable to property for which a taxpayer claims a charitable deduction.

Substantial estate or gift tax valuation understatement. The accuracy-related penalty also applies to substantial estate or gift tax valuation understatements. This penalty is derived from the Code § 6660 penalty under previous law. The previous-law penalty is modified by RRA '89 so that a taxpayer is subject to this penalty only if the value of any property claimed on an estate or gift tax return is 50 percent or less of the amount determined to be correct. The penalty under previous law is also modified by increasing by five times the threshold below which the penalty will not apply—from $1,000 to $5,000.

Gross valuation misstatements. The rate of the accuracy-related penalty is doubled to 40 percent with respect to gross valuation misstatements by taxpayers. Gross valuation misstatements are of three types:

1. Misstatement that is the same as the substantial valuation overstatement, except that the doubling of the rate applies only to valuation overstatements claimed on a taxpayer's return that are 400 percent or more of the amount determined to be correct.

2. Misstatement that is the same as the substantial estate or gift tax valuation understatement, except that the doubling of the rate applies only to valuations claimed on an estate or gift tax return that are 25 percent or less of the amount determined to be correct.

3. Overstatement of pension liabilities, which, as noted previously, is beyond the scope of this service.

Fraud. This penalty applies to the part of any tax underpayment due to fraud and is imposed at a 75 percent rate. The accuracy-related penalty does not apply to any part of a tax underpayment on which the fraud penalty is imposed.

Definitions and special rules. RRA '89 provided special rules that apply to each of the penalties imposed under its new penalty structure:

1. Standardized exception criteria are used for all of the accuracy-related penalties. No penalty will be imposed if reasonable cause for the tax underpayment can be shown, and the taxpayer acted in good faith.

2. An accuracy-related or fraud penalty is imposed only if a return has been filed. This provision is designed to improve coordination between the accuracy-related and failure-to-file penalties.

3. A standard definition of an underpayment is used for all accuracy-related penalties.

RRA '89 repeal of penalties under previous law. RRA '89 repealed the penalties provided under previous law for negligence and fraud, substantial understatement of tax liability, valuation overstatements, and estate and gift tax valuation understatements. It also repealed the negligence rules regarding tax straddles and amounts reported on information returns, as well as the higher interest rate applicable to substantial underpayments resulting from tax-motivated transactions.

(RRA '89 § 7711)

tax preferences See **alternative minimum tax (AMT); AMT preferences.**

tax shelters In general, a promoter of a tax shelter is required to register the shelter with the Internal Revenue Service. For purposes of this requirement, a tax shelter constitutes any investment:

• Regarding which it could reasonably be inferred that, from any representations made regarding a sale of an interest therein or an offer of such an interest, the ratio of deductions from the investment to the amount invested (the "tax shelter ratio") would be more than 2 to 1 at the end of any of the first five years after the date of the first sale offering of an interest therein.

• That must be registered under federal or state securities laws, is sold under a registration exemption under which a notice must be filed with a federal or state securities regulating agency, or is a substantial investment.

Other provisions of the Internal Revenue Code also apply with respect to tax shelters, such as use of the accrual method of accounting, the at-risk rules, the passive loss rules, and certain penalty provisions that apply to the shelters themselves. For example, a penalty applies with respect to overvaluations of property involved.

(Temp. Reg. § 301.6111–1T; Code § 6707; CCH ¶ 40,885)

tax straddles The Internal Revenue Code prevents taxpayers from using straddles to defer taxable income or to change ordinary income or short-term capital gain into long-term capital gain.

For purposes of these rules, a *straddle* is any set of offsetting positions, with specific statutory exceptions, made up of covered call options and contract optioned stock. A *position* is an interest in actively traded personal property other than stock and may include a forward futures contract or an option. An *offsetting position* is a position that substantially reduces an investor's risk of loss from holding another position.

General Rules

Deduction of losses from straddle positions involving actively traded personal property, other than stock, is generally limited to the excess amount of losses over unrecognized gains on offsetting positions. Gains and losses on regulated futures contracts are reported by taxpayers using a "mark-to-market" rule corresponding to the daily settlement system employed in determining margin requirements by US exchanges on which commodity futures are traded.

A taxpayer's risk of loss related to personal property is substantially reduced if one or more positions with respect to personal property are held by the taxpayer. Such positions may be treated as offsetting even if the property is not of the same kind. A straddle may also be made up of two positions that do not constitute the same type of property interest—for example, a cash position in a commodity and a futures contract covering the same amount of that commodity.

Offsetting positions include the following:

- Positions in the *same* personal property, either the commodity itself or in a commodity contract, as long as the positions' values bear an inverse relationship. In general, this relationship exists where one position's value increases as the value of the other declines. Such positions are also deemed offsetting if the property involved is in a substantially altered form, as long as the positions' values bear an inverse relationship.

- Positions in debt instruments with similar maturities, as long as the positions' values usually bear an inverse relationship.

- Positions whose sale is represented as involving offsetting positions, regardless of whether the positions are called "butterfly," or "spread," or "straddle."

- Positions for which the total margin amount required is typically lower than the margin amount required for each separate position.

Deduction Rules

The deductibility of losses on straddle positions not under a mark-to-market system is limited to the amount that such losses exceed *unrecognized* gains on offsetting straddle positions, even if such gains are unrealized.

Gains and losses from Section 1256 contracts to which the mark-to-market rules apply are calculated by marking such contracts to market. If such contracts constitute capital assets, any gain or loss is treated as 60 percent long-term capital gain or loss and 40 percent short-term capital gain or loss.

Losses are deferred on straddles in the amount by which the taxpayer has unrecognized gains in offsetting straddle positions. When a taxpayer disposes of one or more straddle positions and realizes a loss, the deductible amount is the amount by which the loss exceeds any unrecognized gain on offsetting positions acquired prior to the disposition of the loss position(s). This deferral rule does not apply to losses on positions identified as straddles (see the following discussion of identified straddles), and gains and losses on such straddles are netted. Losses on such straddles are considered incurred no earlier than the date on which all such straddle positions are closed by the taxpayer.

Any losses deferred are carried forward to the next taxable year. They are subject to the deferral rule in that year. Deferred losses are recognized in the first taxable year in which the taxpayer has no unrealized appreciation in any offsetting positions acquired prior to the disposition of the loss position. If more than one unrealized gain position offsetting the loss position and not part of an identified straddle was acquired before disposition of the loss position, the loss is allocated among unrealized gain positions.

The loss deferral rule applies to personal property that is actively traded. For this purpose, personal property includes stock only when it is offset by a buy or sell option with respect to actively traded stock, or where a shareholder of a corporation formed or availed of for the purpose of taking positions in personal property holds offsetting positions.

Wash sale rules.   Wash sale rules provided in the Internal Revenue Code also generally apply to tax straddles. Under these rules, if a taxpayer has an unrealized loss on one position in a straddle and an unrealized gain on the other position, disposes of the loss position, and immediately replaces it for the purpose of maintaining a balanced position to protect the gain, the loss is nondeductible. The loss deduction is deferred, and the deferral rule does not apply since new property is substituted in the straddle. These rules apply to any person who is not a dealer in stock or securities.

Short sale rules.   Taxpayers generally are prohibited from making a short-term gain into a long-term gain through the use of offsetting straddle positions that do not involve substantially identical property. This prohibition, as prescribed by regulations similar to short sale rules, involves suspension of the commencement of the holding period of any straddle positions under the loss deferral rule.

Under such rules, a commodity futures contract is treated the same as the short sale of a long futures contract for the same commodity, or the short sale of the commodity.

Interest and carrying charges. Interest and carrying charges incurred by a taxpayer to buy or carry personal property are required to be added to the cost of such personal property. In general, other charges required to be added to the property's cost are reduced by dividends on stock included in the straddle, market discount, and acquisition discount includable in income. The following items also are taken into account before capitalization under this rule: The deduction of short sale expenses is disallowed in certain cases, and net direct interest with respect to market discount bonds is deferred, as is interest on short-term debt.

Mark-to-market rule. The loss deferral, short sale, and wash sale rules described do not apply to straddles that are totally made up of Section 1256 contracts. Gain or loss on any such contract at the end of a year is reported by a taxpayer on the basis of the mark-to-market system used by the US commodity futures exchanges for purposes of determining daily gains and losses of investors.

For purposes of this rule, a Section 1256 contract includes any regulated futures contract, foreign currency contract, nonequity option, or dealer equity option. Also, a "regulated futures contract" includes:

- A contract requiring delivery of personal property or an interest therein.
- A contract for which the deposit amount required and the amount available for withdrawal are based on a mark-to-market system.
- A contract traded on a commodity futures exchange recognized by the Internal Revenue Service or subject to rules prescribed by the Commodity Futures Trading Commission (CFTC) or any board of trade recognized by the IRS.
- A foreign currency contract traded in the interbank market and delivery of a foreign currency subject to trading through a regulated futures contract, as long as the contract has an arm's-length price in accordance with interbank market prices.

Also, for purposes of this rule, a *nonequity option* is any option traded on, or subject to, the rules of a recognized exchange or board of trade. Such an option does not include a right to acquire stock from the issuing corporation. A *dealer equity option* involves certain listed options held by dealers in options.

All commodity futures contracts held by a taxpayer that are not closed out are considered under this rule as if closed out at fair market value as of the last day of the year. Gains and losses on such positions are considered 60 percent long-term and 40 percent short-term. This treatment applies regardless of the holding period of the commodity futures contract. At the time that the commodity futures contract is closed out, usually in the following year, the resulting gain or loss is adjusted, for tax purposes, to reflect the gain or loss reflected in the preceding year. A maximum tax of 33 percent applies, with the ratio of long-term to short-term gain being immaterial.

Mixed Straddles

These are straddles made up of Section 1256 contracts and other property. When the straddle is identified as such by a taxpayer, the taxpayer may elect to have the part of the straddle made up of Section 1256 contracts excluded from the mark-to-market rule. A taxpayer may also:

- Offset gains and losses from mixed straddle positions by identifying each mixed straddle to be so treated, or
- Set up a mixed straddle account for a class of activities with respect to which gains and losses are recognized and offset on a periodic basis.

For either of these alternatives, 60 percent long-term and 40 percent short-term taxation applies only to net straddle gain or loss related to Section 1256 contracts. With respect to Section 1256 contracts, no more than 50 percent of any net gain can be treated as long-term capital gain, and no more than 40 percent of any net loss can be treated as short-term capital loss.

In general, an election related to mixed straddles is effective only with respect to the taxable year for which it is made. The election is made on Form 6781 by the due date of the return for the immediately preceding taxable year, irrespective of any return filing extensions.

Identified Straddles

The loss deferral rule described earlier does not apply to identified straddles, which are taxed under special rules. To qualify as an identified straddle, a straddle generally must clearly be marked as such on the taxpayer's records before the end of the day it is acquired by the taxpayer, or other time as prescribed by regulations. Losses on positions in an identified straddle are considered incurred no earlier than the date when the taxpayer disposes of all positions making up the straddle.

Hedges

The interest capitalization, loss deferral, short sale, and wash sale rules do not apply to transactions entered into by a taxpayer as hedges. These are designed to limit a taxpayer's risk with respect to transactions engaged in the normal course of a taxpayer's trade or business that produce ordinary income or loss. In general, a transaction qualifies as a hedge only if it is clearly identified as such by the taxpayer before the end of the day on which it is executed.

Deduction of a hedging loss is limited to the taxable income from the related trade or business of the taxpayer, not reduced by such loss. This prohibits ordinary losses from being passed through to limited investors in transactions by traders who are dealers in the property involved.

Note. As this book went to press, the IRS issued temporary and proposed regulations guaranteeing ordinary income and loss treatment for specially defined hedging transactions. (T. D. 8493)

Losses on Regulated Futures Contracts

A three-year carryback is available for losses from regulated futures contracts. The carryback is available to the extent that such losses can be applied against the taxpayer's net commodity futures gains during that three-year period. The carryback is first applied to the earliest year in that period and then to succeeding years, with the amounts carried back subject to 60 percent long-term and 40 percent short-term tax treatment. Losses applied in carryback years are subject to this 60/40 treatment, although a carryback is not available to taxable years ending before June 24, 1981.

Governmental Obligations

Certain governmental obligations, including Treasury bills, are treated as capital assets. Discount on such obligations is treated as interest that is taxable as ordinary income.

Capital Assets

Taxable dispositions of commodity futures and similar holdings that qualify as capital assets are treated as sales or exchanges for tax purposes. The holding period of a commodity futures contract must be tacked on to the holding period of a commodity acquired after June 23, 1981, through a Section 1256 contract.

If a futures contract requires delivery of money rather than a commodity, the termination of the contract (through expiration, lapse, etc.) produces capital gain or loss if it constitutes a capital asset, even if there is no sale or exchange.

(Code §§ 1092, 1256; CCH ¶ 32,100, ¶ 32,700)

tenancy by the entirety This type of property ownership can be created only by a married couple. This type of ownership is not recognized by many states and affords no tax advantages, but it does afford protection against creditors and provides for inheritance of the property upon the death of the co-owner.

tenancy in common This form of property ownership is similar to ownership as joint tenants in that individuals may enter into it with respect to any type of property. However, this form of ownership provides no right of survivorship, no exclusion from the probate process, and no protection from creditors or parties who have judgments against the owner as a result of a court action.

theft losses A loss incurred by a taxpayer as the result of a theft usually may be deducted in the loss year. The deduction rules are the same as those applicable to casualty losses.

(Code § 165; CCH ¶ 9802)

Treasury bills Treasury bills, commonly referred to as T-bills, are short-term debt obligations issued by the US Treasury. They have maturities of 13 weeks, 26 weeks, and 52 weeks, and they can be purchased with a minimum investment of $10,000. Over $10,000, additional purchases can be made in $5,000 increments. The 13-week and 26-week bills are issued weekly, and 52-week bills are issued monthly. These obligations are issued by the Treasury at a discount, and the purchaser receives the face value at redemption. Interest income earned on those bills is taxable for federal income tax purposes but *not* for state and local income tax purposes.

Treasury bills can be purchased from banks and securities brokers, which charge commissions, or directly from a Federal Reserve Bank (or branch). To purchase them from a Federal Reserve Bank, the purchaser must file an application, referred to as a "tender." The tender's price is either competitive or non-competitive. This means that the purchaser either offers a specified price or makes the purchase based on the average of accepted competitive prices.

Treasury bonds and notes These obligations issued by the US Treasury are commonly referred to as T-bonds and T-notes. These obligations are required to be in registered form after 1983. Some pre-1984 obligations, however, are still traded.

Treasury bonds are offered periodically with 10-year, 20-year, and 30-year maturities. Treasury notes are issued monthly with maturities of 2, 4, 5, 7, and 10 years.

Minimum investments for Treasury bonds are $1,000, and additional investments can be made in increments of $1,000. Minimum investments for Treasury notes are $5,000 for notes having maturities of under four years, and $1,000 otherwise. Additional investments in these notes can be made in increments of $1,000.

Treasury bonds and notes can be purchased from banks and securities brokers, which charge commissions, or directly from a Federal Reserve Bank at no fee. The direct purchase is made by use of a tender (See **Treasury bills** for a discussion of "tender").

Interest income earned on these obligations is taxable for federal income tax purposes but *not* for state and local income tax purposes.

(YPG 2.01)

See also **capital asset; capital gains and losses.**

trust Establishment of a trust involves the transfer of property by the grantor (maker) to a trustee for the benefit of beneficiary, such as a family member. The trust can be revocable or irrevocable. There are a number of types of trusts to which special tax rules apply, such as the Clifford trust.

U

US savings bonds Two types of savings bonds are issued by the US government: Series EE bonds and Series HH bonds. Series EE bonds are sold at a discount of 50 percent of the bond's face value. Bond denominations range from $50 to $10,000. A purchaser must hold a bond for six months before it can be redeemed, and face value is paid if it is held until maturity of 10 years.

The interest paid on these bonds, when issued after November 1, 1982, and held for at least five years, is 85 percent of average market yield on US Treasury securities, compounded semiannually. A minimum interest rate of 7.5 percent is guaranteed. The yield is lower if the bond is redeemed early. If the redemption is after one year, the interest is 5.5 percent. The rate increases thereafter as prescribed in redemption tables.

Series HH bonds can only be purchased in exchange for Series EE bonds or their predecessor, Series E bonds. These bonds have 10-year maturities and have denominations of $500, $1,000, $5,000, and $10,000. Also, these bonds are sold at par value, and interest is paid on them semiannually.

Note: Holders of Series E and Series H bonds, the predecessors of the bonds just described, still earn interest on their bonds. However, if the Series E bond held is more than 40 years old, no interest is paid.

Tax Treatment

On Series EE and Series HH bonds, interest earned is taxable income for federal income tax purposes but *not* for state and local income tax purposes. Current interest income on Series HH bonds is taxable when earned. Tax on interest income earned on Series EE bonds may be deferred until redemption. Alternatively, a taxpayer may elect to report the income currently for tax purposes. Such an election is binding on the taxpayer unless the Internal Revenue Service permits a change. (Code § 103; CCH ¶ 6606; YPG 10.01.D, 10.02.C; see also Appendix A)

Education Savings Bonds

An individual taxpayer who redeems a qualified US savings bond in a year in which he or she pays qualified higher education expenses is allowed an income exclusion for the redemption. To qualify, the bond must be issued to an individual reaching age 24 before the issue date and must be a discount bond. Qualified expenses include tuition and fees paid to an eligible institution for the taxpayer, his or her spouse, or an eligible dependent. Such expenses are, in general, reduced by scholarships and other financial aid for education. The exclusion is not available to married individuals filing separate tax returns.
(Code § 135; CCH ¶ 7550)

Note. The exclusion for interest earned on education savings bonds is phased out for holders whose income exceeds certain thresholds, which are adjusted yearly for inflation. Due to a legislative drafting error in RRA '93, the base year for inflation adjustments was changed from 1989 to 1992. This would reduce the 1994 income threshold and eliminate the tax benefit of such bonds for more taxpayers. For 1993, the applicable threshold for modified adjusted gross income is $68,250 for joint return filers and $45,500 for other filers.

W

warrants These are rights, traded on stock exchanges, that enable holders to buy a specific number of shares of a corporation's stock at a specified price during a specified period. Their value is the difference between the price specified and the market value of the related stock. They cease to have value when the period specified expires.

wash sales If a taxpayer incurs a loss on a sale or other disposition of stock or securities, the loss is generally not deductible if, within a 61-day period (i.e., a period beginning 30 days prior to the date of such property's sale or disposition and ending 30 days after that date), the taxpayer acquires or contracts to acquire substantially identical stock or securities. An acquisition of stock or securities by a taxpayer within the statutory 61-day period is not subject to this rule.
(Code § 1091; CCH ¶ 32,080; YPG 2.04.C)

wills These are formal legal documents setting forth a decedent's instructions regarding the settlement of his or her estate. When an individual dies having a will, he or she dies *testate*. In general, the will must meet requirements set forth by the law of the state in which the maker resides. Also, in general, the maker of a will should engage an attorney so that his or her wishes as to the disposition of the property in the estate are carried out. Estate taxes may apply with respect to a decedent's estate, and such taxes may be reduced if the taxpayer makes gifts during life. If a decedent dies without a will, he or she is *intestate,* a status that may involve additional expense and complications in the probate process required under state law.

    See also **estate tax; gift tax; intestacy; probate.**

Revenue Procedure 89–46 (1989–2 C.B. 597)

This document provides a procedure for certain cash-basis taxpayers to obtain expeditious consent from the IRS to change their method of reporting the increase in the redemption value (interest) of Series E or EE U.S. Savings Bonds for federal income tax purposes.

SECTION 1. PURPOSE

The purpose of this revenue procedure is to provide a procedure for certain cash-basis taxpayers to obtain expeditious consent to change their method of reporting the increase in the redemption value (interest) of Series E or EE U.S. savings bonds for federal income tax purposes. Taxpayers complying with this revenue procedure will be deemed to have obtained the consent of the Commissioner to change their method of reporting this income.

SECTION 2. BACKGROUND

.01 Section 454 of the Internal Revenue Code and section 1.454–1(a) of the Income Tax Regulations provide that if the increase in the redemption price of certain non-interest bearing obligations issued at a discount does not constitute income for such year under the cash method of accounting used by the taxpayer in computing taxable income, the taxpayer may elect to treat such increase as constituting income for the year in which such increase occurs. (For this purpose non-interest bearing obligations include Series E or EE U.S. savings bonds.) Any such election under section 454 must be made in the taxpayer's return and may be made for any tax year. The election once made is binding upon the taxpayer with respect to all such obligations, unless the Commissioner permits the taxpayer to change to a different method of reporting income from such obligations pursuant to section 446.

.02 Section 446(e) of the Code and section 1.446–1(e) of the regulations state that, except as otherwise provided, in order to change a method of accounting for federal income tax purposes, a taxpayer must obtain the consent of the Commissioner. Section 1.446–1(e)(3)(i) requires that in order to obtain this consent, a Form 3115, Application for Change in Accounting Method, must generally be filed within 180 days after the beginning of the tax year in which the proposed change is to be made. Section 1.446–1(e)(3)(ii) authorizes the Commissioner to prescribe administrative procedures setting forth the limitations, and conditions deemed necessary to permit taxpayers to obtain consent to change their method of accounting in accordance with section 446(e).

SECTION 3. SCOPE AND OBJECTIVE

.01 This revenue procedure applies to taxpayers who own Series E or EE U.S. savings bonds, have elected under section 454 of the Code to report as income the increase in redemption price occurring in a tax year, and now wish to change their method of accounting to report such income in the taxable year in which the obligation is redeemed, disposed of, or finally matures, whichever is earlier.

.02 A taxpayer shall not be permitted to change its method of accounting pursuant to this revenue procedure during the 5-year period following the year for which a change is made pursuant to this revenue procedure.

SECTION 4. APPLICATION

In accordance with section 1.446–1(e)(3)(ii) of the regulations, the 180-day rule is waived for purposes of this revenue procedure for tax years beginning on or after January 1, 1989. Further, under section 1.446(e)(2)(ii) consent is hereby granted to a taxpayer within the scope of this revenue procedure to change from a method of reporting as income the annual increase in the redemption price of Series E or EE U.S. savings bonds issued at a discount to a method of reporting such increases in the year in which they are realized by disposition, redemption, or upon final maturity, whichever is earlier. This consent is granted for the tax year for which a taxpayer requests a change (year of change) by filing a current Form 3115 in the manner described in section 5 of this revenue procedure and by otherwise complying with the provisions of this revenue procedure.

SECTION 5. MANNER OF EFFECTING THE CHANGE

.01 A taxpayer applying for a change in method of accounting pursuant to this revenue procedure must complete a current Form 3115 and attach it to the taxpayer's federal income tax return for the year of change. The Form 3115 must be attached to a return filed on or before the due date (including extensions), except in the case of certain taxpayers described in section 6 changing their method for 1988. The taxpayer must identify the Series E or EE U.S. savings bonds for which this change in accounting method is requested. No user fee is required for an application filed under this revenue procedure.

.02 In order to assist in the processing of the change in accounting method and to ensure proper handling, reference to this revenue procedure shall be made a part of the Form 3115 by either typing or legibly printing the following statement at the top of page 1 of the Form 3115 "FILED UNDER REV. PROC. 89–46."

.03 The consent to make this change is hereby granted, provided the taxpayer attaches to the completed Form 3115 statements to the following effect:

(1) The taxpayer agrees to report all interest on the obligations acquired during the year of change and for all subsequent tax years when the interest is realized upon disposition, redemption, or final maturity, whichever is earlier; and

(2) The taxpayer agrees to all interest on the obligations acquired before the year of change when the interest is realized upon disposition, redemption, or final maturity, whichever is earlier, with the exception of any interest income previously reported in prior tax years.

.04 No adjustments under section 481 of the Code is to be taken into account with respect to this change.

.05 The signature of the person requesting the change in method of accounting must appear in the space provided for it on the Form 3115. See the signature requirements set forth in the General Instructions attached to a current Form 3115 for those who are authorized to sign Form 3115. A parent may sign on behalf of a minor child. If an agent is authorized to represent the taxpayer before the Service, to receive the original or a copy of correspondence concerning the request, or to perform any other act(s) regarding the application on behalf of the taxpayer, a power of attorney reflecting such authorization(s) must be attached to the application. A taxpayer's representative without a power of attorney to represent the taxpayer as indicated in this subsection will not be given any information about the application.

SECTION 6. EFFECTIVE DATE

This revenue procedure shall be effective for tax years ending after December 30, 1988. However, to take advantage of this revenue procedure for 1988 calendar tax years, taxpayers must have timely filed (i.e., filed within the first 180 days of 1988) a Form 3115 with the National Office of the Internal Revenue

Service for 1988. Any taxpayer that has timely filed a Form 3115 for 1988 may effect a change in method for such year by timely filing an original return, or by filing an amended return, for 1988, and attaching to such return a copy of the Form 3115, including the statements described in section 5.03 and a reference to this revenue procedure, as described in section 5.02.

SECTION 7. INQUIRIES

Inquiries regarding this revenue procedure may be addressed to the Commissioner of Internal Revenue, Attention: CC:IT&A, 1111 Constitution Avenue, N.W., Washington, D.C. 20224.

DRAFTING INFORMATION

The principal author of this revenue procedure is Joseph Donnelly of the Office of Assistant Chief Counsel (Income Tax and Accounting). For further information regarding this revenue procedure, contact Joseph Donnelly on (202) 566–6803 (not a toll-free call).

Depreciation/Cost Recovery Tables

ACRS Cost Recovery Tables for Real Estate

All Real Estate except Low-Income Housing (Generally Applies to Assets Placed in Service after 1980 and on or before 3–15–84)

	1	2	3	4	5	6	7	8	9	10	11	12
Recovery Year					*Applicable Percentage*							
1	12	11	10	9	8	7	6	5	4	3	2	1
2	10	10	11	11	11	11	11	11	11	11	11	12
3	9	9	9	9	10	10	10	10	10	10	10	10
4	8	8	8	8	8	8	9	9	9	9	9	9
5	7	7	7	7	7	7	8	8	8	8	8	8
6	6	6	6	6	7	7	7	7	7	7	7	7
7	6	6	6	6	6	6	6	6	6	6	6	6
8	6	6	6	6	6	6	5	6	6	6	6	6
9	6	6	6	6	5	6	5	5	5	6	6	6
10	5	6	5	6	5	5	5	5	5	5	6	5
11	5	5	5	5	5	5	5	5	5	5	5	5
12	5	5	5	5	5	5	5	5	5	5	5	5
13	5	5	5	5	5	5	5	5	5	5	5	5
14	5	5	5	5	5	5	5	5	5	5	5	5
15	5	5	5	5	5	5	5	5	5	5	5	5
16	—	—	1	1	2	2	3	3	4	4	4	5

Low-Income Housing (Placed in Service after 1980 and before 5-9-85)

	1	2	3	4	5	6	7	8	9	10	11	12
Recovery Year					*Applicable Percentage*							
1	13	12	11	10	9	8	7	6	4	3	2	1
2	12	12	12	12	12	12	12	13	13	13	13	13
3	10	10	10	10	11	11	11	11	11	11	11	11
4	9	9	9	9	9	9	9	9	10	10	10	10
5	8	8	8	8	8	8	8	8	8	8	8	9
6	7	7	7	7	7	7	7	7	7	7	7	7
7	6	6	6	6	6	6	6	6	6	6	6	6
8	5	5	5	5	5	5	5	5	5	5	6	6
9	5	5	5	5	5	5	5	5	5	5	5	5
10	5	5	5	5	5	5	5	5	5	5	5	5
11	4	5	5	5	5	5	5	5	5	5	5	5
12	4	4	4	5	4	5	5	5	5	5	5	5
13	4	4	4	4	4	4	5	4	5	5	5	5
14	4	4	4	4	4	4	4	4	4	5	4	4
15	4	4	4	4	4	4	4	4	4	4	4	4
16	—	—	1	1	2	2	2	3	3	3	4	4

Note: The half-year convention is not used with 18- or 19-year real property. First-year recovery is based on the number of months (using a mid-month convention) the property is in service during the year and the first-year recovery percentage is provided over the number of in-service months.

Low-Income Housing (Placed in Service after 5–8–85; 15-Year 200 Percent Declining Balance, Assuming no Mid-Month Convention)

	1	2	3	4	5	6	7	8	9	10	11	12
Recovery Year					*Applicable Percentage*							
1	13.3	12.2	11.1	10.0	8.9	7.8	6.6	5.6	4.4	3.3	2.2	1.1
2	11.6	11.7	11.9	12.0	12.1	12.3	12.5	12.6	12.7	12.9	13.0	13.2
3	10.0	10.1	10.2	10.4	10.5	10.7	10.8	10.9	11.1	11.2	11.3	11.4
4	8.7	8.8	8.9	9.0	9.1	9.2	9.3	9.5	9.6	9.7	9.8	9.9
5	7.5	7.6	7.7	7.8	7.9	8.0	8.1	8.2	8.3	8.4	8.5	8.6
6	6.5	6.6	6.7	6.8	6.9	6.9	7.0	7.1	7.2	7.3	7.4	7.4
7	5.7	5.7	5.8	5.9	5.9	6.0	6.1	6.1	6.2	6.3	6.4	6.5
8	4.9	5.0	5.0	5.1	5.2	5.2	5.3	5.3	5.4	5.5	5.5	5.6
9	4.6	4.6	4.6	4.6	4.6	4.6	4.6	4.6	4.6	4.7	4.8	4.8
10	4.6	4.6	4.6	4.6	4.6	4.6	4.6	4.6	4.6	4.6	4.6	4.6
11	4.6	4.6	4.6	4.6	4.6	4.6	4.6	4.6	4.6	4.6	4.6	4.6
12	4.5	4.6	4.6	4.6	4.6	4.6	4.6	4.6	4.6	4.6	4.6	4.6
13	4.5	4.5	4.6	4.5	4.6	4.6	4.6	4.6	4.6	4.5	4.6	4.6
14	4.5	4.5	4.5	4.5	4.5	4.5	4.5	4.6	4.6	4.5	4.5	4.5
15	4.5	4.5	4.5	4.5	4.5	4.5	4.5	4.5	4.5	4.5	4.5	4.5
16	0.0	0.4	0.7	1.1	1.5	1.9	2.3	2.6	3.0	3.4	3.7	4.1

Expensing and Depreciation for "Listed Property"

Date Placed in Service	1990 Maximum
After 6–18–84 and before 1–1–85	$6,000
After 12–31–84 and before 4–3–85	6,200
After 4–2–85 and before 1–1–87	4,800
After 7–31–86 and before 1–1–87 if MACRS elected	1,475
After 12–31–86 and before 1–1–88	1,475
After 12–31–87 and before 1–1–89	2,450
After 12–31–89	2,660

Note: For autos placed in service during 1990, the maximum depreciation deduction for 1991 is $4,200. For 1992 it is $2,550 and then $1,475 for each succeeding year.

18-Year Real Property (Placed in Service after June 22, 1984 and before May 9, 1985)

	Month Placed in Service											
Year	1	2	3	4	5	6	7	8	9	10	11	12
1	9%	9%	8%	7%	6%	5%	4%	4%	3%	2%	1%	0.4%
2	9	9	9	9	9	9	9	8	9	10	10	10
3	8	8	8	8	8	8	8	8	9	9	9	9
4	7	7	7	7	7	8	8	8	8	8	8	8
5	7	7	7	7	7	7	7	7	7	7	7	7
6	6	6	6	6	6	6	6	6	6	6	6	6
7	5	5	5	5	6	6	6	6	6	6	6	6
8–12	5	5	5	5	5	5	5	5	5	5	5	5
13	4	4	4	5	4	4	5	4	4	4	5	5
14–17	4	4	4	4	4	4	4	4	4	4	4	4
18	4	3	4	4	4	4	4	4	4	4	4	4
19		1	1	1	2	2	2	3	3	3	3	3.6

18-Year Real Property (Placed in Service after March 15 and before June 23, 1984)

	Month Placed in Service										
Year	1	2	3	4	5	6	7	8	9	10–11	12
1	10%	9%	8%	7%	6%	6%	5%	4%	3%	2%	1%
2	9	9	9	9	9	9	9	9	9	10	10
3	8	8	8	8	8	8	8	8	9	9	9
4	7	7	7	7	7	7	8	8	8	8	8
5	6	7	7	7	7	7	7	7	7	7	7
6	6	6	6	6	6	6	6	6	6	6	6
7	5	5	5	5	6	6	6	6	6	6	6
8–12	5	5	5	5	5	5	5	5	5	5	5
13	4	4	4	5	5	4	4	5	4	4	4
14–18	4	4	4	4	4	4	4	4	4	4	4
19		1	1	1	2	2	2	3	3	4	

19-Year Real Property

	Month Placed in Service											
Year	1	2	3	4	5	6	7	8	9	10	11	12
1	8.8%	8.1%	7.3%	6.5%	5.8%	5.0%	4.2%	3.5%	2.7%	1.9%	1.1%	0.4%
2	8.4	8.5	8.5	8.6	8.7	8.8	8.8	8.9	9.0	9.0	9.1	9.2
3	7.6	7.7	7.7	7.8	7.9	7.9	8.0	8.1	8.1	8.2	8.3	8.3
4	6.9	7.0	7.0	7.1	7.1	7.2	7.3	7.3	7.4	7.4	7.5	7.6
5	6.3	6.3	6.4	6.4	6.5	6.5	6.6	6.6	6.7	6.8	6.8	6.9
6	5.7	5.7	5.8	5.9	5.9	5.9	6.0	6.0	6.1	6.1	6.2	6.2
7	5.2	5.2	5.3	5.3	5.3	5.4	5.4	5.5	5.5	5.6	5.6	5.6
8–12	4.7	4.7	4.8	4.8	4.8	4.9	4.9	5.0	5.0	5.1	5.1	5.1
13	4.2	4.3	4.3	4.4	4.4	4.5	4.5	4.5	4.5	4.6	4.6	4.7
14–18	4.2	4.2	4.2	4.2	4.2	4.2	4.2	4.2	4.2	4.2	4.2	4.2
19	0.2	0.5	0.9	1.2	1.6	1.9	2.3	2.6	3.0	3.3	3.7	4.0

18-Year Real Property (Placed in Service after June 22, 1984, Other than Low-Income Housing) for which Alternate ACRS Method over an 18-Year Period Is Elected

	Month Placed in Service					
Year	1–2	3–4	5–7	8–9	10–11	12
1	5%	4%	3%	2%	1%	0.2%
2–10	6	6	6	6	6	6
11	5	5	5	5	5	5.8
12–18	5	5	5	5	5	5
19	1	2	3	4	5	5

18-Year Real Property (Placed in Service after March 15 and before June 23, 1984; Low-Income Housing Placed in Service after March 15, 1984) for which Alternate ACRS Method over an 18-Year Period Is Elected

	Month Placed in Service						
Year	*1*	*2–3*	*4–5*	*6–7*	*8—9*	*10–11*	*12*
1	6%	5%	4%	3%	2%	1%	0.5%
2–10	6	6	6	6	6	6	6
11	5	5	5	5	5	5	5.5
12–18	5	5	5	5	5	5	5
19		1	2	3	4	5	5

19-Year Real Property for which Alternate ACRS Method over a 19-Year Period Is Elected

	Month Placed in Service											
Year	*1*	*2*	*3*	*4*	*5*	*6*	*7*	*8*	*9*	*10*	*11*	*12*
1	5.0	4.6	4.2	3.7	3.3	2.9	2.4	2.0	1.5	1.1	0.7	0.2
2–13	5.3	5.3	5.3	5.3	5.3	5.3	5.3	5.3	5.3	5.3	5.3	5.3
14–19	5.2	5.2	5.2	5.2	5.2	5.2	5.2	5.2	5.2	5.2	5.2	5.2
20	0.2	0.6	1.0	1.5	1.9	2.3	2.8	3.2	3.7	4.1	4.5	5.0

GENERAL DEPRECIATION SYSTEM

200 or 150 Percent Declining Balance Switching to Straight-Line—3, 5, 7, 10, 15, 20
Years (Half-Year Convention)

			Recovery Period			
	3-Year	5-Year	7-Year	10-Year	15-Year	20-Year
Recovery Year			Depreciation Rate			
1	33.33	20.00	14.29	10.00	5.00	3.750
2	44.45	32.00	24.49	18.00	9.50	7.219
3	14.81	19.20	17.49	14.40	8.55	6.677
4	7.41	11.52	12.49	11.52	7.70	6.177
5		11.52	8.93	9.22	6.93	5.713
6		5.76	8.92	7.37	6.23	5.285
7			8.93	6.55	5.90	4.888
8			4.46	6.55	5.90	4.522
9				6.56	5.91	4.462
10				6.55	5.90	4.461
11				3.28	5.91	4.462
12					5.90	4.461
13					5.91	4.462
14					5.90	4.461
15					5.91	4.462
16					2.95	4.461
17						4.462
18						4.461
19						4.462
20						4.461
21						2.231

Straight-Line—27.5 Years (Mid-Month Convention)

Recovery Year	Month Placed in Service											
	1	*2*	*3*	*4*	*5*	*6*	*7*	*8*	*9*	*10*	*11*	*12*
	Depreciation Rate											
1	3.485	3.182	2.879	2.576	2.273	1.970	1.667	1.364	1.061	0.758	0.455	0.152
2	3.636	3.636	3.636	3.636	3.636	3.636	3.636	3.636	3.636	3.636	3.636	3.636
3	3.636	3.636	3.636	3.636	3.636	3.636	3.636	3.636	3.636	3.636	3.636	3.636
4	3.636	3.636	3.636	3.636	3.636	3.636	3.636	3.636	3.636	3.636	3.636	3.636
5	3.636	3.636	3.636	3.636	3.636	3.636	3.636	3.636	3.636	3.636	3.636	3.636
6	3.636	3.636	3.636	3.636	3.636	3.636	3.636	3.636	3.636	3.636	3.636	3.636
7	3.636	3.636	3.636	3.636	3.636	3.636	3.636	3.636	3.636	3.636	3.636	3.636
8	3.636	3.636	3.636	3.636	3.636	3.636	3.636	3.636	3.636	3.636	3.636	3.636
9	3.636	3.636	3.636	3.636	3.636	3.636	3.636	3.636	3.636	3.636	3.636	3.636
10	3.637	3.637	3.637	3.637	3.637	3.637	3.636	3.636	3.636	3.636	3.636	3.636
11	3.636	3.636	3.636	3.636	3.636	3.636	3.637	3.637	3.637	3.637	3.637	3.637
12	3.637	3.637	3.637	3.637	3.637	3.637	3.636	3.636	3.636	3.636	3.636	3.636
13	3.636	3.636	3.636	3.636	3.636	3.636	3.637	3.637	3.637	3.637	3.637	3.637
14	3.637	3.637	3.637	3.637	3.637	3.637	3.636	3.636	3.636	3.636	3.636	3.636
15	3.636	3.636	3.636	3.636	3.636	3.636	3.637	3.637	3.637	3.637	3.637	3.637

Straight-Line—27.5 Years (Mid-Month Convention)(Continued)

					Month Placed in Service						
1	*2*	*3*	*4*	*5*	*6*	*7*	*8*	*9*	*10*	*11*	*12*
					Depreciation Rate						

Recovery Year	1	2	3	4	5	6	7	8	9	10	11	12
16	3.637	3.637	3.637	3.637	3.637	3.637	3.636	3.636	3.636	3.636	3.636	3.636
17	3.636	3.636	3.636	3.636	3.636	3.636	3.637	3.637	3.637	3.637	3.637	3.637
18	3.637	3.637	3.637	3.637	3.637	3.637	3.636	3.636	3.636	3.636	3.636	3.636
19	3.636	3.636	3.636	3.636	3.636	3.636	3.637	3.637	3.637	3.637	3.637	3.637
20	3.637	3.637	3.637	3.637	3.637	3.637	3.636	3.636	3.636	3.636	3.636	3.636
21	3.636	3.636	3.636	3.636	3.636	3.636	3.637	3.637	3.637	3.637	3.637	3.637
22	3.637	3.637	3.637	3.637	3.637	3.637	3.636	3.636	3.636	3.636	3.636	3.636
23	3.636	3.636	3.636	3.636	3.636	3.636	3.637	3.637	3.637	3.637	3.637	3.637
24	3.637	3.637	3.637	3.637	3.637	3.637	3.636	3.636	3.636	3.636	3.636	3.636
25	3.636	3.636	3.636	3.636	3.636	3.636	3.637	3.637	3.637	3.637	3.637	3.637
26	3.637	3.637	3.637	3.637	3.637	3.637	3.636	3.636	3.636	3.636	3.636	3.636
27	3.636	3.636	3.636	3.636	3.636	3.636	3.637	3.637	3.637	3.637	3.637	3.637
28	1.970	2.273	2.576	2.879	3.182	3.485	3.636	3.636	3.636	3.636	3.636	3.636
29	0.000	0.000	0.000	0.000	0.000	0.000	0.152	0.455	0.758	1.061	1.364	1.667

Straight-Line—31.5 Years (Mid-Month Convention)

	Month Placed in Service											
Recovery Year	1	2	3	4	5	6	7	8	9	10	11	12
	Depreciation Rate											
1	3.042	2.778	2.513	2.249	1.984	1.720	1.455	1.190	0.926	0.661	0.397	0.132
2	3.175	3.175	3.175	3.175	3.175	3.175	3.175	3.175	3.175	3.175	3.175	3.175
3	3.175	3.175	3.175	3.175	3.175	3.175	3.175	3.175	3.175	3.175	3.175	3.175
4	3.175	3.175	3.175	3.175	3.175	3.175	3.175	3.175	3.175	3.175	3.175	3.175
5	3.175	3.175	3.175	3.175	3.175	3.175	3.175	3.175	3.175	3.175	3.175	3.175
6	3.175	3.175	3.175	3.175	3.175	3.175	3.175	3.175	3.175	3.175	3.175	3.175
7	3.175	3.175	3.175	3.175	3.175	3.175	3.175	3.175	3.175	3.175	3.175	3.175
8	3.175	3.174	3.175	3.174	3.175	3.174	3.175	3.175	3.174	3.175	3.175	3.175
9	3.174	3.175	3.174	3.175	3.174	3.175	3.174	3.175	3.175	3.175	3.174	3.174
10	3.175	3.174	3.175	3.174	3.175	3.174	3.175	3.174	3.174	3.175	3.175	3.175
11	3.174	3.175	3.174	3.175	3.174	3.175	3.174	3.175	3.175	3.174	3.174	3.174
12	3.175	3.174	3.175	3.174	3.175	3.174	3.175	3.174	3.174	3.175	3.175	3.175
13	3.174	3.175	3.174	3.175	3.174	3.175	3.174	3.175	3.175	3.174	3.174	3.174
14	3.175	3.174	3.175	3.174	3.175	3.174	3.175	3.174	3.174	3.175	3.175	3.175
15	3.174	3.175	3.174	3.175	3.174	3.175	3.174	3.175	3.175	3.174	3.174	3.174
16	3.175	3.174	3.175	3.174	3.175	3.175	3.175	3.174	3.174	3.175	3.175	3.174
17	3.174	3.175	3.174	3.175	3.174	3.175	3.174	3.175	3.175	3.174	3.174	3.175

Note on RRA '93: The Revenue Reconciliation Act of 1993 lengthened the recovery period for determining the depreciation deduction as to nonresidential real property from 31.5 to 39 years, generally effective for property placed in service on or after May 13, 1993. See the Foreword on RRA '93.

Straight-Line—31.5 Years *(Mid-Month Convention) (Continued)*

Recovery Year	Month Placed in Service											
	1	2	3	4	5	6	7	8	9	10	11	12
						Depreciation Rate						
18	3.175	3.174	3.175	3.174	3.175	3.174	3.175	3.174	3.175	3.174	3.175	3.174
19	3.174	3.175	3.174	3.175	3.174	3.175	3.174	3.175	3.174	3.175	3.174	3.175
20	3.175	3.174	3.175	3.174	3.175	3.174	3.175	3.174	3.175	3.174	3.175	3.174
21	3.174	3.175	3.174	3.175	3.174	3.175	3.174	3.175	3.174	3.175	3.174	3.175
22	3.175	3.174	3.175	3.174	3.175	3.174	3.175	3.174	3.175	3.174	3.175	3.174
23	3.174	3.175	3.174	3.175	3.174	3.175	3.174	3.175	3.174	3.175	3.174	3.175
24	3.175	3.174	3.175	3.174	3.175	3.174	3.175	3.174	3.175	3.174	3.175	3.174
25	3.174	3.175	3.174	3.175	3.174	3.175	3.174	3.175	3.174	3.175	3.174	3.175
26	3.175	3.174	3.175	3.174	3.175	3.174	3.175	3.174	3.175	3.174	3.175	3.174
27	3.174	3.175	3.174	3.175	3.174	3.175	3.174	3.175	3.174	3.175	3.174	3.175
28	3.175	3.174	3.175	3.174	3.175	3.174	3.175	3.174	3.175	3.174	3.175	3.174
29	3.174	3.175	3.174	3.175	3.174	3.175	3.174	3.175	3.174	3.175	3.174	3.175
30	3.175	3.174	3.175	3.174	3.175	3.174	3.175	3.174	3.175	3.174	3.175	3.174
31	3.174	3.175	3.174	3.175	3.174	3.175	3.174	3.175	3.174	3.175	3.174	3.175
32	1.720	1.984	2.249	2.513	2.778	3.042	3.175	3.174	3.175	3.174	3.175	3.174
33	0.000	0.000	0.000	0.000	0.000	0.000	0.132	0.397	0.661	0.926	1.190	1.455

200 or 150 Percent Declining Balance Switching to Straight-Line—3, 5, 7, 10, 15, 20 Years (Mid-Quarter Convention—Property Placed in Service in First Quarter)

Recovery Year	Recovery Period					
	3-Year	5-Year	7-Year	10-Year	15-Year	20-Year
	Depreciation Rate					
1	58.33	35.00	25.00	17.50	8.75	6.563
2	27.78	26.00	21.43	16.50	9.13	7.000
3	12.35	15.60	15.31	13.20	8.21	6.482
4	1.54	11.01	10.93	10.56	7.39	5.996
5		11.01	8.75	8.45	6.65	5.546
6		1.38	8.74	6.76	5.99	5.130
7			8.75	6.55	5.90	4.746
8			1.09	6.55	5.91	4.459
9				6.56	5.90	4.459
10				6.55	5.91	4.459
11				0.82	5.90	4.459
12					5.91	4.460
13					5.90	4.459
14					5.91	4.460
15					5.90	4.459
16					0.74	4.460
17						4.459
18						4.460
19						4.459
20						4.460
21						0.557

200 or 150 Percent Declining Balance Switching to Straight-Line—3, 5, 7, 10, 15, 20
Years (Mid-Quarter Convention—Property Placed in Service in Second Quarter)

	Recovery Period					
	3-Year	*5-Year*	*7-Year*	*10-Year*	*15-Year*	*20-Year*
Recovery Year			Depreciation Rate			
1	41.67	25.00	17.85	12.50	6.25	4.688
2	38.89	30.00	23.47	17.50	9.38	7.148
3	14.14	18.00	16.76	14.00	8.44	6.612
4	5.30	11.37	11.97	11.20	7.59	6.116
5		11.37	8.87	8.96	6.83	5.658
6		4.26	8.87	7.17	6.15	5.233
7			8.87	6.55	5.91	4.841
8			3.33	6.55	5.90	4.478
9				6.56	5.91	4.463
10				6.55	5.90	4.463
11				2.46	5.91	4.463
12					5.90	4.463
13					5.91	4.463
14					5.90	4.463
15					5.91	4.462
16					2.21	4.463
17						4.462
18						4.463
19						4.462
20						4.463
21						1.673

200 or 150 Percent Declining Balance Switching to Straight-Line—3, 5, 7, 10, 15, 20 Years (Mid-Quarter Convention—Property Placed in Service in Third Quarter)

	Recovery Period					
	3-Year	5-Year	7-Year	10-Year	15-Year	20-Year
Recovery Year			Depreciation Rate			
1	25.00	15.00	10.71	7.50	3.75	2.813
2	50.00	34.00	25.51	18.50	9.63	7.289
3	16.67	20.40	18.22	14.80	8.66	6.742
4	8.33	12.24	13.02	11.84	7.80	6.237
5		11.30	9.30	9.47	7.02	5.769
6		7.06	8.85	7.58	6.31	5.336
7			8.86	6.55	5.90	4.936
8			5.53	6.55	5.90	4.566
9				6.56	5.91	4.460
10				6.55	5.90	4.460
11				4.10	5.91	4.460
12					5.90	4.460
13					5.91	4.461
14					5.90	4.460
15					5.91	4.461
16					3.69	4.460
17						4.461
18						4.460
19						4.461
20						4.460
21						2.788

200 or 150 Percent Declining Balance Switching to Straight-Line—3, 5, 7, 10, 15, 20 Years (Mid-Quarter Convention—Property Placed in Service in Fourth Quarter)

	Recovery Period					
	3-Year	5-Year	7-Year	10-Year	15-Year	20-Year
Recovery Year			Depreciation Rate			
1	8.33	5.00	3.57	2.50	1.25	0.938
2	61.11	38.00	27.55	19.50	9.88	7.430
3	20.37	22.80	19.68	15.60	8.89	6.872
4	10.19	13.68	14.06	12.48	8.000	6.357
5		10.94	10.04	9.98	7.20	5.880
6		9.58	8.73	7.99	6.48	5.439
7			8.73	6.55	5.90	5.031
8			7.64	6.55	5.90	4.654
9				6.56	5.90	4.458
10				5.74	5.91	4.458
11					5.90	4.458
12					5.91	4.458
13					5.90	4.458
14					5.91	4.458
15					5.90	4.458
16					5.17	4.458
17						4.458
18						4.459
19						4.458
20						4.459
21						3.901

Index

A

Accelerated cost recovery system (ACRS), 181–84
Acceleration of tax deductions, x
Accounting methods, 184
Accounting periods, 184–85
Accrual basis, 185
Acquisition discount, 185
Adjustable rate mortgages (ARM), 254
Adjusted basis, 196
Adjusted gross income, 185
Age 55, exclusion available for home sellers over, 40–42
Aggregation rules, 191
Allocable installment indebtedness (AII), 221
Allocation of debt, 50–52
Alternative depreciation system (ADS), 186
Alternative minimum tax (AMT), 121–29
  adjustments, 122, 126–27, 187
  alternative minimum taxable income (AMTI), 121
  charitable contribution of appreciated property, 127–28
  computation of, 125–26
  credit, 123–24, 187
  definition, 186
  depreciation, 125
  elections, 124–25
  exemptions, 123, 187–88
  foreign tax credit, 124, 188
  foreign taxes, 127
  incentive stock options, 128
  intangible drilling costs, 125, 128
  itemized deductions, 126
  local taxes, 127
  net operating losses, 124, 125, 188–89
  passive activity losses, 127
  percentage depletion, 129
  personal exemptions, 126
  personal interest, 127
  preferences, 122–23, 127–29, 189
  private activity bonds, 35
  standard deduction, 126
  state taxes, 127
  tax-exempt interest income, 128
American depositary receipts (ADRs), 186

AMT; *see* Alternative minimum tax (AMT)
Annuities
  definition, 189–90
  joint and survivor annuities, 229–230
  minimum distribution requirements, 94
  substantially equal periodic payments exception, qualifying for, 91
Annuity contracts, 105
Anti-churning rules, 190
Applicable installment obligations (AIOs), 220–21
At-risk rules, 153–63, 190–93
  activities to which rules apply, 154
  aggregation rules, 191
  amount at risk, 155–58, 192–93
  amount not at risk, 157–58
  constructive ownership rules, 157
  deductible losses, 160–61
  disposition of activities, 162–63
  foreclosure proceedings, disposition through, 162
  gifts, disposition through, 162–63
  interplay with other tax rules, 161
  loan repayments, effect of, 159–60
  loss carryovers, 161
  loss recapture, 162
  nonrecourse debt, 158, 159–60
  partnerships, 266
  property encumbered by debt, 156
  purpose of, 153
  qualified nonrecourse financing for real estate, 158–59
  real estate, application to, 154–55, 158–59, 192
  recapture rules, 193
  recourse loans, 159
  related person loans, 156–57
  sale of interest, 162
Average benefits test for self-employed retirement plans, 87

B

Bad debt, defined, 193
Balloon mortgages, 255
Bankruptcy, 194–95

Trusts — *Cont.*
  charitable remainder trusts, 204
  Clifford trusts, 204
  Crummey trusts, 176, 207
  definition, 115
  estimated tax, 212
  inter vivos trusts, 225
  life insurance trusts; *see* Life insurance trusts
  QTIP trusts, 282
  qualified Subchapter S trusts (QSSTs), 177
  rabbi trusts, 282–83
  real estate investment trusts, 283–85
  Section 2503(b) trusts, 175–76
  Section 2503(c) trusts, 175
  Totten trusts, 172
  transfers to minor child, 174–76

U

Undertaking, 137–39
  dissimilar activities, combination of, 140
  location, 138
  oil and gas, 139
  professional service, 140
  rental and nonrental operations, combined, 138–39
  same interest, controlled by, 139
  separating, 141–42
  similar, 139
Uniform Gifts to Minors Act, 172–74

Uniform Transfers to Minors Act, 174
Union, IRA with, 72
Universal life insurance, 104
U.S. savings bonds, 172, 313–14
  kiddie tax, minimizing, 168–69
  series EE, x, 36–37
  series HH, 36–37

V

Valuation tables, 320–33

W

Warrants, defined, 314
Wash sales, 314
  avoiding, xi
  rules, 33–34, 308
Whole life insurance, 104, 235–36, 237–38
Wills, 315
Wrap-around mortgages, 256

Y

Yachts; *see* Personal residence, sale of
Year-round planning guide tax-saver checklist, ix–xiv